FISHING ATLAS TO
SOUTH EAST QUEENSLAND
NAVIGATION & BEACON DIRECTORY

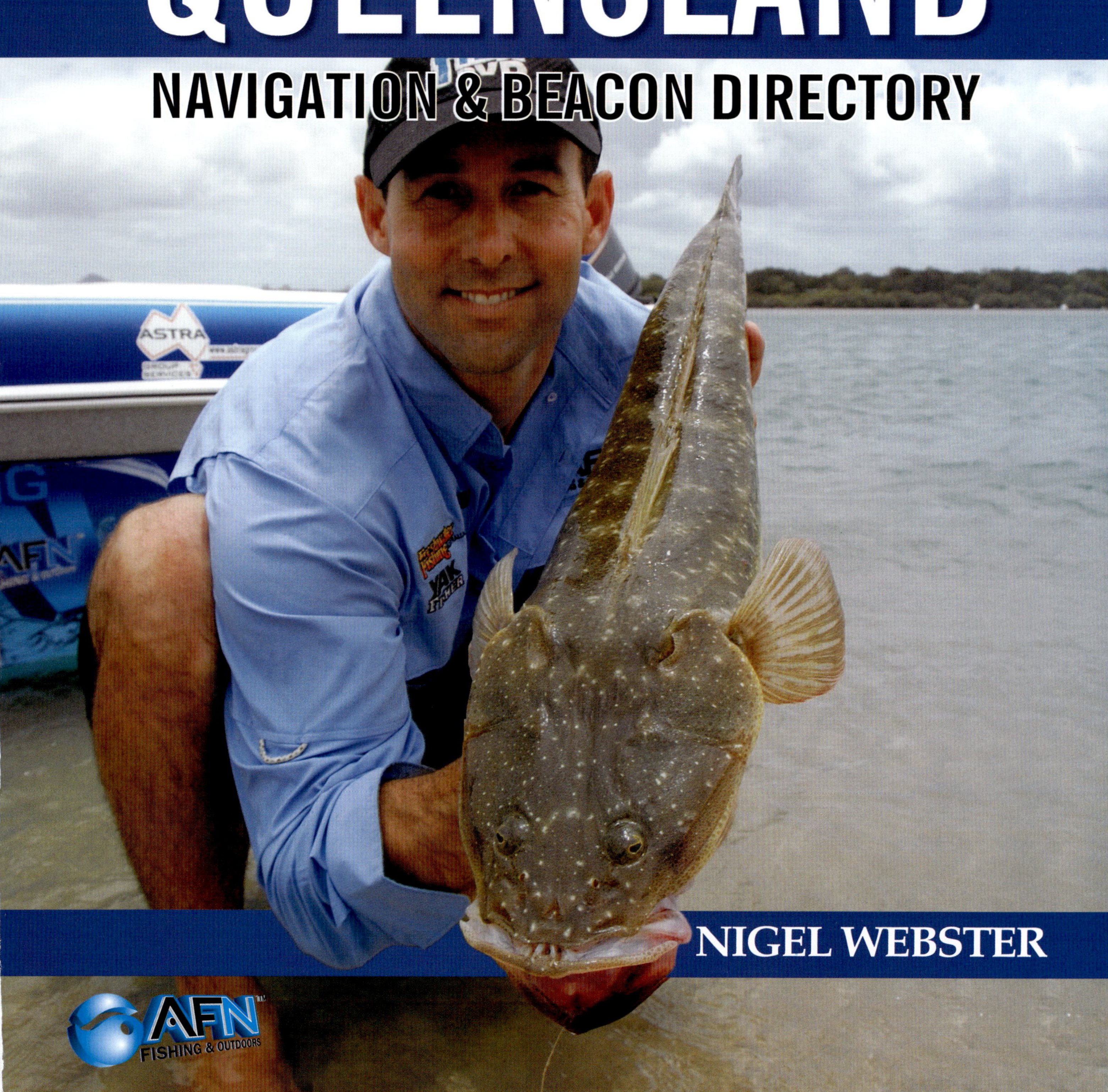

NIGEL WEBSTER

AFN FISHING & OUTDOORS

ACKNOWLEDGEMENTS

This book would not have been possible without the assistance of several parties.

The production team at Australian Fishing Network, work tirelessly to develop a range of fishing media products; a large book always puts added strain on the team. Bill Classon and Debbie Sheldon-Collins have provided guidance on the direction of the book from its concept. Joy Eckermann has done an incredible job deciphering my maps and information and as such has developed first-class fishing maps throughout the south-eastern corner of this State. The layout of the book is a credit to her ability to pull together a great looking book. Our Managing Editor had the un-enviable task of editing this book and making good sense of my writing.

The south-eastern corner of Queensland is blessed with a huge amount of water to explore and fish. It would take any angler decades to become familiar with half of it! I am fortunate to be able to fish with many of the respected anglers that live, fish and write about this great part of the coast. These anglers have kindly contributed much of their hard-earned lessons about where and how to fish particular locations throughout the area. The information gathered added to the already comprehensive data that was compiled by Leeann Payne and Gordon Macdonald in the development of the AFN Moreton Bay and Gold Coast Fishing Maps. Many thanks are extended to Ben Madin, James Clarke, Michael Geary, Steve Wilson, Mike Connolly, Anthony Wishey, Chris Britton, Robert Kwiatkowski, John Palermo, Guy McConnell, Ben Godfrey, Mick Horn, Roderick Walmsley, David Hodge and Thomas Seebach.

Many authors will testify to the amount of family time that is lost when developing a book. I extend a big heartfelt thank you to Stephanie, Lachlan and Abby for all your patience throughout the production of this title.

A great number of anglers communicated the need for a fishing guide book that would encompass the entire south-eastern corner of Queensland. You also told us what you most wanted to see in such a book. Thank you for the guidance; it has greatly assisted us in the development of this publication. I hope we have given you a product that will serve you well and add huge value to your fishing experience.

First published 2012
Revised and updated 2015
Revised and updated 2018
Reprinted 2021, 2024

Published and distributed by
Australian Fishing Network
PO Box 544 Croydon, Victoria 3136
Telephone: (03) 9729 8788
Email: sales@afn.com.au
www.afn.com.au

ISBN: 9781 8651 3350 8

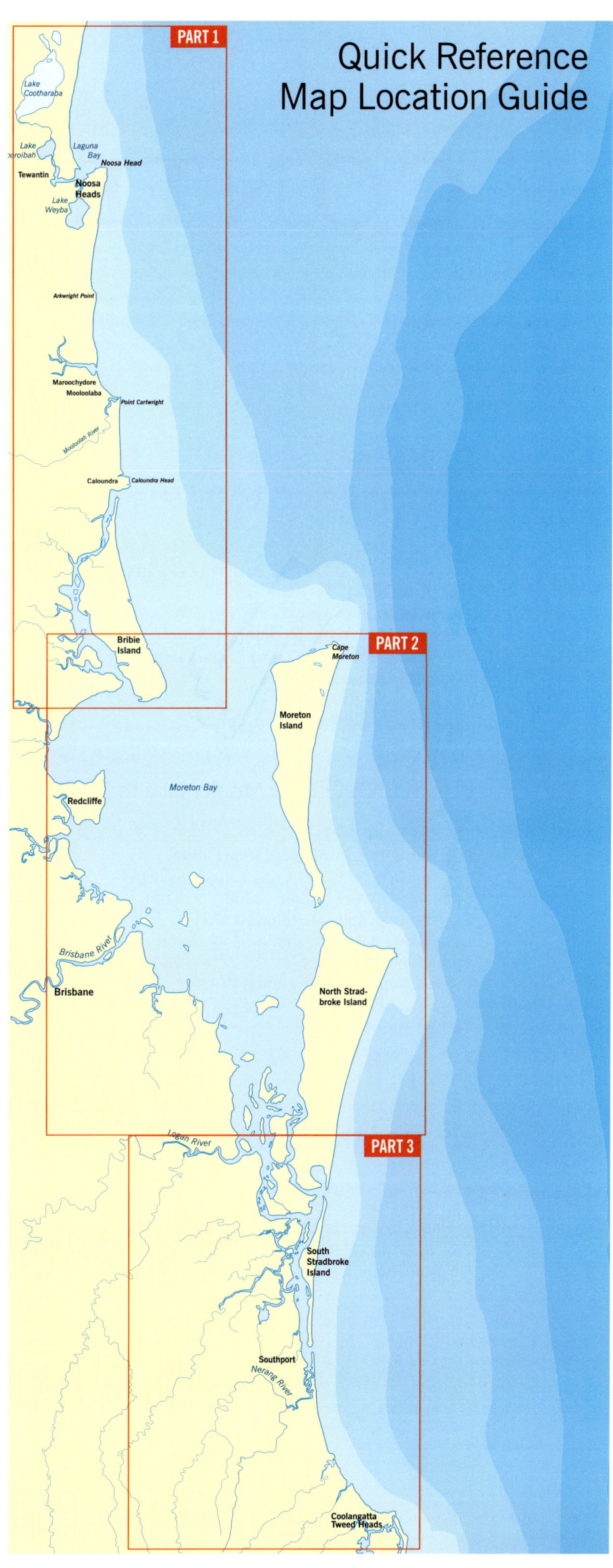

Quick Reference
Map Location Guide
PART 1
Lake Cootharaba
Laguna Bay
Noosa Head
Tewantin
Noosa Heads
Lake Weyba
Arkwright Point
Maroochydore
Mooloolaba
Point Cartwright
Mooloolah River
Caloundra
Caloundra Head
Bribie Island
PART 2
Cape Moreton
Moreton Island
Moreton Bay
Redcliffe
Brisbane River
Brisbane
North Strad-broke Island
Logan River
PART 3
South Stradbroke Island
Southport
Nerang River
Coolangatta
Tweed Heads

CONTENTS

LEGEND FOR MAPS

Navigations Aids

Port When lighted exhibits Starboard When lighted exhibits

Beacons, Bouys

CARDINAL MARKS Indicate navigable water for the area beyond the mark in the direction depicted.

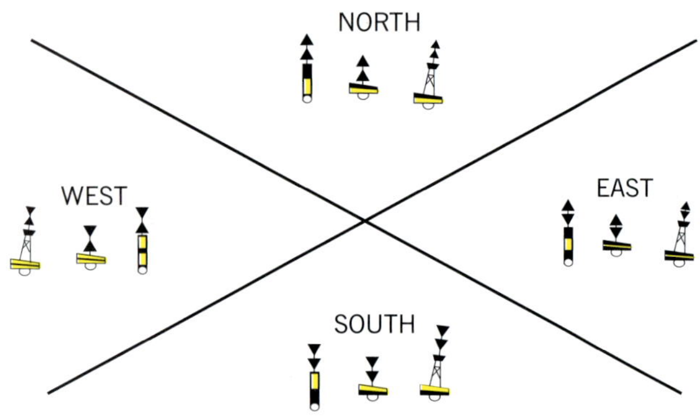

Lighted marks all exhibit a WHITE light.

SPECIAL MARKS Indicate several features (eg: pipe outfall) where navigable water is usually evident from the map.

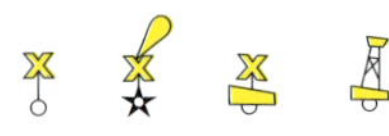

When lighted exhibits

ISOLATED DANGER MARKS Are stationed over a submerged hazard. KEEP CLEAR.

When lighted exhibits

SAFE WATER MARKS

When lighted exhibits

MARINE PARK BUOYS

Symbols

 0 – 1 m

 1 – 2 m

 2 – 5 m

Over 5 m

Extensive areas of mangroves

Approximate areas of drying mud and sand banks

Saltpan

Notable drop-off and channel waters

Sand, mudflat, shallow

Shallow, weeded broken bottom

Marine National Parks

Natural vegetation and structure

Toilet

Camping

Broken reef, bottom gravel, coffee rock

Boat ramp

Solid unbroken reef, rock

Submerged rock

Waterway sign

INTRODUCTION

I have been living and fishing in the south-eastern corner of Queensland for over a decade. The move was made to this wonderful area because it offered so much for a fishing journalist. The location provides a wealth of water and fishing opportunity. Add to this, the benefit that these waters really are the mixing zone for southern and northern species. How many major Australian cities offer a fishing backdrop that provides top class fishing for a range of species that includes the likes of Spanish mackerel, longtail tuna, snapper, threadfin salmon and bass? There really is much to love about this part of the Australian coastline. This corner of the State is heavily populated with anglers for a reason. The area offers extensive waterways with a great variety of sporting fish for the recreational angler to target. This book was daunting to plan due to the fact that local Brisbane waterways are vast, with so many options available to anglers of all disciplines. To properly cover the fishing content required by the recreational angler, we called upon some of the very best local anglers to provide their hard-earned knowledge on their local fishing haunts and favourite techniques. Local information developed by anglers such as Leeann Payne and Gordon Macdonald was also drawn upon to ensure we didn't lose any of the previous hard work undertaken to outline available fishing options in the south-east Queensland area.

A broad geographical area has been covered in this publication. The waters of the south-eastern corner have been broken into parts to make it easier to digest the huge amount of information carried within this book. Chapter One and Two cover the northern and southern halves of the Sunshine Coast. Chapter Three details the north-western regions and rivers of Moreton Bay while Chapter Four covers the rest of the Bay. Chapter Five describes the locations throughout the Jumpinpin area and Chapter Six contains information on the Gold Coast and surrounding systems. Chapter Seven provides information on all the offshore fishing locations and options available from north of Noosa to the Queensland border at the Tweed.

This book aims to provide a complete and accurate account of the available fishing locations for the recreational angler. Information has been provided on the type of structure available in all locations as well as the species most commonly found in any given place, the seasonal patterns of local fish and also some of the most common ways to catch them. This book will provide a great starting place for any angler wishing to get out and catch fish on Brisbane and district waters. If you are an experienced angler, we have done our utmost to provide you with information from some of our best local anglers; this will assist you to explore some of the many other options available that you may have been considering but have not yet tried or experienced.

Much of the waters illustrated within this book belong to the Moreton Bay Marine Park as described in the Queensland Government publication *Moreton Bay Marine Park – A Users Guide (2010)*. The publication describes four dominant zones of recreational fishing use classification. These include Marine National Park (Green Zone), Conservation Park (Yellow Zone), Habitat Protection (Dark Blue Zone) and General Use (Light Blue Zone). If you plan to fish recreationally in the boundaries of the Moreton Bay Marine Park, it is recommended that familiarity with the aforementioned publication or updated versions is gained. The maps produced for the purpose of this book have highlighted the approximate position of Green Zones (no fishing) at the time of production. These are likely to change in the future and anglers will be required to stay abreast of any changes. The other zonings stipulate various requirements of recreational anglers choosing to fish within designated boundaries. It is the responsibility of anglers to identify these zones and fish within the legal requirements as stipulated by the Queensland Government for these zones.

General Disclaimers, Safety Disclaimers and References

Information published in this book should be used as a guide only. AFN offers no warranty of the reliability of data contained in the maps and GPS coordinates displayed within this book when being used for navigational purposes. Water depths, landforms and location of navigational markers shown on maps have all been thoroughly reviewed on the water at the time of publication. However, the precise location of this data cannot be guaranteed due to factors including but not limited to the changing nature of the marine environment. Mariners should always be aiming to use the latest available information when navigating the waters detailed in this book. Published GPS coordinates have been obtained from reliable sources and although every effort has been made to verify accuracy, the precise location of data cannot be guaranteed. Data pertaining to the location and type of navigational marker shown on our fishing maps has been obtained from on-water observations and those published by Maritime Safety Queensland (Beacon to Beacon Guide information that falls under the Creative Commons licence 3.0). The State of Queensland, Department of Transport and Main Roads (Maritime Safety Queensland) is the original owner and copywrite holder of the approximate location of and type of navigational marker shown within this publication. The State of Queensland, Department of Transport and Main Roads (Maritime Safety Queensland) does not endorse this product.

Navigational aid data obtained from the State of Queensland, Department of Transport and Main Roads (Maritime Safety Queensland) and used within this publication must only be used in conjunction with the following Disclaimer.

DISCLAIMER

When using the Beacon to Beacon Guide booklets and/or the maps contained therein for commercial or non-commercial purposes, the Department of Transport and Main Roads (Maritime Safety Queensland) gives no warranty of any kind whether express, implied, statutory or otherwise in respect to the availability, accuracy, currency, completeness, quality or reliability of the information or that the information will be fit for any particular purpose or will not infringe any third party Intellectual Property rights and the liability (including without limitation, liability in negligence, negligent misstatement and pure economic loss) of the Department of Transport and Main Roads (Maritime Safety Queensland) for any direct, indirect or consequential loss, damage, cost or expense howsoever resulting from the use of, or reliance on, the information is entirely excluded.

PART 1

THE SUNSHINE COAST ESTUARY AND BEACH

ABOVE: First light is a great time to be fishing the Noosa Headland.

The Sunshine Coast is situated an easy drive north of Brisbane. Often confused by tourists with the Gold Coast, the two destinations are in reality poles apart. The Sunshine Coast is far removed from the hustle and bustle of the Gold Coast; many parts of this area are just progressing beyond sleepy beach suburb status. The area offers a huge amount of fishing water to travelling and local anglers. This extends from Bribie Island at the northern tip of Moreton Bay to the Noosa north shore that stretches towards Rainbow Beach and Double Island Point. The Bruce Highway north of Brisbane crosses many of the feeder systems that supply the Sunshine Coast estuaries with water. The fact that most of these crossings offer quality fishing for bass, mangrove jack, flathead, tarpon and bream is a testament to the fact that fishing in the estuary systems proper is pretty good as well! The Sunshine Coast offers great shorebased and boat/kayak fishing around developed centres and the wild areas that remote parts of the coast still offer. This potential to catch good fish close to tourist hotspots as well as off the beaten track for the more adventurous angler, entices fishers of all persuasions back to the area again and again.

The local estuary systems offer miles of water that are well worth exploring. Developed river mouths often give way to mangrove wilderness in the upper reaches of the estuaries. These systems provide good mangrove jack, trevally, flathead, whiting, estuary cod, tarpon and bass fishing in summer. Winter provides equally good fishing for bream, big tailor, trevally and jewfish. The rock and beach anglers are treated to top winter fishing for big bream, tailor, trevally, dart, jewfish and reef species. Summer offers plenty of whiting, flathead and dart, and occasionally a tussle with a larger pelagic such as tuna, mackerel or cobia where access to deeper water exists.

For this book, the Sunshine Coast has been split into two key areas. Chapter One will cover all the detail of the northern half of the coastline and Chapter Two will explore every kilometre of the southern part. If a slightly more laid back atmosphere is your cup-of-tea, then the Sunshine Coast is the place for you.

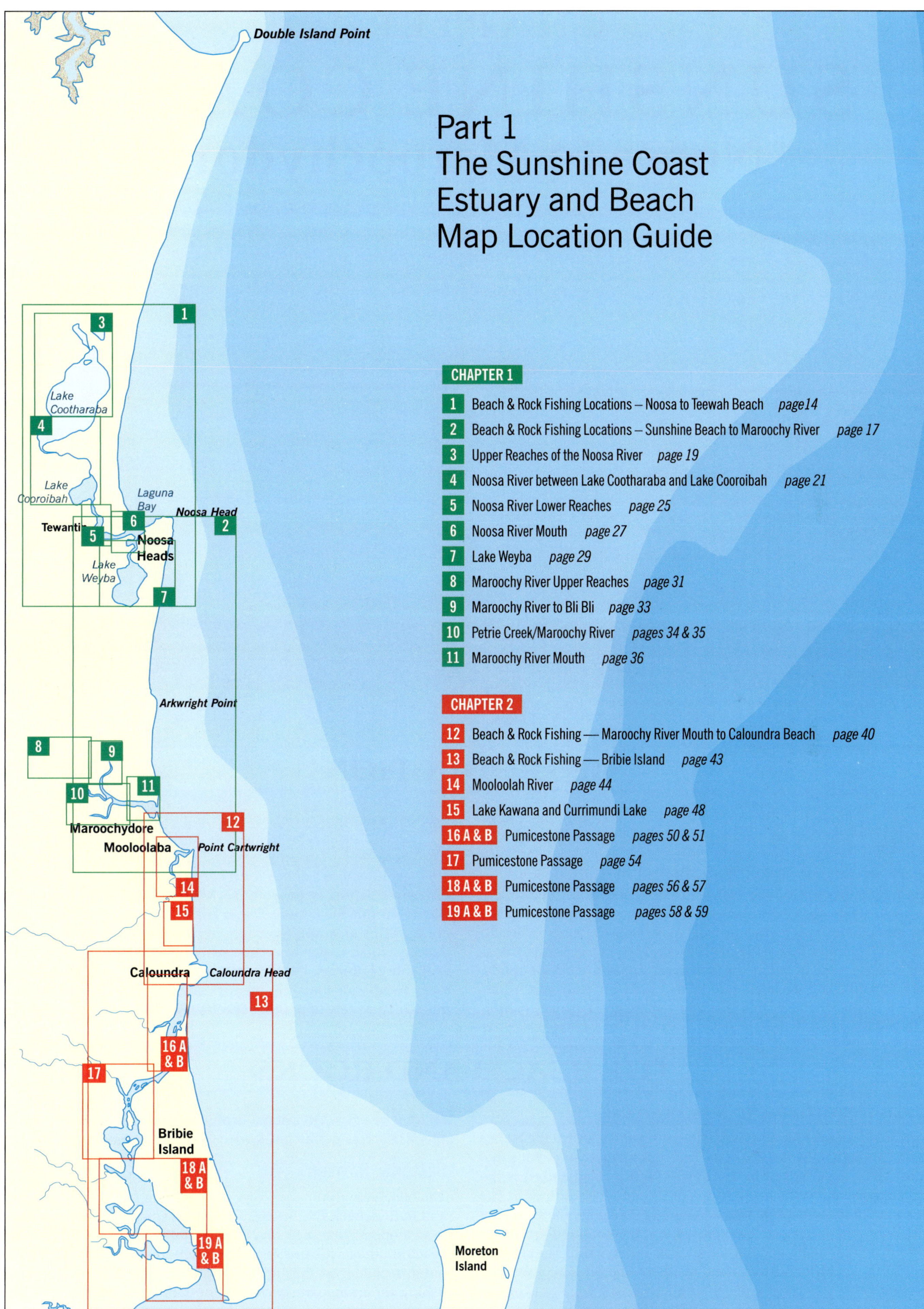

Part 1 The Sunshine Coast Estuary and Beach Map Location Guide

CHAPTER 1

CHAPTER 2

CHAPTER 1

SUNSHINE COAST
Noosa to Maroochydore

ABOVE: An angler enjoys the solitude of the beach between Noosa and Double Island Point.

INTRODUCTION

Situated in the northern half of the Sunshine Coast, the waters around Noosa and Maroochydore are prestigious tourist destinations that also offer a lot for the recreational angler. The northern extent of the Sunshine Coast remains one of the last well-populated areas before the highway north takes the traveller to more sparsely populated ones. The immediate areas to the north of Noosa such as Rainbow Beach, Tin Can Bay and other settlements around the Fraser Island Coast will remind you of what the Sunshine Coast townships might have looked liked decades ago. Within only an hour and a half drive north of Brisbane, this area offers some good estuary fishing together with some top class beach and rock angling.

The two estuary systems that can be found in this area are the Noosa and Maroochy rivers. These systems enter the ocean amongst kilometres of beautiful beach that offers some of the most renowned fishing in the country. Many travelling anglers on their way to sample the famous Fraser Island fishing immediately to the north of this area, unknowingly bypass first class fishing beaches that are much easier to access. Although there is not a wealth of available platforms, the long beaches in this area are truncated by rocky headlands that offer the rock angler plenty of opportunity to mix with a variety of popular species.

THE BEACH AND ROCKS

NOOSA NORTH SHORE TO MAROOCHYDORE

Top quality beach fishing exists to the north and south of the Noosa area. Although there is some of the best rock fishing on the Sunshine Coast to be experienced in the way of Noosa Headland, it is the endless beaches on the north shore, or those to the south of Noosa Headland that most excite the shorebased exponents. Kilometres of surf, sand and gutters can be explored, and it is common to look far to your right and left, and not see another rod in hand! The beaches provide a wealth of northern and southern species. Tailor, bream, whiting, dart, tarwhine, flathead and jewfish are regular captures on local beaches. Occasional captures of mackerel, tuna and exotic species such as permit and bonefish are also not unheard of.

SEASONAL PATTERNS

The beach environment offers good fishing for most of our bread and butter species throughout the year. That being said, if you ask local anglers what their favourite time of year to fish the rocks and beach is, they will uncategorically tell you that it is spring. The months of August through to December offer superb shorebased fishing for a range of species. Tailor are in good numbers through this period and offer the angler a chance to tangle with extra large specimens. Quality bream, dart, tarwhine, whiting and flathead all feature well in a spring time angler's catch. The jewies start to get active around the shorelines through late winter and really hit their straps in September and October. Summer offers more opportunity to tangle with some bigger pelagics as they occasionally push into the surf zone and close to the rocky headlands to feed. Throw in other options like the odd squire, sweetlip and drummer off the rocks and these locations will always have something on offer for you.

BEACH AND ROCK FISHING LOCATION GUIDE

MAP 1 NO.1 NOOSA NORTH SHORE – TEEWAH BEACH

(BREAM, DART, FLATHEAD, WHITING, TAILOR, JEWFISH, TARWHINE)

This beach fishing location offers one of the most accessible, remote style fishing for the Brisbane angler. The road through Tewantin will take you to the ferry crossing where cars can be transported across river before heading to the beach. This road will transport you to First Cutting, where anglers are offered the opportunity to travel a regulated sand motorway for 50 km or so. Anglers with 4WD vehicles are able to travel from First Cutting south towards Noosa (approx 5 km) and north towards Double Island Point and Rainbow Beach.

The beach offers kilometres of top class surf fishing with endless numbers of gutters and water to explore. Standard surf fishing practices apply with bait anglers producing much of the catch. Baits such as pipis, worms, pilchards and strip baits provide the opportunity to clash with resident bream, whiting, dart, flathead, tailor and jewfish. These days it is more common to find better jewfish in the areas between Teewah and Double Island, but they continue to surprise by showing up in various locations. This area is largely demarcated by the location of some impressively tall and ancient sand dunes. These sandy escarpments begin to take on an orange colouration and are known as the 'Coloured Sands'. A good tip for anglers fishing this stretch is to stay mobile until fish are encountered. It is not uncommon to find the fishing better along specific stretches of this beach for a period of time. For example, some periods will demonstrate that the fishing is much better in the area between Teewah and the Noosa River, and at other times the fishing is best from the Coloured Sands and on to the north. Local anglers stay mobile until they find the fish. A good strategy practiced by locals is to drive the beach at low tide and mark good looking gutters and steeper sections of beach on a hand held GPS unit. As the tide starts to flood, anglers then return to these marks to fish the best of the structure.

During summer, the pelagic season hits full swing and at times rampaging schools of spotted and school mackerel, longtail tuna, the odd cobia and golden trevally will move into the surf zone for a feed. Surf anglers are known to land some impressive pelagics at these times! Casting and high speed retrieving slugs through the surf zone is also a popular pursuit for anglers chasing pelagics in summer or tailor on a winter's day with a good westerly wind at your back.

MAP 1 NO. 2 NOOSA HEADLAND

(FLATHEAD, BREAM, TAILOR, JEWFISH, SQUIRE)

Rock fishing is not the most commonly practised form of angling in the area, however the Noosa Headland provides one of the best rock fishing platforms on the Sunshine Coast. The location provides the basis from which shorebased anglers can target fish traversing the deeper water off the headland. Patches of reef and gravel exist in bottom areas off the Headland which hold various species of fish at times. The wash zones around the headland hold good numbers of bream, trevally, jewfish and the odd drummer. The pick of the season for all of these species off the rocks is late winter into early spring.

Large flathead also frequent the sandy, rocky fringe areas during this part of the year. Bait anglers using live fish baits around reefy and wash zones are in with the chance of catching jewfish and big flathead. Night time bait fishing is a favoured technique for the serious jewfish anglers who use the Noosa Headland as their base for recording some impressive captures. Late winter and spring also provide some good angling for squire sized snapper and sweetlip by anglers fishing with baits and soft plastics around areas of visible reef. Boat anglers targeting the wash zones with soft plastics and blades have had fabulous sessions on big bream, trevally and other surprises like kingfish and jewfish.

It is not uncommon to see pelagic species like mackerel and tuna coming within casting distance at times when these fish are in abundance. Anglers casting slugs from the platform and high speed spinning, or floating out livebaits, can take some surprising catches at times.

With top class walking tracks around most of the Headland, it is astonishing that the area is not fished with much more vigour than is typically seen. As always, great care must be taken when fishing the rocks as it remains a dangerous place to fish in certain conditions.

MAP 1 & INSET: AREAS OF INTEREST

NOOSA GROYNE BEACH

(BREAM, DART, FLATHEAD, WHITING, TAILOR)

Tucked between the Noosa Headland and the mouth of the Noosa River is a smaller section of beach. The beach area is separated by a rockwall positioned in the middle of the beach between Noosa and the river mouth. This rockwall marks the old position of the Noosa River mouth. The stretch of sand to the south of the rockwall is Noosa Beach and the sand stretch to the north is commonly known as the Noosa Groyne Beach. Few anglers spend time fishing on Noosa Beach as it forms a popular tourist location. However, the location of the Groyne Beach means anglers wishing to target the beach without travelling too far from Hastings Street, are only required to travel a few hundred metres. The beach is easy walking distance from Noosa and offers rarely fished beach waters. Bait anglers will commonly tangle with bread and butter species like bream, whiting, dart and flathead. Beach anglers here have intercepted pelagics like tailor and the occasional mackerel as they move in and out of the river during peak tides.

LITTLE COVE, BOILING POT AND TEA TREE BAY

(BREAM, DART, FLATHEAD, WHITING, TAILOR)

The sections of the Noosa Headland closest to Noosa Beach are popular tourist destinations, and as such, anglers targeting these areas need to fish early or late in the day to fool resident fish. Bait and lure fishing close to the rocks during the low light periods of the day produce some good captures of bread and butter species. Late winter produces some great flathead fishing in these areas. Pilchard, prawn or live baits, or alternatively 'hopping' a soft plastic lure off the bottom is the way to go if you do choose to target these flathead.

DOLPHIN POINT TO HELLS GATE

(FLATHEAD, BREAM, TAILOR, JEWFISH, SQUIRE, GARFISH)

The rock areas around Granite Bay, the end of the headland: Hells Gate and the southern side of Alexandria Bay are targeted most by local anglers. These locations offer access to some deeper water and the chance to tangle with larger fish holding or moving past the ends of the headland. There are several patches of rocky reef and

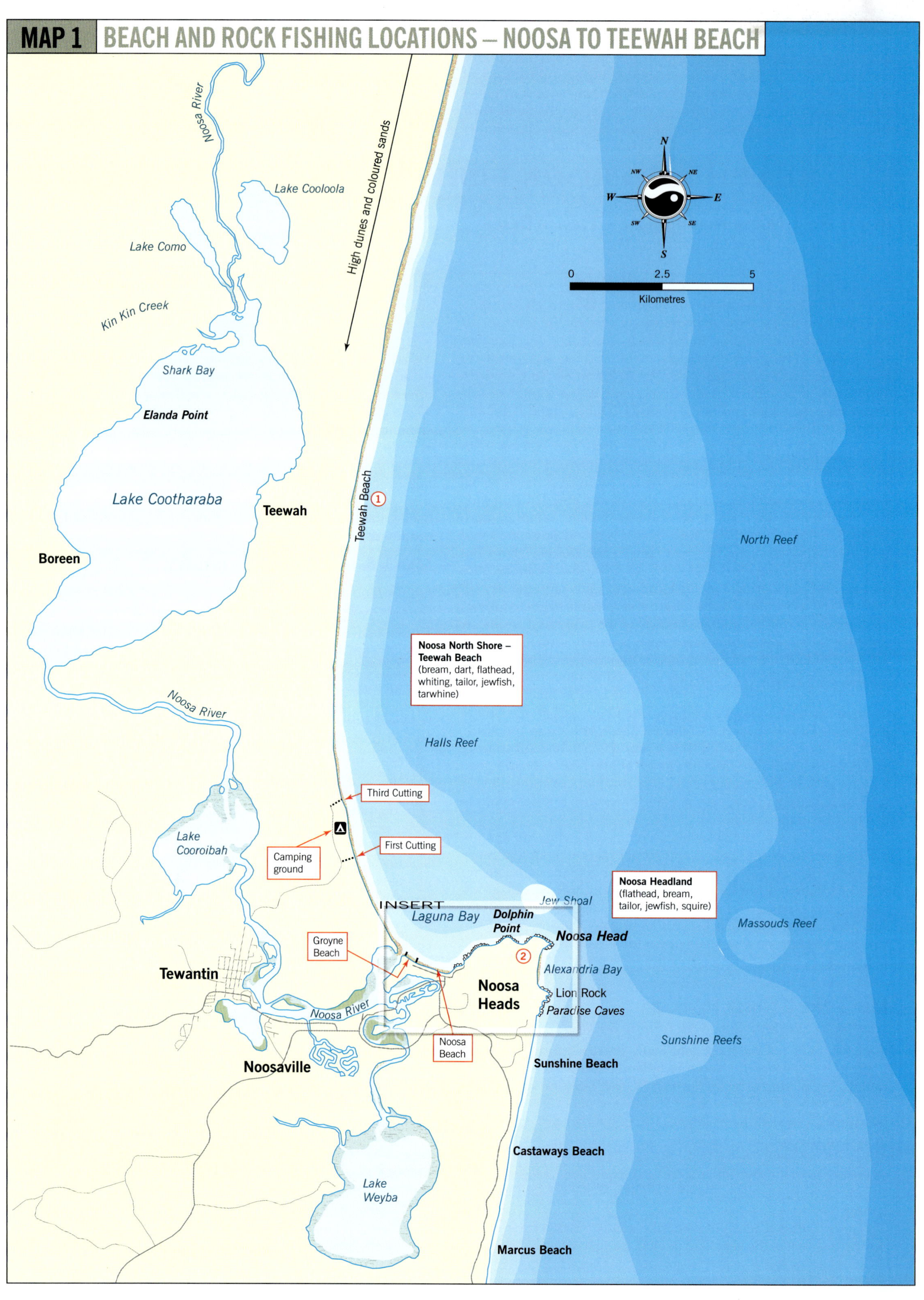

MAP 1 BEACH AND ROCK FISHING LOCATIONS – NOOSA TO TEEWAH BEACH
Noosa River
Lake Cooloola
Lake Como
High dunes and coloured sands
Kin Kin Creek
Shark Bay
Elanda Point
Lake Cootharaba
Teewah
Teewah Beach
1
Boreen
N
NW
NE
W
E
SW
SE
S
0
2.5
5
Kilometres
North Reef
Noosa North Shore – Teewah Beach
(bream, dart, flathead, whiting, tailor, jewfish, tarwhine)
Noosa River
Halls Reef
Third Cutting
Lake Cooroibah
First Cutting
Camping ground
INSERT
Jew Shoal
Noosa Headland
(flathead, bream, tailor, jewfish, squire)
Laguna Bay
Dolphin Point
Noosa Head
Massouds Reef
Groyne Beach
2
Tewantin
Alexandria Bay
Noosa Heads
Lion Rock
Paradise Caves
Noosa River
Noosa Beach
Sunshine Reefs
Noosaville
Sunshine Beach
Castaways Beach
Lake Weyba
Marcus Beach

ABOVE: An angler soaks a bait off the end of Noosa Headland.

bommie structure situated in casting distance from these locations. These structures fish particularly well when they are covered by some wash created through increased swell. Anglers should be warned that weather generated swell makes the areas around the ends of the headland a dangerous place to fish at times. Winch Cove is tucked into the corner of Granite Bay and these waters often host some great garfish fishing during the winter months. Although the bread and butter species are commonly caught in the area, many anglers spend time around the extremities of the headland primarily targeting squire and jewfish.

Alexandria Bay *(flathead, bream, tailor, whiting, dart)*

Tucked between the bounding north and south rock extremities of the Noosa Headland is the secluded Alexandria Bay. The beach is rarely fished by anglers due to the requirement to walk some distance to access it. However, anglers choosing to make the walk, will often find some good fishing for our common bread and butter beach species. The beach is usually host to some good gutters, particularly on the northern end tight against the Hells Gate rocks. Bait fishing for common beach species is the way to go here.

Lion Rock to Paradise Caves *(flathead, bream, tailor, jewfish, squire)*

This area fishes much the same as the Hells Gate area. The rocks are easily accessed from Sunshine Beach and enables anglers the opportunity to cast a line into deeper waters. The reefy waters of Sunshine Reef are proximal to these areas and are host to some of the best coral trout fishing on the Sunshine Coast – so you never know what you might tangle with when fishing from the rocks in this area! There is typically a solid gutter running alongside the rocks immediately to the south of the Paradise Caves location. This area will always hold a few good fish during the low light periods of the day.

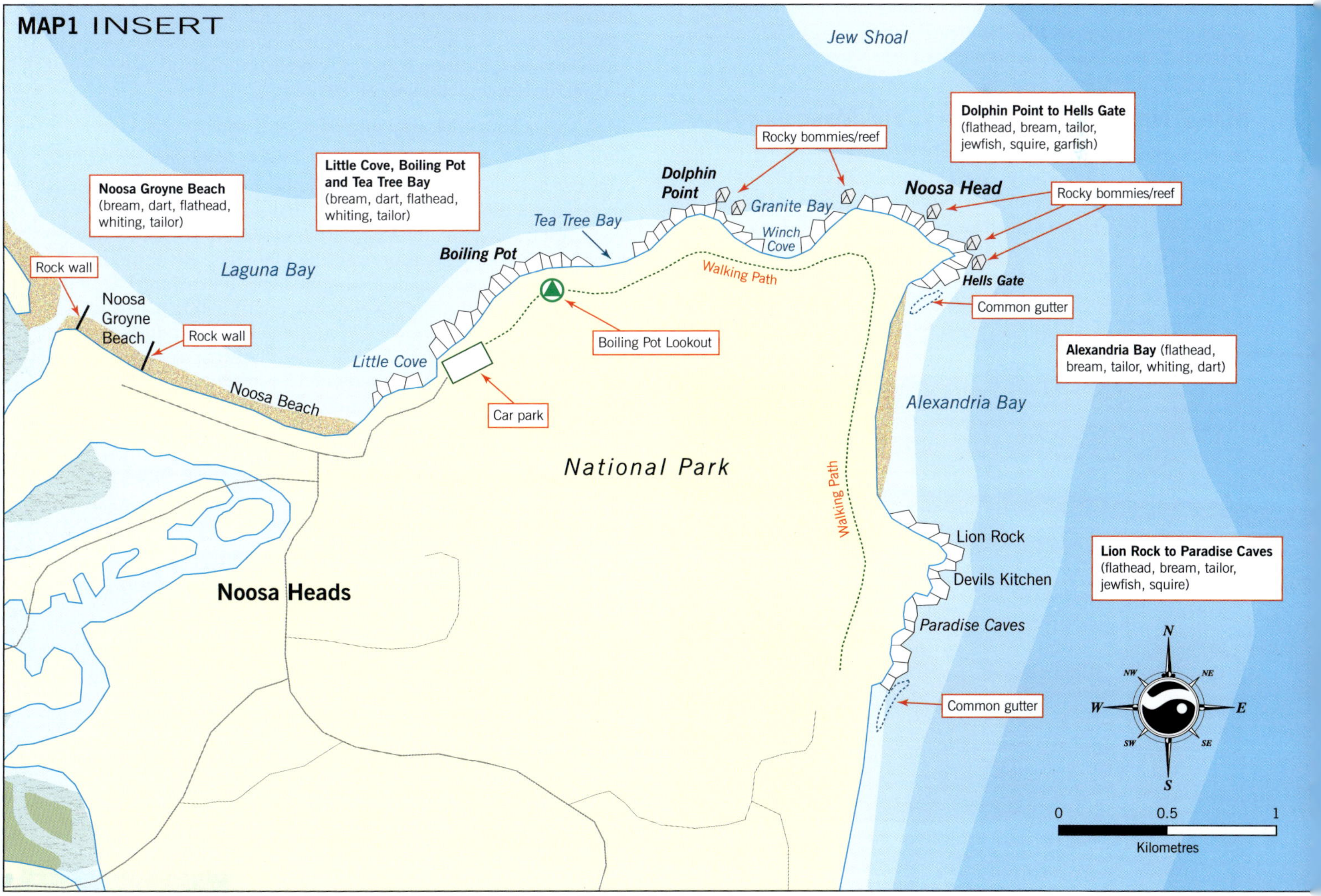

MAP1 INSERT

Jew Shoal

Dolphin Point to Hells Gate (flathead, bream, tailor, jewfish, squire, garfish)

Rocky bommies/reef

Little Cove, Boiling Pot and Tea Tree Bay (bream, dart, flathead, whiting, tailor)

Noosa Groyne Beach (bream, dart, flathead, whiting, tailor)

Dolphin Point

Granite Bay

Noosa Head

Rocky bommies/reef

Tea Tree Bay

Winch Cove

Boiling Pot

Walking Path

Hells Gate

Laguna Bay

Rock wall

Noosa Groyne Beach

Rock wall

Common gutter

Boiling Pot Lookout

Alexandria Bay (flathead, bream, tailor, whiting, dart)

Little Cove

Noosa Beach

Car park

Alexandria Bay

National Park

Walking Path

Lion Rock

Lion Rock to Paradise Caves (flathead, bream, tailor, jewfish, squire)

Noosa Heads

Devils Kitchen

Paradise Caves

Common gutter

N NE E SE S SW W NW

0 0.5 1

Kilometres

Map 2 No. 1 Sunshine Beach to Coolum
(Bream, Dart, Flathead, Whiting, Tailor, Jewfish, Tarwhine)

The beaches to the south of Noosa and down towards Coolum offer a similar style of fishing to Teewah Beach. The locations are less remote to access, however it is still rare to have to share your water with another angler. The same species frequent the beaches here as to the north of Noosa and can be targeted in the same manner. Early morning sessions produce good results on bream, dart, whiting, flathead, tailor and jewfish. The majority of jewfish seem to come from the stretch of beach between Peregian Beach and Coolum, but don't let that put you off. Never ignore any good looking water in the Sunshine vicinity – particularly around the rocky northern zones. Jewies will always become more active in the beach and rock areas following periods of heavy rainfall and some dirty water pushing out of local estuaries.

Map 2 No. 2 Coolum – Point Arkwright
(Flathead, Bream, Tailor, Jewfish, Squire)

The rocky platforms to the south of Coolum Beach provide some good fishing for shorebased anglers. Point Perry to Point Arkwright provides access to deeper water rock and sand structure. This structure is host to a variety of species including bream, flathead, smaller sweetlip and cod, jewfish and squire. Pelagic fare such as tailor are an option when they are moving through the area in abundance. Popular fishing locations include the rocks at Point Arkwright, Yaroomba and the deeper gutter often situated to the south of Point Arkwright that extends towards the beach at Yaroomba. Bait fishing techniques using pilchard, fish strip baits, squid and live bait are popular and effective in this location. Targeting the bottom parts of the water column with soft plastics lures and the upper parts while high speed spinning with metal lures accounts for some good fish for lure anglers. The location is susceptible to poor weather and care must be taken when fishing here when there is a swell running into the rocks.

Map 2 No. 3 Coolum Beach to the Maroochy River
(Bream, Dart, Flathead, Whiting, Tailor, Jewfish, Tarwhine)

There are typically plenty of surf gutters that will hold some good fish along this stretch of beach. The standard south-east Queensland beach fare will all be present. Anglers fishing this area catch plenty of quality dart with some good whiting, tarwhine, flathead, tailor and the odd jewfish thrown in to spice things up. Popular techniques include bait fishing through the day for dart, bream, whiting and flathead, while the serious big fish anglers tend to hit the beach after dark for big bream, tailor and jewies. Anglers will often find that the fishing is improved in certain gutters within this stretch so it can pay to maintain a mobile approach.

ABOVE: Big sand whiting are popular targets on the beach.

ABOVE: A well presented bait in a near-shore gutter is often productive in these parts.

Map 2 Areas of Interest

Mudjimba Coffee Rock
(Bream, Dart, Flathead, Whiting, Tailor, Jewfish, Tarwhine)

The beach waters around Mudjimba are host to significant sections of coffee rock that extends right up and on to the beach. This structure can be a haven for a variety of predators at times. This easily accessed location fishes very well at times and in particular, during the low light periods of the day.

Maroochy River Mouth and North Shore
(Bream, Dart, Flathead, Whiting, Tailor, Jewfish, Tarwhine)

The beach waters to the north of the Maroochy River can be accessed via the North Shore Road that will take anglers past the Twin Waters location. Remote car parks will enable access to some good beach fishing spots around the Maroochy River mouth. The most subtle structure in the area is the rocky Pincushion Island that sits abroad the Maroochy River mouth area. Casting baits and lures in the channels that are etched around the island produce good fish for anglers. These areas and the beach gutters that sit adjacent to the Maroochy River mouth are renowned for producing quality jewfish when they become active in the area. This often happens after some good rain and through the late winter and spring months. These waters are also well known for producing quality tailor and trevally as well as good bream, whiting, dart and flathead. Some cracking bream are taken in the area during the winter spawning periods. Best results are often experienced in low light periods of the day and night time.

The Sandbags *(Bream, Dart, Flathead, Whiting, Tailor)*

The southern corner of the Maroochy River mouth and the northern extremity of the beach at Maroochydore are home to some unique structures. Four lines of sandbags protrude from the beach and out into the water in an attempt to reduce erosion. The structures deflect some of the current that moves through the area and provide deeper patches of water immediately around these structures. The location is always home to a few predators that produce some excitement for local anglers. Some quality winter bream, tailor and trevally are caught in the area and there are always a few decent dart, whiting and the odd flathead about.

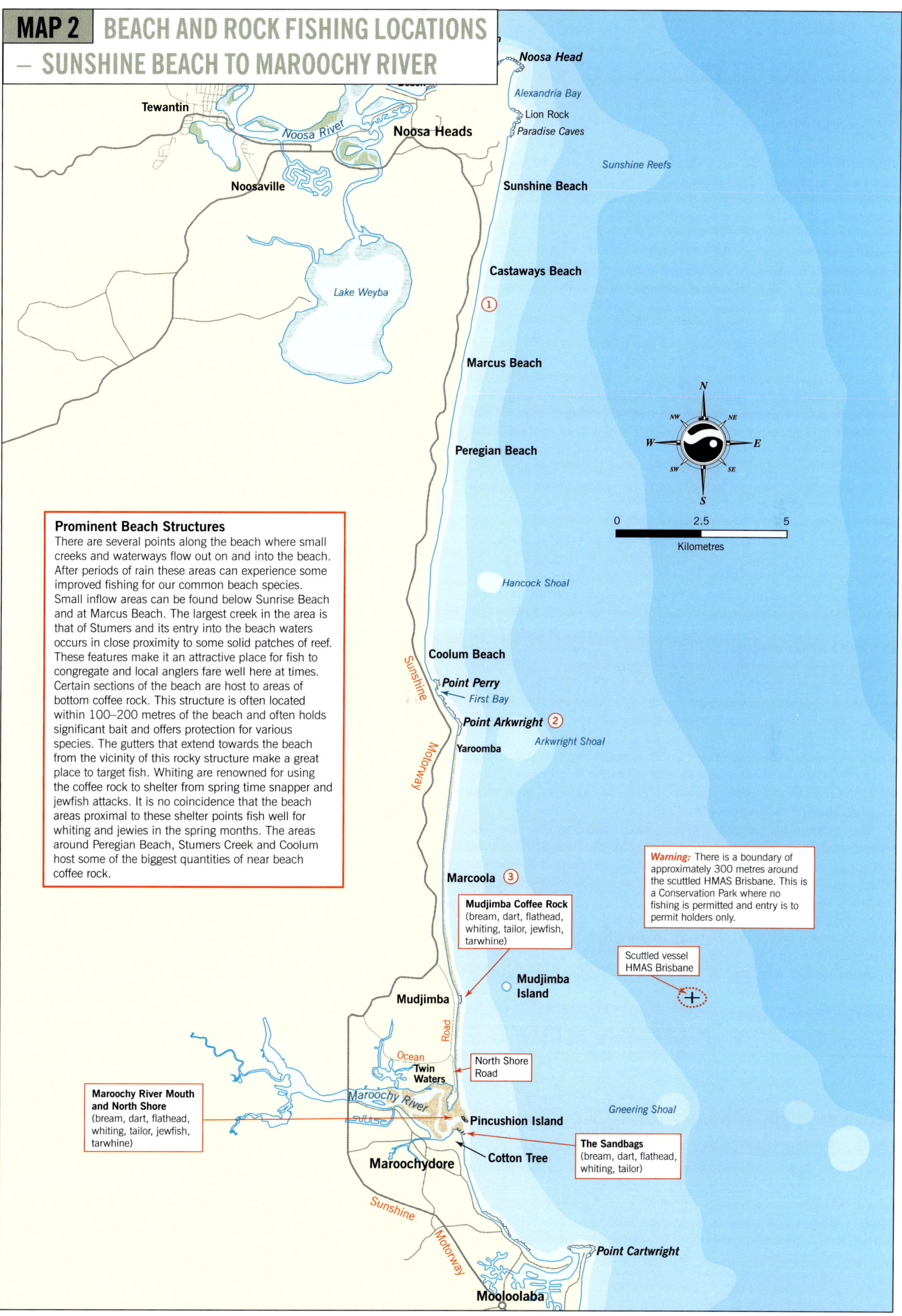

MAP 2
BEACH AND ROCK FISHING LOCATIONS – SUNSHINE BEACH TO MAROOCHY RIVER
Noosa Head
Alexandria Bay
Lion Rock
Paradise Caves
Tewantin
Noosa River
Noosa Heads
Noosaville
Sunshine Reefs
Sunshine Beach
Lake Weyba
Castaways Beach
1
Marcus Beach
N
NW
NE
W
E
SW
SE
S
Peregian Beach
0
2.5
5
Kilometres
Prominent Beach Structures
There are several points along the beach where small creeks and waterways flow out on and into the beach. After periods of rain these areas can experience some improved fishing for our common beach species. Small inflow areas can be found below Sunrise Beach and at Marcus Beach. The largest creek in the area is that of Stumers and its entry into the beach waters occurs in close proximity to some solid patches of reef. These features make it an attractive place for fish to congregate and local anglers fare well here at times. Certain sections of the beach are host to areas of bottom coffee rock. This structure is often located within 100–200 metres of the beach and often holds significant bait and offers protection for various species. The gutters that extend towards the beach from the vicinity of this rocky structure make a great place to target fish. Whiting are renowned for using the coffee rock to shelter from spring time snapper and jewfish attacks. It is no coincidence that the beach areas proximal to these shelter points fish well for whiting and jewies in the spring months. The areas around Peregian Beach, Stumers Creek and Coolum host some of the biggest quantities of near beach coffee rock.
Hancock Shoal
Coolum Beach
Sunshine
Point Perry
First Bay
Point Arkwright
2
Yaroomba
Arkwright Shoal
Motorway
Warning: There is a boundary of approximately 300 metres around the scuttled HMAS Brisbane. This is a Conservation Park where no fishing is permitted and entry is to permit holders only.
Marcoola
3
Mudjimba Coffee Rock
(bream, dart, flathead, whiting, tailor, jewfish, tarwhine)
Scuttled vessel
HMAS Brisbane
Mudjimba Island
Mudjimba
Road
Ocean
Twin Waters
North Shore Road
Maroochy River Mouth and North Shore
(bream, dart, flathead, whiting, tailor, jewfish, tarwhine)
Maroochy River
Pincushion Island
Gneering Shoal
The Sandbags
(bream, dart, flathead, whiting, tailor)
Cotton Tree
Maroochydore
Sunshine
Motorway
Point Cartwright
Mooloolaba

THE NORTHERN SUNSHINE COAST ESTUARY SYSTEMS

Noosa and Maroochy River Estuary Patterns

Many of our common bread and butter estuary species as well as some of the more exotic ones, can be caught throughout the year. However, certain seasonal patterns are prevalent. Summer in the estuaries provides the pick of the fishing for species such as the mangrove jack. The warmer months also provide great flathead, trevally and whiting fishing. Winter has some bigger spawn run bream in the system combined with larger tailor and trevally at times. Surface fishing for the bigger tailor and trevally is a pastime of many local anglers. Spring time typically sees the jewfish and bigger flathead more active.

The Noosa River

The Noosa River and its associated tributaries are host to similar species of fish to neighbouring estuaries along the Sunshine Coast. The Noosa River varies slightly in that its headwaters reach up into more remote and inaccessible locations than nearby systems like the Maroochy, Mooloolah and Pumicestone Passage systems. The upper Noosa River is protected from outboard motors, is difficult to access by road and sustains healthy populations of wild bass. The system works its way to more populated domains as it works through several lake environments and gradually begins to broaden as it nears the entrance. The system is largely shallow today, which differs from the 'good old days'. Locals in the area tell stories of 15 metre depths through the lower channel areas in the days prior to the system being diverted to make way for beach side development and the famous Hastings Street. The average size of dominant fish species in the system has dropped a lot from those good old days, but the estuary continues to host some exciting recreational angling for locals and tourists alike.

The upper Noosa River is host to some quality bass fishing for anglers prepared to travel by boat or dirt track to these upper reaches. In higher flow periods and in winter, bass will work further down the system but their home is typically the upper reaches. These areas are also host to good numbers of tarpon, smaller trevally and some of the usual suspects like mangrove jack and bream. The odd barramundi and threadfin salmon will show up for anglers in the upper reaches, but these captures are far less common than a few decades ago.

The remainder of the Noosa River holds value for the recreational angler in that commonly caught species include bream, whiting, flathead, trevally (big eye, giant, golden and diamond), tailor and moses perch. Although you have to work a bit harder for them, there are reasonable numbers of mangrove jack, tarpon, mulloway, estuary cod and javelin fish. Rare captures continue to be barramundi, the very occasional threadfin salmon and luderick. Winter in the Noosa still has a few luderick showing up on the lower rockwall, and this area continues to be one of the most northern places where this species can be caught in Australia. The crab enthusiasts are often out on the river with mud crabs a popular target.

Facilities

The Noosa area caters reasonably well for touring anglers although there is room for some improvement! The area offers plenty of accommodation for touring anglers within easy reach of shops, restaurants and most importantly tackle stores and boat ramps. Quality boat ramps are available for all sizes of boats at Noosaville and Tewantin. Sand ramps can be found at Tewantin and adjacent to the Ferry Crossing up-river of Tewantin.

Commercial Fishing

It is sad that old photos on Noosa hotel walls showcase magnificent fish that were caught in local systems. Giant trevally weighing 10–20 kg that once frequented the Noosa system are now a thing of the past. Although it is reasonable to expect that commercial fishing practices continue in local systems, it is hard to believe that commercial fishing to the extent with which it is carried out in places such as the Noosa River is allowed to continue. Several licences are still active in the system and allow nursery areas for fish to be netted methodically for prawns every year with a large toll on local fish species. Not to say that fishing quality in the system has degraded purely as a result of commercial fishing. Urbanisation, the altering of direction of the lower Noosa River and the affect of recreational angling pressures have all taken a toll on fish populations in the estuary. The degradation of the food chain and available habitat combined with the shallowing of this estuary appear to have had a big impact on the average size of local species over the past decades. A few seasons of more controlled fishing practices in the Noosa River could see the rebirth of one of the most impressive tourist angling destinations in the Brisbane area were it allowed to happen.

FACT BOX

CHARTERS AND GUIDED FISHING

There are several options available for anglers wishing to be guided in the area. A good mix of inshore charter service is available in the Noosa area. If you are interested in a lure fishing the river contact well-known local identity Andy Phipps of "Phippsy's Smooth Water Charters" – *www.phippsy.com.au*

A river based charter that offers a mix of bait and lure fishing can be found by contacting Chris of "Noosa River Fishing Safaris" – *www.fishingnoosa.com.au/riverfishingsafaris.htm*

If you are after a spot of fishing and crabbing then contact the team at "Noosa River Fishing and Crab Tours" – *www.noosafishingandcrabtours.com.au*

NOOSA RIVER LOCATION GUIDE

Map 3 No.1 Noosa River Upper reaches

(Bass, tarpon, trevally)

The Noosa River upstream from Fig Tree Point are prime bass waters. The waters adjacent to the 'Narrows' are made of tight bends and are characterised by snaggy and reeded banks. The catch in these parts consists mainly of bass as well as tarpon and a few big eye and giant trevally. The bankside structure consists of steeper and undercut bank with overhanging foliage and reeds. This type of structure makes angling a little difficult. Techniques that are favoured here include casting lures such as spinnerbaits, beetlespins and small hardbody minnow patterns. Accurate casting and getting those lures into the shade will improve the catch rate. The stretch of the river above the Narrows is a little wider in places and is host to more open bankside structure. Anglers fishing baits around the snags typically target these reeded banks more than the lurecasting brigade.

As you traverse the system above Harrys Camp the river tends to meander more, making for some bendy but scenic travel. There

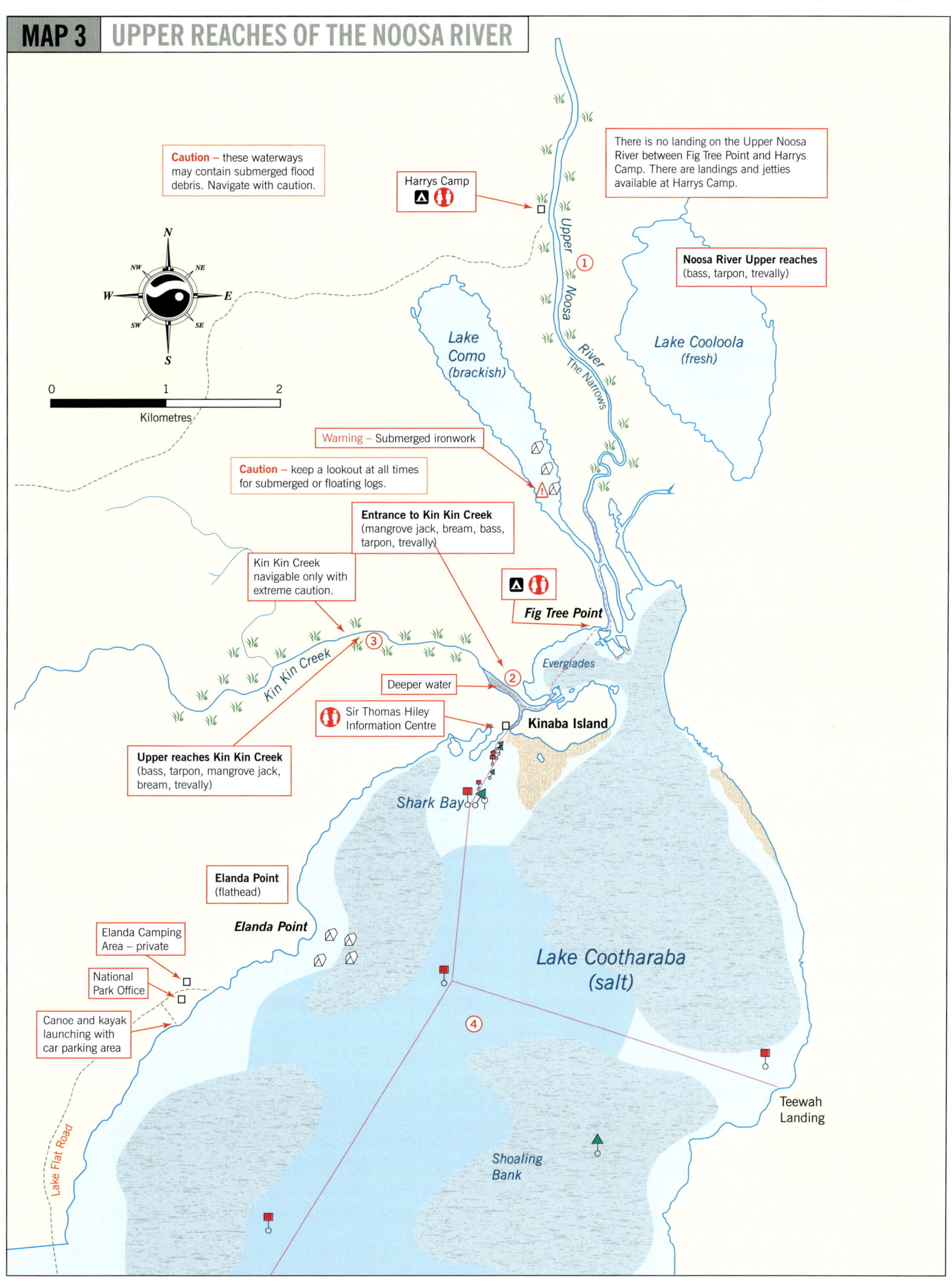
MAP 3 UPPER REACHES OF THE NOOSA RIVER
Caution – these waterways may contain submerged flood debris. Navigate with caution.
Harrys Camp
There is no landing on the Upper Noosa River between Fig Tree Point and Harrys Camp. There are landings and jetties available at Harrys Camp.
Upper Noosa River
The Narrows
Noosa River Upper reaches (bass, tarpon, trevally)
Lake Como (brackish)
Lake Cooloola (fresh)
N
NE
E
SE
S
SW
W
NW
0
1
2
Kilometres
Warning – Submerged ironwork
Caution – keep a lookout at all times for submerged or floating logs.
Entrance to Kin Kin Creek (mangrove jack, bream, bass, tarpon, trevally)
Kin Kin Creek navigable only with extreme caution.
Fig Tree Point
Everglades
Kin Kin Creek
Deeper water
Sir Thomas Hiley Information Centre
Kinaba Island
Upper reaches Kin Kin Creek (bass, tarpon, mangrove jack, bream, trevally)
Shark Bay
Elanda Point (flathead)
Elanda Point
Elanda Camping Area – private
National Park Office
Canoe and kayak launching with car parking area
Lake Cootharaba (salt)
Teewah Landing
Shoaling Bank
Lake Flat Road
1
2
3
4

are regulations on the use of outboard motors from the Campsite 3 area so check current regulations before boating in the area. Summer will typically have the bass further upriver and they are great candidates for targeting with surface lures, particularly if there has been good cicada activity.

Map 3 No. 2 Entrance to Kin Kin Creek
(Mangrove jack, bream, bass, tarpon, trevally)

Kin Kin Creek provides deeper water in the stretches where it begins to mix with Lake Cootharaba. Overhanging vegetated banks provide undercut structure and fallen timber homes for predators like mangrove jack, bream, bass, tarpon and trevally. Some of these banks provide difficulty for the angler and require skilled casting techniques with lures often having to be 'skipped' in under tight structure. Getting lures and bait into the shade is the key to catching local inhabitants. Soft plastics, lipless crankbaits and bibbed hardbody lures all take fish in the area. Drifting live herring, diver whiting and mullet baits or dead baits of pilchard and prawn into the snags is also a popular technique up here. Night time baitfishing is effective in these stretches but it will attract the attention of local bull sharks. The odd barramundi is also known to pop up in this area. A man-made channel was dredged through the Kin Kin Creek peninsular to make Kinaba Island. The bankside structure looks very natural today but the channel does not fish as well as the entrance to Kin Kin Creek.

Map 3 No. 3 Upper Reaches Kin Kin Creek
(Bass, tarpon, mangrove jack, bream, trevally)

The creek begins to shallow as the angler traverses its upper reaches. That said, there are still deeper sections, some sneaky little rock bars and some tempting bankside structure. After rain, it has been known to run surprisingly clear. Bass become more common the further upriver the angler travels. Casting lures and baits around the snags while staying mobile is an effective approach.

Map 3 No. 4 Lake Cootharaba

Lake Cootharaba is a large, shallow expanse that becomes shallower by the year. It can become a dangerous option for small boats caught in the middle of the lake in a strong southerly. The area is worked over extensively by nets when the prawns show up each season and as such is an unreliable fishery.

Areas of Interest

Elanda Point *(Flathead)*

Land based anglers fishing the margins around Elanda Point target local rocky structure for the odd flathead.

Map 4 No. 1 Lake Cootharaba Outlet – Channel and Beacons *(Flathead, bream, whiting)*

The main structure in the area consists of channels and beacons that are targeted by boat and shorebased anglers. These structures can be targeted during the run-out tide with baits and soft plastics for flathead, bream and whiting.

Map 4 No. 2 Noosa River between the Lakes
(Bream, trevally, flathead, mangrove jacks)

The stretch of river between Lake Cootharaba and Lake Cooroibah is a favoured haunt for many locals. The river provides attractive, challenging and often exciting fishing. Bankside structure consists of undercut style banks that contain a wealth of fallen tree and submerged timber structure. Bankside depths are often in the metre range with the channel dropping down to 3–5 m in the middle. Bait

ABOVE: Fishing the bankside snags is a popular pastime in the upper Noosa River.

and local predators use the bankside structure for protection and feeding purposes.

Many anglers fishing this stretch of the river target the feisty mangrove jack at which times other species become an exciting bycatch. The odd barramundi and threadfin salmon are known to be caught here. Unfortunately, these captures are nowhere near as common as they used to be.

Anchoring and drifting live and dead baits into snags or drifting likely looking banks with bait is effective here. Favourite baits include live herring, mullet, whiting and prawn with dead prawn and pilchard baits also effective. Trolling diving hardbody lures to 2–4 m depths or drifting while casting soft plastics or lipless style lures accounts for good fish around the snags. Summer surface luring in low light periods is effective but is not for the faint-hearted! A secret when fishing this stretch is to look for clusters or groups of fallen snags and then work them meticulously. If larger patches of bait are congregating around certain parts of the stretch, then focus your efforts there.

Areas of Interest

Mouth of Tronsons Drain
(Mangrove jack, trevally, estuary cod)

At certain times of the year, bait will be found congregating around the entrance to this outlet at which time lures and baits fished through the area will often attract the attention of predators.

Extensive Rock Bar Above Johns Landing
(Mangrove jack, trevally, estuary cod, bream, flathead, soapy jewfish)

Approximately 500 m up-river of Johns Landing, anglers watching a sounder will notice a stretch of solid reef bottom structure. The

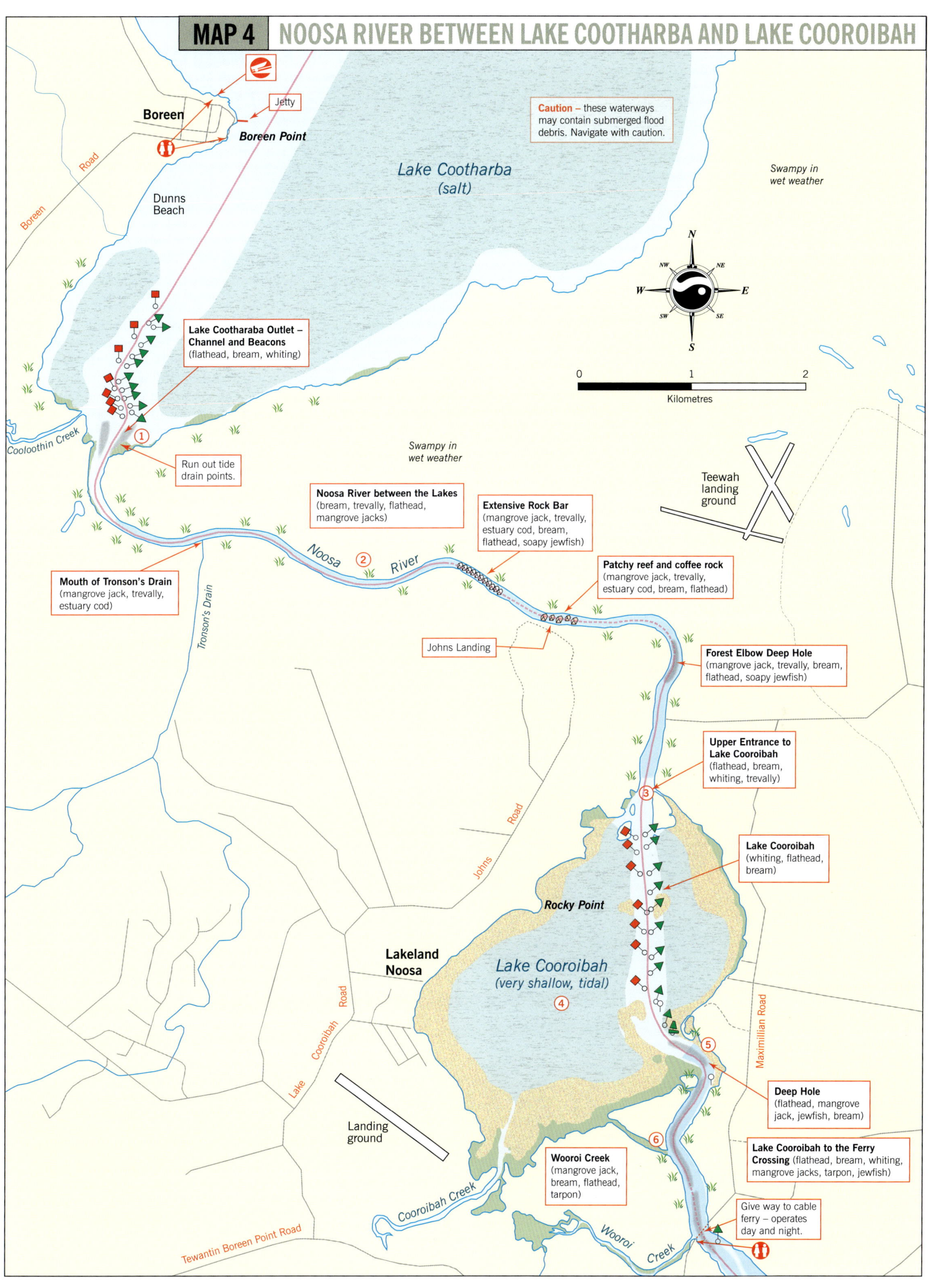
MAP 4 NOOSA RIVER BETWEEN LAKE COOTHARBA AND LAKE COOROIBAH
Jetty
Boreen
Boreen Point
Caution – these waterways may contain submerged flood debris. Navigate with caution.
Lake Cootharba (salt)
Swampy in wet weather
Road
Boreen
Dunns Beach
N
NE
E
SE
S
SW
W
NW
0
1
2
Kilometres
Lake Cootharaba Outlet – Channel and Beacons (flathead, bream, whiting)
1
Cooloothin Creek
Run out tide drain points.
Swampy in wet weather
Teewah landing ground
Noosa River between the Lakes (bream, trevally, flathead, mangrove jacks)
Extensive Rock Bar (mangrove jack, trevally, estuary cod, bream, flathead, soapy jewfish)
Noosa
2
River
Mouth of Tronson's Drain (mangrove jack, trevally, estuary cod)
Patchy reef and coffee rock (mangrove jack, trevally, estuary cod, bream, flathead)
Tronson's Drain
Johns Landing
Forest Elbow Deep Hole (mangrove jack, trevally, bream, flathead, soapy jewfish)
Upper Entrance to Lake Cooroibah (flathead, bream, whiting, trevally)
3
Road
Johns
Lake Cooroibah (whiting, flathead, bream)
Rocky Point
Lakeland Noosa
Lake Cooroibah (very shallow, tidal)
4
Road
Cooroibah
Lake
Maximillian Road
5
Deep Hole (flathead, mangrove jack, jewfish, bream)
Landing ground
6
Wooroi Creek (mangrove jack, bream, flathead, tarpon)
Lake Cooroibah to the Ferry Crossing (flathead, bream, whiting, mangrove jacks, tarpon, jewfish)
Cooroibah Creek
Wooroi
Creek
Give way to cable ferry – operates day and night.
Tewantin Boreen Point Road

bottom in this area consists of solid rocky bottom varying from 2–6 m in depth. You will notice the current irregularities as water is pushed up off the structure. The rock bar can claim a lot of gear when first fishing the area, but if you get the hang of trolling lures or drifting and hopping soft plastics and lipless crankbaits across the structure, you have a chance of catching some quality fish. Bait anglers anchoring and fishing baits down current to prime parts of the rock bar also fare well. Use the sounder to locate drop-off sections holding fish and focus your efforts there. Don't ignore the shoreline snags sitting alongside the rock bar vicinity and aim to fish the periods when the tide is just starting to run or beginning to ease in velocity.

Johns Landing Broken Reef

(Mangrove jack, trevally, estuary cod, bream, flathead)

Patchy rock structure exists on the bottom adjacent to the Johns Landing Private Camping Facility. The spot is popular for shorebased anglers and produces fish for anglers fishing baits and lures in the area.

Forest Elbow Deep Hole

(Mangrove jack, trevally, bream, flathead, soapy jewfish)

This corner provides one of the deeper holes in the stretch of the river. The shoreline structure adjacent to the hole accounts for some quality mangrove jack when conditions account for increased activity levels. A good indication of effective times to fish the hole is when fish can be seen stacking up on the drop-off to the hole when sounding the area with your fishfinder. Trolling deeper diving hardbody lures through the hole has accounted for some good fish. Drifting live baits through the hole and drifting while jigging soft plastics and lipless lures such as blades will also provoke attention from local predators.

ABOVE: Mangrove jack are a popular target in the Noosa River.

Map 4 No. 3 Upper Entrance to Lake Cooroibah

(Flathead, bream, whiting, trevally)

The outlet of the river into Lake Cooroibah consists of sand islands and shallower channel areas separated by some deeper channels. During the incoming tide, fish tend to move out of the channels and feed in the shallows. As the tide turns and runs out, fish retreat to the channels and await passing food. This area is favoured for drifting live baits or jigging soft plastics for the usually common flathead. Bream, trevally and whiting are often caught while fishing in this manner.

Map 4 No. 4 Lake Cooroibah

(Whiting, flathead, bream)

A thin and marked channel runs through the middle of the lake. Outside of this channel, the lake is largely very shallow. Most anglers fishing the shallows are targeting whiting on the run-in tide. Fishing worm, yabby and prawn baits in slightly deeper sections or fishing surface lures across the shallows are good ways to catch these tasty fish. Small stickbaits fished consistently with a 'walk-the-dog' style retrieve (no pauses) across the surface are a favoured approach in the area. This is particularly the case when the prawns are about.

Map 4 No. 5 Lake Cooroibah Outlet – Deep Hole

(Flathead, mangrove jack, jewfish, bream)

The Noosa River below Lake Cooroibah changes slightly in character. The system begins to broaden and different species become more common. Anglers will encounter more tailor and fish of a larger average size than found upriver. The big eye and giant trevally start to become bigger and are joined by some of their cousins such as the golden and diamond trevally. Fish such as javelin fish and jewfish also become more predominant in the lower reaches.

Lake Cooroibah drains into the lower Noosa River and this location is demarcated by a deep hole. The fishfinder will show soundings of a sudden drop-off that is host to scattered, submerged timber structures. The drop-off ledge often shows evidence of fish holding on the ledge. Traditionally jewfish have been targeted with some success in this location. Although not as common these days, jewies are still available in this location and are joined by some of the other local predators such as mangrove jack and the odd big flathead. Anchoring up-current of the hole and drifting live baits down the drop-off produces some good fish each year. Lure anglers spend time drifting over the drop-off and presenting jigged soft plastics and lipless style lures like blades to fish holding off the ledge areas. When using soft plastics don't be shy to use bigger offerings like 5–7 inch lures. Larger grub (tailed) style soft plastics in the 6 inch size will also draw attention from local predators when smaller offerings are not working. Boats with front mounted electric motors make this job so much easier these days!

Map 4 No. 6 Lake Cooroibah to the Ferry Crossing

(Flathead, bream, whiting, mangrove jack, tarpon, jewfish)

The banks are lined with mangroves and occasional fallen timber throughout this stretch of river. Bankside water is typically one metre deep and falls away to 4 m around the middle of the river. Sounding the water will show the odd mid-water structure lying on the bottom. Finding these areas while drifting with live baits or jigged lures will tempt predators holding around the available structure. The odd jewfish and jack are caught in this area after succumbing to excessive boat pressure in the Deep Hole and falling back further in the river. If you get to the Deep Hole to find a lot of boats, don't be put off. Use this to your advantage by drifting back downstream as you may be pleasantly surprised to find some good fishing to yourself!

Area of Interest

Wooroi Creek (mangrove jack, bream, flathead, tarpon)

The creek that enters the Noosa River immediately above the Ferry Crossing is largely shallow, opening into an occasional deeper section. Mangrove lined and secluded banks provide some good flathead, mangrove jack, tarpon and bream fishing. Drifting with the tide and casting lures to bank structure is a favoured approach here. Don't be afraid to bring a few crab pots with you, particularly after some rain.

Map 5 No. 1 Channel beneath Ferry Crossing
(flathead, bream, whiting)

It is well worth drifting a bait or lure on the run-out tide for species holding in the channel or along its sandy edges. Flathead are the mainstay, however some reasonable bream and whiting can be found on the sand edges and up in the shallows when the tide is building.

Map 5 No. 2 The Ski Run Channel
(flathead, bream, jewfish, tailor, trevally, tarpon, mangrove jack)

This stretch of water is the local ski run and is favoured by fast boats and skiers during summer. The bank drops into water that reaches 4–5 m deep in places, which is quite deep for the Noosa River. The channel is home to the odd chunky piece of rocky structure and as such hosts various predatory fish throughout the year. Drifting through the channel is a favoured way of covering ground and showing your offering to as many fish as possible. Fish will often 'stage' in certain parts of the channel so a mobile approach works well. Bait anglers targeting fish here mostly use live offerings of whiting, mullet and herring. Lure anglers either troll the bank line where diving lures are kept close to bottom, or drift while casting and retrieving various lure types such as soft plastics, bibbed and non-bibbed lures. If several boats are anchored around Makepeace Island, try drifting this patch of ground.

Areas of Interest

Old Ferry and Moorings at Makepeace Island
(flathead, bream, jewfish, tarpon, mangrove jack)

The moorings and old ferry lodged against the eastern side of Makepeace Island provide good structure on a deeper corner. At stages when the tide is not pushing too strongly, these areas make great places to drift and cast a well placed lure. Soft plastics and blades jigged in the shaded zones are often belted by holding predators. Some surprisingly good mangrove jack and jewfish have been caught in amongst the resident bream. The island is owned by Sir Richard Branson who visits quite regularly. If you are fishing off the island and catch a glimpse of Sir Richard feel free to give him a wave!

Deeper corner opposite Makepeace Island
(flathead, bream, jewfish, tailor, trevally, tarpon, mangrove jack)

A naturally vegetated bank drops into 2–4 m of water in the area immediately opposite Makepeace Island on the western bank. It provides the first bit of deeper water downstream from the big sandbanks below the ferry crossing. At various times of the year, bait and predators will shelter in this hole. It is a bit unpredictable, but when the fish are there, the fishing can be exciting. Bait anglers will often anchor up current of the hole and cast live and dead baits into deeper sections. Lure anglers often drift across the hole and work lures from the bankside drop-off and out into the deeper water. Jigging soft plastics and bladed lures produces good fish here every year. Flathead and bream are a mainstay in the hole, but are often joined by trevally, soapy jewfish, the occasional jack and tarpon. The turns of the tide are good times to be fishing the area.

Above: Flathead hold along any quality bottom structure in this part of the system.

Sheep Island drop-off (flathead, bream)

The waters immediately to the southern side of Makepeace and Sheep islands are shallow mud and weed flats. Many travellers end up pushing their way back out of here! The ledge where the flats drop into deeper water (1–2 m) holds some decent flathead at times. Some locals troll diving minnows along the drop for flathead awaiting a feed off the flats. Run-out tide is a prime time to target the area.

Map 5 No. 3 Tewantin Shallows
(flathead, Bream, Whiting)

This area between Sheep Island and the town of Tewantin is shallow weeded flats. It is rare to see anglers fishing in these shallows despite the fact that some good fish can be caught here. A rising tide and water up over the flats will usually have some good bream, flathead and whiting moving into the area, particularly in the summer months. Anglers in smaller boats find it easy to drift over the shallows while casting surface lures. Small cup face poppers or walk-the-dog retrieves with surface stickbait lures will get interest from predators hunting the flats – particularly when the prawns are on the go!

The ledge where these flats drop off into the channel sees a lot of tidal movement pushing against the obstruction. Anglers will often find the bream and trevally thick in this area. By working through the smaller ones, anglers will find some good fish in amongst the schools.

Map 5 No. 4 The Tewantin Gravel Patch

(Flathead, Bream, Jewfish, Tailor, Trevally, Estuary Cod, Tarpon, Mangrove Jack)

This is often one of the busiest stretches of the river to fish for boat traffic, but can be well worth the effort. A quality boat ramp is located on the western side, immediately above Noosa Harbour. The area consists of gravel/coffee rock bottom structure in 1–2 m of water and is usually host to a wealth of predators. Early in the day, prior to the boat traffic picking up, is the pick of the times to fish this stretch. The rocky bottom runs around the entire corner and drops into a 3–4 m hole on the inner corner at the starboard beacon.

A Warning Marker on the western side demarcates a chunk of old ballast material dropped by the big boats that used to traverse the Noosa River with cargo. This structure is a haven for moses perch and will usually hold a jack or two for the first one to cast a lure at it for the day.

The turns of the tide make for good fishing throughout the gravel patch and favoured approaches include drifting with baits and lures. Much of the structure is accessible to the shorebased angler. Bait anglers prefer fishing the deeper corner, and either anchoring or drifting live and dead baits through the area. Lure anglers typically drift with the tide while jigging soft plastics and harder lures off the bottom. The water is shallow enough to retrieve a bibbed lure and keep it close enough to the bottom to attract attention from predators. Fishing surface lures through the area during low light periods will usually have something coming up to investigate your offering! A good tip when using lures in the area is to try to experiment with lure size. Different sized lures will have varying results at certain times of the year, and this often has a lot to do with the size of the available food supplies.

Map 5 No. 5 Tewantin Channel

(Flathead, Bream, Jewfish, Tailor, Trevally, Estuary Cod, Tarpon, Mangrove Jack)

The area consists of gravelly bottom in the middle areas of the channel that runs down the river immediately out from the vicinity of Noosa Marina. The structure is an extension of that found upriver and local anglers fish this area in much the same way. This location has been known to produce a good flathead and jewfish for anglers fishing the turn of the tide. Boat anglers drifting the channel will find it well worthwhile putting some casts around the many houseboats anchored alongside the channel.

The southern bank, accessed from Hilton Esplanade, provides some good shorebased fishing. Anglers have ready access to some deeper water with plenty of moored boats and some good bottom structure in places. Anglers walking the banks have done well here.

Areas of Interest

Noosa Marina

(Flathead, Bream, Javelin Fish, Trevally, Mangrove Jack)

The areas within the Noosa Marina are restricted to fishing, but the structure is home to a lot of feisty predators. These fish can be targeted on the outer edges of the infrastructure by boat and shorebased anglers. Targeting the fish during the lower light periods and into the night is definitely the way to go in this location. Surface and sub-surface lures cast tight against structure and worked back out is a favourite approach here. Fishing the lights after dark can produce some exciting action at times.

Noosa Harbour Bridge Hole *(Flathead)*

Doonella Lake is a large and very shallow stretch of water. The extensive shallow mud flats are hard for most boats to traverse and are mainly the home to crabbers dropping off pots at high tide. The lake drains into the Noosa River through the Hilton Terrace Bridge at Noosa Harbour. The area immediately above and below the bridge is home to a deeper hole of 1–3 metres. As the tide begins to push out through the area, the resident flathead often become active. Shorebased anglers and boaties can target these fish with some success in the area during suitable conditions. Anglers targeting the bridge pylons with bait and lures will encounter flathead, trevally and bream.

The adjacent shallow extents of Lake Doonella are hard to access due to water depth. However, they are a great place to target mud crabs as long as you plan to put-in and retrieve your pots at the top of a run-in tide.

Map 5 No. 6 Goat Island

(Bream, Whiting, Flathead, Tailor)

The water between Goat Island and the north shore is home to acres of shallow weeded flats. In summer, these flats are home to plenty of bream, whiting and the odd good flathead. The location is often a sheltered spot when the wind is blowing, and is best on a rising tide. A channel runs along the north shore side and anglers in boats can drift through this region and cast to weeded areas on either side. The most effective approach across these shallows is to cast and retrieve surface lures. Fish hunting the flats on a run-in tide will quickly and aggressively attack a well presented surface lure fished across the shallows. Some good whiting and bream fall to this technique here every year.

Areas of Interest

Hole Beneath Goat Island

(Bream, Flathead, Trevally, Javelin Fish)

The flats on the eastern side of Goat Island drop into a slightly deeper hole that lies adjacent to the north shore bank. A run-out tide is a great place to target fish in this hole. It is rare to see anglers fishing the structure but it does produce fish for locals prepared to spend some time here. Anchoring above the hole and fishing live and dead baits into the area produce some good bread and butter species. Live prawns, yabbies and worm baits usually produce a fish or two here. Small soft plastics and blades will also turn up fish for the lure angler.

Right: The Noosa Marina holds good bream and jacks; ensure you fish only on the outside of the area!

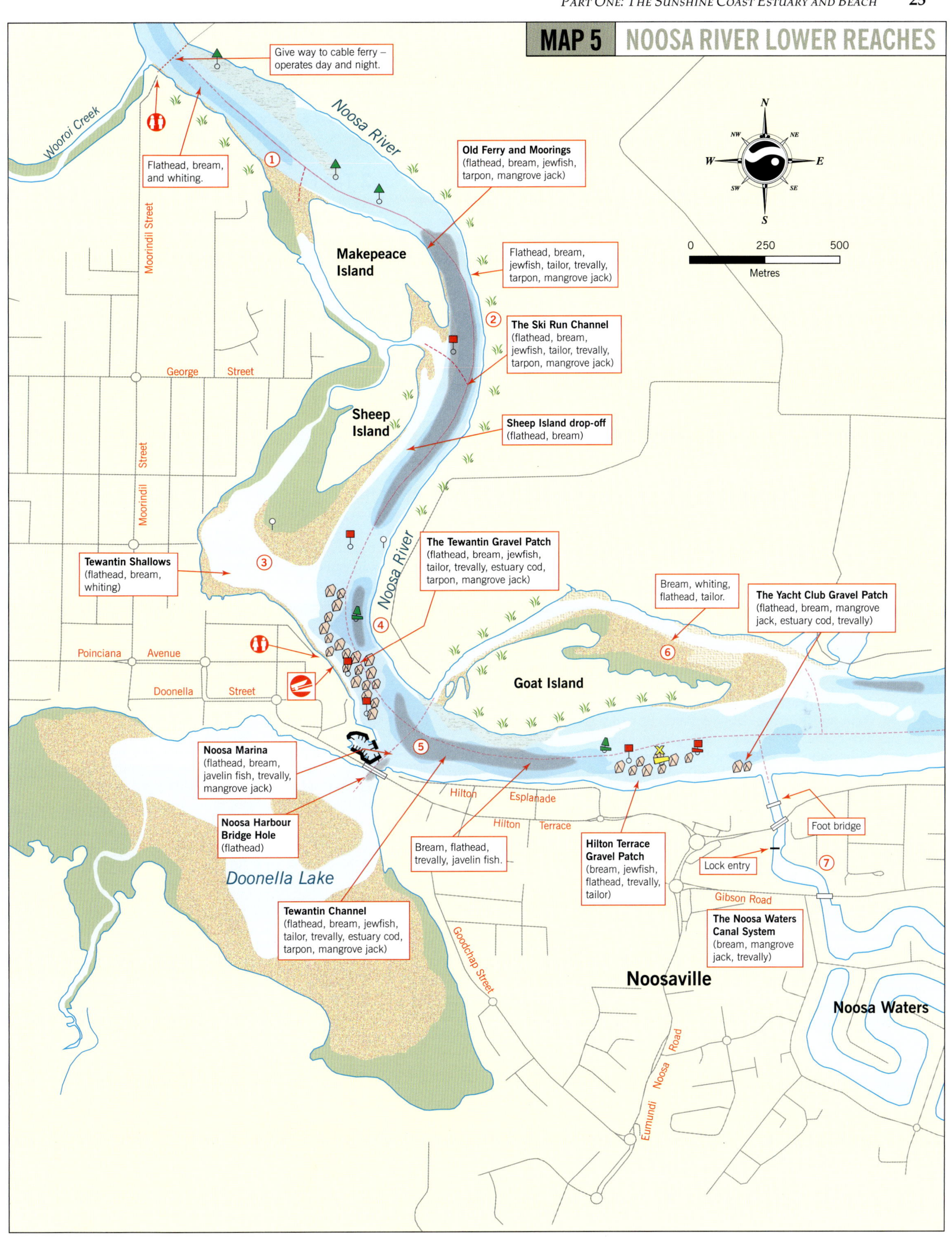
MAP 5 NOOSA RIVER LOWER REACHES
Give way to cable ferry – operates day and night.
Wooroi Creek
Noosa River
Flathead, bream, and whiting.
Old Ferry and Moorings (flathead, bream, jewfish, tarpon, mangrove jack)
Moorindil Street
Makepeace Island
Flathead, bream, jewfish, tailor, trevally, tarpon, mangrove jack)
The Ski Run Channel (flathead, bream, jewfish, tailor, trevally, tarpon, mangrove jack)
George Street
Sheep Island
Sheep Island drop-off (flathead, bream)
Moorindil Street
Tewantin Shallows (flathead, bream, whiting)
The Tewantin Gravel Patch (flathead, bream, jewfish, tailor, trevally, estuary cod, tarpon, mangrove jack)
Noosa River
Bream, whiting, flathead, tailor.
The Yacht Club Gravel Patch (flathead, bream, mangrove jack, estuary cod, trevally)
Poinciana Avenue
Doonella Street
Goat Island
Noosa Marina (flathead, bream, javelin fish, trevally, mangrove jack)
Noosa Harbour Bridge Hole (flathead)
Hilton Esplanade
Hilton Terrace
Bream, flathead, trevally, javelin fish.
Hilton Terrace Gravel Patch (bream, jewfish, flathead, trevally, tailor)
Foot bridge
Lock entry
Doonella Lake
Tewantin Channel (flathead, bream, jewfish, tailor, trevally, estuary cod, tarpon, mangrove jack)
Gibson Road
The Noosa Waters Canal System (bream, mangrove jack, trevally)
Goodchap Street
Noosaville
Noosa Waters
Eumundi Noosa Road
N
NE
E
SE
S
SW
W
NW
0
250
500
Metres
1
2
3
4
5
6
7

Hilton Terrace Gravel Patch

(Bream, Jewfish, Flathead, Trevally, Tailor)

A warning marker denotes a patch of rocky bottom structure on the southern side of the channel between Goat Island and Noosaville. The structure is easiest fished from a boat, but anglers accessing the river through Hilton Esplanade can reach the outer extents with a good cast. Fishing the area during low light periods and preferably as the tide begins to move following a change produces the best results. The area is quite shallow, and fishing lures across the structure while drifting with the tide has produced good fish for anglers. Winter bream fishing can be very good through this patch of ground, when small, well presented soft plastics are readily fought over by some good fish!

Map 5 No. 7 The Noosa Waters Canal System

(Bream, Mangrove Jack, Trevally)

A few hundred metres above the intersection of the canal system and the Noosa River, the water is locked by a private gate set-up. Only local boating residents have pass key access. Access to the area can be gained from the road side in places, which enables shorebased and kayak anglers the opportunity to fish the waters. The area is host to some great bream and mangrove jack fishing around the abundant shoreline structure. Kayak anglers trolling diving minnows through the canals produce some great jacks each season, particularly during the hours of darkness. Be aware of local bull sharks as there are some sizeable ones caught here occasionally. Also, be aware to respect people's property and privacy when fishing the area, as residents are rightfully protective of their space!

Area of Interest

The Yacht Club Gravel Patch

(Flathead, Bream, Mangrove Jack, Estuary Cod, Trevally)

Between the locked canal gate system and the Noosa River, a stretch of easily accessed water can be found. This area is fished by many landbased anglers and accounts for good bream, whiting and the occasional jack. This is a good place to target mudcrabs after a spell of rain. The canal system enters the Noosa River alongside the Noosa Yacht and Rowing Club. A patch of rocky ground clothes the western corner of the man-made channel that enters the river immediately opposite the Yacht Club. This is a great shorebased location, where anglers fishing baits and lures can catch some good fish. Early morning bait anglers using live offerings have taken some good jacks and trevally in this area. The channel and bridge here also provide good shorebased fishing and crabbing locations.

Map 6 No. 1 The Noosaville Jetty Run

(Bream, Trevally, Flathead, Mangrove Jack, Tailor)

The stretch along Gympie Terrace is home to dozens of jetties and pontoons. These floating structures host good numbers of resident species and much of the fishing can be accessed from land and boat. Many shorebased anglers spend time fishing into the middle of the channel and bother only small fish. The cunning shorebased angler gets offerings into any available shade and some exciting captures occur! Shorebased anglers will find that many jetties are locked, however there is still plenty of space to cast a lure and bait against the structures that provide shade and shelter.

The low light periods and a run-out tide provide the best opportunity to catch fish in these areas. Casting accuracy and allowing the tide to work lures into the prime locations are the way to catch fish here. Most anglers fishing these areas stay mobile and continue to put soft plastic and sinking hardbody lures against and under the available structure. Sinking lures right into the shady depths and then twitching them back out is a sure way to produce an aggressive reaction. Smaller live and dead baits such as prawns will also tempt resident fish.

Houseboats anchored down the middle of the channel provide some handy structure in an otherwise sandy channel. Low light periods and during the run-out tide are good times to cast a lure to fish holding around these floating structures. Lures that can be cast tight against the structure and allowed to sink to the shade stand the best chance of being eaten by local predators. Be mindful to not strike someone else's property when fishing in this manner.

Map 6 No. 2 The Frying Pan

(Trevally, Tailor, Whiting, Bream, Flathead)

The waters directly opposite Munna Point are host to a huge expanse of sand flats. These flats envelope much of the water between Munna Point and the mouth of the Noosa River. The western shoreline truncating the flats is host to a channel that runs along this shoreline and is known as the Frying Pan region. The adjacent flats are home to plenty of fish, but there are also plenty of predators that happily feed in the channel. Fishing either side of the channel will provide some good catches of trevally, tailor, bream and flathead. Low light periods and as the tide starts to move are favoured times to fish here.

Winter fishing in the Frying Pan with big surface lures is renowned for producing some XOS tailor and some bigger giant and golden trevally. Retrieving surface and sub-surface lures from the shallow bank and flat areas and out into deeper water is a common and effective strategy. Hopping big soft plastics over the drop-offs has produced some big flathead in the spring and summer months. Baitfishing the area with worms, yabbies and prawns around the drop-off areas is a favoured technique for solid spring and summer whiting. These speedsters are also effectively targeted here with smaller surface lures.

Area of Interest

The Frying Pan Flats *(Whiting, Flathead, Bream)*

There are plenty of sand flat areas around the Frying Pan that extend all the way towards Munna Point. The flats are channelled and contain the odd snag that has drifted down river and become lodged in the sand. The flats are home to some good whiting, bream and flathead. Anchoring on the edge of the flats and baitfishing with live or dead prawns, yabbies and worms will bring some good whiting and bream undone. Many boat and kayak anglers enjoy drifting or wading the flats and retrieving small surface and diving lures. Resident whiting, bream and flathead produce some entertaining and tasty fishing. Peak times for the flats are spring and summer, and are best on a rising tide.

Map 6 No. 3 Noosa River Mouth Rockwall Hole

(Bream, Flathead, Whiting, Trevally, Tailor, Luderick)

A rockwall has been developed along the southern bank of the mouth to prevent erosion. The wall is flanked by a deeper hole that continues to run out into the ocean, and can be fished by boat and shorebased anglers. This hole provides action for bait anglers targeting bream, flathead and whiting. The tidal flow can cause difficulty for anglers so aim to target the periods of lessened tidal flow. The area provides some luderick action during the cooler months for anglers that want to experience some of the most northern luderick fishing available. Float and weed fishing is the favoured approach.

Area of Interest

Noosa River Mouth Channel Snags

(Bream, Flathead, Trevally, Mangrove Jack, Tailor)

The southern bank running upriver from the mouth of the Noosa River provides a snag lined channel. The tide can push strongly through the area, but the available structure is home to some quality predators. Anglers in the know use low light periods of

MAP 6 NOOSA RIVER MOUTH
CORAL SEA
Teewah Beach
Caution – these waterways may contain submerged flood debris. Navigate with caution.
Warning – Noosa bar and inlet should not be crossed except with local knowledge.
Bar Crossing
Noosa River Mouth Channel Snags (bream, flathead, trevally, mangrove jack, tailor)
Laguna Bay
North Head
The Frying Pan (trevally, tailor, whiting, bream, flathead)
Groyne
Noosa Parade Jetties and Canals (bream, trevally, mangrove jacks)
Frying Pan
The Spit
Groyne
Rockwall Hole (bream, flathead, whiting, trevally, tailor, luderick)
Noosa Beach
NOOSA INLET
Woods Bay (trevally, tailor, flathead, whiting)
Hastings Street
Woods Bay
0 250 500
Metres
Woods Bay Spit
Noosa Sound
Parade
Noosa
Channel
Heads
Noosa
Noosa Sound (trevally, tailor, flathead, mangrove jack)
Ricky Ricardo's Hole (trevally, tailor, flathead, bream)
Woods Bay Spit Channel (trevally, bream, estuary cod, mangrove jacks, tailor)
Noosa Heads Channel (trevally, tailor, flathead, mangrove jack)
DPI Bank Channel (flathead, bream, whiting)
Munna Point
Munna Bridge Hole
Munna Bridge Area (flathead, trevally, tailor, bream, jewfish, jacks)
Creek
River
The Noosaville Jetty Run (bream, trevally, flathead, mangrove jack, tailor)
Noosa Parade
Weyba
Drive
Pelican Beach
Weyba Hole (flathead, bream, whiting, trevally, jewfish, javelin fish)
Terrace
Keyser Island Flats
Noosa
Noosa
Road
Gympie
Weyba Mangrove Banks (flathead, mangrove jack)
Keyser Island
Weyba
Keyser Island Flats
Ross Island
Hay Island
Keyser Island Flats
Keyser Island Flats (whiting, bream, flathead)
Weyba Road Bridge
Weyba Road
Weyba Creek Footbridge
Weyba Creek (flathead, bream, whiting, trevally, mangrove jack)
Lake Weyba Drive
Weyba Mangrove Banks (flathead, mangrove jack)
Weyba Creek

ABOVE: The Noosa River produces the odd chunky GT.

minimal tidal flow to target solid trevally, jacks and the occasional barra. Drifting the bank and fishing soft plastic and hardbody lures into the snags is an effective technique. You will lose some gear but the rewards can be worth the angst. Anchoring above snags and fishing live fish baits into the timber is also an effective technique in the area. There is little room for error when fishing here, and many good fish are hooked and lost remarkably quickly!

Map 6 No. 4 Noosa Sound

(TREVALLY, TAILOR, FLATHEAD, MANGROVE JACK)

Once upon a time, the Noosa River channel used to run straight through this area and along Noosa Parade to the ocean. The diversion means the channel now etches out its course around the head of this sandy peninsular and can be fished by boat and shorebased anglers. The channel is up to 4 m deep in places and has some solid snags on the bottom. Winter will see a brigade of anglers fishing surface lures in the low light (and cold) periods of the day. Some solid tailor and trevally fall every year to this approach. Fishing soft plastics and sinking hardbody lures through winter and summer will produce a variety of predators if you can stop them before the snags! Boat anglers drifting with live fish baits through the channel take some big flathead and jacks each season. The tidal flow often pushes through the area, and bait is typically held up along the edges of the flow. Putting lures across this zone is a sure way to tangle with a local tailor or trevally.

Areas of Interest

Ricky Ricardo's Hole *(TREVALLY, TAILOR, FLATHEAD, BREAM)*

The well-known restaurant Ricky Ricardo's on the southern bank shoreline, is close to a deeper section of the river. This area is often referred to by locals as Outer Woods Bay. This hole is home to predatory fish year-round. Winter surface luring is favoured here for big tailor and trevally. Summer lure and bait fishing produces some good flathead, bream and the occasional jack. The hole is accessible to the shorebased angler from Noosa Parade.

Woods Bay Spit Channel

(TREVALLY, BREAM, ESTUARY COD, MANGROVE JACK, TAILOR)

A channel often exists in the region opposite the Woods Bay Spit. The channel hugs the Noosa Parade rockwall that is host to pontoons and housing. The area is most accessible by boat, but anglers fishing from The Woods Bay Spit can target fish in the channel. Low light periods provide some exciting fishing as larger predatory fish feed on local bait around the rockwall and floating structure. Surface and sub-surface lures cast and retrieved around the rock wall and structure can be very effective. Baitfishing with live bait will tempt aggressive local species like trevally and jacks.

Map 6 No. 5 Woods Bay

(TREVALLY, TAILOR, FLATHEAD, WHITING)

Some deeper water exists in the often sheltered area of Woods Bay. At times, boat and shorebased anglers are treated to some great fishing in this region of the river. During winter, this becomes the domain of the early morning surface lure angler. Big, blooping retrieves and exhilarating surface strikes, big tailor and trevally are a signature of this area during the cold months. During summer, lure and bait fishing will produce some good fish. Some sizeable whiting and flathead fall to shorebased bait anglers each summer. The location will often throw in a few surprises such as a barra, soapy jewfish or the odd average sized queenfish.

Areas of Interest

Noosa Parade Jetties and Canals

(BREAM, TREVALLY, MANGROVE JACK)

Private jetties are situated in the deeper channel that runs along Noosa Parade and up to the Sheraton. The shoreline on the southern side of Noosa Parade forms a host of canals with plenty of pontoon and jetty structures. These pontoons and jetties are home to plenty of bream, trevally and the odd jack. Spring and summer provide some good bream fishing around this structure. Drifting while casting and retrieving lures is a favoured approach here. As always, be mindful of people's properties and move on if requested to do so by property owners.

Map 6 No. 7 Munna Bridge Area

(FLATHEAD, TREVALLY, TAILOR, BREAM, JEWFISH, MANGROVE JACK)

The Munna Bridge Hole is a deeper hole that spreads out in the area beneath the Munna Point Bridge. The deeper water extends as a deeper channel to the east and around the back of the Noosa Heads area. The shoreline immediately adjacent to Munna Bridge is a favourite shorebased spot for anglers targeting mangrove jack. Live baiting in the hole and around the bridge pylons in the dark and during low light periods of the day produces jacks routinely. There is often a good supply of bait in the hole and lure anglers drifting and casting soft plastics, blades and bigger lipless crankbait style lures can tempt a big flathead, jewfish or jack from the local waters.

Areas of Interest

Noosa Heads Channel

(TREVALLY, TAILOR, FLATHEAD, MANGROVE JACK)

The channel that runs behind the Noosa Parade canal systems attains depths of up to 5 metres in places. It is possible to find large amounts of bait stacked up in this channel at times. When this occurs, the predators are rarely far away. The area can be home to some fantastic surface activity at times, as trevally, tailor and other species gorge on available bait. The bankside structure in the vicinity is also home to the occasional mangrove jack and other species such as tarpon. Once upon a time, this was a favourite location to target threadfin salmon. Casting and retrieving lures is an effective manner to tangle with local species, as is drifting or anchoring with live fish baits.

DPI Bank Channel *(FLATHEAD, BREAM, WHITING)*

Immediately up-river from Munna Point Caravan Park and within the Noosa River, a 2–4 m channel runs down the southern river bank in the vicinity of the DPI Station. The channel is home to some good fish at times. Anglers drifting the channel in boats or fishing from the shore fare well here. Live fish, prawn and worm baits produce many of the good fish taken here each year. Anglers fishing bigger fish baits off the Munna Point area take the odd good bull shark.

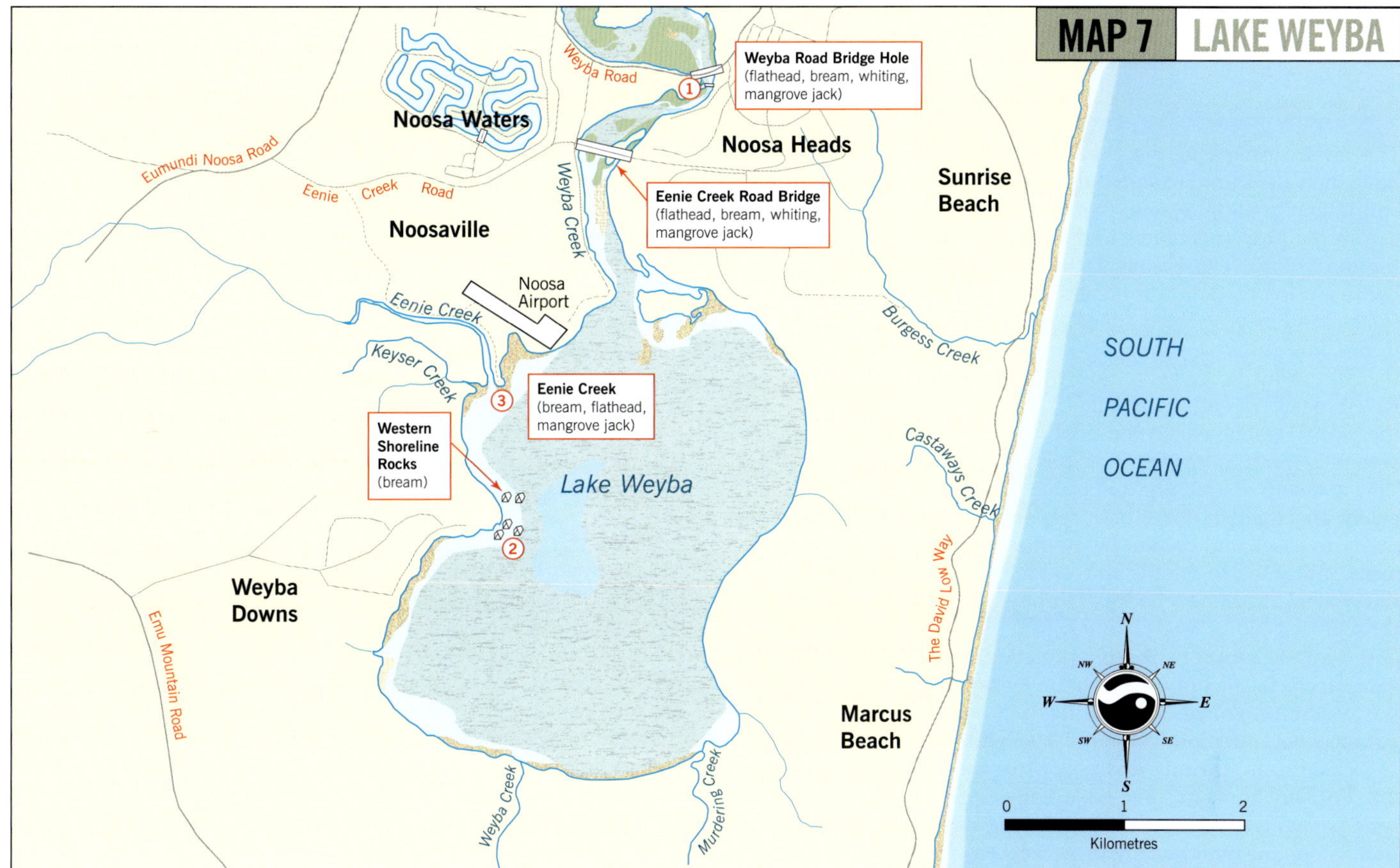

Map 6 No. 8 Weyba Creek
(flathead, bream, whiting, trevally, mangrove jack)

Lake Weyba empties into the Noosa River via Weyba Creek. The creek meanders its way to the Noosa River through expansive mangrove lined banks and over extensive sandy shallows. Although difficult to navigate in sections, the waters of Weyba Creek produce a variety of predators to keep recreational anglers returning.

Areas of Interest

Weyba Hole
(flathead, bream, whiting, trevally, jewfish, javelin fish)

Above the first major turn of the lower Weyba Creek waters, anglers will encounter a deeper hole. Locally referred to as Weyba Hole, this deeper patch of water is home to several species year-round. This location often surprises, and was traditionally a go-to spot for threadfin salmon. Boat anglers are able to drift or anchor and fish live and dead baits into the hole. Lure anglers target the location in much the same way as at the Munna Bridge Hole.

Keyser Island Flats *(whiting, bream, flathead)*

The waters around the Keyser Island and Weyba Channel are host to expansive weedbed and mud flats. These flats are usually the home of the crabber chasing quality mud crabs. However, a rising tide in these waters will find predators such as whiting, flathead and bream very receptive to a surface lure or lightly weighted prawn or worm bait. Areas of the flats are accessible to the shorebased angler through Noosa Parade and Weyba Road.

Weyba Mangrove Banks *(flathead, mangrove jack)*

Weyba Creek is host to some extensive undercut style mangrove lined banks. These undercuts provide great host structure for flathead, mangrove jacks and other species such as moses perch. Live baiting with whiting, mullet and herring along the banks or drifting and retrieving soft plastic and hardbody lures in these areas is a good way to tangle with these fish. Low light periods where the tide is not pushing too hard produces best results.

Map 7 No. 1 Weyba Road Bridge Hole
(flathead, bream, whiting, mangrove jack)

A deeper channel and hole extends around the old and new bridge close to Weyba Road. This is a popular shorebased location where live baiting and lure anglers are able to target fish in the channel and around the bridge pylons. Low light and night time live baiting produce several jacks and big flathead each season.

Up-river of the bridge, anglers will enter the shallow and expansive Lake Weyba. This body is very shallow and difficult to navigate. 6 knot speed restrictions make the drive across the lake a long one. Despite its shallow waters, the lake does hold some quality if hard to access fish.

Map 7 No. 2 Western Shoreline Rocks *(bream)*

The western shoreline of Lake Weyba holds a couple of notable fishing locations. A small peninsular on this shoreline lies adjacent to some rocky structure. This shorebased spot provides some good bream fishing during low light periods when the tide is rising. Local rocky shores attract resident bream as water pushes into the area. Fishing baits of prawn and worm produces good results.

Map 7 No. 3 Eenie Creek
(bream, flathead, mangrove jack)

This shallow creek offers some access for shorebased anglers and kayak anglers. The creek provides scenic fishing but the propensity for the entrance to remain shallow and to silt up at low tide results in tough fishing in stagnating waters at times. That said, some anglers do experience some 'remote style' jack fishing around the snags when only minutes from home!

Area of Interest

Eenie Creek Road Bridge at Weyba Creek
(flathead, bream, whiting, mangrove jack)

This area is one of the last deeper sections to fish when travelling up Weyba Creek and fishes similar to the Weyba Road Bridge area.

THE MAROOCHY RIVER

The river systems of the Sunshine Coast although similar, all have their own unique signature. The Maroochy River is a broad and largely shallow system that gently meanders its way through a mix of bush vegetation and farmland towards its mouth at Maroochydore. The system is broadly characterised by natural banks and many shallow mud and sand banks. The Maroochy River system and its associated tributaries can be broadly grouped into upper, mid and lower zones. 23 km above the mouth of the system the Maroochy River splits into the North and South Maroochy Rivers near to Yandina and the Bruce Highway. The junction of the two rivers is near to the tidal limit of this waterway and the waters up-river of this point include the upper zone of the system. This area and the picturesque waters that characterise its up-river extent are largely home to bass, tarpon and the odd brackish water mangrove jack and bream. Below the confluence of the two river arms and down to the Bli Bli township includes the mid zone of the system. The Maroochy River throughout its mid zone meanders through flat lying floodplain territory. Banking against farmland and a lot of natural bankside vegetation, the system is joined by several creeks including Coolum, Eudlo and Petrie creeks. As the system progresses through the mid zone, the usual estuarine suspects become more common. The bankside structure is home to jacks, bream, trevally and cod while the mud and sand drop-off zones are home to some good flathead. The Maroochy River is well known for some good jewie fishing with some of the deeper holes along the river hosting these fish year-round. The propensity for the mid zone of the system to include floodplain runoff means this section of the estuary are often darkly coloured. Don't let this put you off exploring up the system as there is some good fishing to be had in these waters. The lower zone of the system includes the waters from beneath Bli Bli and down towards the mouth of the Maroochy River. The lower zone includes some deeper sections of river, canal developments and a broad estuarine delta where the river meets the sea. The lower zone is typically characterised by clearer waters due to a more direct influence from the sea. This zone is the most popular area for recreational anglers to practice their passion. This section of the system is home to bream, whiting, flathead, tailor, trevally, mangrove jack and jewfish to name some of the more popular suspects intercepted by anglers.

Facilities

Maroochydore is an easy 1 hour drive from Brisbane and contains all the services a recreational angler could wish for. Anglers will find a thriving coastal town that offers a good mix of accommodation styles and comforts for the traveller. There are plenty of options for the shorebased and boating angler in the area. Below Bli Bli there are four boat ramps. Three ramps can be found on the southern river bank at Picnic Point Esplanade, above the highway bridge and on Eudlo Creek at Fisherman's Road. A boat ramp can also be found at Muller Park on the northern bank just below the David Low Bridge at Bli Bli. A further boat ramp can be found up-river at Lake Dunethin off the Bli Bli Road.

THE MAROOCHY RIVER LOCATION GUIDE

Map 8 No.1 Maroochy River Upper Reaches *(Bass, Tarpon, Mangrove Jack)*

The Maroochy River splits at this point to form the North and South Maroochy Rivers. This point approximates the broad location where ocean tides begin to have little influence on the system and anglers begin to encounter brackish and freshwater species.

Areas of Interest

North Maroochy River *(Bass, Tarpon, Mangrove Jack)*

The North Maroochy River is targeted more by recreational anglers than the nearby South Maroochy River. This arm of the system pushes up past Ninderry and runs parallel with the Bruce Highway. The arm is a beautiful stretch of water that is shallow for much of its extent. As such, it offers the most opportunity for anglers using small craft such as kayaks and canoes. The land adjacent to the Ninderry Road Bridge is the most common point used by kayak anglers to access the system. Above and below this point the waters are largely covered by thick vegetation and a plethora of places for predatory fish to hide. Anglers fishing in these waters spend most time casting lures for predominantly bass and lesser numbers of mangrove jack and the odd tarpon. Casting lures tight against available structure is a good way to get a response from feisty local bass. Popular techniques involve casting surface lure and using walk-the-dog retrieves during the summer months. Sub-surface lures including small spinnerbait profile lures, hardbody lures and soft plastics are productive when fished around structure.

South Maroochy River *(Bass, Tarpon, Mangrove Jack)*

The South Maroochy River does not provide the large amount of fishing geography as provided by the northern arm. Above the confluence of the two arms, the South Maroochy River works its way up past Yandina where it is eventually truncated by the Wappa Falls Dam. Much of this stretch of water makes for tough fishing in shallow water. The occasional bass and lesser numbers of mangrove jack are caught by anglers here.

Map 8 No. 2 Maroochy River – Lake Dunethin Stretch *(Flathead, Bream, Mangrove Jack)*

Below the North and South Maroochy rivers confluence, the Maroochy River meanders through farmland and joins Lake Dunethin. The river consists of shallower waters in these areas and some care must be taken when navigating by boat. The bankside drop-off provides an ideal location to target flathead and bream with lures and baits. The shoreline structure holds the odd jack, and closer to the Bruce Highway Bridge, the occasional bass.

Areas of Interest

Caboolture Creek

The mouth of Caboolture Creek offers some good bankside fishing with plenty of natural structure to hold a few fish. The odd scattering of rock structure exists in the channel in these parts. Above the entrance to Caboolture Creek and below at Browns Rocks, anglers can find patches of reef that usually hold fish. These areas cause motor props some heartache on lower tides so travel with care!

Lake Dunethin

A big run-out tide can provide some increased activity from resident fish around the entrances to Lake Dunethin and Boggy Creek on the opposite side of the channel. Bankside structure and harder structure such as Dunethin Rock are good places to cast a bait and lure during these periods. Jigging prawn style soft plastics or the real thing around local structure during these run-out tides produces some good flathead and bream for anglers. The summer months produce a few good jacks for anglers targeting these areas.

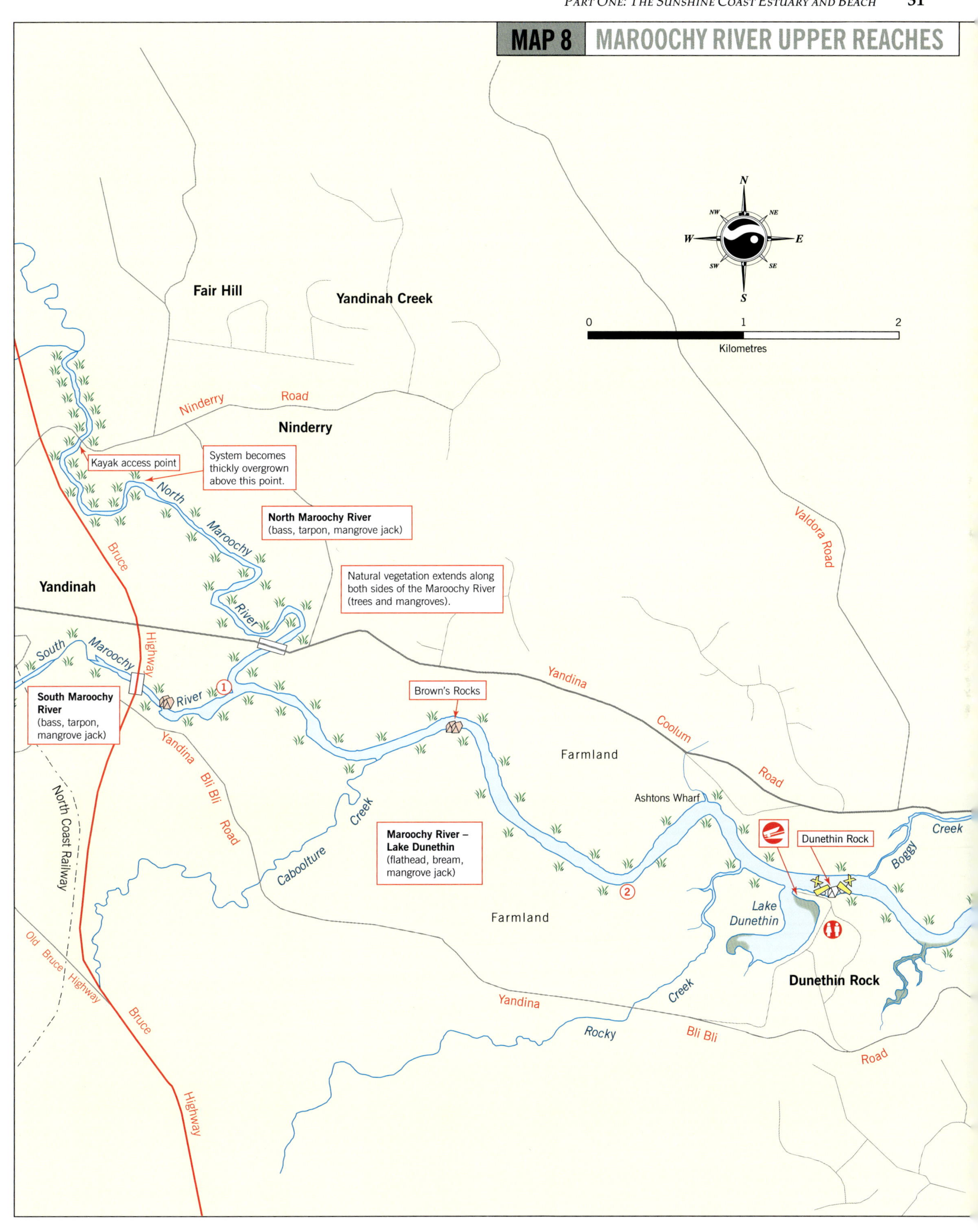
MAP 8 MAROOCHY RIVER UPPER REACHES
N
NW
NE
W
E
SW
SE
S
0
1
2
Kilometres
Fair Hill
Yandinah Creek
Ninderry
Road
Ninderry
Kayak access point
System becomes thickly overgrown above this point.
North Maroochy River
North Maroochy River (bass, tarpon, mangrove jack)
Natural vegetation extends along both sides of the Maroochy River (trees and mangroves).
Yandinah
Bruce
Highway
South Maroochy River
South Maroochy River (bass, tarpon, mangrove jack)
1
Brown's Rocks
Yandina
Coolum
Road
Valdora Road
Farmland
Ashtons Wharf
Yandina Bli Bli Road
North Coast Railway
Caboolture Creek
Maroochy River – Lake Dunethin (flathead, bream, mangrove jack)
2
Dunethin Rock
Boggy Creek
Lake Dunethin
Farmland
Dunethin Rock
Old Bruce Highway
Bruce
Highway
Yandina
Rocky
Creek
Bli Bli
Road

Map 9 No. 1 Cane Train Bridge
(FLATHEAD, MANGROVE JACK)

This section of the mid zone of the Maroochy River fishes much the same as areas upriver. Natural bankside structure and drop-off areas provide some good catches for anglers prepared to put some time into fishing the location.

Map 9 No. 2 Small Creek Bend
(FLATHEAD, MANGROVE JACK, JEWFISH)

The river takes a strong turn in the area of Small Creek. Local anglers often concentrate efforts in this area for a good reason. The location is home to plenty of quality fish holding structure. The channel in this location hosts a good mid-river rock bar in slightly deeper water and in close proximity to creek inflows and good bankside structure. These structures are worth targeting with hardbody and soft plastic lures when chasing flathead, bream, jacks and the odd jewie and cod. There are a few lucky anglers that take the occasional barra from this location. Live baits fished around the rocks and snags during low light hours have produced some good fish for anglers.

Map 9 No. 3 Confluence Coolum Creek
(FLATHEAD, MANGROVE JACK)

Thick vegetation abounds either side of the Maroochy River and up along the banks of Coolum Creek. The water is largely shallow through the area but the natural banks and secluded nature of the waters provide solitude and a few fishing surprises for anglers prepared to explore. The drop-off areas and natural bankside structure provide shelter and feeding points for fish such as flathead and jacks.

Map 9 No. 4 Bli Bli Islands Stretch
(FLATHEAD, BREAM, MANGROVE JACK, JEWFISH, WHITING)

The river above and below the Bli Bli Islands is host to some deeper patches of water. The natural bankside structure and shallow water island areas that drain into these deeper points on the run-out make these waters a prime place to target quality flathead, the occasional jack and jew. The winter and spring months often produce good numbers of soapy sized jewie and the occasional larger specimen in these deeper areas. Turn of the tide periods and particularly following some decent rainfall are prime times to find active jewies in the area. Anglers fishing deeper jigged soft plastics and live baits during lower light periods report the best of the catches.

Local anglers often spend time around the island sand flats targeting whiting. Through the warmer months these flats can fish well for whiting on surface lures or live baits of prawn and worm.

Map 9 No. 5 Cook Rd Bend and David Low Way Bridge
(FLATHEAD, BREAM, MANGROVE JACK, ESTUARY COD, TREVALLY, JEWFISH)

The pylons of the David Low Way Bridge always host a variety of predators. Although the water can be quite shallow through the bridge area, there are deeper channels that produce some good fish. The deeper waters around the bridge contain coffee rock bottom in places and this all combines to produce a great fish holding location. Fishing hardbodied lures, soft plastics or baits tight against the pylons should produce fish for anglers wetting a line at turning tide and low light periods. There are a number of pylons to fish under the bridge and bream anglers will often find good numbers of fish moving between and holding against these structures. Rocks adorn the walls on either side of the river here, and offer the shorebased angler some good fishing. There is a boat ramp immediately downriver of the bridge on the Muller Park side of the river. The channel waters, bridge and rock structures produce a variety of fish each year that includes the likes of bream, jacks, jewies, estuary cod, trevally and tailor. The shallow sandflat areas around the bridge also produce some great whiting fishing at times for anglers fishing a making tide.

The river drops into some deeper water a few hundred metres above the bridge. This deeper water wraps around a productive bank that extends around the corner on the eastern shoreline. A mix of timber and rocky structure can be located along this bank near to the point where the bank drops into deeper water. Anglers drifting along the bank during low light periods and casting lures tight against the bank, then working them out into deeper water report some good catches. The standard culprits are invariably holding along this wall and include bream, flathead, jewies and the odd jack. Diving hardbody, bladed and soft plastic lures all work well here if fished productively against and along fish holding structure. Live and dead baits will also produce some good fish. Anglers fishing baits during the night hours report some good catches here.

ABOVE: Bridges and rocky banks in the area always hold a mangrove jack or two.

LEFT: The Maroochy River holds some good mangrove jacks in places.

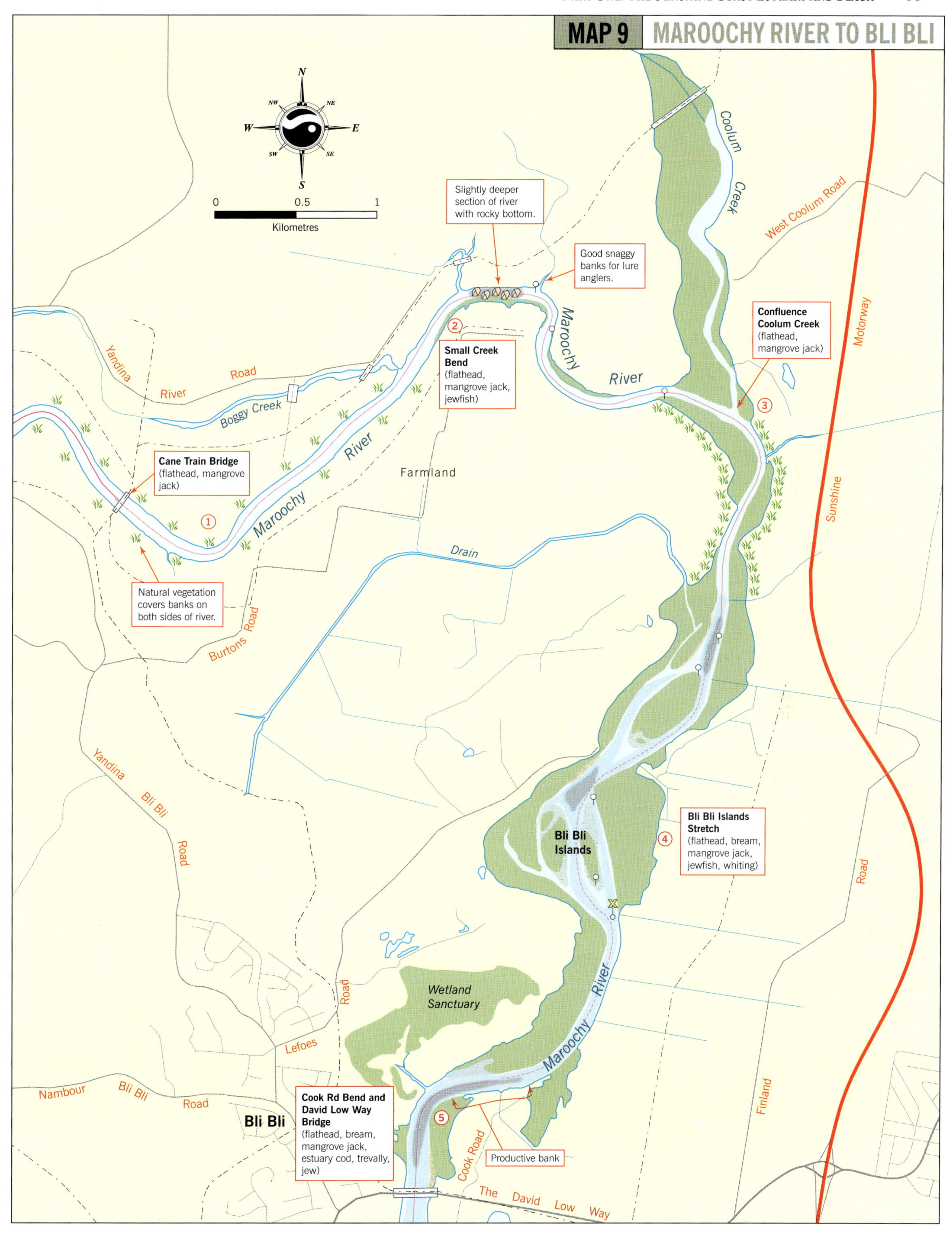
MAP 9
MAROOCHY RIVER TO BLI BLI
N
NW
NE
W
E
SW
SE
S
0
0.5
1
Kilometres
Slightly deeper section of river with rocky bottom.
Good snaggy banks for lure anglers.
Confluence Coolum Creek (flathead, mangrove jack)
Small Creek Bend (flathead, mangrove jack, jewfish)
Cane Train Bridge (flathead, mangrove jack)
Natural vegetation covers banks on both sides of river.
Bli Bli Islands Stretch (flathead, bream, mangrove jack, jewfish, whiting)
Cook Rd Bend and David Low Way Bridge (flathead, bream, mangrove jack, estuary cod, trevally, jew)
Productive bank
Coolum Creek
West Coolum Road
Motorway
Sunshine
Road
Maroochy River
Yandina River Road
Boggy Creek
Farmland
Drain
Burtons Road
Yandina Bli Bli Road
Bli Bli Islands
Wetland Sanctuary
Lefoes Road
Nambour Bli Bli Road
Bli Bli
Cook Road
The David Low Way
Finland
1
2
3
4
5

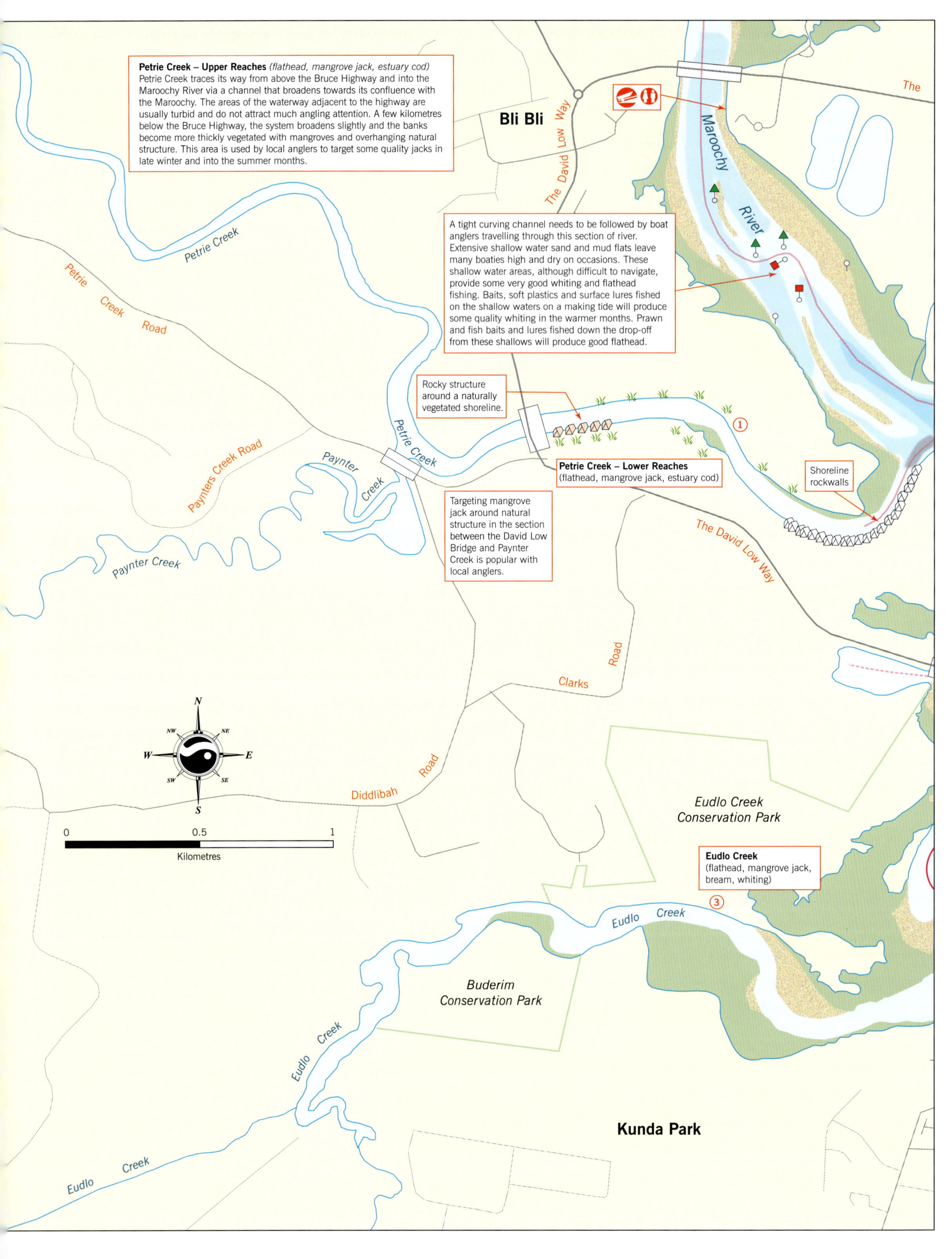

Petrie Creek – Upper Reaches *(flathead, mangrove jack, estuary cod)*
Petrie Creek traces its way from above the Bruce Highway and into the Maroochy River via a channel that broadens towards its confluence with the Maroochy. The areas of the waterway adjacent to the highway are usually turbid and do not attract much angling attention. A few kilometres below the Bruce Highway, the system broadens slightly and the banks become more thickly vegetated with mangroves and overhanging natural structure. This area is used by local anglers to target some quality jacks in late winter and into the summer months.
Bli Bli
The David Low Way
Maroochy River
The
A tight curving channel needs to be followed by boat anglers travelling through this section of river. Extensive shallow water sand and mud flats leave many boaties high and dry on occasions. These shallow water areas, although difficult to navigate, provide some very good whiting and flathead fishing. Baits, soft plastics and surface lures fished on the shallow waters on a making tide will produce some quality whiting in the warmer months. Prawn and fish baits and lures fished down the drop-off from these shallows will produce good flathead.
Petrie Creek
Petrie Creek Road
Rocky structure around a naturally vegetated shoreline.
1
Petrie Creek
Paynter Creek
Paynters Creek Road
Petrie Creek – Lower Reaches
(flathead, mangrove jack, estuary cod)
Shoreline rockwalls
Targeting mangrove jack around natural structure in the section between the David Low Bridge and Paynter Creek is popular with local anglers.
Paynter Creek
The David Low Way
Clarks Road
N
NE
E
SE
S
SW
W
NW
0
0.5
1
Kilometres
Diddlibah Road
Eudlo Creek Conservation Park
Eudlo Creek
(flathead, mangrove jack, bream, whiting)
3
Eudlo Creek
Buderim Conservation Park
Eudlo Creek
Kunda Park
Eudlo Creek

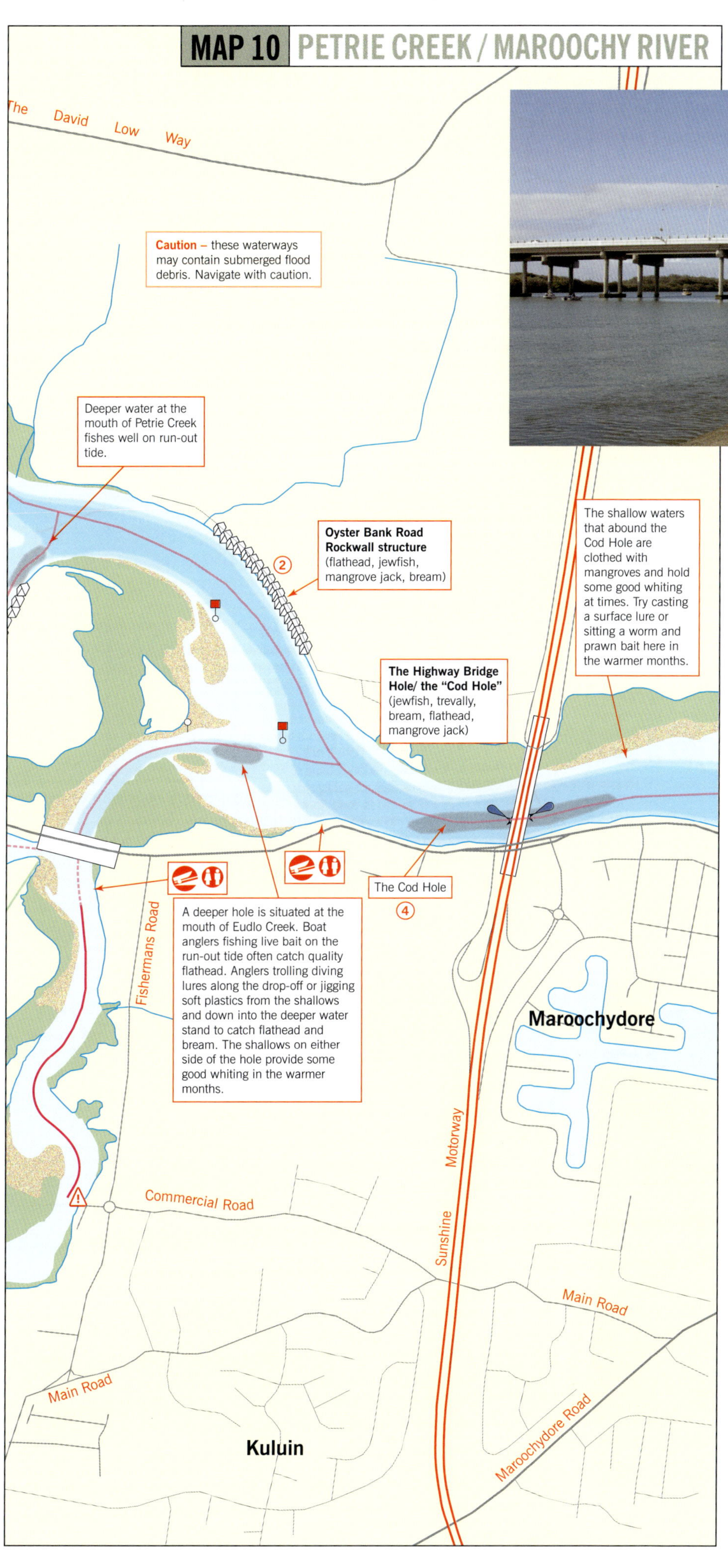

ABOVE: The 'Cod Hole' is a popular place for shorebased and boating anglers to wet a line.

Map 10 No. 1 Petrie Creek – Lower Reaches

(Flathead, mangrove jack, estuary cod)

The lower sections of Petrie Creek are fished more heavily because they are readily accessible to boat and shorebased anglers. The waters between Paynter Creek and the mouth of Petrie Creek host plenty of bridge pylons, natural bankside and some solid rock structure. The pylons at Petrie Creek Road and the David Low Way Bridge host some good jacks, as does the rock structure on the southern bank immediately below the David Low Way Bridge. A good length of bankside rockwall structure clothes much of the lower southern bank and is well worth a fish. These structures produce good mangrove jack and flathead fishing for anglers that read the seasons and tides well. Late winter and into summer provide good fishing for these species as well as estuary cod and lesser numbers of trevally, bream and whiting. Anglers fishing live baits and larger lures tight against the available structure are in with a good chance of tangling with jacks and flatties. But be warned, the jacks here know how to find their way home in very short time! The deeper hole at the mouth of Petrie Creek is a good place to fish the run-out tide. Anglers fishing live and dead prawn and fish baits record some good flathead and mangrove jack here. Lower light periods of the day combined with the start of the run-out provide active fish for anglers in position at this time. The shallow water around this area produces some good whiting fishing for anglers fishing baits and lures. Small surface lures fished quite quickly across the shallows tempts some good fish, as does a well presented worm and prawn bait.

Map 10 No. 2 Oyster Bank Road Rockwall *(Flathead, jewfish, mangrove jack, bream)*

The northern bank opposite the Petrie Creek and Eudlo Creek mouth areas is home to a solid rockwall. The channel waters drop to depth immediately out from the rocky bank. In the midst of the tide, this area is prone to strong current, however around the tidal changes, the location is known to produce some quality flathead and jewfish. The warmer months produce a few jacks from the location, while winter spawn bream will sometimes school in the area. This location offers equal opportunity to boat and shore-based anglers. Anglers fishing with live and dead bait report good catches here every year. Alternatively, lure anglers that fish with sinking lures such as soft plastics, blades or lipless crankbaits take some good fish holding against the drop-off. Trolling anglers towing diving lures along the drop-off take good flathead and jacks where they are offered an un-obstructed trolling line.

Map 10 No. 3 Eudlo Creek

(Flathead, Mangrove Jack, Bream, Whiting)

The navigable reaches of Eudlo Creek form a broad channel that consists of mainly shallower waters that sit above a mud, sand and weeded bottom. The shallow waters are etched with deeper channels and these waters can provide some good fishing. The banks of Eudlo Creek are quite heavily vegetated and as such provide some solid structure for fish to hold and feed around when the tide is up. As the run-out tide drains water from these shallows, fish retreat to the deeper channels and feed on food falling from the flats. This 'drain' style fishing provides well for anglers in the know. These shallow mud flat areas are often a few degrees warmer than other areas of the system, and as such often provide active mangrove jack, flathead and whiting when other adjacent locations are fishing more quietly. This is particularly the case in late winter. Although baits will produce fish in these areas, it is lure anglers that are on the move and retrieving lures through much of the available area that produce the best catches. Lures that represent small baitfish and prawn profiles typically produce well.

Above: Flathead are a popular target in the lower reaches.

Map 10 No. 4 The Highway Bridge Hole/ the 'Cod Hole'

(Jewfish, Trevally, Bream, Flathead, Mangrove Jack)

The highway bridge moves Sunshine Coast traffic across one of the deeper and larger holes in the system. Locally this hole is known as the 'Cod Hole'. This deeper patch of water produces a lot of fish for boat and shorebased anglers. The deeper water stretches approximately 100 m above and below the highway bridge. It is a popular spot and as such the fish can be cautious and tough to catch at times. However, for anglers prepared to fish during low light hours and through the night, some good fish are there to be caught. Anglers that coordinate their efforts with tide change periods stand a greater chance of tangling with larger local fare. Anglers using local live fish bait, prawns, worms or fresh dead baits stand to tangle with resident fish. Alternatively, jigging soft plastics or sinking lure types along the drop-off areas and around pylon structures produces good fish for anglers. Deeper diving lures trolled through the Cod Hole have also produced fish for anglers able to troll a consistent line. The area is renowned for producing some quality jewies each year, and is a haunt for local jewfish anglers that are serious about catching a few. Winter and spring are good times to tangle with larger jewie, particularly if there are good numbers of mullet in the river. The Cod Hole also produces quality bream and flathead as well as the odd jack, estuary cod and grunter. The deeper water and bridge structure attracts and holds good quantities of bait at times, and when the pelagics have moved into the river, some good trevally and tailor will be taken here. Targeting these fish with quickly retrieved metal lures and soft plastics will attract the attention of these speedsters.

Map 11 No. 1 Lower Cod Hole

(Flathead, Bream, Whiting)

The lower sections of the Cod Hole downriver of the highway bridge have the water becoming increasingly shallower. These shallower sections do not attract as much angling attention as the deep water near to the bridge. This can be a sneaky spot to take some quality flathead, bream and the odd jewfish that are trying to escape the ruckus occurring immediately upriver. The same techniques that produce fish in the other sections of the Cod Hole will produce here. Anglers targeting whiting and flathead fare well at times on the shallows along the northern bank immediately proximal to these sections of the Cod Hole. Surface lures, worms and prawn baits produce some sizeable summer whiting, while soft plastics jigged down the drop-off into deeper water produce flathead on the run-out tide.

Map 11 No. 2 Twin Waters Banks

(Flathead, Bream, Whiting, Mangrove Jack)

The Maroochy River waters adjacent to the Twin Waters canals provide great bread and butter species fishing. The outlet to the canals provides a ready source of food that have predators lurking in the nearby waters. This makes for a popular landbased fishing location, with shorebased anglers able to target flathead, bream and whiting over the adjacent shallow water flats. Boat anglers produce some good fish when fishing in the channel that runs just off the shallows that hug the shoreline. The footbridge and rockwall at the entrance to the canal system is always home to a few jacks. Live baiting and hitting dark corners with lures provides some solid hook-ups and quite often some monumental dustups!

Map 11 No. 3 Boardwalk Banks

(Flathead, Bream, Whiting, Trevally, Tailor)

The Board Walk Banks are also known as the Black Bank area. A channel cuts through shallow water flats producing a sweeping

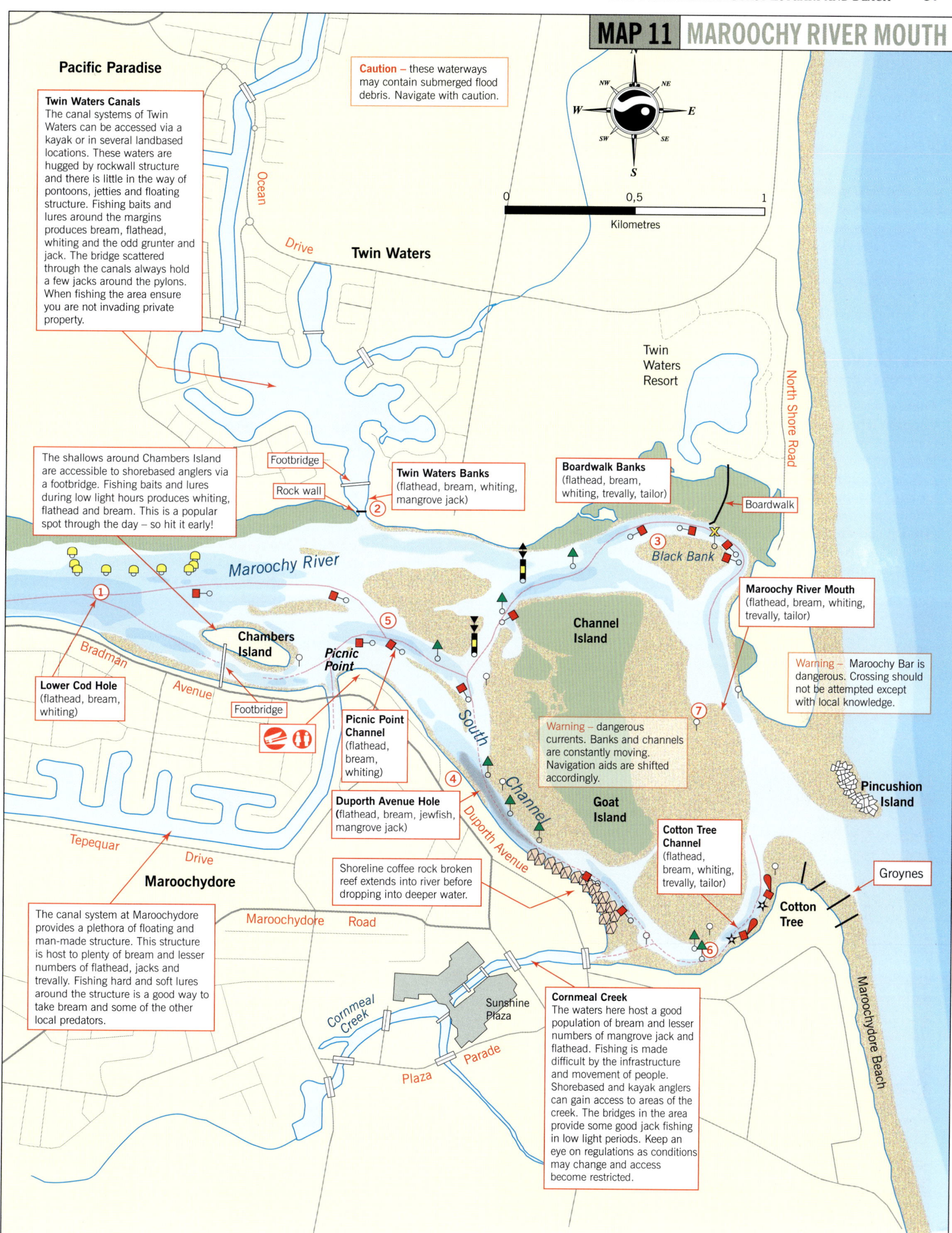

MAP 11 MAROOCHY RIVER MOUTH
Pacific Paradise
Twin Waters Canals
The canal systems of Twin Waters can be accessed via a kayak or in several landbased locations. These waters are hugged by rockwall structure and there is little in the way of pontoons, jetties and floating structure. Fishing baits and lures around the margins produces bream, flathead, whiting and the odd grunter and jack. The bridge scattered through the canals always hold a few jacks around the pylons. When fishing the area ensure you are not invading private property.
Caution – these waterways may contain submerged flood debris. Navigate with caution.
N
NW
NE
W
E
SW
SE
S
0
0,5
1
Kilometres
Ocean
Drive
Twin Waters
Twin Waters Resort
North Shore Road
The shallows around Chambers Island are accessible to shorebased anglers via a footbridge. Fishing baits and lures during low light hours produces whiting, flathead and bream. This is a popular spot through the day – so hit it early!
Footbridge
Rock wall
Twin Waters Banks (flathead, bream, whiting, mangrove jack)
Boardwalk Banks (flathead, bream, whiting, trevally, tailor)
Boardwalk
Maroochy River
Black Bank
Maroochy River Mouth (flathead, bream, whiting, trevally, tailor)
Channel Island
Chambers Island
Picnic Point
Bradman
Avenue
Lower Cod Hole (flathead, bream, whiting)
Footbridge
Picnic Point Channel (flathead, bream, whiting)
Warning – Maroochy Bar is dangerous. Crossing should not be attempted except with local knowledge.
Warning – dangerous currents. Banks and channels are constantly moving. Navigation aids are shifted accordingly.
South Channel
Pincushion Island
Goat Island
Duporth Avenue Hole (flathead, bream, jewfish, mangrove jack)
Duporth Avenue
Cotton Tree Channel (flathead, bream, whiting, trevally, tailor)
Groynes
Cotton Tree
Tepequar
Drive
Maroochydore
Shoreline coffee rock broken reef extends into river before dropping into deeper water.
Maroochydore
Road
The canal system at Maroochydore provides a plethora of floating and man-made structure. This structure is host to plenty of bream and lesser numbers of flathead, jacks and trevally. Fishing hard and soft lures around the structure is a good way to take bream and some of the other local predators.
Cornmeal Creek
Sunshine Plaza
Plaza
Parade
Cornmeal Creek
The waters here host a good population of bream and lesser numbers of mangrove jack and flathead. Fishing is made difficult by the infrastructure and movement of people. Shorebased and kayak anglers can gain access to areas of the creek. The bridges in the area provide some good jack fishing in low light periods. Keep an eye on regulations as conditions may change and access become restricted.
Maroochydore Beach

corner in the northern bank of the estuary. This is a popular flathead location. Spring fishing often has numbers of fish congregating here as part of the annual spawning process. Wading the shallows or drifting in a boat while casting lures that allow the angler to bump the bottom regularly will often tempt these aggressive fish.

This corner channel often holds concentrations of baitfish in winter and anglers fishing here will encounter trevally and tailor that are busy hunting this bait. Small metal lures, soft plastics and surface lures such as poppers and stickbaits often provide some exciting fishing when the predators are holding up in the channel.

The shallow water areas provide good whiting and bream fishing in the warmer months. Casting hardbodied lures across the shallows or sitting worm and prawn baits in strategic positions will often produce good numbers of cruising fish. Aim to target darker sections of sea grass as these areas are used by resident fish to feed with some level of protection. A building tide is optimal when pursuing these bread and butter species.

MAP 11 NO. 4 DUPORTH AVENUE HOLE
(FLATHEAD, BREAM, JEWFISH, MANGROVE JACK)

The waters adjacent to Duporth Avenue are also known as the South Channel. The southern bank that runs parallel to Duporth Avenue contains some of the most prominent fish holding structure in the lower sections of the river. Shoreline jetties sit on top of a coffee rock and mud ledge that drops suddenly into deeper water. This structure continues downriver to the point where Cornmeal Creek enters the system. Jewfish, flathead, bream and the odd jack and estuary cod are caught by anglers fishing lures or live and dead baits in the deeper waters along the drop-off. Boat anglers using bait will often anchor at the upriver end of the deeper water and fish baits back into the hole on the run-out tide. Winter provides some great action on schooling bream both in the deeper water and up on top of the coffee rock ledge. Drifting the shoreline and fishing with soft plastics, diving hardbodied lures and blades provides some good fishing for sizeable bream when they are schooled up. Where good concentrations of bait can be found holding here, do not be surprised to encounter trevally and tailor.

ABOVE: Whiting haunt the shallows in the area and love a worm bait or worm style soft plastic.

ABOVE: Look for deeper sections of the river if targeting school jewfish.

MAP 11 NO. 5 PICNIC POINT CHANNEL
(FLATHEAD, BREAM, WHITING)

The waters immediately out from Picnic Point provide some good fishing for bread and butter species. A slightly deeper channel cuts through sand flats and the area is fed by waters running from the nearby canal system on a run-out tide. The area is home to good numbers of flathead, bream and whiting in the summer months.

MAP 11 NO. 6 COTTON TREE CHANNEL
(FLATHEAD, BREAM, WHITING, TREVALLY, TAILOR)

A channel runs along the southern bank towards the mouth of the Maroochy River. This channel is close to extensive shallow water flats and provides some good shorebased fishing on the start of the run-out tide. Peak tidal flow periods make for difficult fishing due to current, however the area is worth inspecting, as many of the fish that cruise the local flats will retreat back into this channel as the tide runs out. Jigging soft plastics with the tidal flow, or fishing stationery baits will produce fish holding in the channel. Winter provides some good tailor and trevally fishing in this area.

MAP 11 NO. 7 MAROOCHY RIVER MOUTH
(FLATHEAD, BREAM, WHITING, TREVALLY, TAILOR)

The eastern side of Channel and Goat Islands form an extensive area of sand flats and sea grass beds cut by a channel that snakes towards the mouth of the system. The channel and shallows through this area and down towards Pincushion Island provide some good fishing for bread and butter species. The warmer months produces flathead in the shallows and channel waters while there are plenty of bream and whiting cruising the flats on the building tide. The channel waters down towards Pincushion Island produce trevally and tailor in the cooler months.

CHAPTER 2

SUNSHINE COAST

Mooloolaba to Bribie Island and the Pumicestone Passage

ABOVE: The ocean view from Mooloolaba towards Caloundra.

INTRODUCTION

The southern half of the Sunshine Coast is becoming increasingly populated. A growing tourism trade and northern urban sprawl from Brisbane has this pretty part of the coastline buzzing for much of the year. This stretch of coastline incorporates the townships of Mooloolaba and Caloundra. There are kilometres of spectacular beach, plenty of estuary fishing options, some great deep water ocean access and the unique Pumicestone Passage that separates Bribie Island from the mainland. The popularity of waterfront living has resulted in the development of a plethora of small to medium sized urban lake and canal systems. This means that there are fishing opportunities for every angler regardless of whether you prefer a weekend spot of shorebased angling or chasing big critters far offshore. This section of coast breaches the northern extents of Moreton Bay and offers a great deal for the likes of Sunshine Coast, Brisbane and touring anglers alike.

THE BEACH AND ROCKS

MAROOCHYDORE TO BRIBIE ISLAND

The shoreline between the Maroochy River mouth and Caloundra offers kilometres of access to beach and scattered rock fishing platforms. Anglers that venture on to Bribie Island are offered some less populated beach fishing as these areas are slightly harder to access than beaches on the mainland. The fishing area off Bribie Island extends down around the northern corner of Moreton Bay and these waters hold year-round bread and butter species as well as the odd pelagic species 'passing by'.

The seasonal beach fishing patterns in this section of the coast are similar to those encountered in the northern half of the Sunshine Coast. Bread and butter species are available all year round, however spring is a popular time to catch good numbers of bream, whiting, flathead, dart and tarwhine. Late winter and spring are the months to tangle with tailor and jewfish. As the seasons progress into the warmer months the tailor become bigger with the largest specimens usually being reported in October and November. The summer months offer the rare opportunity to tangle with pelagic speedsters such as tuna and mackerel species.

MAP 12 BEACH AND ROCK FISHING – MAROOCHY RIVER MOUTH TO CALOUNDRA BEACH

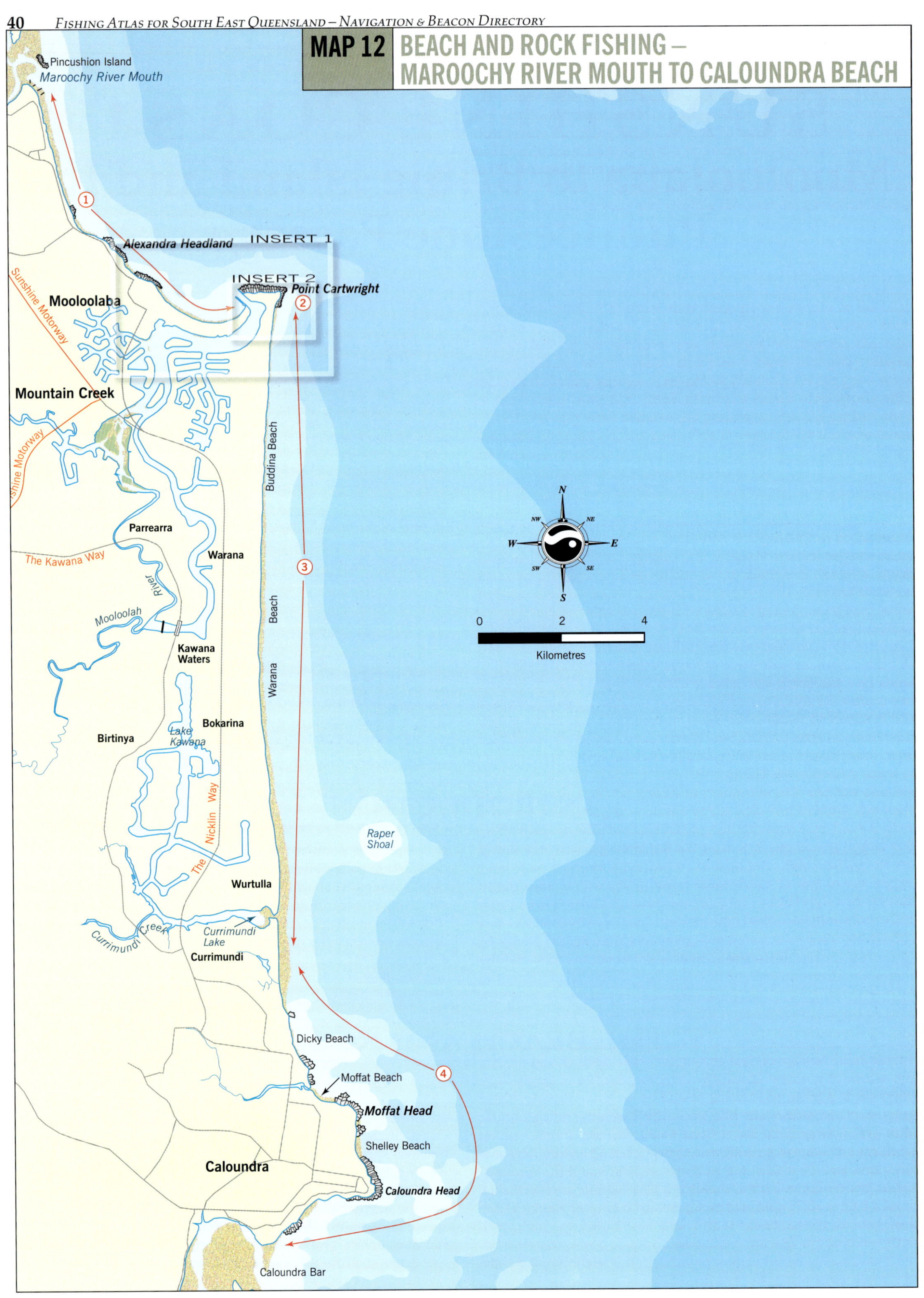

BEACH AND ROCK FISHING LOCATION GUIDE

Map 12 No.1 Maroochy River Mouth to Mooloolah River Entrance *(Bream, Dart, Flathead, Whiting, Tailor)*

There are plenty of sandy beach and rock fishing locations to choose from in this stretch of water. Shoreline gutters and exposed coffee rock clusters will hold early morning and evening bream, whiting, dart and flathead. Alexandra Headland can be used as a fishing platform in mild weather. Anglers fishing baits and soft plastic lures in visibly deeper water around rocks often snare bream, flathead and the odd squire and sweetlip. Through the months of January to March, the offshore waters within the bay are usually alive with baitfish and predators such as mackerel and tuna. These fish can occasionally be reached from this platform by anglers casting long and high speed spinning with metal lures (slugs). This is typically a first hour of light proposition. This technique accounts for plenty of tailor each year for anglers prepared to get out on the rocks and cast a lure.

The rocky shores and beach front of Mooloolaba is located immediately to the south of Alexandra Headland. This stretch accounts for bread and butter species, however it is a popular tourist spot and anglers have to compete with many other beach users through much of the day and night.

Goat Island
Maroochy River Mouth
Aerodrome Road
Alexandra Headland
Sunshine Motorway
Mooloolaba
Point Cartwright
N NE E SE S SW W NW
0 0.5 1
Kilometres
The western rock wall along the mouth of the Mooloolah River presents a good platform for targeting bread and butter species. The corner of the beach holds plenty of bottom coffee rock. This structure attracts some quality winter gar, summer bream, flathead, whiting and the odd tailor and tuna.
MAP12 INSERT 1

Map 12 No. 2 Point Cartwright *(Bream, Flathead, Tailor, Jew)*

The rock platform at Point Cartwright provides a good fishing platform in suitable weather conditions. The best location for fishing includes the area immediately off the most eastern point of the headland. Easy access to deeper water can be found directly off the point and immediately to the north-east. Areas to the north and south of this are more prone to increased wave activity in most conditions, making it more dangerous for anglers. There is often deeper water off the end of the headland and this often wraps the southern rocks of the headland and extends towards the Kawana Beach end of the rocky platform. This deeper water hosts bream, flathead and the occasional jewfish, squire and sweetlip. Most popular techniques here include casting pilchard, squid and worm baits into deeper water. Targeting

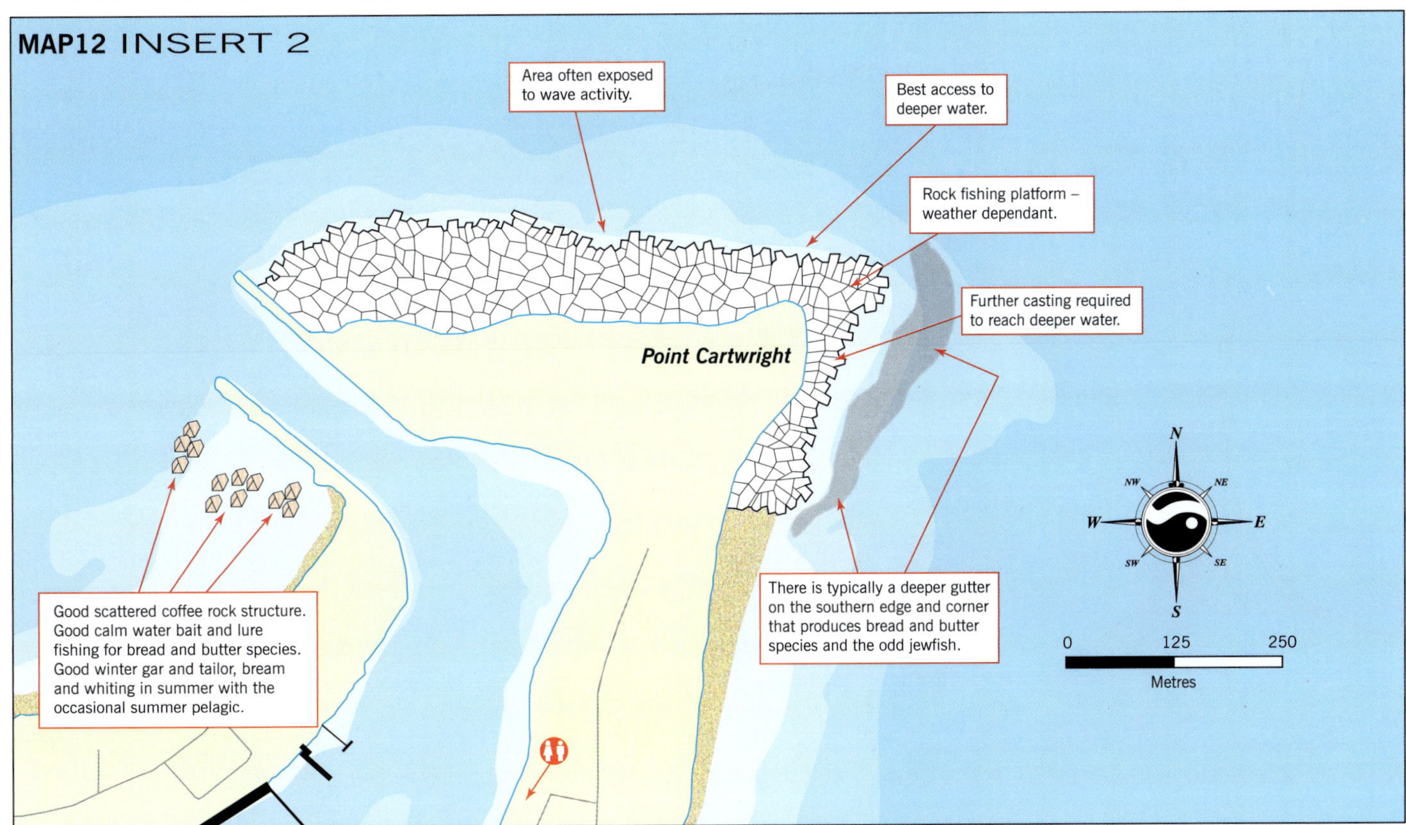

jewies with live and dead baits at night produces some good fish for anglers prepared to fish the rocks at night. Extreme caution should be applied when fishing here in low light hours.

Pelagic species such as tailor, trevally, mackerel and tuna are also caught here by anglers practicing high speed spinning techniques. Low light fishing often produces the best fishing results for pelagic species. Using braided lines, employing long casts and letting heavy metal slugs sink for a period before retrieving them as fast as possible will produce fish if they are in casting range.

MAP 12 No. 3 WARANA BEACH STRETCH
(BREAM, DART, FLATHEAD, WHITING, TAILOR)

There are usually plenty of near-shore gutters to be found in the stretch of beach between Point Cartwright and Currimundi. Fishing pilchard, gar, fish strip baits and worms in the available gutters on a building tide will produce bream, dart, tarwhine, whiting, flathead and tailor. Low light hours will provide the better fishing and increase the chances of tangling with larger fare such as jewies.

MAP 12 No. 4 CURRIMUNDI TO CALOUNDRA BEACH STRETCH
(BREAM, FLATHEAD, WHITING, TAILOR, SQUIRE, JEW)

The beach between Currimundi and Caloundra provides more shoreline rock structure around where anglers can target a variety of species. Rocky promontories at either end of Dicky Beach, Moffat Beach and Shelley Beach provide plenty of options for local shorebased anglers. The usual suspects such as bream, flathead and whiting can be taken on baits fished in deeper water around rocky structure. The near-shore reef also offers anglers fishing larger baits such as pilchard, gar and squid, the option of taking squire, sweetlip, and the odd jewfish and tailor when they are in season. The water around the headland at Caloundra is home to Moffat Beach and Kings Beach corners, to the north and south respectively. The structure immediately off the Moffat Beach corner consists of shallow reef and can be prone to wave activity. When able to fish here, anglers can use baits and soft plastic lures to target reef fare such as squire, sweetlip and cod. The Kings Beach corner forms the most eastern extrusion of the Caloundra Headland and offers access to deeper water. Here, anglers are able to target reef species as well as bream, tailor and jewfish. Low light periods of the day produce the best results.

MAP 13 No. 1 NORTHERN BRIBIE ISLAND – OCEAN SIDE
(BREAM, DART, FLATHEAD, WHITING, TAILOR, JEWFISH)

The most accessible ocean beaches along the outer edge of Bribie Island can be found along the northern and southern ends of the sand island. Access to the northern tip can be had by boating across Pumicestone Passage or driving across the bridge at the southern end of the island. The road in the south can be followed to the beach where access to the north is possible via 4WD and with a permit (issued by Queensland Parks and Wildlife Service). The northern strip is renowned for having the better formed surf gutters and with the outflow associated with the nearby Caloundra Bar, usually holds some good fish. The close proximity to the Pumicestone Passage entrance means there are often spawning congregations of fish through the winter and spring months. Good numbers of bream, whiting and flathead can be taken here during these periods. Winter time tailor and spring and summer time dart, tarwhine and a few quality jew are also caught here by anglers each year. Baits of pilchard, gar, flesh strip bait and worms produce most of the fish.

MAP 13 No. 2 SOUTHERN BRIBIE ISLAND – OCEAN SIDE
(BREAM, DART, FLATHEAD, WHITING, TAILOR, JEWFISH, TUNA, MACKEREL)

The southern ocean beach areas of Bribie Island can be accessed via the Bribie Island bridge. Beach travel will require 4WD and a permit. Although there are often several locations that offer good fishing, locals focus a lot of time in the Skirmish Point area. Water movement in the area is known for producing deeper sections of water close to shore. This structure is home to good numbers of whiting, bream, dart and flathead. The area also attracts pelagic predators from November onwards. Anglers casting for distance with metal slugs and employing high speed retrieves are known to catch mackerel and tuna species when they are within range. Visible signs of bait being pushed to the surface are usually a good indication that large predators, tailor and trevally may not be too far away! Worm and flesh baits are a good way to tempt bread and butter fare in gutters.

ABOVE: The Caloundra Bar is used by boats to access the adjacent offshore waters. Caution should be applied when using this bar.

MAP 13 BEACH AND ROCK FISHING – BRIBIE ISLAND
Caloundra
Caloundra Head
Golden Beach
1
The Skids
Bribie Island
Mission Point
Donnybrook
Welsby
White Patch
Toorbul
Banksia Beach
Bellara
Woorim
Bongaree
Pebble Beach
Sandstone Point
Skirmish Point
2
Red Beach
SouthPoint

MAP 14 MOOLOOLAH RIVER
Mooloolaba
Caution – when bar shoals temporary aids to navigation are placed to mark the approach to the entrance channel.
Near-shore rock and reef structure.
Shallow water with occasional patch of broken reef.
Point Cartwright
Good shorebased fishing for mangrove jack, trevally and flathead under and around the bridge structure.
Mooloolaba Beach
Deeper and shallow water coffee rock reef.
Good flathead fishing in deeper water at the start of the run-out tide.
Mayes Canal
Tuckers Creek
Minyama Island
Mooloolah River
Deeper water with broken coffee rock bottom is situated close to shore. This is a good shorebased location to target winter bream, tailor, trevally and gar. Livebaiting here at night is known to produce the odd jack, jewie and cod.
Suburban lakes fed by Mountain Creek provide a sheltered place to target bream, mullet and tarpon. Local fly anglers frequent these areas when the tarpon are active. Good family fishing locations.
Sunshine Motorway
Good mangrove jack water exists around the bridge structure. The area also fishes well for bream, flathead and trevally.
These deeper water areas provide good fishing for flathead and school jewfish. Bait and lures fished around the start of the run-out tide often produce best results.
Brisbane Road
Mooloolah Island
Mountain Creek
Good shorebased fishing for mangrove jack around the bridge structure. Lures and live baits fished during the low light hours in spring and summer produces good fish.
Scattered rock bar structure along parts of the channel.
Buddina
Minyama
Pacific Boulevarde
Point Cartwright Drive
The Nicklin Way
Parrearra Channel
Mountain Creek canal system.
Footbridge
The Sunshine Motorway Bridge and surrounding bridges and pontoons provide plenty of structure for jacks. Lures and baits work well for aggressive resident fish.
Lock and weir
Deeper water and rocky structure on corner provides good fishing for bream, mangrove jack and estuary cod.
Wyuna Canal
Parrearra
Deeper water and rocky structure on corner provides good fishing.
The Kawana Way
Warana
Oceanic Drive
Rocky shoreline structure provides good fishing for bream, mangrove jack and estuary cod.
N
NE
E
SE
S
SW
W
NW
0
0.5
1
Kilometres
The weir provides structure and variable water flow that attracts species such as trevally, queenfish and mangrove jack. The area produces some good tarpon in the warmer months.
The bridges are popular places to target jacks, bream and trevally.
Weir
Mooloolah River

THE SOUTHERN SUNSHINE COAST ESTUARY SYSTEMS

There are several estuary and urban lake waterways to fish in this beautiful stretch of coastline. These waters offer a diverse and exciting mix of southern and tropical species. The Mooloolah and Pumicestone Passage systems bond smaller systems, including Currimundi Lake and its associated canal systems. Although the area is now well populated, the local waters continue to produce some great fish for anglers that are familiar with some good technique, know where to start fishing and when to be there.

Spring and summer are popular periods to fish for bread and butter species in the estuary and beach. Big flathead, bream and whiting are mainstays of the spring recreational fishing scene. On the beach they are joined by dart and the odd tarwhine. Warming waters are usually associated with improved mangrove jack fishing in the estuary however there are certain anglers that are effective at catching these fish in winter. Certain locations offer summer time shorebased anglers the chance of tangling with bigger pelagics such as mackerel and tuna. Late winter and spring are popular times to target the elusive jewfish. Winter periods produce big tailor, trevally and squire in shoreline reef systems and congregations of bigger spawning bream in the estuary.

THE MOOLOOLAH RIVER

The Mooloolah estuary is a relatively small system that is fed by the Mooloolah River and Mountain Creek. These feeder systems are largely populated throughout and as the estuary proper broadens, it becomes home to canal systems and plenty of man-made structure. The entrance to the sea is one of the best deep water access points in the northern Brisbane region and as such is used by many boat anglers each year to head out into the deep blue. Although the estuary is used a lot by sea going boaties, the system provides some great fishing for anglers choosing to stay and fish the river. Towards the mouth, the vast amount of man-made structure is home to a variety of predators. These include the standard estuarine fare, as well as a few pelagic surprises from time to time. As anglers venture upriver past the highway bridge, the scenery takes on a more natural look. The natural structure is home to bread and butter species as well as tropical aggressors such as jacks and cod.

FACILITIES

The estuary is easily navigable for much of its area and provides many options for boat and shorebased anglers. There are many points from which to gain shoreline access to good fishing locations. There are good quality ramps located at the lower end of either side of the estuary. These ramps are home to plenty of parking but are popular when good weather arrives on a warm weekend. A smaller ramp is situated further upriver near the highway bridge.

FACT BOX

CHARTERS AND GUIDED FISHING

Guided fishing of the Mooloolah River is available with Robert Smith of South Queensland Charter Services.
Contact 0407 574 868 or *info@sqcs.com.au*

MOOLOOLAH RIVER LOCATION GUIDE

MAP 14 NO. 1 MOOLOOLAH RIVER MOUTH *(BREAM, FLATHEAD, TAILOR, TREVALLY, JEW)*

There are quality rockwalls either side of the Mooloolah River entrance into the ocean. Anglers use these platforms to target fish occupying real estate in the mouth regions of the system. The slightly deeper water that sits tight against the rocks is always home to some good fish. Occasionally, wave activity will produce white water around the seaward reaches of the rockwalls. These conditions are prime for tempting active bream and other predators beneath the protective foam cover. Anglers that fare well from these areas are mostly fishing baits and jigging soft plastics in the waters close to the base of the rocks. Fishing weights that are just light enough to get a hook to the bottom is a key to catching quality fish. The subtle drifting of bait or lure around the rocks (with available current) is needed to fool cautious local fish. Anglers that fish through the night and in the early and late periods of the day fare best in this area. Popular locations include the near-shore reef to the southern end of the eastern wall. This is a popular spot for bream anglers. If you are in the hunt for a school jewfish, then try fishing in the waters just off the southern end of the western wall. The area between the base of the wall and back towards the first moored yachts is home to a deeper hole. This hole is a great place to find a jewie at the turn of the tide on a new or full moon. Fishing the hours of darkness will improve your chances. This hole is also home to some good winter spawn bream.

RIGHT: Mooloolah River mouth offers deep water ocean access.

MAP 14 NO. 2 MOOLOOLAH RIVER MOUTH – CORNER BAY *(BREAM, WHITING, TREVALLY, TAILOR, JEW)*

The last corner of the system, before the river drains into the sea is occupied by a shallow bay. The shallows are home to sand and broken coffee rock reef. These shallows are also home to yabbies and the edge of the shallows is demarcated by a sharp drop into the deeper waters of the channel. This structure makes it a haven for a variety of species. This is a popular spot to target bream and whiting in the shallows. Building and high tide stages often have some good bream feeding in this area. This commonly happens in low light periods of the day, before bright sunlight and boat traffic pushes the fish back into the channel. Worm, prawn, yabby and fish baits can be used to tempt fish here. Anglers wading and casting with lightly weighted soft plastics and small shallow diving hardbody lures can also catch some good fish. Anglers targeting the deeper drop-off area are known to catch flathead, tailor and trevally, as well as the odd jewie.

Map 14 No. 3 Harbour Parade Coffee Rock Ledge
(BREAM, FLATHEAD, TAILOR, TREVALLY, JEWFISH)

The waters at the end of Harbour Parade feature a shallow shoreline sand flat. These waters drop into a deeper channel that hosts broken coffee rock structure. This is a popular shorebased and boat fishing location. The area is used by spawning bream that congregate in winter. Anglers using blades and heavily weighted soft plastics fare well on good sized bream when they are holed up here. The structure is attractive to schools of baitfish which in turn attracts predators like tailor, trevally and school jewfish. This is a popular location for anglers casting surface lures for winter tailor and trevally. This hole, as well as others found in these lower reaches is known for yielding some surprise captures. Local anglers report the odd queenfish, mangrove jack and hairtail as rare but not uncommon captures here.

Map 14 No. 4 Mooloolaba Spit Moorings
(BREAM, MANGROVE JACK, TAILOR, TREVALLY, JEWFISH)

The inner corner of Mooloolaba Spit houses an extended area of boat mooring infrastructure. The area hosts deeper water and is home to large boats and the local commercial fishing fleet and processing areas. This all combines to provide a location with great fish holding potential. There are some limited shorebased fishing options in the area where foot bound anglers can put baits and lures into tight structure. The area is used extensively by boat anglers to target fish holding tight against the extensive wood and moored boat structures.

Talking with local commercial fishers uncovers the fishing surprises this location holds. Fishers here talk of sightings of the odd Spanish mackerel and cobia cruising through the deeper water structure looking for a feed. These fish have obviously found their way to the area: attracted by the natural berley trail this area provides in the way of the fish processing areas. Likewise, this area attracts big bream, jacks, cod and some sizeable trevally and jewfish. The outer edges of the moorings are used by anglers to target winter jewie. Recent seasons have produced some night and daytime hairtail so anything is possible in this location. Summer evening and morning sessions are used to throw larger lures and baits tight against structure for jacks. Winter anglers spend time fishing light-weight soft plastics, blades and diving hardbody lures tight against structure to tempt winter time bream. The key is fishing offerings from the top to the bottom of the water column to find where concentrations of fish are holding.

Note: There are quality boat ramps situated on either side of the river in this area. The northern shoreline hosts two ramps adjacent to the Mooloolaba Coast Guard. A multiple lane ramp also exists on the southern shore off Harbour Parade. This ramp is also a popular place for shorebased anglers to target bread and butter species.

Map 14 No. 5 The Wharf Marina
(BREAM, MANGROVE JACK, TREVALLY, ESTUARY COD)

This location hosts deeper water and a plethora of submerged structure in the way of rocks and timber pylons. Parts of the area are closed to fishing so keep an eye out for signs indicating access restrictions. Local anglers spend time in this area casting lures around the vast amount of structure. The deeper water and shade are home to some quality fish: including bream, trevally, jacks and cod. The location provides a corner that is situated slightly out of the current flow, and this provides a good holding spot for baitfish. This being the case, the predators are never far away. The fishing can be surprisingly good here when the Mooloolaba Spit Moorings are not fishing that well, so keep this location as a backup plan. Be warned when casting expensive lures here as there is no guarantee you will get them back!

Map 14 No. 6 Kawana Waters Canal System
(BREAM, WHITING, FLATHEAD, MANGROVE JACK, TAILOR, TREVALLY, JEWFISH)

The canal system on the southern side of the estuary is home to plenty of structure. This structure provides shelter for resident prey and predators. There are deeper sections of water, shallow yabby beds and plenty of floating and pylon structures to keep a variety of species happy. Structure that provides some form of shade and deeper water will be home to bream, mangrove jack and trevally. Casting lures around the structure or fishing live bait (particularly at night) is a favoured way to target these species here. Splashy surface lures fished across the canals at night produces some quality jacks and trevally every year. The shallows and drop-off areas provide good bream, flathead and whiting fishing. Soft plastic lures, prawn, yabby, fish and worm baits are a good option. Deeper sections of water are located at the entrance to some of the canal arms. This structure is a good place to target flathead and the odd school jewfish. Fishing baits at the start of the run-out tide is often a good strategy. Where this tide period can be combined with first or last light of the day, anglers will often experience improved catch rates.

Map 14 No.7 Mooloolah Canal System
(BREAM, WHITING, FLATHEAD, MANGROVE JACK, TREVALLY)

The canal system fishes much the same as the canal system on the other side of the estuary. Any structure that provides shade will host bream, trevally and jacks. The canal walls and sand stretches will hold whiting, bream and flathead. The bridges at the entrance to the system provide some good fishing for jacks when combined with lower light periods of the day. The entrance to the canals demarcates some slightly deeper water. This hole provides some good flathead fishing at the start of the run-out tide. Fishing with live baits and jigging soft plastics are techniques used by local anglers to score some good fish here. The shallows adjacent to the deeper water provide some good fishing for whiting in summer. Fishing with yabby, prawn and worm baits is a favoured way of taking these fish.

Map 14 No. 8 Mooloolah Island
(BREAM, WHITING, FLATHEAD, MANGROVE JACK, TREVALLY)

The channel is slightly deeper in this section directly below the Sunshine Motorway Bridge and McKenzie Bridge. The water immediately below the bridges is home to a small boat ramp and provides good access for shorebased anglers. The deeper water and abundance of man-made structure here provides good fishing opportunities for bream, flathead, mangrove jack, trevally and the occasional queenfish. Local anglers target quality jacks around the bridge structures in the low light hours and through the night.

Map 14 No. 9 Parrearra Channel
(BREAM, MANGROVE JACK, TREVALLY, ESTUARY COD, QUEENFISH, TARPON)

The channel is a unique patch of water that is locked to public boating by a loch. A further weir controls water flow into the top of the channel where water from the upper Mooloolah River enters. The channel provides good fishing for shorebased, kayak and authorised boating anglers. A street directory will show the many access points whereby shorebased anglers can gain access to the channel to wet a line. The channel is a solid stretch of water that is constrained by rockwalls throughout much of its length. A combination of bridges, rocks, deeper water and man-made structure make this water a haven for a variety of predators. The channel is fed by several inflow points in the way of the weirs and feeder pipe systems (eastern shoreline). The rockwalls and bridges in the area account for plenty of jacks, trevally, cod and bream each season. Local anglers find that when water rushes into the channel through the various feeder points it provides great fishing for trevally, queenfish and tailor. The upper reaches of the channel make for good tarpon fishing, particularly in the warmer months.

Map 14 No. 10 Mooloolah Estuary Confluence

(Bream, Whiting, Flathead, Mangrove Jack, Trevally, Estuary Cod)

The estuary splits into two smaller arms at this point. The area forms the confluence of the Mooloolah River and Mountain Creek. The area immediately above the bridges forms a unique location that hosts mangrove islands and split channel water. The edges adjacent to the mangroves host natural vegetation and yabby bed structures. These areas are prime places to target whiting and flathead. The channel hosts some good patches of broken reef and coffee rock. This is particularly the case in the area immediately upriver of the bridges. The drop-off and rocky structures produce some quality jacks, bream, trevally and cod every year. Jigging soft plastics and live baits account for most of these fish.

Map 14 No. 11 Upper Mooloolah River

(Bream, Mangrove Jack, Estuary Cod, Trevally)

The Mooloolah River above its confluence with Mountain Creek takes on a different form. The system becomes narrower and begins to meander significantly, among banks that are made up of natural vegetation. The channel here is mostly shallow; however, the tight corners of the upper system are often host to deeper water. There are several sections of rocky bank structure in this upper section. Anglers fishing this section of river are predominantly targeting bream and jacks. Significant by-catch includes trevally, the odd estuary cod and flathead. Fishing live baits in low light hours or casting and retrieving hardbody lures and jigging soft plastics through the day accounts for most fish caught here. For best results focus efforts on the deeper sections adjacent to solid rock or timber and overhanging structures. The Kawana Way Bridge produces some quality jacks for anglers targeting fish around the solid structure.

Map 14 No. 12 Mountain Creek

(Bream, Whiting, Flathead, Mangrove Jack, Trevally)

The creek is largely shallow and at times a very muddy system. However, the area does produce some good fish for anglers. The stretch of water including the bridges to the confluence with the Mooloolah River produces most of the fish caught in this area. The solid structure provided by the three bridges over Mountain Creek and the canal system are used by jacks and bream to shelter and feed. The shallow mangrove banks directly opposite the canal system are a great spot to target whiting and flathead in the summer months. Mountain Creek provides water for several urban lakes located to the north of the creek. These waters are easily accessed from the street and provide some sheltered fishing for species such as bream, mullet and tarpon.

Right: The jetty structures along the river are often home to quality jacks.

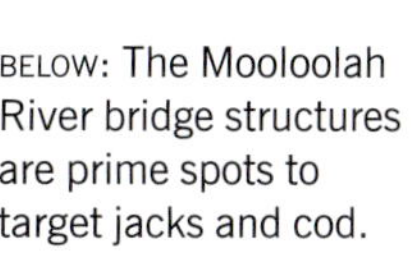

Below: The Mooloolah River bridge structures are prime spots to target jacks and cod.

LAKE KAWANA AND CURRIMUNDI LAKE

The stretch of land between the Mooloolah River and Pumicestone Passage entrance at Caloundra is home to some unique urban estuary fishing. Currimundi Lake is fed by Currimundi Creek and is open to the ocean via a shallow entrance. This means the waterway does not experience strong tidal flows. The lake makes its way inland through a mix of natural vegetation and man-made structure. Currimundi Lake feeds the body of water known as Lake Kawana which occupies the backwaters farthest from the ocean entrance. This body of water is picturesque and although densely populated around its boundaries, provides some good fishing. The waters can be accessed via many shorebased locations and through the use of small boats and kayaks. This is a popular family destination and it is common to see a good number of families enjoying some fishing close to suburbia.

FACILITIES

Currimundi Lake is host to a small boat ramp on the southern margin mid-way between the bridge and lake entrance. There is a good little café on the southern side of the lake entrance that is great for mum and dad to get a coffee whilst the kids fish or swim.

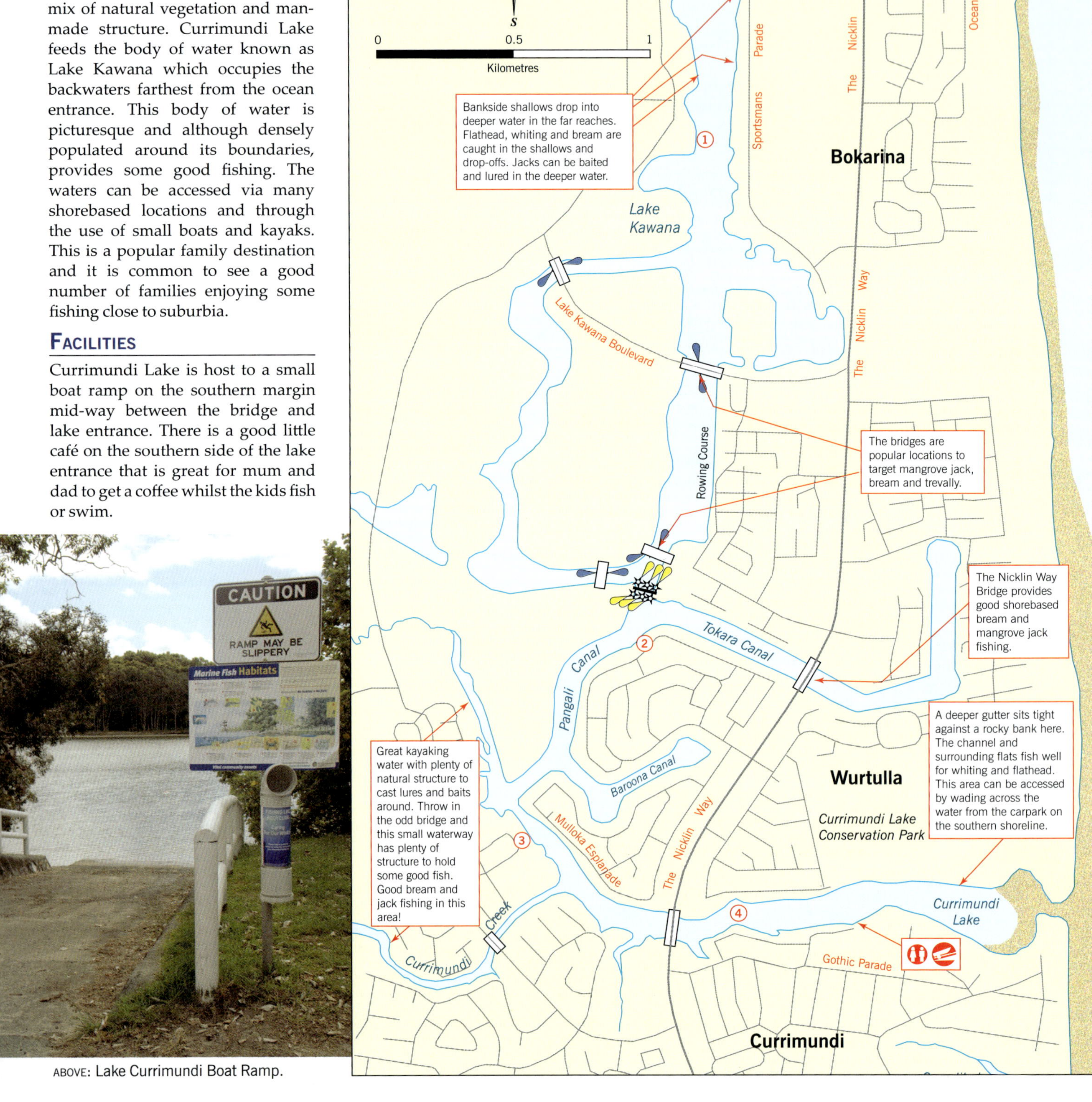

ABOVE: Lake Currimundi Boat Ramp.

LAKE KAWANA AND CURRIMUNDI LAKE LOCATION GUIDE

MAP 15 NO. 1 LAKE KAWANA

(BREAM, WHITING, FLATHEAD, MANGROVE JACK, TREVALLY)

The waters of Lake Kawana provide a host of options for shorebased and kayak anglers. Bridges, bankside structure and deeper patches of water hold good numbers of bream, flathead, whiting, trevally and mangrove jack. Popular approaches include fishing live bait and surface lures at night for trevally and jacks in the warmer months. The banks and shallow sections are home to yabbies and as such provide good lure and bait fishing for bread and butter species. Worm, yabby and whitebait are popular bait choices in this patch of water.

MAP 15 NO. 2 CURRIMUNDI LAKE CANAL SYSTEM

(BREAM, WHITING, FLATHEAD, MANGROVE JACK, TREVALLY)

The upper reaches of Currimundi Lake below Lake Kawana form a series of canals. Pangali Canal links two dead end canals in the way of Tokara and Baroona canals. The canals are accessible via boat and kayak and provide some good fishing for bread and butter species, trevally and the odd mangrove jack. Bait fishing for bream, whiting and flathead or casting lures around the available jetty structure are popular approaches. The best fish are often caught early in the day or at the night when the canals are at their quietest.

MAP 15 NO. 3 CURRIMUNDI LAKE – UPPER REACHES

(BREAM, MANGROVE JACK, TREVALLY)

Thick vegetation surrounds much of this scenic part of the lake. There are several access points for the shorebased angler and this area makes for great kayak fishing water. There is plenty of natural structure to hold bream, jacks and trevally. Summer lure fishing here can be well worth the time spent to explore the waterway. Livebaiting around the snags during low light periods and into the night produces some good jacks. However, casting soft plastics and hardbody lures around the structure is popular with anglers that frequent the area. Early morning surface lure fishing here can provide some surprisingly great sessions. Don't let the proximity of this location to major roads lead you to believe there isn't some good fishing to be had here!

MAP 15 NO. 4 CURRIMUNDI LAKE – LOWER REACHES

(BREAM, WHITING, FLATHEAD, MANGROVE JACK, TREVALLY)

This stretch of the lake broadens as it nears its confluence with the sea. The waterway is relatively shallow, contains banks lined with natural vegetation and is a popular spot with weekend anglers and sightseeing. There is plenty of shorebased access to the water here and a small boat ramp on the southern bank provides access for boat anglers. The bridge is home to plenty of pylons and provides good fishing every year for jacks, trevally, bream and flathead. Live bait fishing around the bridge at night is a good way to tangle with local jacks. The sandy shallows and drop-offs in the lower sections of the lake provide good fishing for whiting, flathead and bream. The lower bank on the north shoreline hosts some slightly deeper water and the surrounding flats are a good place to target whiting and flathead. Favourite approaches include bait fishing with worms, prawns and yabby, or fishing soft plastics and small hardbody lures for flathead and whiting. A dedicated brigade of anglers is now targeting summer whiting on small stickbait style surface lures.

ABOVE: The Highway Bridge at Lake Currimundi is a popular spot to target species such as jacks.

PUMICESTONE PASSAGE

The Pumicestone Passage is an extensive and popular waterway that separates the mainland from Bribie Island. The waterway is urbanised around its northern and southern reaches. The northern urban development includes the towns of Pelican Waters, Golden Beach and Caloundra, where the Passage drains into the ocean and demarcates the northern extent of Bribie Island. The southern end of Pumicestone Passage is the site where the estuary drains into Moreton Bay. The Bribie Island shores at the entrance are home to the towns of Bongaree, Bellara and White Patch. Across the bridge to the mainland side of the Passage, anglers will find the towns of Pebble Beach, Toorbul, Meldale and Donnybrook. The Pumicestone Passage is fed by numerous small to medium size creeks. These include Lamerough, Bells, Halls, Coochin, Saltwater, Hussey, Glass Mountain, Bullock, Elimbah and Ningi Creeks. Pumicestone Passage offers many kilometres of scenic waterway that is home to plenty of natural structure and a variety of piscatorial and marine wildlife. For this reason there are zones of Marine Park located within the Passage where local wildlife is protected. Anglers fishing the Passage will find a variety of options available throughout the year and can also be treated to special encounters with plenty of turtles and the local dugongs. Local fishers will testify to the waterway throwing some challenges in the way of excessive drift weed and murky waters prevailing through periods of the year. However, the wealth of water to fish, quality structure, good numbers and variety of local fish on the doorstep of Brisbane, mean resident anglers keep this place a well kept secret.

FACILITIES

There are few boat ramps in the middle sections of Pumicestone Passage, however there are plenty of quality boat ramps scattered around the northern and southern extents of the waterway. There are two ramps at Caloundra around the Caloundra Coast Guard establishment. The entrance to the Pelican Waters system is proximal to three ramps and a further ramp can be found at the southern extent of the suburbs on Bells Creek. In the south: Donnybrook, Meldale and Toorbul have ramps in close reach to local anglers. There are several ramps either side of the Bribie Island bridge. A ramp on the western side can be found at Spinnaker Sound Marina and over to the east of the channel. Ramps are located at the Bribie Island Volunteer Marine Rescue and further down towards the jetty at Bongaree.

MAP 16 A
PUMICESTONE PASSAGE
Caloundra
Bullock Beach
Caloundra Coast Guard
Warning – Caloundra Bar dangerous. Crossing should not be attempted except with local knowledge.
The influence of the Caloundra Bar often leaves a deeper channel situated adjacent to shoreline rocks. Low light periods and a turning tide often produce jewfish, tailor and bream for shorebased bait anglers. Winter and spring provides the best fishing here.
Good channel fishing waters.
N
NE
E
SE
S
SW
W
NW
0
0.5
1
Kilometres
Lamerough Creek
Golden Beach
Rocks
Blue Hole
Shorebased anglers fishing lures and baits in deeper sections of the channel take some big flathead and bream in winter and spring. The start of the run-out tide is a prime time to target big flathead here. Jigging 5 to 7 inch soft plastics close to the bottom will tempt the bigger fish.
Deeper water with shoreline timber structure produces flathead, jacks and trevally in summer with bream and the odd luderick in winter. Fish soft plastics or baits around the base of fallen structure for big flathead, jacks, trevally and bream. Weed and worm baits will produce luderick when they are holed up here.
Pelican Waters Boulevard
Lamerough Canal
Lake Magellan
Landsborough Parade
Passage
Pumicestone
A deeper rock wall lined hole exists here. The area produces bream, flathead, trevally, good numbers of mangrove jack and the occasional jewfish. Fishing with live bait at the start of the run-out tide is often productive. Live baits fished at night produces the best of the jack fishing.
Pelican Waters
This section of the channel catches water draining from the shallows and is locally renowned as a great place for bait anglers to target school jewfish, bream and flathead. The bottom of the run-out tide is the prime time to be fishing here.
Bells Creek
Upriver of this area provides good fishing for mangrove jack, bream and flathead. Fishing live baits, hardbody and soft plastic lures around bankside structure are good options here. Late winter and early spring are good times to be targeting jacks.
Bribie Island National Park
Bribie Island
South Pacific Ocean
1
2
3
4
5
6

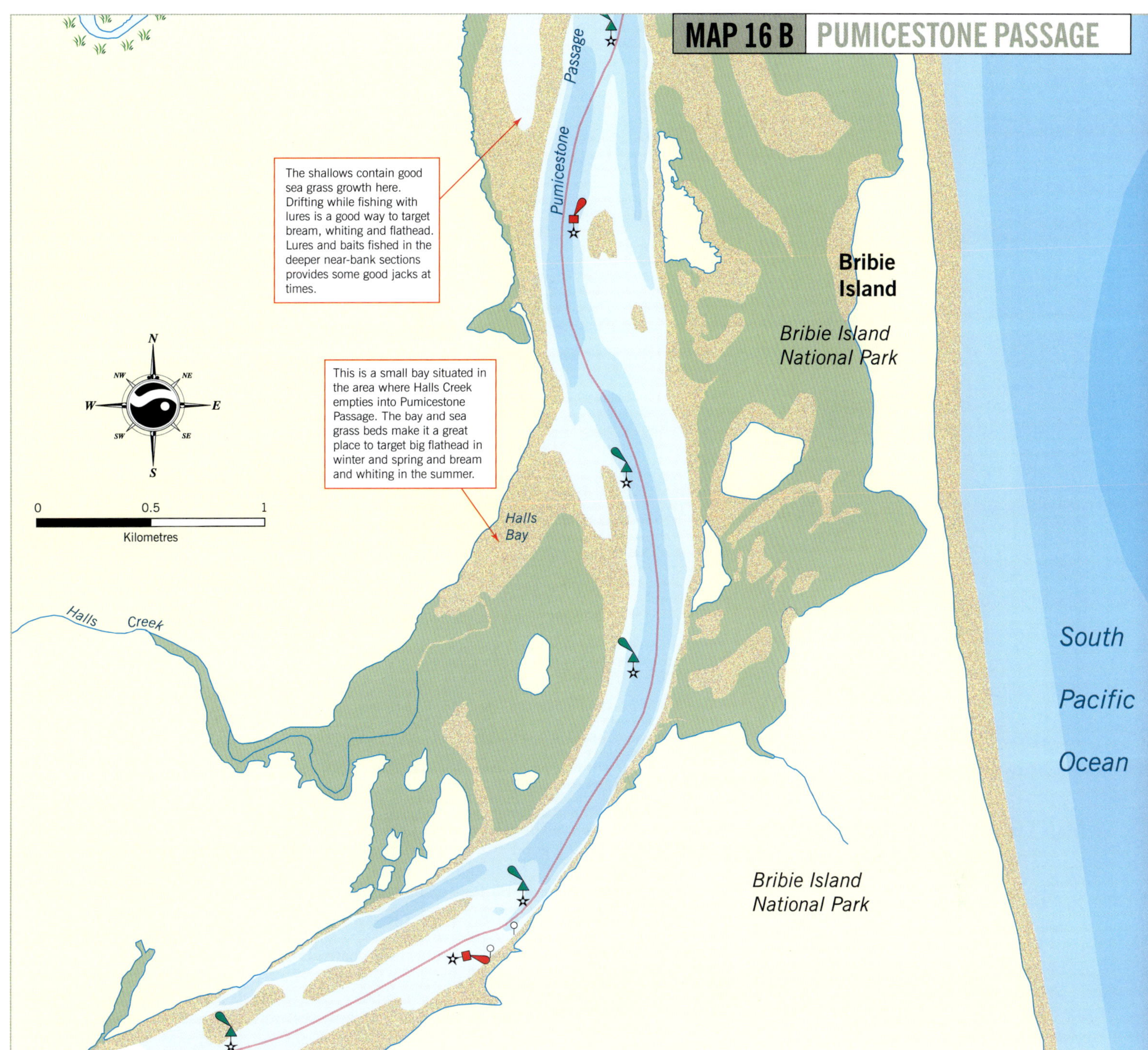

PUMICESTONE PASSAGE LOCATION GUIDE

Map 16A No. 1 Caloundra Bar

(FLATHEAD, BREAM, TAILOR, JEWFISH, WHITING, TREVALLY)

The Passage empties into the sea via a relatively wide channel in this spot. The channel turns sharply at Caloundra and this ensures there are always some deeply etched gutters lining the bottom around the mouth area. The exact location of these gutters changes somewhat with the seasons, but there is usually some deeper water to be found here. This water with patchy bottom reef areas and rocky structures along the northern shoreline provide good shelter for local predators and bait. The location is well known for producing some big flathead, bream, tailor, jewfish and fewer whiting and trevally. This is a popular weekend fishing spot and it is not uncommon to find the area packed with shorebased and boat anglers on a weekend when the weather is fine. The channel is prone to strong tidal flow here. A good strategy if you are serious about catching some quality fish in this location is to hit the water early or late in the day when the tide is turning. The Bulcock Beach and Boardwalk area and north around the headland provides good shorebased fishing in close proximity to deeper water containing reef structure. This area fishes well for a variety of species and includes a few surprises such as winter luderick and the odd reef fish. Anglers using pilchard, worm, yabby and prawn baits fare well on bread and butter species in the general area. Jigging blade and soft plastic lures in deeper water is a proven method for taking some good bream and flathead. Anglers targeting flathead around the drop-off on either side of the channel encounter some big fish every spring. Fishing with big baits and lures and keeping them close to the bottom is a key to catching these bigger fish.

ABOVE: The waters around the estuary mouth at Caloundra are popular with boating and shorebased anglers.

Map 16A No. 2 Golden Beach Channel

(Flathead, bream, whiting, tailor, trevally, mangrove jack, luderick)

The area inside the northern tip of Bribie Island and opposite Golden Beach hosts a deeper channel cutting through expansive sand and sea grass flats. The channels within the shallow water are always shifting but this area always holds a good variety of fish.

The deeper channel waters that hug the Golden Beach shoreline are a great place to target flathead, bream and whiting. Shorebased anglers fishing with baits produce good catches of these fish here.

ABOVE: Golden trevally are often caught around Golden Beach.

The sand and sea grass shallows in this stretch of water are home to good numbers of flathead, whiting, bream and trevally in summer. Fish use the protection of sea grass to get up in the shallows and feed on local yabby, prawn and baitfish. Drifting across the flats and fishing surface and diving hardbody lures is a popular way to catch these fish here. Some big golden trevally are caught on these flats and surrounding channels every summer. Bait fishing and jigging soft plastics in the channel and drop-off areas produces good flathead, trevally and tailor. The channels inside Bribie Island hold big flathead in spring and the surrounding shallows provide good fishing for big whiting in summer. A run-out tide for the flathead and a making tide for whiting is preferred.

The Golden Beach channel abuts and erodes the sands of Bribie Island opposite the Gemini and Moorings Beach Resorts. The location provides some deeper water with sunken timber structures. The spot is popular among local anglers through the seasons. Spring and summer fishing produces quality flathead, mangrove jack, trevally and estuary cod. The cooler months provide anglers with a chance to tangle with spawn bream and the odd luderick.

Map 16 No. 3 Pelican Waters Canal System

(Bream, mangrove jack, flathead, whiting, trevally)

Pelican Waters is a large canal system that offers resident fish plenty of man-made structure to call home. The bridges, floating pontoons and pylons offer predatory species a place to shelter and ambush prey. The canals are a great place to explore by boat or kayak. The bridges offer a few landbased options. Anglers casting hardbody and soft plastic lures around the structure catch bream, jacks, trevally and flathead during the day. Night fishing offers anglers fishing with big surface lures or live bait the chance to tangle with species such as jacks and trevally.

MAP 16A NO. 4 PELICAN WATERS CHANNEL
(BREAM, FLATHEAD, WHITING, TREVALLY)

The Pumicestone Passage channel that runs past Pelican Waters is deepest on the western shoreline. The channel transitions into sand and sea grass flats on the Bribie Island side of the channel. The channel and flats fish well for bream, flathead and whiting as well as some bigger fare such as trevally and the odd jewfish. Drifting the shallow sea grass beds while retrieving hardbody and soft plastic lures is a great way to take flathead, bream and whiting. The channel offers good bait and lure fishing for flathead, bream, whiting, trevally and the occasional jewfish. The jetty south of the Pelican Waters entrance is a good shorebased spot to get in amongst the action.

MAP 16A NO. 5 BELLS CREEK
(BREAM, FLATHEAD, JEWFISH, WHITING, MANGROVE JACK)

The entrance to the creek is scoured to form a deeper hole. Shorebased bait anglers fish through the night and during low light hours to take some handy catches of bream, flathead and school jewfish when they are schooled up here. Upriver of the entrance, the creek is made up of shallow sand banks that drop into deeper holes in places. The sand banks fish well for whiting while the drop-off ledges fish well for flathead and bream. The middle to upper reaches of the creek are clothed in mangroves. The deeper banks with overhanging natural structure fish well for mangrove jack, bream and flathead. This creek can be a sneaky place to take advantage of some good late winter and spring fishing before everyone else hears that they are biting. As the water temperature warms, the fish become increasingly active.

ABOVE: Shallow hardbody lures fished around the shallows will produce bream.

ABOVE: Solid jacks will hold along much of the shoreline structure in this part of the world.

MAP 16A NO. 6 LOWER BELLS CREEK CHANNEL
(BREAM, FLATHEAD, JEWFISH, WHITING, MANGROVE JACK)

The Pumicestone Passage channel to the south of the Bells Creek mouth begins to shallow and lose clarity. The channel runs between bankside shallow flats and sea grass beds. The channel is shallower than that to the north. The area can provide anglers with frustrating fishing at times as the channel becomes full of floating weed. Deeper sections within the channel and bankside shallows hold some good fish at times. Anglers fishing worm, pilchard, yabby and prawn baits fare well on bream, whiting, flathead and in late winter and spring the odd school jewfish.

MAP 17 NO. 1 WESTAWAYS CREEK AND CHANNEL
(FLATHEAD, BREAM, WHITING, JEWFISH, MANGROVE JACK)

Westaways Creek enters the Pumicestone Passage in this area. A deeper channel runs along the southern Pumicestone Passage bank where the creek enters the system. This area of bank is largely Green Zone. The channel is mostly utilised by local fishers to target bream, whiting and flathead. Anchor based fishing with live and dead bait is a favoured approach. Fish baits, worm, prawn and nippers will entice local predators.

The northern bank has a deeper section in amongst extended shallow water sea grass beds. The flats are a great place to target whiting and bream in summer. A building tide and a bit of southerly wind chop will produce the best fishing here. The deeper water adjacent to this bank is known to produce the occasional jack and school jewfish. Early morning fishing with soft plastics and bibbed hardbody lures should encourage reaction from these predators.

MAP 17 NO. 2 COOCHIN CREEK
(FLATHEAD, BREAM, WHITING, MANGROVE JACK)

Coochin Creek is an impressive fishing location. This relatively small creek provides great fishing for bream, whiting and flathead, and is a favoured haunt for local anglers chasing mangrove jack. Coochin Creek enters the Pumicestone Passage at the end of a long, straight and broad stretch of water. Saltwater Creek enters Coochin Creek in the middle of this stretch. This patch of water produces very good fishing for whiting and bream in summer and flathead in spring and summer. Upriver of the broad straight, the creek takes its first ninety degree turn. The waters from this point and up into the far upper reaches of Coochin Creek are the place to target jacks. Casting lures and baits tight against backside structure is the way to tangle with these fierce creatures. The far upper reaches are well known for producing a few jacks in the middle of winter, so this is not a summer only jack fishery.

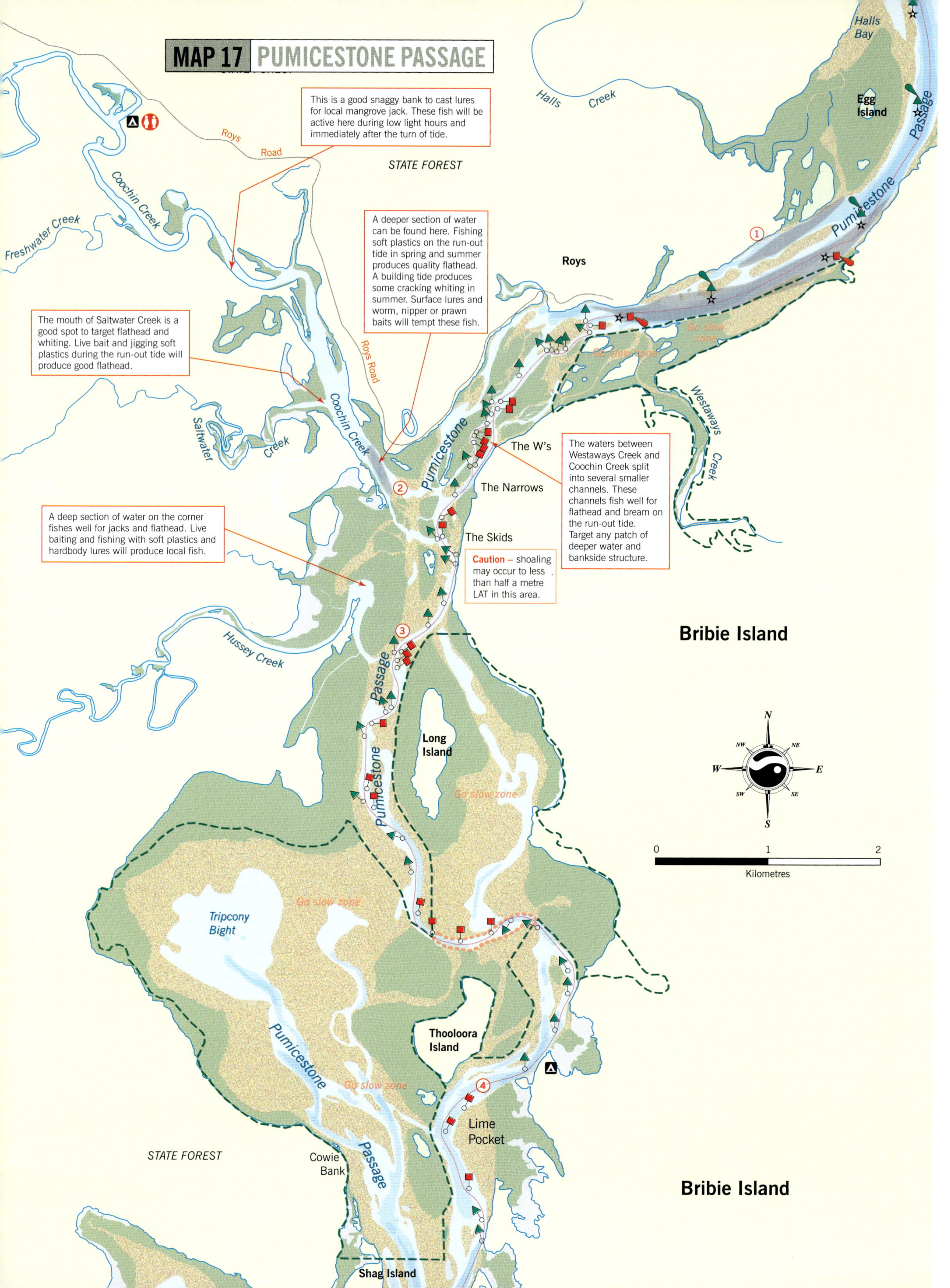
MAP 17 PUMICESTONE PASSAGE
This is a good snaggy bank to cast lures for local mangrove jack. These fish will be active here during low light hours and immediately after the turn of tide.
A deeper section of water can be found here. Fishing soft plastics on the run-out tide in spring and summer produces quality flathead. A building tide produces some cracking whiting in summer. Surface lures and worm, nipper or prawn baits will tempt these fish.
The mouth of Saltwater Creek is a good spot to target flathead and whiting. Live bait and jigging soft plastics during the run-out tide will produce good flathead.
The waters between Westaways Creek and Coochin Creek split into several smaller channels. These channels fish well for flathead and bream on the run-out tide. Target any patch of deeper water and bankside structure.
A deep section of water on the corner fishes well for jacks and flathead. Live baiting and fishing with soft plastics and hardbody lures will produce local fish.
Caution – shoaling may occur to less than half a metre LAT in this area.
Halls Bay
Egg Island
Halls Creek
Roys Road
STATE FOREST
Coochin Creek
Freshwater Creek
Roys
Pumicestone Passage
Go slow zone
Westaways Creek
Saltwater Creek
The W's
The Narrows
The Skids
Hussey Creek
Bribie Island
Long Island
Tripcony Bight
Thooloora Island
Lime Pocket
Cowie Bank
Shag Island
STATE FOREST
0
1
2
Kilometres
N
S
E
W
NW
NE
SW
SE
1
2
3
4

Map 17 No. 3 Hussey Creek *(flathead, bream, whiting, mangrove jack)*

Hussey Creek and the local waters of the Pumicestone Passage fish well at times for flathead, whiting, bream and the odd jack. Deeper sections of banks that contain some structure will hold jacks in these parts. The upper sections of Hussey Creek are a great place to explore with a kayak and do provide some good fishing for jacks in summer. The area borders on protected Green Zone so be careful where you fish in this area.

Map 17 No. 4 Thooloora Island Channel *(flathead, bream, whiting)*

Much of the western channel waters are protected Green Zone in this location. The eastern and deeper sections of the channel fish well for flathead, bream and whiting. The channel markers here fish well for bream holding against the base of these structures at times. Jigging soft plastics and blades around the structure will tempt these fish. Flathead will hold against the edge of sandbanks on the run-out tide. Drifting while jigging soft plastics across the drop-off works well for these ambush style predators.

Map 18A No. 1 Glass Mountain Creek and Pumicestone Passage Channel *(flathead, bream, whiting, mangrove jack)*

Glass Mountain Creek and the adjacent areas of Pumicestone Passage contain myriad sand flats etched in places by channel water. Glass Mountain Creek makes for shallow water navigation at times, but exploration up the system can be well worth the effort. The lower reaches provide a haven for whiting and bream on the flats and flathead along the drop-off areas. The areas where the channel cuts into the bankside vegetation are worth fishing. Bait and lure fishing here will provide bream, flathead and the odd jack. The upper reaches of the creek are quite narrow in places, but the waters provide some good mangrove jack fishing at times.

The channel waters around the confluence of Glass Mountain Creek and Pumicestone Passage provide deeper water structure for bream, flathead and the odd school jew. An early morning run-out tide often has bait and predators stacked up in this area. Fishing baits and jigging soft plastics around the drop-off points produces some good flathead.

Map 18A No. 2 Poverty Bank Ledge *(bream, flathead, trevally, mangrove jack, estuary cod)*

A few hundred metres north of Poverty Point, a red channel marker demarcates a coffee rock ledge. Mud, sand and scattered coffee rock drops into 3 to 4 m of water just off this ledge. The shallows and deeper water around this ledge fish well for bream, flathead and the odd mangrove jack and school jewfish. The ledge is a great holding point for bait and as such a variety of species of fish have shown up here, so be prepared for the odd surprise! Anglers that fare well in this location either anchor along the ledge and fish bait, or drift along the structure and fish with lures. Live and dead fish baits or prawns, worms and nippers will tempt local predators. Bibbed hardbody lures, blades and soft plastics when worked over the ledge and down along the face of the structure will provide good results. The best fishing occurs as the tide starts to run along the ledge. Peak tidal flow makes the location a tough one to fish.

There are several other locations in the area that are worth fishing. The mangrove edge adjacent to the ledge fishes well at the top of the tide. Fish that hold on the ledge move into these shallow areas to feed when the water inundates the surrounding flats. A submerged rocky point can be found to the north of the ledge and this fishes well for bream and flathead when water is pushing over the top of it. The channel waters and drop-off points in the area fish well on the bottom of the run-out tide.

Map 18A No. 3 Donnybrook Shallows *(bream, flathead, whiting)*

The township of Donnybrook overlooks extensive sand and weed shallows. Local shallows and channel waters wrap the prominent Little Goat Island. The area produces consistent catches of bream, whiting and flathead. A rising tide will provide good options for targeting bream and whiting that are feeding in the shallows. Fishing worm, prawn, nipper or fish (mullet, tailor or bonito) strip baits on the edge of the channel and shallow margins is a great way to tempt these fish. Lure anglers often choose to drift across the flats and cast and retrieve shallow diving hardbody lures and soft plastics. Surface lures work well here in summer for both bream and whiting. Prawn imitation hard and soft lures work well in this location. A run-out tide can also fish well around Donnybrook. Anglers that consistently catch fish on the run-out tide are good at reading the water and specifically targeting the channel waters that cut through the shallows. Fish will retreat to specific parts of these channels as the water leaves the shallows. Anglers that traverse these areas will eventually find concentrations of fish holding in deeper channels. Present a bait or lure that matches the food supply draining from the shallows and you'll have a fish on in short time!

Map 18A No. 4 Gallaghers Bank *(bream, flathead, whiting, trevally, tailor)*

The eastern bank that runs along Gallagher Point provides plenty of structure to host resident bream, flathead and whiting. Natural bankside vegetation sits above a sandy foreshore that drops into several metres of water in the channel. The drop-off is often clothed in weed and the location produces some big bream, flathead and whiting at various stages throughout the year. Drifting the bank and hopping soft plastics from the shallow water and down into the channel produces good numbers of fish. A coffee rock ledge exists to the south of Gallagher Point and this location produces good fish on the turn of the tide. Bait anglers are often found anchored up in this location as it produces good bread and butter species and the odd school jewfish.

Map 18A No. 5 Bullock Creek *(bream, flathead, whiting, mangrove jack)*

The creek produces bream and flathead along the channel drop-off areas and whiting across the shallow flats. Although shallow at times, the limited waters of the upper reaches produce the odd mangrove jack around the near-bank drop-offs and natural bankside structures. The mouth of the creek fishes well for flathead on the run-out.

Map 18B No. 6 Elimbah Creek *(bream, flathead, whiting, mangrove jack)*

Elimbah Creek drains into Pumicestone Passage via a tightly marked channel and through extensive sand and weed shallows. The channel markers in the area are well worth targeting for bream holding at the base of these hard structures. The shallows are a haven for bream and whiting and these fish are often targeted on the building tide. Baits of worms and nippers produce some good fish, as does drifting while casting shallow diving and surface hardbody lures. Overcast and windy conditions produce the best flats fishing. Drifting with the wind at your back and making long casts before retrieving back to your feet is a very successful approach. Better quality fish often use the poor weather conditions to actively feed across the shallows without a strong threat of predation.

Upstream from the mouth of Elimbah Creek, the waterway is a mix of interspersed deeper holes separated by shallow sandbanks. The deeper water and drop-off points fish well for flathead, bream and the odd mangrove jack and cod while the shallows produce good summer whiting and bream. Man-made structures, rocky bottom and natural bankside vegetation provide structure that

MAP 18 A PUMICESTONE PASSAGE

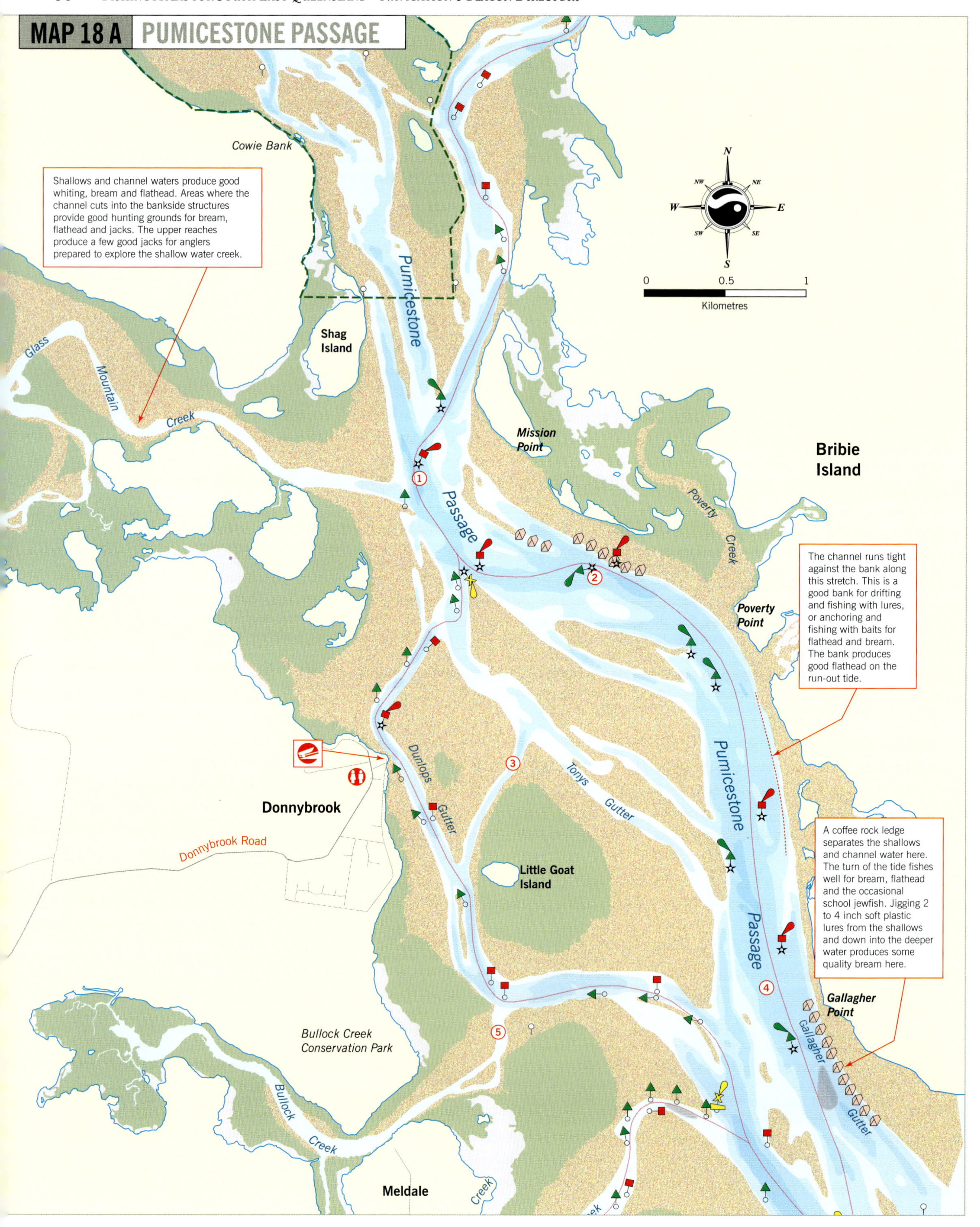

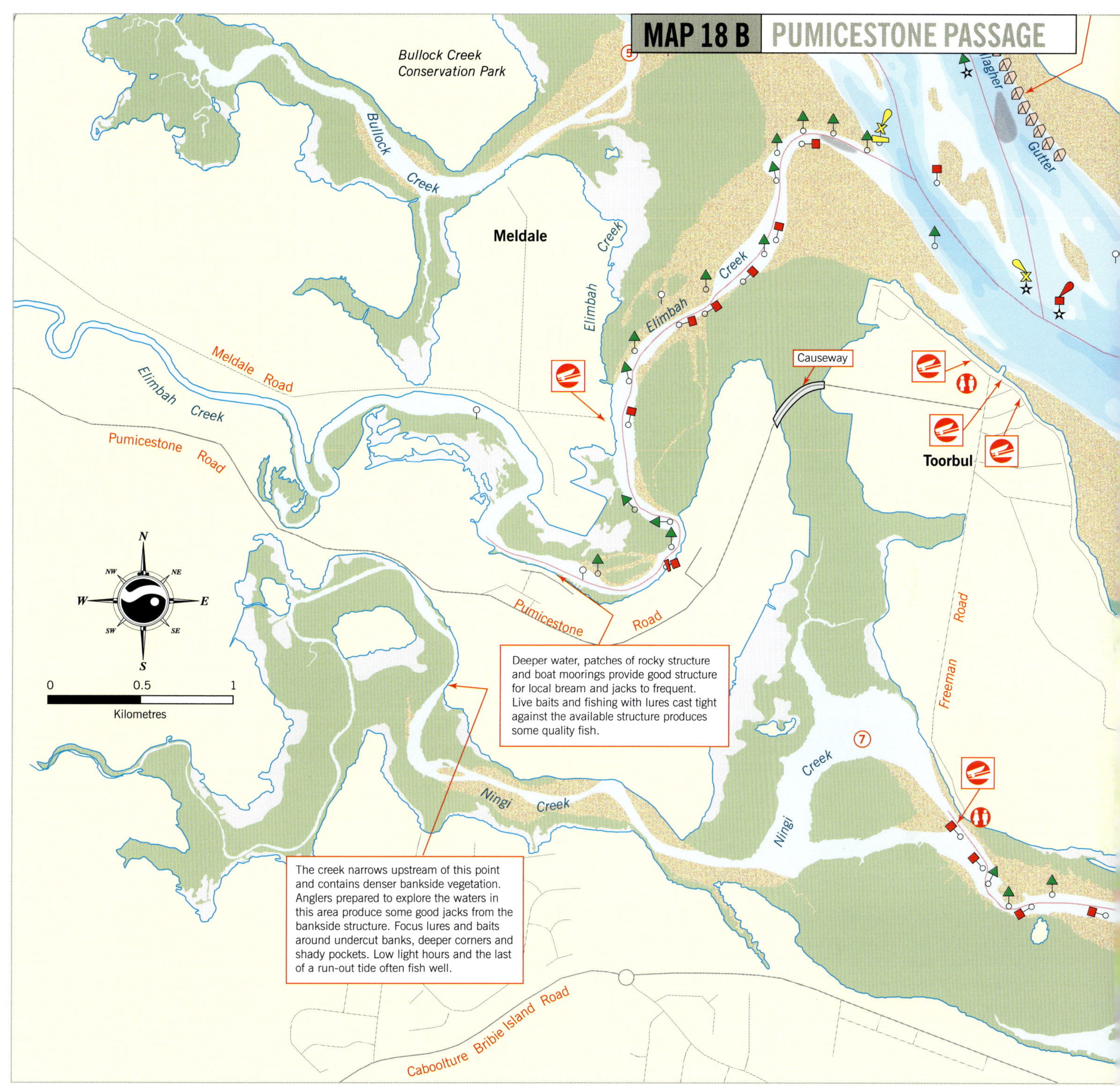

often holds mangrove jack. The upper reaches of Elimbah Creek produce good numbers of jacks in late winter and throughout summer. Fishing during the bottom of the run-out tide and through the night often yields the best results on these aggressive predators. Live baiting and fishing with diving hardbody lures are favoured means for taking these fish here.

Map 18B No. 7 Ningi Creek Middle to Upper Reaches *(Bream, Flathead, Whiting, Mangrove Jack)*

Ningi Creek is well known amongst local anglers as being a good producer of mangrove jacks. This picturesque waterway consists of a channel bordered by mangroves and lined by oyster racks in varying states of repair throughout its lower reaches. The channel waters and bankside structure provide plenty of shelter to keep resident jacks, bream, flathead, whiting and cod happy. Local anglers find fishing with live bait through the night in the upper reaches to be particularly effective when targeting jacks. Anglers drifting and casting hardbody and soft plastic lures tight against the bankside structure also fare well on local jacks. Low light periods and the turn of the tide produces the best fishing for mangrove jack. Bream, trevally and flathead are common bycatch for anglers targeting jacks in the upper reaches.

The middle reaches of Ningi Creek produce some good flathead and bream fishing. Bream are commonly found in the shallows during the building tide as there is plenty of available sand and weed flat country in the creek. The channel waters are popular places to target flathead on the run-out tide. The fishing in the creek really starts to fire when the prawns are in abundance here.

MAP 19A No.1 WHITE PATCH BANK
(FLATHEAD, BREAM, WHITING)

A sand and mud bank along the foreshore of the White Patch location drops into a deeper channel. The bottom contains weed and scattered coffee rock. The drop-off produces bream, flathead and summer whiting at times. Fish strip baits, worms and nippers produce good catches of bread and butter species. Fish tend to congregate here on the run-out tide.

MAP 19A No. 2 TOORBUL FLATS
(FLATHEAD, BREAM, WHITING, TAILOR, TREVALLY)

Toorbul sits to the western side of extensive weed and sand flats. These flats are bound to the south by Ningi Creek and to the east by Shag Island. Good numbers of bream, whiting and at times tailor and trevally will get up on to this ground on a building tide. Several deeper channels cut through these flats and fish use these pathways to access the flats. Anglers positioning themselves at the

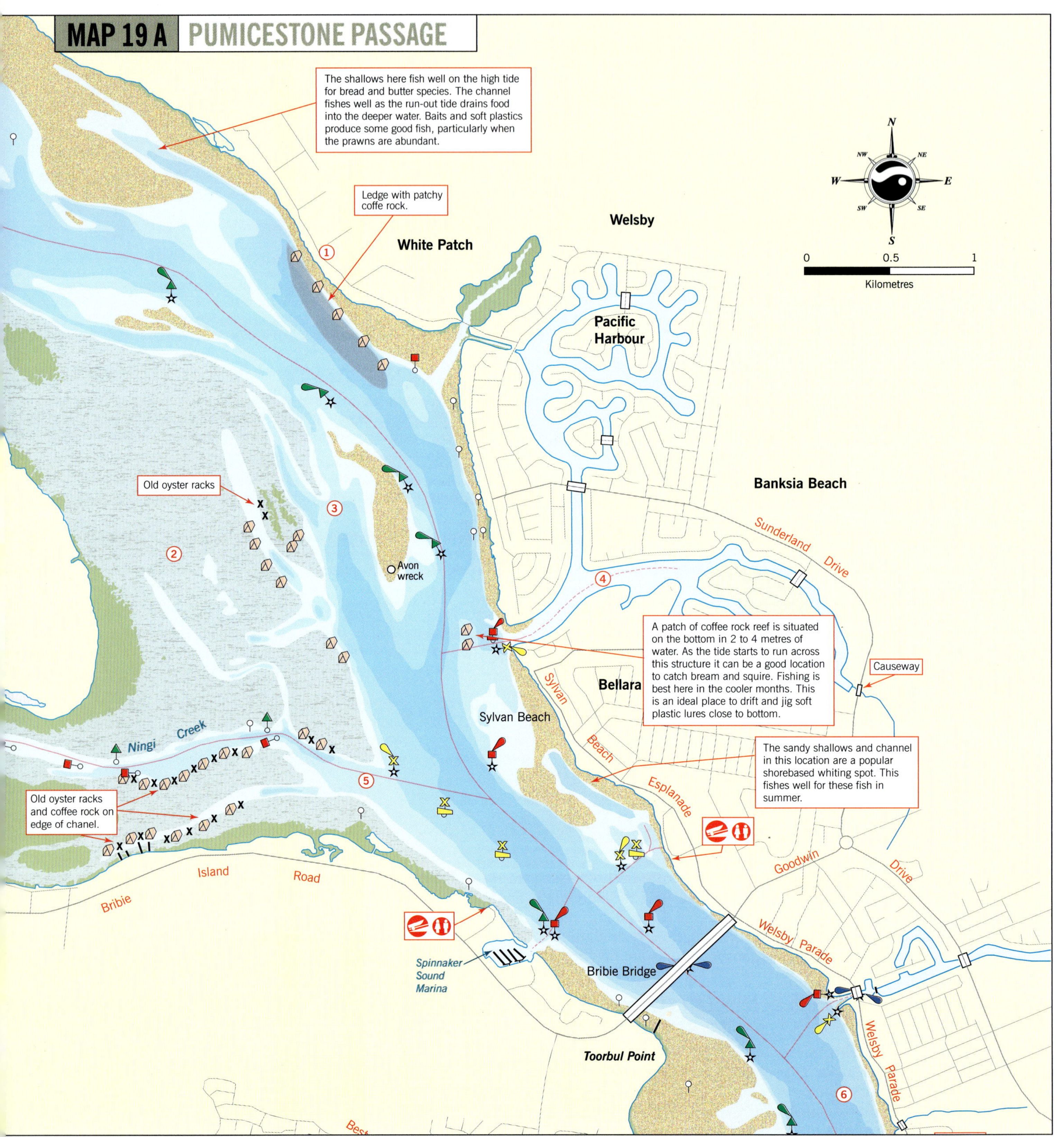

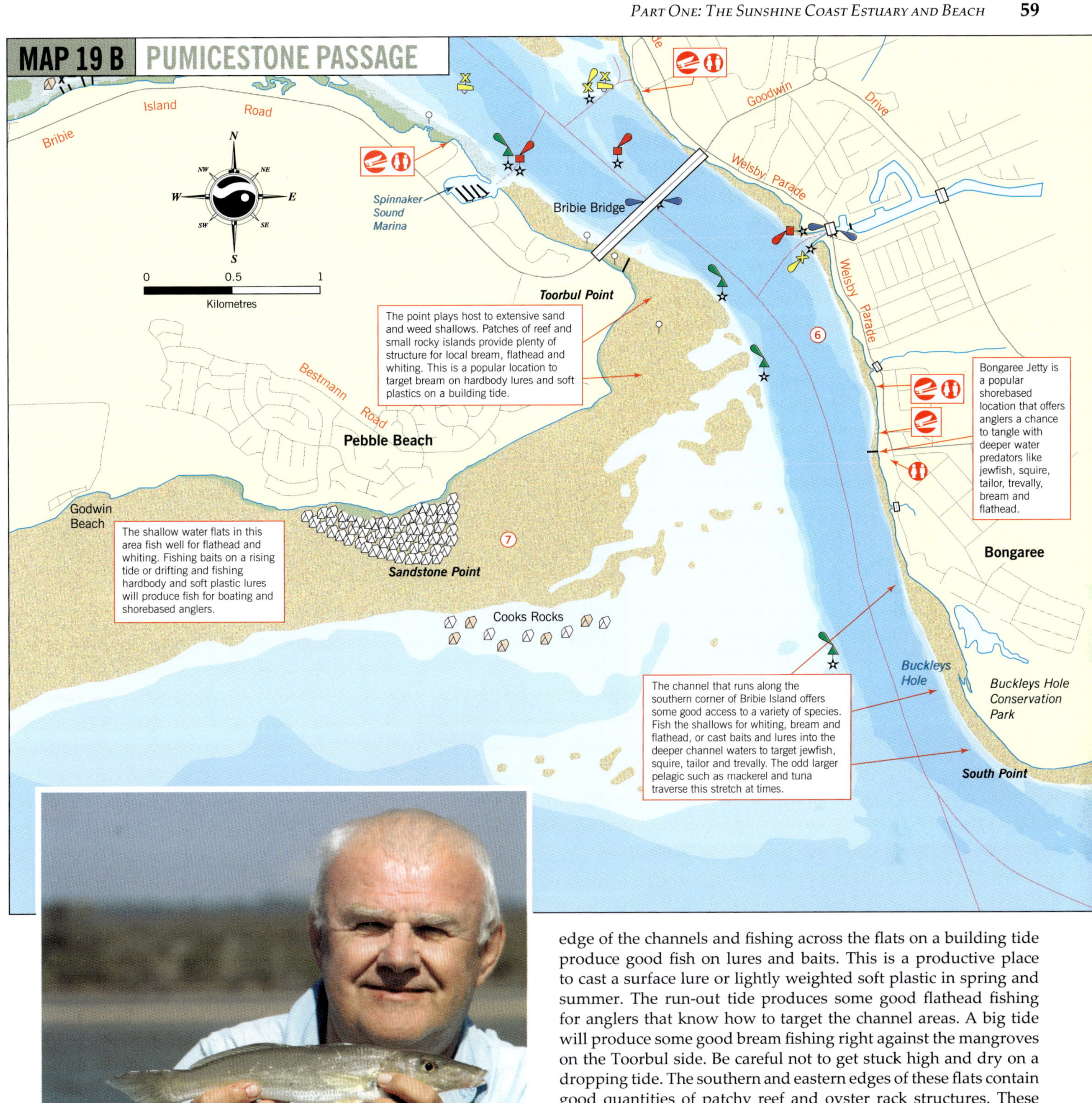

ABOVE: Whiting are popular species to target on the Pumicestone Flats.

edge of the channels and fishing across the flats on a building tide produce good fish on lures and baits. This is a productive place to cast a surface lure or lightly weighted soft plastic in spring and summer. The run-out tide produces some good flathead fishing for anglers that know how to target the channel areas. A big tide will produce some good bream fishing right against the mangroves on the Toorbul side. Be careful not to get stuck high and dry on a dropping tide. The southern and eastern edges of these flats contain good quantities of patchy reef and oyster rack structures. These locations are a haven for big bream when the tide is up and over these areas. The fish here love a well presented lure retrieved across available structure. Be prepared to be 'owned' by some of these fish on the way to losing some tackle!

Map 19A No. 3 Toorbul Channel

(Flathead, bream, whiting, trevally, tailor, mangrove jack, squire)

The Pumicestone Passage channel waters to the east of the Toorbul flats provide some good fishing for a variety of species. As waters recede from the shallows, a lot of predatory fish and available food supply such as prawns and baitfish move into the channel. The drop-off point into the channel is often clothed in weed which makes it a prime structure to target fish during the run-out stages of the tide. The drop-off into the western side of the channel opposite White Patch, around Shag Island and the Avon Wreck are good places to start searching for fish. Channel waters are typically several metres deep here. These areas hold good numbers of bream, flathead, whiting and tailor as well as trevally at times. The rocky outcrops that sit along the edge of the shallows to the south of Shag Island fish well around the top of the tide. Bream are a prime target in these locations. The eddy effect in the channel areas around Shag Island and the Avon Wreck, results in bait being held up here from time to time. In the event that good bait supply can be found, the predators won't be far away. The sandy shores on the eastern bank adjacent to the Bribie Island Canals fishes well for whiting. This is a popular shorebased spot in summer. A patch of bottom coffee rock reef is located a few hundred metres out from the entrance to the Bribie Island Canals. This reef fishes well for flathead in summer and bream in the winter. It is one of the areas within the Pumicestone Passage that you will catch legal squire. Patches of coffee rock located along the bottom of the deeper parts of the channel will produce the odd squire and sweetlip. Anglers targeting these spots with baits and soft plastics encounter these fish when they are holding in the channel. Squire are most commonly found here during late winter and sweetlip during the summer months.

Map 19A No. 4 Bribie Island Canals

(Flathead, Bream, Whiting, Trevally, Tailor, Mangrove Jack)

The Bribie Island Canals host a plethora of man-made structure in shallow and deeper water. This provides a haven for species such as bream, mangrove jack and trevally. Anglers targeting these areas will also come across whiting and flathead. A popular approach to fishing the area includes boating through the canals and casting lures around available structure. Retrieving deep diving hardbody lures through shady spots produces some good fish, as does dropping slow sinking soft plastics tight against structure. Surface lures cast into the shallows and retrieved into deeper water and alongside structure tempts some good fish through the warmer months. Treat local property with respect when fishing this area and the canal inhabitants will welcome you back the next time.

Map 19A No. 5 Ningi Creek Mouth and Pumicestone Passage Channel

(Flathead, Bream, Whiting, Trevally, Mangrove Jack)

The entrance of Ningi Creek into Pumicestone Passage is a popular location for local anglers to target resident species. Substantial shallow water sand and weed flats drop into a deeper channel where Ningi Creek drains into the Passage. The edge of the channel is host to oyster rack and broken reef structures. The available structure along this stretch of water screams fish to the angler. A

RIGHT: Big tailor are a prize when fishing the southern entrance to Pumicestone Passage.

BELOW: Chopper tailor are a favourite among many local beach anglers.

popular approach involves targeting this edge structure on the building tide and then targeting the deeper sections of the drop-off when the tide pushes out. The hard structure produces good bream for anglers drifting and casting lures. Lures and baits fished along the drop-off produce some very good flathead here, as well as trevally, tailor and the odd jack.

The channel areas of the Pumicestone Passage out from the mouth of Ningi Creek hold patches of broken reef on the bottom. These structures hold squire in the winter and sweetlip in the summer. The sandy beach on the eastern side of the channel, immediately opposite the mouth to Ningi Creek, is a popular shorebased whiting spot in summer.

Map 19B No. 6 Southern Pumicestone Passage Channel *(Flathead, Bream, Whiting, Trevally, Tailor, Mangrove Jack, Squire, Jewfish)*

The bridge linking Bribie Island to the mainland is a dominant structure that sits at the top of this popular stretch of water. The bridge is a popular haunt for bait and lure anglers targeting a variety of species. The turn of the tide is a prime time to be fishing this structure. Anglers that fish the bridge during low light and through the night produce some of the best results. Live fish baits, strips of tailor, mack tuna and bonito or blades and soft plastic lures fished around the pylons will entice resident predators. The bridge is well known for producing regular captures of bream, jewfish, trevally, tailor, squire and sweetlip. Winter produces the best of the jewfish, squire, trevally and tailor fishing. Bream can be caught year -round and summer fishes best for sweetlip.

The eastern edge of the channel running from the bridge to the southern tip of Bribie Island hosts a sandy drop-off that falls into 6 to 10 m in places. The bottom holds patches of broken reef that play host to bait and a variety of predators. The channel is a popular spot for shorebased and boating anglers to target bream, squire, jewfish, sweetlip, flathead, tailor and trevally. The sandy shoreline produces some good whiting fishing through summer. Popular locations along this stretch include the Bongaree Jetty and the channel waters out from Buckleys Hole. Popular dead baits through this area include prawns, yabbies and worms for bream and whiting, and pilchards, tailor or bonito for bigger predators. Anglers drifting with the tide and hopping soft plastics along the bottom produce good fish along this stretch.

ABOVE: Big bream congregate on the shallows around the southern parts of Pumicestone Passage.

ABOVE: Shoreline ledges and coffee rock will hold school jewfish.

The shallow shoreline immediately to the south west of the bridge and out from Toorbul Point produces some good fishing for bread and butter species. The location holds some rocky islands and the shallows consist of mixed weed, sand and gravel. A high tide fishes well for bream and flathead around the hard structure. The drop-off around the shallows fishes best on the run-out. This is a prime location for anglers targeting bream on small hardbody lures.

Map 19B No. 7 Sandstone Point Flats *(Flathead, Bream, Whiting, Trevally, Squire)*

The waters off Sandstone Point comprise of shallow sand and weed flats with scattered reef and small rocky islands. There are also small areas of remnant oyster rack structure to be found here. The foreshores around Sandstone Point are used by shorebased anglers to target whiting on a high tide. Baits of worms and nippers will entice these fish and the cruising bream that frequent the location. The rocky island and oyster rack structures are only a high tide fishing option as they are high and dry at low tide. Shallow riding boats and kayaks are the vessel of choice for anglers wishing to target fish in these areas. Targeting bream, flathead and whiting with hardbody and soft plastic lures is a popular approach in this location. A retreating tide should see anglers heading into deeper waters off the flats to target fish, such as the area around Cooks Rocks. This location consists of structure in 3 to 4 m of water and is a popular spot for winter anglers targeting bay squire.

PART 2

MORETON BAY

ABOVE: Lure fishing shallow reef around Bird Island.

Moreton Bay is an extensive waterway that is protected by the influence of two large sand islands. North Stradbroke Island lies to the south of Moreton Island and the two isles are separated by approximately 3.5km. These large chunks of sand protect Moreton Bay from the ocean swell. The largest entrance into Moreton Bay can be found to the north where Moreton Island is separated from Bribie Island by a distance of approximately 15km. This stretch of water consists of myriad sand banks and channels. The shipping route into Port of Brisbane meanders through this area and the main channel is shared by large ships and a variety of pelagic species that call the channel markers home for periods of the year. Much of the waters that separate Moreton Bay from the ocean consist of shallow sandy bottom. Access to the sea by boaters consists of navigating dangerous waters at times. Many boats have come to grief in these ocean bar environments over the years.

The bay itself holds little hard structure in relation to the broad size of the waterway. The reef structure that can be found includes that around some of the islands within the waterway, occasional bottom rubble and some patchy shoreline rock. Several artificial reefs have been installed to provide added habitat to local marine species. Local fish hold on any available reef, ledge, mangrove and man-made structure.

The shores of Moreton Bay are host to one of Australia's biggest cities. Urban sprawl has resulted in rapid population growth along the edge of this scenic waterway over the past decades. Today, Moreton Bay supports a large recreational and commercial fishing community. The local fishing has suffered the affects of long term commercial and recreational fishing, however, every year, the waterway continues to produce some top quality fishing. The geographical location of Moreton Bay provides a great mix of southern and northern fish species. The area fishes well for pelagic species such as mackerel, tuna, trevally, tailor, kingfish and cobia to name a few. The location also provides great reef fishing options for the likes of snapper, jewfish, sweetlip, cod and occasional tropical species like tusk fish and nannygai. The bread and butter brigade is kept happy with good numbers of bream, flathead and whiting available through many parts of the bay. The rivers and creeks that feed Moreton Bay provide some unique estuary fishing in places. Although bream, flathead and whiting are common captures, the rivers offer good fishing for well sought after species such as mangrove jack, jewfish, squire and lesser numbers of the prized threadfin salmon and occasional barramundi. The brackish and freshwater reaches of the rivers are well known for some quality bass and golden perch fishing.

Seasonal influences affect the fishing in Moreton Bay. Various pelagic species call the area home during the warmer months while winter and spring times are renowned as providing the best of the reef fishing. Moreton Bay fishing 'die-hards' include anglers like Mike Connelly. Mike summarises one of the keys to catching fish in Moreton Bay as being the ability to find concentrations of bait. His law of the Bay is as follows,

> *"The type and movement of bait can vary between the north and south of Moreton Bay. If you can establish the right patterns of movement and find the bait, you will find the predatory fish you are targeting".*

Key factors for catching fish in the Bay also include locating and understanding the structure that fish prefer, and the influence of the tides in those particular areas.

Local anglers have to battle aggressively these days to protect their right to fish Moreton Bay. Although protection is necessary in some areas, radical green movements threaten to remove much of Moreton Bay from the reaches of the recreational fisher. These movements and over-zealous commercial fishing in prime nursery areas are the biggest long term threat for recreational fishing in this popular location. Although some argue the 'Green Zoning' of the bay is excessive, there is certainly benefit in protecting key areas of the waterway. Voting sensibly in the years to come will hopefully provide us with a good balance of resource protection and accessible fishing water.

This part of the book has been divided into geographical sections to enable easy perusal of the areas you are most interested in fishing. Chapter Three includes a detailed look at all the available fishing spots in the North Western Bay and rivers, Chapter Four covers the North Eastern and Southern Moreton Bay regions.

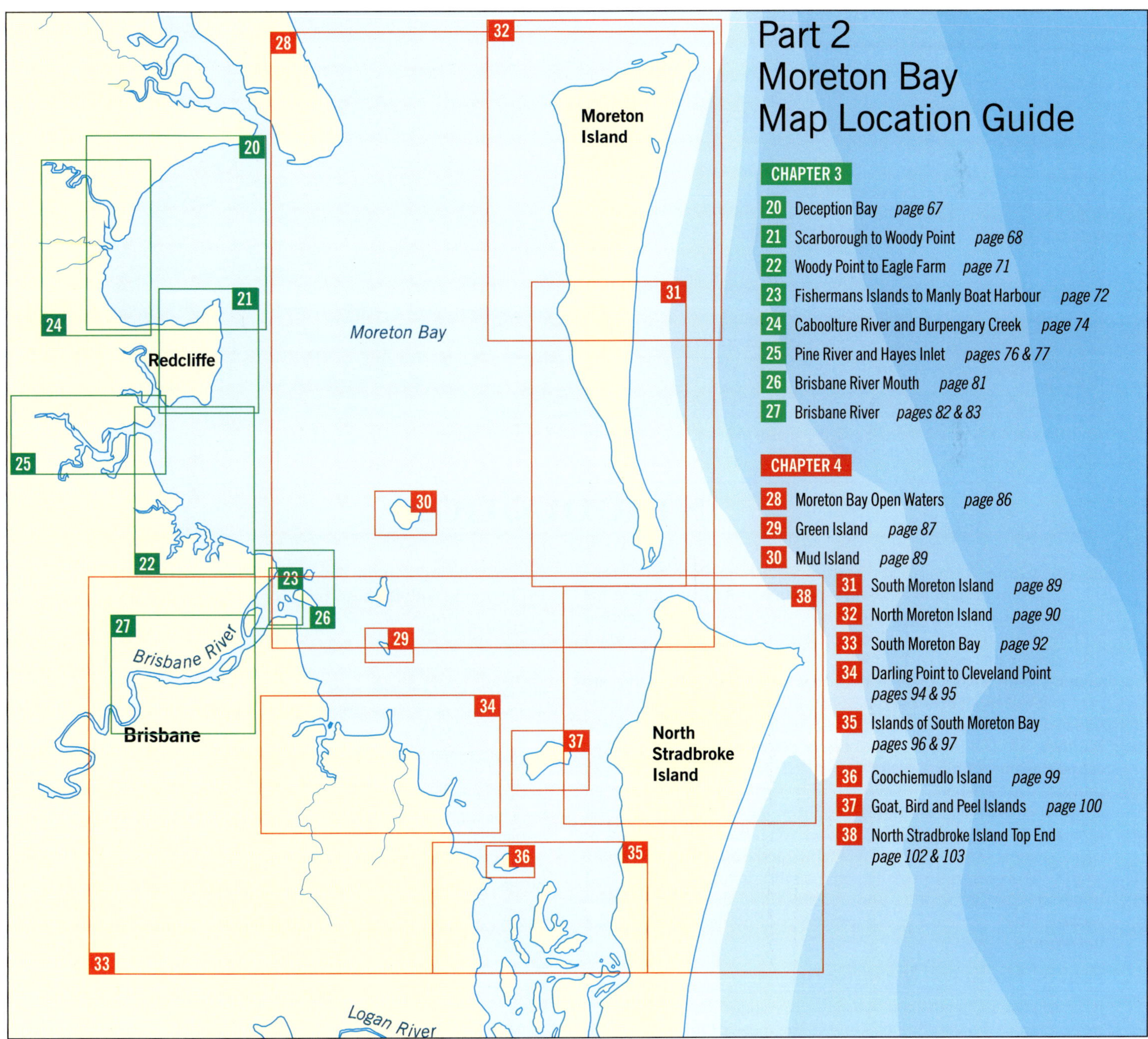

CHAPTER 3

NW MORETON BAY & RIVERS

Sandstone Point to Redland Bay

Including Deception Bay, Redcliffe, Sandgate, Manly and the Caboolture, Pine and Brisbane Rivers

ABOVE: Moreton Island and the shipping channel of Moreton Bay provide the backdrop for some remarkably good fishing.

INTRODUCTION

This Moreton Bay margin stretching from Sandstone Point on the far northern shoreline to Redland Bay in the south, comprises a varied mix of rocky shore interspersed with mud, sand and weeded bottom. It is cut in places by significant estuaries in the way of the Caboolture, Pine and Brisbane River systems. The shallow bay waters that straddle the shoreline are host to a variety of bread and butter, reef and sporadic pelagic fare. Green Zones reduce some of the fishing area along this shoreline but there are still plenty of options for the recreational angler. The estuary systems offer a variety of species, some of which are very unique. The Brisbane River threadfin salmon population is an enigma as these fish are rarely caught in any of the surrounding systems. The mangrove jack and occasional barramundi taken in these systems serve to remind us that we geographically border the tropics. The estuaries provide some quality fishing for bread and butter species and in the upper reaches of all these systems bass become more common and populations of golden perch are not uncommon.

Fishing Notes for Moreton Bay

As this chapter begins our journey of Moreton Bay, it is worth gaining an understanding of some of the more prominent species targeted throughout the bay and what approaches are most likely to put you in with the best chance of getting connected.

Snapper: Can be targeted with baits and artificials. Quality fresh baits fished with a minimum of lead will put you in the box seat. Due to the relative shallowness of Moreton Bay waters, a basic running ball sinker rig and 2/0 to 4/0 baitholder pattern hooks will present fresh fillet baits, squid and pilchard pieces well. A fresh whiting head with skeleton attached will work exceptionally well for the larger snapper around the bay islands and along prominent ledges and contours.

Soft plastics work exceptionally well and almost any 3 to 5 inch plastic will entice the average snapper up to 3kg. Larger plastics to 7 inches are ideal for targeting those trophy fish that can reach 10 kg in weight. Lipless crankbaits, Clouser flies, minnow lures and several other offerings can all work at any given time.

Bream: Fresh baits are ideal however frozen offerings including mullet gut, fowl gut, squid, prawns, pilchards and flesh baits will also work for these scavengers. Keep baits lightly weighted and hook sizes between #2 and 2/0 for best results with a running sinker rig on 2 to 5kg line. Many small minnow lures, plastics, surface lures and flies will also entice strikes from these plucky little fighters. Quality fish over 30cm in length are mainly caught in the cooler months but can show up at any time. They are readily spread throughout most shallow reef areas, beaches and estuarine systems.

Flathead: These are probably one of the easiest species to catch on either baits or lures. Usually if it passes within sight of the flathead they will have a crack at it. Drifting the channels during low tide or on the tops of the flats during the higher stages with baits will increase your chances of encountering a flathead. The lower stages of the falling tide is the time to be working the edges of prominent banks and channels with minnow lures, plastics or Clouser flies. Flathead are plentiful in numbers, easy to hook and land but be careful of their spikes when handling them.

Sweetlip: Most sweetlip are encountered by anglers targeting snapper, as they are found in similar areas and will eat the same offerings. They seem more prevalent on fresh baits with gar and mullet fillets and fresh squid being prime offerings. Grass sweetlip are the most common and many larger specimens are lost due to their tenacious and powerful fighting ability once hooked. Their prime white flesh makes them a welcome catch.

Threadfin salmon: This prized species has really made its presence known in the Brisbane River and will take lures, flies and live baits. Popular artificials include lipless crankbaits, stickbait style plastics and blade lures. These are usually worked with small hops along the edges of the drop-offs into the main channel of the Brisbane River although fish have been caught mid-stream as they feed on the prawn schools. Working lures and flies around the lights shining onto the water further up the river also pays dividends at night. Live prawns, mullet, herring, pike and squid will also work and threadfin have been taken on these from many locations by both landbased and boating anglers. With the average fish around the metre mark they are great fun on spin or baitcasting gear loaded with 6 to 10kg braided line.

Whiting: These tasty morsels are fun to catch and mouth watering to eat. Moreton Bay's numerous flats and shallow channels make ideal habitat for both winter and summer whiting. Live worms on a long-shank hook and a light sinker on 2 to 4kg line is all that is required. Thin, tenderised strips of squid and peeled prawn tails will also work well as do Gulp Sandworms. Whiting will often hit small clear poppers in shallow areas, especially around weed beds although a stealthy approach and good presentation is paramount. A welcome by-catch, whiting are sometimes caught on small minnow lures targeted at flathead.

Sharks: Moreton Bay and the surrounding waterways are home to large numbers of sharks, predominately whalers. Many anglers target these specifically in the bay by drifting large whole fish baits into a tuna oil slick. Whalers, hammerheads and tiger sharks of all sizes respond to this approach. In the creeks and rivers, baits such as live mullet and catfish will attract the attention of whalers, especially bull sharks. The warmer months see heightened and more aggressive behaviour from sharks in the Moreton Bay area.

Cobia: Black kingfish are more prevalent in the bay during the latter months of the year where they can be caught on live baits including yakkas, slimey mackerel, whiptails, sand crabs and many other larger baits. With the quality fish around the 20kg mark and specimens to over 45kg showing up at times, a minimum of 15kg main line, 100lb monofilament leaders and 8/0 live bait or circle hooks are required for a positive outcome. Any areas in the northern half of the bay where baitfish and small reef species congregate (around beacons, ledges, coffee rock and rubble grounds) is worth trying during this period.

Mackerel: School mackerel and spotted mackerel are heavily targeted due to their fighting ability and tasty white fillets. Surface feeding schools can be targeted with chrome slices and a high-speed retrieve. Slow trolling with either rigged pilchards or small chrome spoons behind a paravane can produce results when the mackerel are a little deeper. Jigging chrome slices and drifting pilchards on ganged-hook rigs around the beacons in the northern bay is another successful ploy, especially during the warmer months. Spanish mackerel are occasionally taken inside the bay however best results will be obtained in the waters around Cape Moreton and off Point Lookout.

Tuna: Just like mackerel, surface feeding schools of tuna (longtail, mack and frigate) can be found anywhere throughout the bay, where they can be caught using high-speed retrieves and chrome slices. Fly fishermen often achieve more consistent results using intermediate lines and small imitate-the-bait flies such as surf candies, bay bait and polar-fibre minnows. Live yakkas and slimy mackerel fished around the beacons in the northern bay will often gain the attention of longtail tuna (to 30kg) and larger mack tuna (to 9kg). The longtail tuna are tenacious fighters and palatable if eaten Japanese style however both mack and frigate tuna are usually only kept for bait purposes.

Estuary cod: Usually found around structure such as rock walls, reefs and other man-made structures, estuary cod will eat a broad array of lures, flies and baits; both alive and dead. Both the black spot and gold spot estuary cod are relatively pleasing to the palate and can reach sizes to over 15kg, however specimens in the 1kg to 3kg bracket are more common in Moreton Bay and the surrounding waterways that feed it.

Trevally: Several species of trevally, especially GT and bigeye can be caught around the bay islands and in most creeks and canals, especially around prominent structure. Most are less than 2kg in weight but are good sport on light spin gear, baitcasters or fly rods. They will eat a broad array of live baits and most baitfish and prawn imitating lures and flies. An occasional golden trevally to 10kg can be caught on live baits fished around the beacons and artificial reefs in the northern bay.

Mangrove jack: Highly prized as both a sports fish and table fare, the mangrove jack will eat a broad array of lures such as hardbody minnows, soft plastics and lipless crankbaits as well as most baitfish profiled flies. Live baits are best; however mangrove jacks will sometimes engulf fresh dead baits as well. Try around structure in any of the mangrove creeks as well as the canal systems for most consistent results. Mangrove jacks are often landed on lighter line by anglers targeting bream however line classes above 6kg are preferred for a more positive outcome on this species, which likes to hunt in ambush around structure and can be a dirty fighter, yet is exceptional eating.

Mulloway: Mulloway are a sought after and highly prized species. Fishing live baits such as large mullet and pike around the deeper channels, ledges and holes in the estuarine systems is a good ploy. Jigging shad style plastics and lipless crank baits in these same areas, as well as casting them to the lighted areas around bridges and other structure at night will also produce results on fish which can reach over 30kg in weight but are more common at weights below 10 kg.

Dart: These plucky fighters are mainly confined to the eastern facing beaches of Moreton and Stradbroke islands and around the whitewater of headlands where they can be caught on baits such as worms, pippies and squid strips, and occasionally small soft plastics. They are great table fare when eaten fresh, although most are less than 1kg in weight.

Tailor: One of the most highly sought after table fish, especially during the cooler months, tailor will respond to many small baitfish profile metals, hardbody minnows and even flies. In saying that, most are commonly targeted on pilchards rigged on ganged hooks fished around areas such as the surf beach gutters, headlands and the mouth of major estuarine systems.

Crabs: Although around all year, the warmer months are best for crabbing as these crustaceans are more active during these months and the carapace is full of tasty white meat. Setting a few safety pots baited with fish frames, chicken carcasses or other scented baits will entice any crabs in the area. For sand crabs, set your pots along the ledges around the bay islands and in any gutters and channels in the bay and also at the mouths of major estuarine and creek systems. Mud crabs are usually found from the mouths of these same systems, right up to the upper saltwater reaches. Pots set along the deeper mangrove banks, in prominent holes and at the mouths of feeder creeks and gutters are likely to produce the goods.

Squid: These tasty cephalopods can be caught on both prawn-style squid jigs as well as squid jags baited with pilchards and other whole fish baits, suspended under a float. During the cooler months they can be caught in a variety of locales however targeting weed beds, rock walls and shallow rubble or reef areas that are covered with good clean water will heighten your chances of success. Tigers, arrows and bottle squid can all be caught around such areas as well as cuttlefish at times.

Prawns: Greasy prawns can be caught in most creek and river systems throughout the whole of the year and are highly prized bait for a broad array of species. During the latter part of summer and early autumn, good numbers of banana and tiger prawns enter the bay and systems flowing into them where they can be targeted with cast nets from landbased locations as well as boats. Often a limit of 10kg of prawns can be cast-netted in under an hour when they are around.

THE NORTH WESTERN SHORELINE AND BAY WATERS

The North Western Moreton Bay shoreline covers an extensive area. This margin extends through several waterside suburbs. These townships are generally equipped with good local boat ramps and access options for the shorebased angler.

The beauty of fishing the bay margins is that there is always a fishing option available, no matter what the season. Many popular species can be caught here year-round; only the size and number of available fish will vary with the seasons. Bream, flathead and whiting are year-round propositions. Bigger bream are a good chance in the cooler months and the better flathead show up in spring and into summer. The shallow flats provide good sand whiting in the summer months and diver whiting in winter. Snapper can be caught throughout the year. The average size fish are in the 35 to 45cm range however better numbers of bigger fish can be caught along the shallow reef systems during winter and spring. The shoreline as a pelagic fishery produces good tailor and trevally during winter and spring and the odd mackerel and tuna during the warmer months.

FACILITIES

Boat ramps in the northern areas include those found at Beachmere, Deception Bay and in Scarborough Boat Harbour. The Scarborough ramp consists of a three lane ramp in good condition that is protected from prevailing wind and in easy launching distance from many popular spots in the area.

Boat ramps in the Redcliffe area can be found at Queens Beach, Margate, Woody Point and Clontarf Beach. The Clontarf Beach ramp supports three launching lanes that are in good condition and protected from much of the prevailing wind. Be wary of shallow rocks as you enter and exit the ramp area.

In the Brambles Bay area, two lane ramps are located at Shorncliffe and Nudgee. The channel from the Nudgee ramp and out into the bay is narrow and tough to access at the bottom of a low tide.

A popular boat ramp near the mouth of the Brisbane River is located on the southern side of the bridge that accesses Fisherman Islands. The ramp is a double lane ramp and offers access to the river and out into Moreton Bay. Access from the ramp to the Brisbane River is attained by passing beneath the bridge. A high tide can make this difficult for larger boats.

FACT BOX

CHARTERS AND GUIDED FISHING

(CORRECT AT TIME OF PUBLISHING)

Several charter operators offer anglers fishing trips in Moreton Bay.

Brisbane Bay Tours operate from Manly and can be contacted on 0431332468 or through the website *brisbanebaytours.com.au*

Reel Easy Charters operate out of Redcliffe and can be contacted on 07 3880 3312 or through the website *reeleasycharters.com.au/about_us*

Sean Conlan Moreton Bay Charters

Incredible Charters operate out of Scarborough and fish throughout the area. They can be contacted on 07 3203 8188 or the website *incrediblecharters.com.au*

THE NORTH WESTERN SHORELINE AND BAY LOCATION GUIDE

MAP 20 NO. 1 BEACHMERE SHORELINE AND GODWIN BEACH

(WHITING, FLATHEAD, BREAM)

The foreshores adjacent to Beachmere and Godwin Beach comprise of sand and mud bottom. The soft bottom material along this stretch of foreshore has been sculptured by water movement. Subtle deeper water gutters can be found near to shore throughout this area. A building tide will often bring bread and butter species into these holes to feed. Shorebased anglers using baits of yabbies and worms fare well on whiting here. Ensure no fishing is carried out within the Green Zone when wetting a line in the area adjacent to Godwin Beach.

MAP 20 NO. 2 DECEPTION BAY

(MACKEREL, TUNA, DIVER WHITING)

The waters of Deception Bay fish well for a variety of species. Pelagic species such as spotted mackerel and longtail and mackerel tuna chase baitfish into the outer edges of the bay during the summer months. A mobile approach whereby boat anglers stay on the move and fish around visible signs of surface feeding activity is recommended. Casting and high speed retrieving metal lures around these signs of surface activity is a good way to hook one of these speedsters.

The bottom fishing for diver whiting during the winter months can be very good in this part of the bay.

RIGHT: Birds shadow a pack of longtail tuna feeding in Deception Bay. The Redcliffe shoreline in the background attracts a variety of reef and pelagic species.

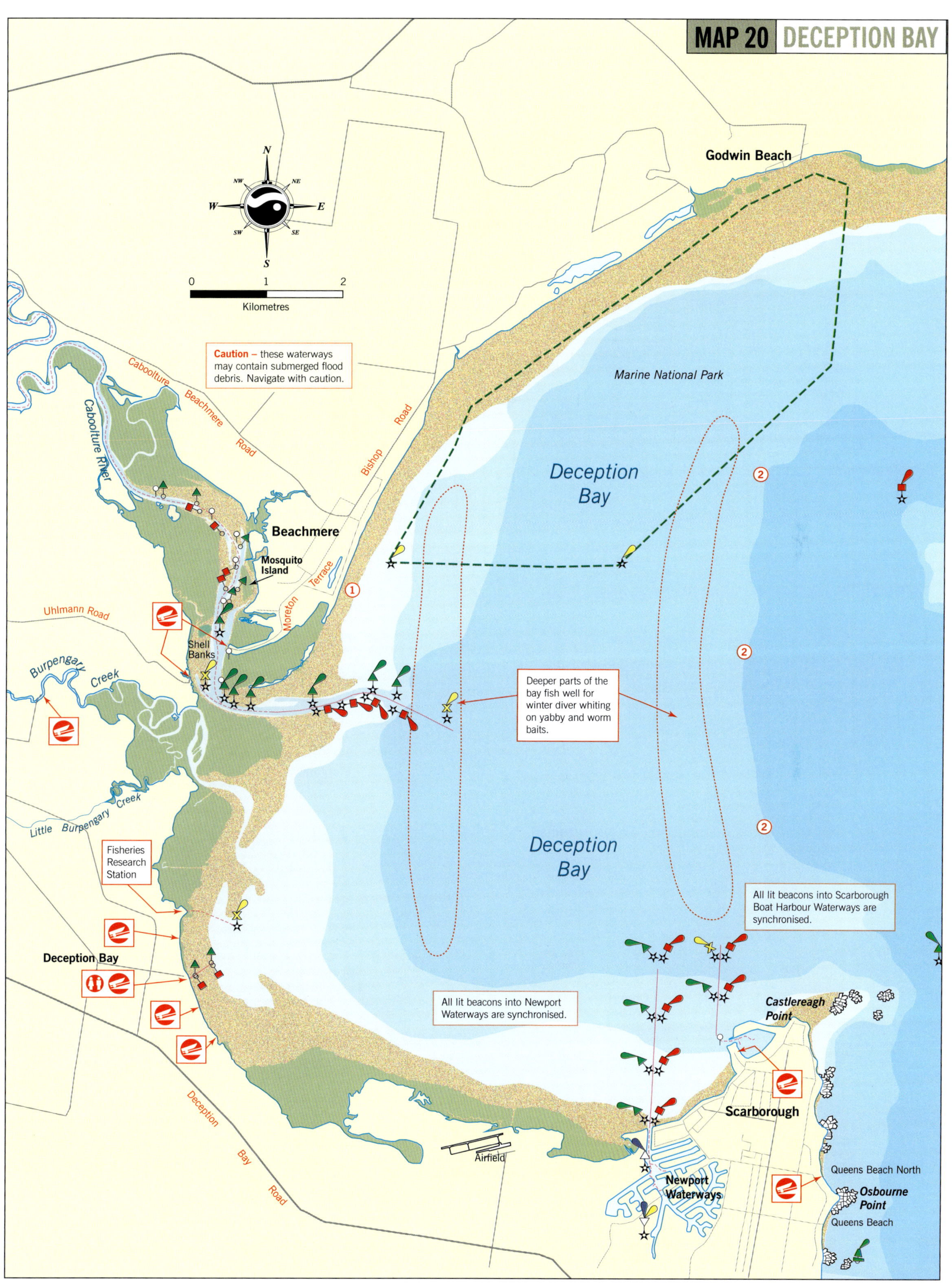
MAP 20 DECEPTION BAY
N
NE
E
SE
S
SW
W
NW
0
1
2
Kilometres
Godwin Beach
Caution – these waterways may contain submerged flood debris. Navigate with caution.
Marine National Park
Caboolture Beachmere Road
Caboolture River
Bishop Road
Deception Bay
Beachmere
Mosquito Island
Moreton Terrace
Uhlmann Road
Shell Banks
Burpengary Creek
Deeper parts of the bay fish well for winter diver whiting on yabby and worm baits.
Little Burpengary Creek
Fisheries Research Station
Deception Bay
All lit beacons into Scarborough Boat Harbour Waterways are synchronised.
Castlereagh Point
All lit beacons into Newport Waterways are synchronised.
Deception Bay Road
Scarborough
Airfield
Newport Waterways
Queens Beach North
Osbourne Point
Queens Beach

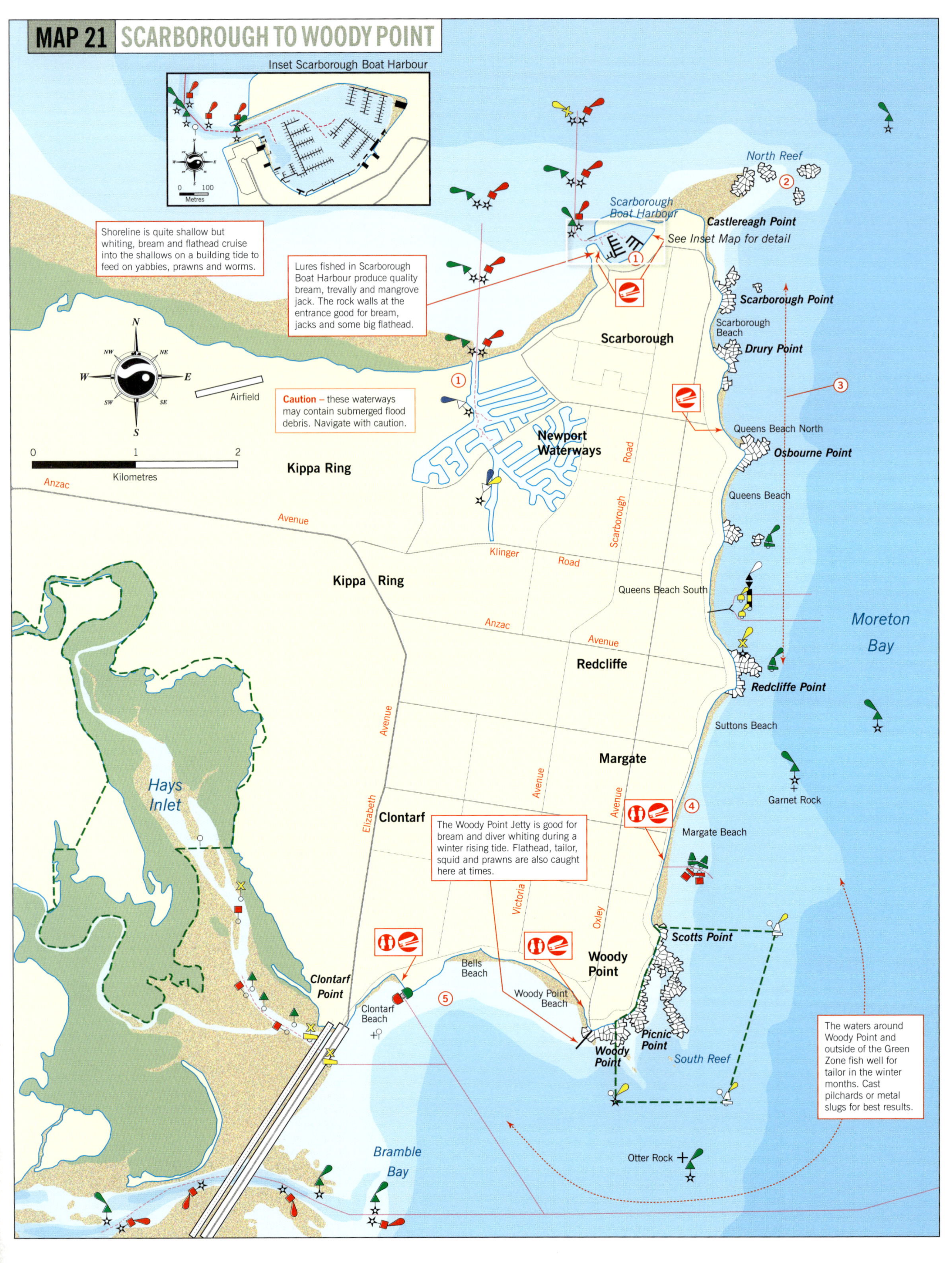
MAP 21 SCARBOROUGH TO WOODY POINT
Inset Scarborough Boat Harbour
0 100
Metres
North Reef
Scarborough Boat Harbour
Castlereagh Point
See Inset Map for detail
Shoreline is quite shallow but whiting, bream and flathead cruise into the shallows on a building tide to feed on yabbies, prawns and worms.
Lures fished in Scarborough Boat Harbour produce quality bream, trevally and mangrove jack. The rock walls at the entrance good for bream, jacks and some big flathead.
Scarborough Point
Scarborough Beach
Drury Point
Scarborough
Airfield
Caution – these waterways may contain submerged flood debris. Navigate with caution.
Newport Waterways
Queens Beach North
Osbourne Point
0 1 2
Kilometres
Kippa Ring
Anzac
Avenue
Road
Scarborough
Queens Beach
Klinger
Road
Kippa Ring
Queens Beach South
Moreton Bay
Anzac
Avenue
Redcliffe
Redcliffe Point
Suttons Beach
Avenue
Margate
Garnet Rock
Hays Inlet
Avenue
Avenue
Elizabeth
Clontarf
The Woody Point Jetty is good for bream and diver whiting during a winter rising tide. Flathead, tailor, squid and prawns are also caught here at times.
Margate Beach
Victoria
Oxley
Scotts Point
Woody Point
Clontarf Point
Bells Beach
Clontarf Beach
Woody Point Beach
Picnic Point
Woody Point
South Reef
The waters around Woody Point and outside of the Green Zone fish well for tailor in the winter months. Cast pilchards or metal slugs for best results.
Otter Rock
Bramble Bay

Map 21 No. 1 Newport Waterways Canal System

(Bream, trevally, mangrove jack)

The canal system at the back of Scarborough is home to plenty of bream and fewer trevally and mangrove jacks. These predators hold tight against the local structure and ambush unsuspecting prey. Casting lures along the retaining walls, around and under floating man-made structure is a great way to hook some of these fish. Casting and retrieving hardbody and soft plastic lures is a favoured approach here. Avoid striking resident's property with lures and boats to keep the peace between locals and anglers.

Area of Interest

Shoreline beach areas are a great place to target whiting and the odd cruising bream and flathead. Fish respond well to surface and diving hardbody lures, soft plastics and baits of yabby, worm and prawn. Near-shore rocks can be reached in places with a good cast. These structures will hold solid bream and the odd squire at times.

Map 21 No. 2 Scarborough Reef System

(Bream, snapper, tailor, sweetlip, cod)

A moon-shaped section of hard reef extends from the tip of the Scarborough peninsular. This is a popular location for many boat and kayak anglers. Despite the attention this place receives; it fishes well for much of the year. Fish migrating down the northern flanks of the bay find this a protective staging point that offers quality structure. Two common approaches are applied here to good effect. Anglers choose to anchor away from the reef and cast baits of pilchard, squid, strip bait or live bait. Snapper, sweetlip, tailor, bream and the odd bigger pelagic are caught by the bait brigade here. Alternatively, boat anglers opt to drift and cast lures or fly. Diving hardbody lures and soft plastics are popular here. Bumping the reef with lures results in good catches of bream, snapper and sweetlip. Winter provides the best of the bream and snapper fishing and the sweetlip turn on the action during summer. Snapper are commonly in the 35 to 45cm range but some big fish upwards of 55cm are caught here every year. Bream make a habit of owning lures cast to them around the sharp reef at Scarborough. Outside of the immediate reef, anglers will catch longtail tuna and various mackerel species through the warmer months.

Map 21 No. 3 Scarborough to Redcliffe Shoreline

(Bream, whiting, flathead, snapper, sweetlip, cod)

A coarse sandy shoreline broken in numerous places by short rocky platforms stretches from Scarborough to Redcliffe. This is a popular fishing location for shorebased, boating and kayak anglers. Fishing from the shore offers anglers the opportunity to target a variety

BELOW: The harbour at Scarborough hosts good boat ramps and plenty of fish attracting structure.

RIGHT: Scarborough Reef produces top class lure and bait fishing for bream and other reef species. (PHOTOGRAPH BY DEAN SILVESTER)

of structure. The beaches offer good whiting, flathead and bream fishing. Many submerged rocky structures can also be reached by shorebased anglers casting a bait and lure. Shorebased anglers can cash in on some exciting summer surface luring for whiting and bream. Boat and kayak anglers that drift and cast lures around the large amount of structure in the area produce some good bream, snapper, sweetlip and flathead. Casting soft plastic lures into reef patches in 2–4m of water is a popular way to target snapper along this shoreline. Fishing around the turn of the tide in low light hours produces snapper year-round and the occasional brute in winter and spring. Lightly weighted baits of pilchard and squid will also produce good fish in these areas.

Map 21 No. 4 Margate to Woody Point Shoreline

(Bream, whiting, flathead, snapper, sweetlip, tailor)

There are less reef areas in the waters off Margate than contained in those immediately to the north; however, the small patches of reef in this area still produce some good snapper, bream and the odd sweetlip. The deeper waters off this area and extending to the south produce some good catches of tailor during winter. These fish gather here to feed on baitfish holding on the outer reef edges. The shallow shoreline waters fish well for whiting, bream and flathead. These areas are a popular place for landbased anglers to soak baits of pilchard, yabbies and wriggler worms. The southern areas of this location border Green Zone so be mindful to avoid fishing to the south-west of Scotts Point.

Map 21 No. 5 Woody Point to Clontarf Beach Shoreline *(Bream, whiting, flathead, tailor)*

The western side of the Woody Point peninsular curls around to the Houghton Highway Bridge and holds some good rock and beach structure. Near-shore reef and beach shallows produce good bream, flathead and whiting every year. The waters become very shallow in places, particularly towards the bridge and care should be taken when boating. The shallow rocky bottom is a magnet for bream. Anglers casting lures in this area fare well on sizeable bream at times. The shorebased scene provides some good bait fishing for whiting.

Map 22 No. 1 Houghton Highway Bridge

(Bream, flathead, whiting)

The bridge provides plenty of solid structure to host resident fish. The combination of many pylons in shallow and deeper water, some of which contains patchy reef, is a Mecca for a variety of species. The bridge is popular with boat and kayak anglers that move from pylon to pylon and cast lures. Bream, flathead and the odd mangrove jack and cod are taken on hardbody and soft plastic lures fished tight against the structure. Bumping diving hardbody lures against the bottom and the pylons is a popular technique with lure anglers here. Alternatively, fishing baits close to the channel and pylons will produce fish. The channel areas around the bridge fish well at times for whiting, flathead, trevally and tailor. The waters through the area can be very shallow in places. A finesse approach is often required to catch fish here. This means fishing as lightly as possible and casting from a distance so as to avoid spooking fish.

Map 22 No. 2 Nudgee Waters

(Bream, flathead, whiting, mangrove jack)

The waters around Nudgee are relatively shallow throughout, however they do offer some useful fishing. The Shorncliffe area to the north is restricted to a large degree by Green Zone. The backwaters of Cabbage Tree Creek and Nundah Creek are removed from Green Zone protection and offer bait and lure anglers the chance to catch a few bream, flathead, whiting and the odd jack. Kedron Brook Floodway runs through the Nudgee area and offers similar fishing options to Cabbage Tree and Nundah Creek. The Floodway offers shore and boat access. Bait and lures fished around the mangroves will produce some good flathead, bream and the occasional jack. Local anglers target these fish predominantly by using live baits fished during the low light hours of the day. The Nudgee foreshores host plenty of shallow mud-bank structure. A building tide fishes well for whiting and flathead. Worm, prawn and fish flesh baits are favoured when targeting these species here. Similar fishing can be encountered all the way south to the Brisbane River mouth. The area can be quickly affected by the onshore wind that can push into this area. The location of the Brisbane Airport in the midst of this area makes it a busy destination that discourages many anglers from fishing extensively in this spot.

LEFT: The rocky shoreline from Redcliffe to Wood Point attracts some big bream and snapper. Surface luring for bream is popular here.
(PHOTOGRAPH BY DEAN SILVESTER)

MAP 22 WOODY POINT TO EAGLE FARM

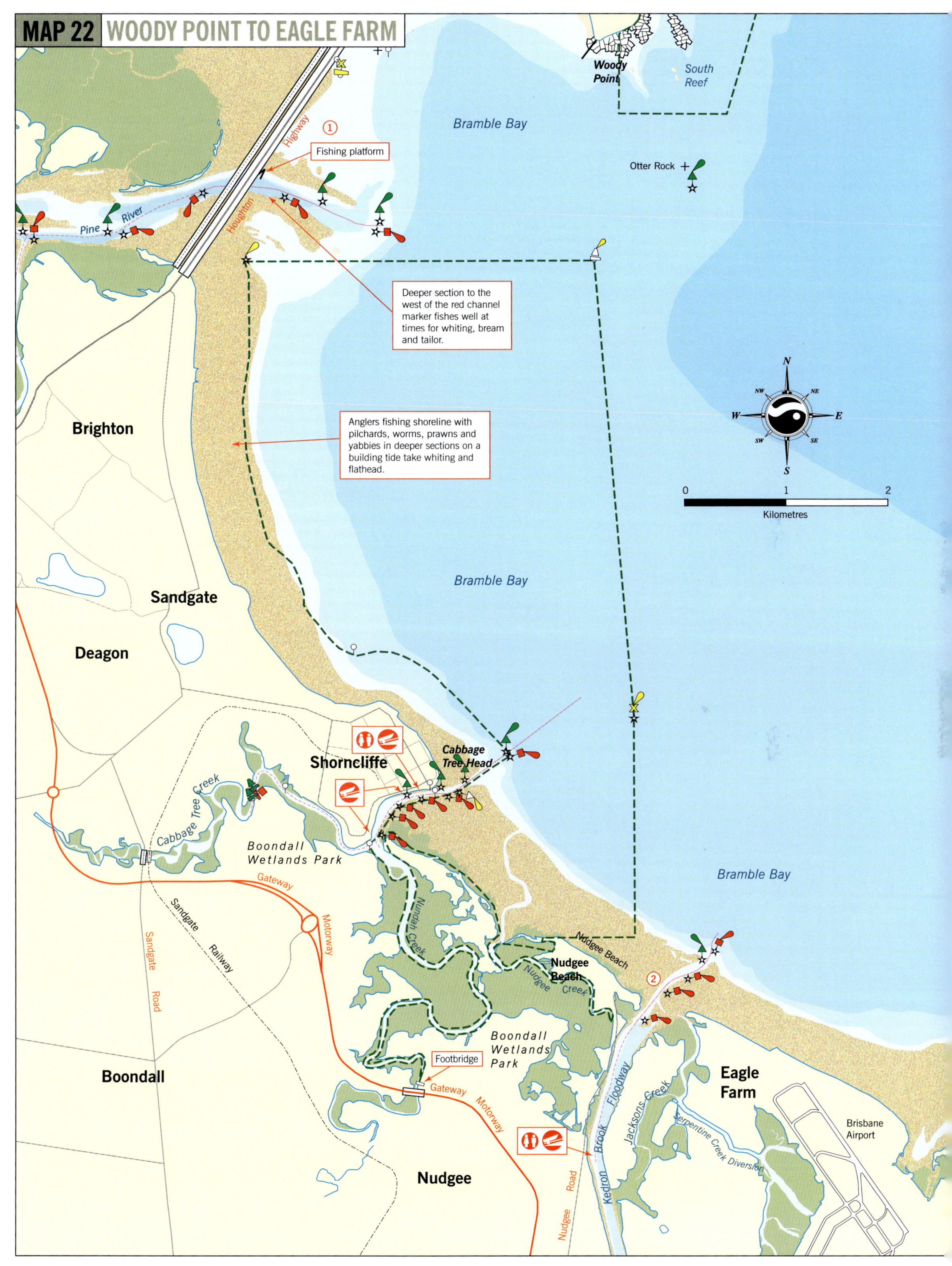

MAP 23 FISHERMAN ISLANDS TO MANLY BOAT HARBOUR

MAP 23 NO. 1 FISHERMAN ISLANDS FLATS *(BREAM, FLATHEAD, WHITING)*

The water to the south of Fisherman Islands is home to extensive mud and weeded shallows. This is a great location to explore with a small boat or kayak. The water depth averages between 1–3m for much of this area. The shallows extending from this point and south to Wynnum are home to extensive worm beds. Local wormers are often found here gathering bait at low tide as worms are obviously a popular bait to use when targeting local fish. These flats are popular hunting grounds for flathead, bream and whiting. Drifting across the area and fishing with soft plastics and surface lures produce good numbers of fish. Alternatively, anchoring a boat and fishing bait in the deeper sections within the flats tempts local predators. A good strategy when targeting flathead and bream here includes focussing efforts in the deeper water channels during the run-out tide. The eastern edge of these flats intersects the Fisherman Islands retaining walls and is home to cruising squire at times.

MAP 23 NO. 2 FISHERMAN ISLANDS AND LYTTON CHANNEL *(BREAM, FLATHEAD, WHITING, JEWFISH, TAILOR)*

The shallows that extend between Fisherman Islands and Lytton are cut by a deeper channel. This channel provides a boating pathway into deeper bay waters. The weed and mud flats adjacent to the channel provide some quality fishing for flathead, bream and whiting. These fish move up on to the shallows as the tide builds and then retreats with the run-out tide. Predicting fish movement will give anglers the upper hand when it comes to catching them. Soft plastics and hardbody lures produce fish over the shallows as will baits of worm, yabbies, prawn and fish baits. Deeper lures such as blades and soft plastics provide some quality fish from the channel waters. The southern areas of the channel demarcate deeper waters. This section is a prime holding point for larger predators such as jewfish, big flathead and the odd tailor and trevally. Live bait and larger lures fished in the area on the run-out tide produce some good fish here each year. The deeper waters away from the flats fish well for diver whiting in winter. Local worm is a popular bait for these fish.

AREA OF INTEREST

The shallows immediately offshore from Lytton are home to a deeper channel. This gutter drains the shallows into deeper water during the run-out tide. This is a good location to target flathead and bream during the falling tide. Soft plastics and hardbody lures fished around the edge of the channel during a building tide will also produce fish.

MAP 23 NO. 3 WYNNUM FORESHORE *(BREAM, FLATHEAD, WHITING)*

The Wynnum foreshores are home to shoreline mud, sand and weeded shallows. The shallows produce flathead, bream and whiting for shorebased anglers on a building tide. The odd lump of timber and rock structure is often home to a big bream or two. Covering as much water as possible with soft plastics, shallow diving hardbody lures, blades or surface lures often provides success. Positioning worm, yabby and prawn baits will usually draw the attention of cruising predators. Tuning Fork Shoal is located immediately offshore from Wynnum and produces the odd squire for anglers that cast soft plastic lures and baits around the location. The Wynnum Jetty provides a good landbased spot to target bream, whiting and flathead.

Map 23 No. 4 Manly Boat Harbour *(bream, trevally, cod, mangrove jack)*

The wealth of man-made structure in the harbour provides shelter and ambush cover for bream, cod, trevally and mangrove jack. The harbour is easily accessed by small boat and kayak and also offers some shorebased access. There are boat ramps available at either end of the harbour. Casting and retrieving lures tight against available structure is a popular approach to catching fish here.

CABOOLTURE RIVER AND BURPENGARY CREEK LOCATION GUIDE

The Caboolture River and Burpengary Creek enter Moreton Bay in the lower reaches of Deception Bay. These systems are ideal for the shorebased, small boat and kayak angling fraternities. The Caboolture River is a small system that is navigable from the mouth and up towards the weir that is located above the township of Caboolture. First-time boaters on the system are best advised to navigate it during the high tide, until a better understanding of the depth variations is achieved. The river provides some good fishing at times for anglers prepared to put some time into the area. A relatively straight and broad lower section of the river makes way for a tighter meandering waterway upriver. The banks of the river are largely clothed in natural vegetation; targeting this structure with lures and baits produces bread and butter species in the lower reaches and bass in the upper sections. In the seasons following the big floods of 2011 the odd barramundi has been taken in this system so be prepared for the odd surprise when fishing here! The much smaller Burpengary Creek provides a good flathead and bream fishery for anglers prepared to fish in this hard to access location.

Above: Jacks will readily attack lures and baits fished tight to snags in the Caboolture River.

Right: Flathead are a popular target in the area.

Map 24 No. 1 Caboolture River Mouth *(flathead, bream, whiting, tailor, trevally)*

The mouth of the system is a great place to target flathead and bream. Flathead will hold in the deeper sections and along drop-off areas during the run-out tide. Local anglers commonly target these fish throughout the year by drifting with W.A, white or frogmouth pilchards and yabbies. Alternatively, drifting while jigging brightly coloured 3 to 5 inch soft plastic lures along the bottom will produce bites from resident fish. Bream can also be caught here throughout the year; however winter often produces the best catches. Target these fish on a building tide with baits of hardiheads, white and frogmouth pilchards; blades and soft plastic lures fished tight to the bottom produce quality fish at times. The deeper sections of water that run alongside the southern parts of the entrance channel are popular areas to target local fish. The shallow bankside water alongside the river channel fishes well for sand whiting on a building tide. Worms, yabbies and prawns produce the majority of the fish taken here. Pelagic species will also use the entrance of the system to feed on available food supply. Tailor and trevally are often caught here when these species are abundant in the Deception Bay area.

Map 24 No. 2 Boat Ramp Stretch *(flathead, bream, whiting)*

Boat ramps adorn either side of the Caboolture River in this stretch of the system. The southern ramp is accessed via Uhlmann Road through Burpengary. This ramp can be precarious to launch a boat from during the low tide and is less preferred than its northern counterpart located on Moreton Terrace on the other side of the river. The boat ramps make for popular landbase fishing locations. This stretch of the estuary contains deeper channel water that is used by many to moor larger vessels. Adjacent banks contain mud and sand shallows that are home to mangroves. Immediately upriver of the Uhlmann Road boat ramp is significant shallow flats known as Shell Banks. These flats are well worth fishing during the building tide as they fish well for foraging groups of whiting and bream. Baits and shallow and surface hardbody lures will produce fish here. The drop-off separating the deeper channel waters fishes well for flathead throughout this stretch of the system. Drifting while fishing baits or lures is a common practice, as is trolling the deeper water with deep diving lures. Anglers using boats fitted

MAP 24 CABOOLTURE RIVER AND BURPENGARY CREEK

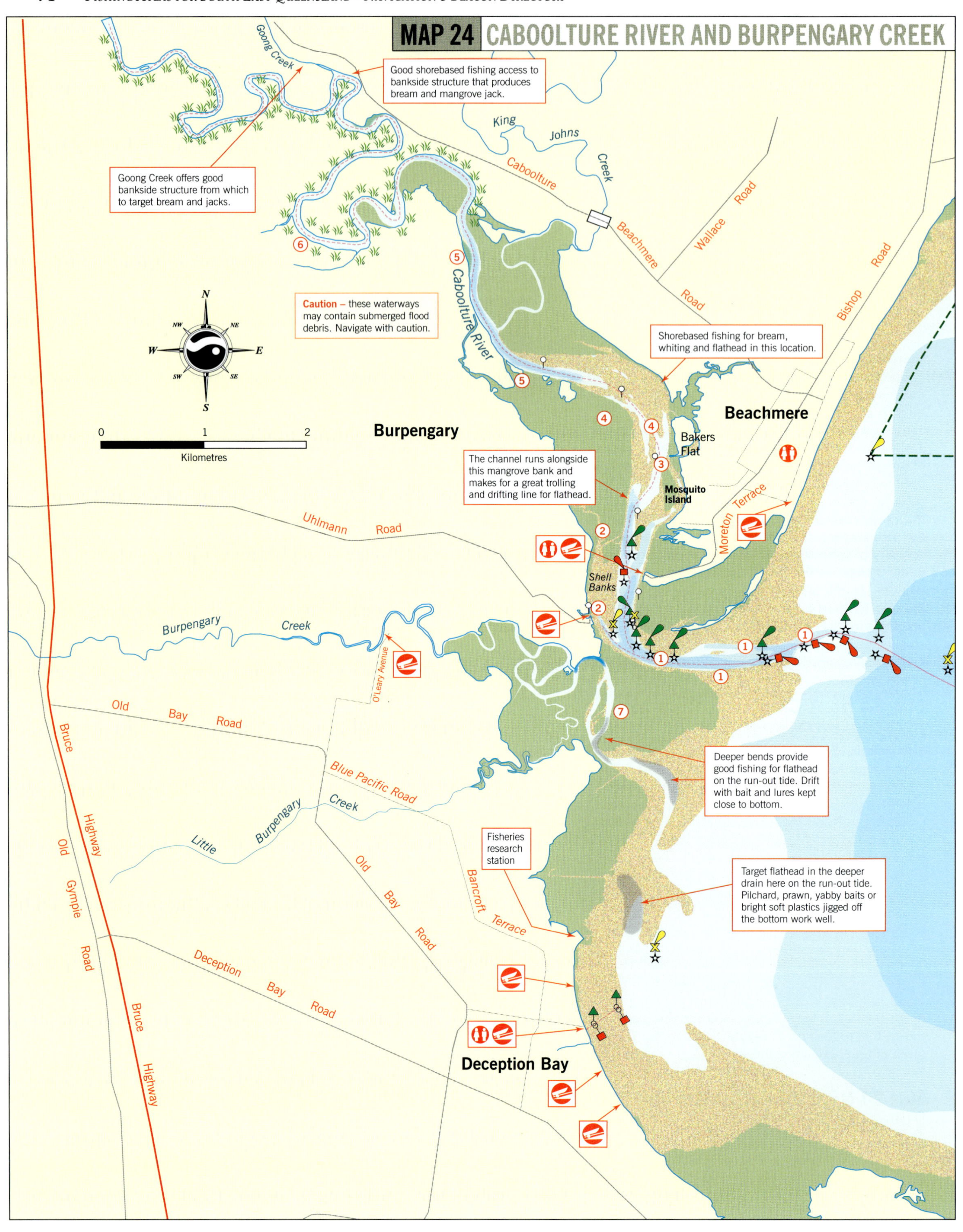

with electric motors can often be found casting lures around the moored boats. These hulls produce bream that shelter and feed beneath the protective structures. Retrieving diving hardbody lures through the shaded areas will produce fish, as will letting slow sinking soft plastics flutter through these zones. This technique will often produce a few surprises in the way of encounters with tailor, trevally and the occasional mangrove jack.

MAP 24 No. 3 MOSQUITO ISLAND
(FLATHEAD, BREAM, WHITING)

Mosquito Island sits in the midst of sand and mud shallows. These shallows are surrounded by channel waters. The deeper sections around the flats are often home to good numbers of flathead. The prime location includes the deeper water positioned immediately to the south of the island. Baits and lures fished through these areas during a run-out tide produce fish more often than not. The shallows become home to bream and whiting during the building tide.

MAP 24 No. 4 BEACHMERE BEND
(FLATHEAD, BREAM, WHITING)

The estuary takes a ninety degree turn above Mosquito Island and at the Beachmere location. The area is home to extensive shallows that are cut by the main channel. The flats make navigating through the area difficult during low tide, but these shallows are home to yabby beds and are always frequented by flathead, bream and whiting. A high but dropping tide is often used to troll diving lures across shallows and through channel waters in this location. This is a great way to show preying flathead a lure or two. Another popular approach is to drift and work baits or lures along the bottom. The building tide fishes well for bream and whiting that come in to shallow water in search of yabbies, prawns and worms.

MAP 24 No. 5 KING JOHNS CREEK STRETCH
(FLATHEAD, BREAM, MANGROVE JACK)

The river here is home to deeper channel waters surrounded by steeper banks and dense bankside vegetation. Bankside and mid-channel snags are great places to target bream and the odd jack. Anglers targeting these structures with lures or live-bait such as mullet or herring fare well when fishing around the turn of the tide. The bank on either side of the river offers deeper ledges that are often shaded by surrounding vegetation. Trolling lures along these banks or drifting and casting lures strategically will produce flathead, bream, mangrove jack and cod. Similar fishing can be found by anglers venturing into King Johns Creek. Strategic lure casting in these areas is made much easier with the use of ancillary tools such as an electric bow-mounted motor.

MAP 24 No. 6 CABOOLTURE RIVER UPPER
(FLATHEAD, BREAM, MANGROVE JACK, BASS, TARPON)

Above the King Johns Creek stretch, the channel shallows somewhat. The structure however remains largely the same. Steeper vegetated banks, fallen timber and mid-river snags provide plenty of host structure for local bream, flathead, mangrove jack and further upriver, bass and tarpon. The two river bends on either side of Monty's Marina offer some great bankside structure that will keep lure and bait anglers busy for hours. These structures are well renowned for holding some stubborn jacks. The Bruce Highway Bridge at Caboolture provides a good option for bait and lure anglers. The most popular approach for anglers fishing in this area includes drifting with the current and casting lures tight against structure. Soft plastic lures sunk into shaded locations and then twitched back towards the angler produces bream and jacks in the lower reaches and bass in the upper sections.

MAP 24 No. 7 BURPENGARY CREEK
(FLATHEAD, BREAM, WHITING, MANGROVE JACK)

Burpengary Creek is a small system and can be difficult to access. Many anglers choose to launch a boat or kayak from the safe locations of the Caboolture boat ramps and access the creek via water. The creek is largely shallow but maintains deeper sections of channel in amongst mangrove lined bankside structure. The deeper sections are often located along bends in the channel and regularly play home to good numbers of flathead. Kayak anglers drifting these sections with baits and lures in tow often take good fish. A run-out tide and a hook kept close to bottom is the key to catching a few here. The building tide will encourage local bream and whiting to get up in the shallows for a feed.

PINE RIVER AND HAYES INLET LOCATION GUIDE

The Pine River is one of the more significant systems that provide great fishing for the northern suburbs. The river enters the Brambles Bay area of Moreton Bay where it combines with waters from Hayes Inlet. Much of Hayes Inlet is protected Green Zone and because of this, most anglers fishing in the area choose to spend their time wetting a line in the Pine River. The Pine is a relatively broad system that offers a variety of sought after recreational species. The bread and butter species are well represented, however anglers fishing in the Pine are treated to regular encounters with mangrove jack, jewfish, cod, trevally and tailor to name a few. The Pine River is a relatively clear system in the lower reaches however the water becomes increasingly discoloured further upriver; this attribute coincides with increased development alongside the banks of the system. The upper reaches of the river are truncated by the Pine River Dam. The dam is stocked with a variety of freshwater species. The dam is responsible for the occasional stocking of the river with species such as bass and golden perch. These fish are regular captures by anglers fishing the upper sections beneath the dam wall. The river provides a variety of structure that host resident species. A key to catching fish in the Pine is to understand where to find these structures and the optimum manner and time in which to fish them.

RIGHT: The upper Pine River reaches hold some good bass. (PHOTOGRAPH BY DEAN SYLVESTER)

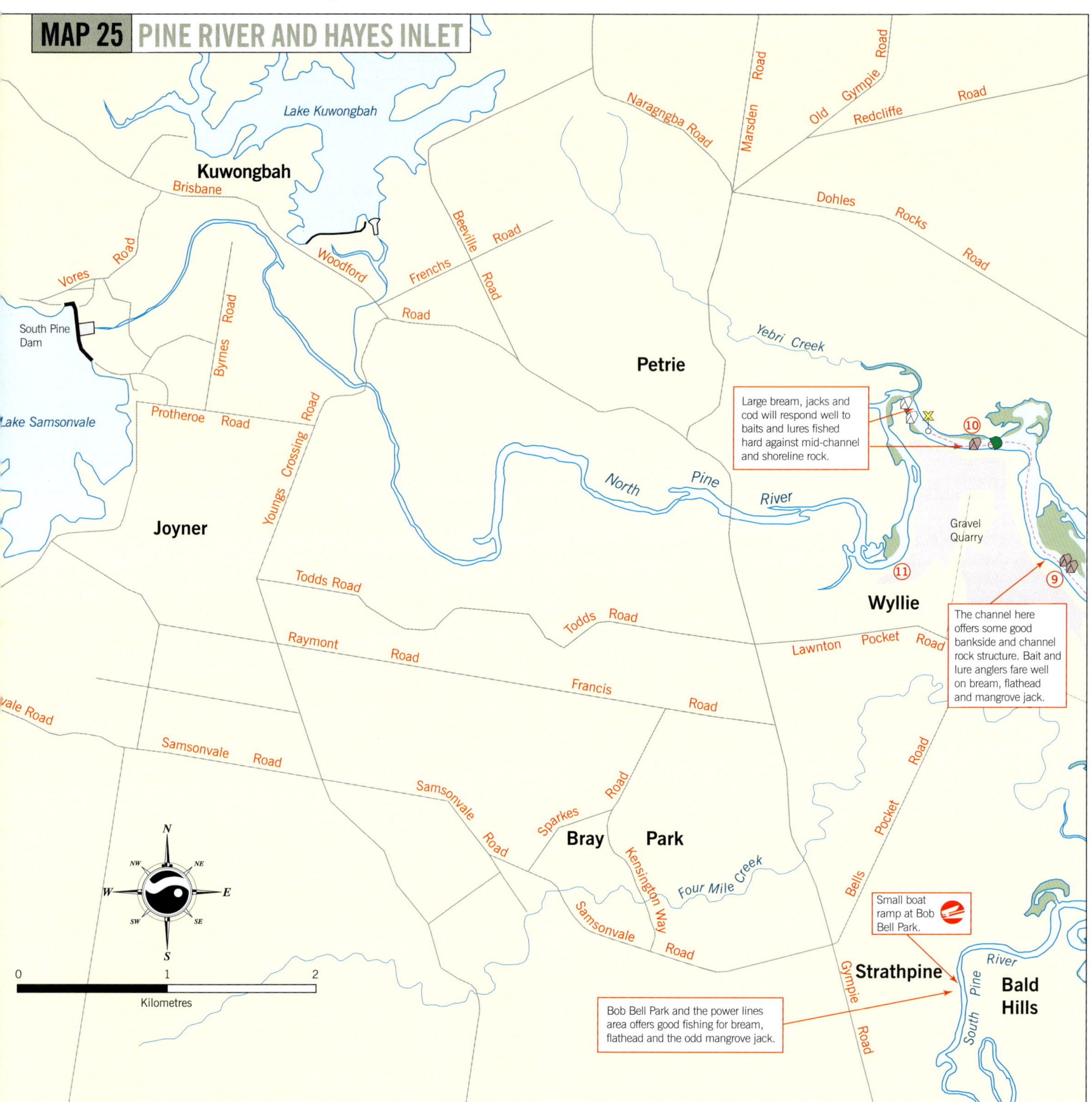

MAP 25 No. 1 HAYES INLET

(FLATHEAD, BREAM, WHITING)

The lower sections of Hayes Inlet are open to recreational fishing. These areas consist of channel waters in the midst of extensive shallow water flats. The channel waters available to fishing provide good flathead. A run-out tide fishes best for these fish and anglers targeting the drop-off margins with baits and lures fare well. The shallows fish well at times for bream and whiting on a building tide. The lower sections of Hayes Inlet fish well for large bream in the winter months. The area is well known for providing some good prawn captures when these tasty crustaceans show up in numbers.

MAP 25 No. 2 PINE RIVER – HOUGHTON HIGHWAY BRIDGE CHANNEL

(FLATHEAD, BREAM, WHITING, JEWFISH, TAILOR)

A deeper channel of the Pine River heads upriver from the Houghton Highway Bridge area. The channel cuts through mangrove lined banks and shallow flats on either side of the system. The channel waters in the lower parts of the Pine are a haven for flathead in the summer and bream and the odd tailor, jewie and luderick in the winter. The bridge hole extends upriver and provides a great place to soak a bait during the turn of the tide. Low light periods of the day when combined with a tide turn can fish very well here. Live

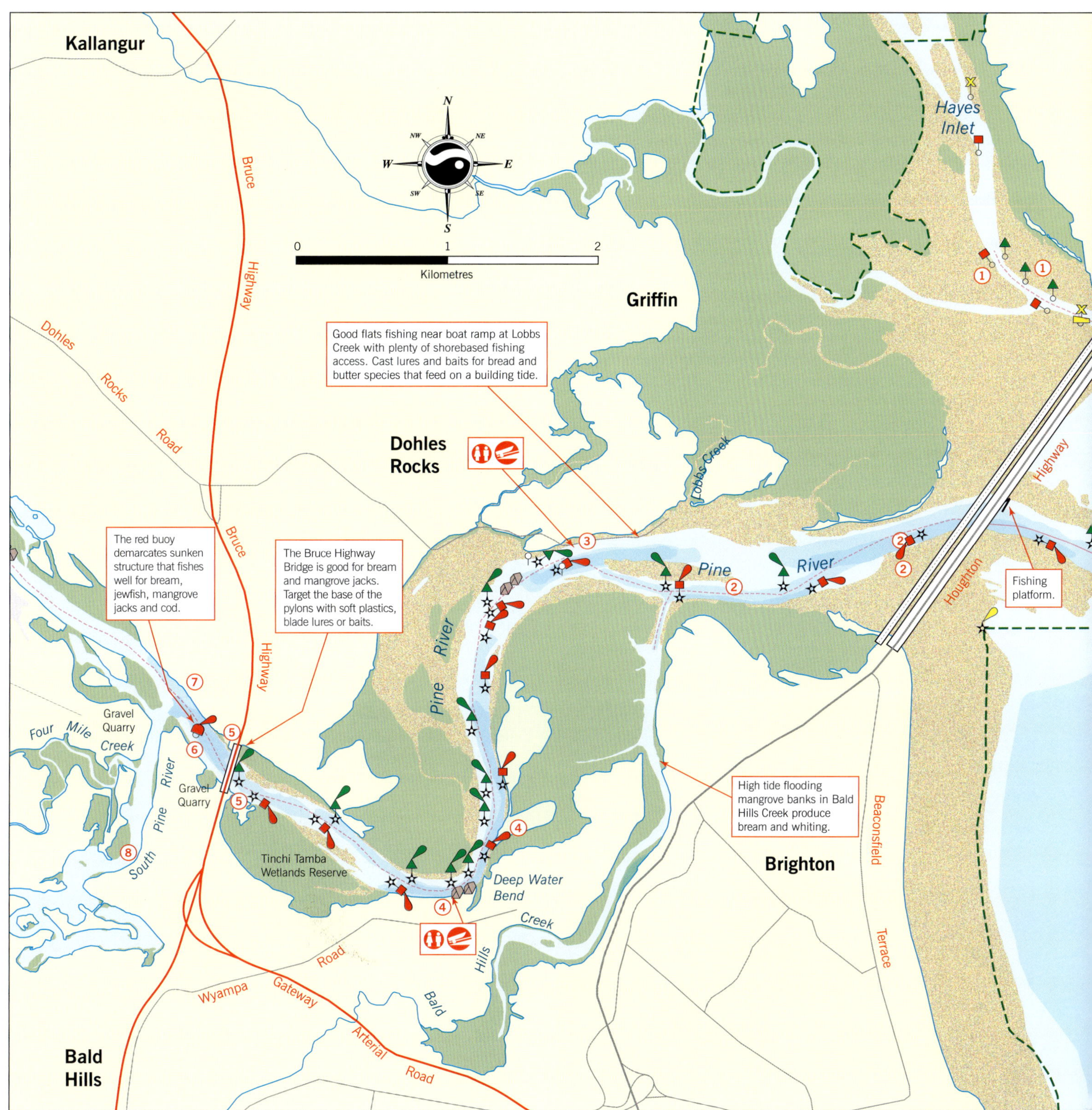

fish baits of prawn, yabbie and worm will tempt resident critters that reside in areas near the hole and the abundant nearby bridge structures. A building tide will see the usual bread and butter suspects heading up on to the flats to feed. Bait and lures fished in prime areas of the shallows will produce bream, flathead and whiting. Target the channel structures within the shallows as they often hold a few good fish.

Map 25 No. 3 Lobbs Creek Bend *(bream, flathead, whiting, tailor, jewfish, luderick)*

A deeper corner is found near to the bank slightly upriver from the confluence of Lobbs Creek and the Pine River. The northern banks to the west and east of this area are home to extensive shallow water flats. The bankside bend immediately adjacent to the upriver extent of the deeper hole contains a good number of submerged and partly submerged rocks. These rocks attract a variety of predators, particularly on a building tide. Tide flow can be strong here at times, so fishing around the turn of the tide for species such as bream is recommended. The deeper waters produce the likes of flathead, bream, tailor and trevally as well as the occasional jewfish and luderick. The surrounding shallows are home to sand, mud and weeded bottom. These areas hold good bream and whiting when well covered with water. The high water drains via several channels. These drains are good places to target flathead on the run-out tide. The location is home to a boat ramp and plenty of shorebased angling access.

Map 25 No. 4 Deep Water Bend
(Bream, Flathead, Whiting, Tailor)

A deeper channel runs along this corner of the river and lies adjacent to public amenities and a shoreline that contains plenty of great fish holding structure. This is a popular location with boat ramp access as well as plenty of places for the shorebased angler to target some good fish. The deeper channel waters combined with the shoreline structure attract a range of species. The most abundant local predator is the bream which thrives around the near-shore rock and timber structure. Soft plastic and hardbody lures fished tight to available structure produces some good fish around those key turn of the tide stages. Bait anglers presenting well positioned pilchard, prawn, worm and yabby baits take consistent catches of bream and lesser whiting and flathead. Other species that provide sport for anglers in this area include jewfish, tailor and the odd mangrove jack and luderick. Summer time jack fishing around the snags can be exciting but often heartbreaking.

Map 25 No. 5 Bruce Highway Bridge
(Bream, Jewfish, Mangrove Jack, Cod)

The Bruce Highway Bridge provides a wealth of solid structure throughout the middle of the river where it crosses the Pine. The bridge is a popular boat and shorebased fishing location. The numerous pylons are home to good numbers of bream and a variety of other larger and nastier critters. Anglers targeting the bridge do best around the top and bottom of the tide. These periods are associated with lower tidal flow and make the area much easier to fish effectively. Popular techniques include fishing soft plastic and blade lures around the base of the pylons. Retrieving diving hardbody lures along the pylons and bumping the concrete structures also produces some quality bream and jacks at times. Anglers targeting the bridge with live bait also catch some good fish from this location. Fishing baits around the bridge during night sessions has produced some solid jewfish and jacks as well as some monumental dust-ups!

Above: Systems such as the Caboolture and Pine produce the odd juvenile barra surprise.

Above: The Pine River contains good deeper water areas that produce quality bream at times.

Map 25 No. 6 The Bruce Highway Bridge Hole
(Bream, Flathead, Jewfish, Mangrove Jack, Cod)

The area upriver of the bridge and adjacent to the southern shoreline is home to a deeper hole in the system. The hole is also home to some great fish holding wreck structures. The use of a sounder and the demarcation of a wreck by a red buoy will assist anglers to find this structure. The hole produces some big flathead around the turn of the tide for anglers fishing with live bait and jigged soft plastics. The wreck structures provide ambush positions for big bream, jacks, jewfish and cod. Anglers dropping live bait on to this structure are often left demoralised by these tough fish that live so close to home. The location does not always rise to occasion but for anglers that are prepared to persist and fish optimal tides and low light periods of the day; the rewards are certainly there to be had.

Map 25 No. 7 Northern Highway Bank
(Bream, Flathead, Mangrove Jack)

A steeper bank that is home to plenty of good fish holding shoreline structure can be located on the northern shore upriver of the Bruce Highway Bridge. This extensive shoreline provides good shelter from the common south and easterly winds and also holds some good fish. Anglers fishing along this bank fare well during a tide turn both early and late in the day. This is a popular boating location and fish are often hard to find during the middle of a weekend day. Drifting along the bank and positioning lures and bait tight against structure will produce resident bream, flathead and the odd jack.

MAP 25 NO. 8 SOUTH PINE RIVER
(FLATHEAD, BREAM, WHITING, MANGROVE JACK)

A short distance upriver of the Bruce Highway Bridge, the Pine River splits to form the South and North Pine River arms. The South Pine River heads directly south towards the township of Strathpine. The first two to three kilometres of river consist of channel waters and mangrove lined flats. Low tide will reveal channel style drains and submerged structures lying beneath the high tide mark. These structures are frequented by flathead, bream and whiting during the higher tide periods. Lure and bait fishing used in conjunction with a mobile approach will see a lot of these fish undone. Boat and kayak anglers targeting fish with lures spend most of their time in the higher reaches towards the Strathpine area. A small boat ramp can be found at Bob Bell Park and this makes an ideal location from which to launch small boats and kayaks. This area also provides a handy place to target fish from the shore. The river in the vicinity of the power lines holds some great mid-channel and bankside structure. These areas hold some great bream and summer time jacks. The run-out tide seems to fish the best for local fish and anglers adopting a drift style approach produce the most fish as they cover the productive looking water. Casting lures tight to structure before retrieving them through likely looking strike zones will provide some exciting fishing.

MAP 25 NO. 9 NORTH PINE RIVER LAWNTON STRAIGHT
(BREAM, FLATHEAD, MANGROVE JACK, COD)

The Lawnton stretch of river upwards of the power lines provides a straight section of channel with some solid bankside structure. The channel provides some broken reef that in combination with the bankside structure offers some good fishing at times. Bait and lure anglers targeting the solid structure produce some big bream, lesser flathead and mangrove jack in the summer months. Trolling the banks and rock areas is productive here.

MAP 25 NO. 10 PETRIE ROCK BAR
(BREAM, JEWFISH, MANGROVE JACK, COD)

The area adjacent to the paper mill at Petrie holds some solid mid-channel rock structure. Waters around the structure provide some good fishing for bream, mangrove jack, jewfish and cod. This location can be tough on tackle so anglers should equip themselves properly. A short distance upriver and on the outer bend of the river, some solid bankside concrete structure can be found. This structure hosts some good fish that can be tempted by well presented lures fished along the wall while drifting with the tide. Anglers that troll diving lures and bump them against any available rock in the area fare well on a range of species.

MAP 25 NO. 11 NORTH PINE RIVER UPPER REACHES
(BREAM, BASS, GOLDEN PERCH, MANGROVE JACK)

The river between the railway crossing at Petrie and the dam wall becomes increasingly fresh. Kayak and shorebased anglers target this area in search of the odd bream, jack, bass and golden perch. The river becomes shallow in places but deeper sections, rock and bankside structure provide plenty of haunts to cast a lure for an aggressive mixture of fish. Local bass anglers keep this area a well kept secret.

BRISBANE RIVER LOCATION GUIDE

The Brisbane River is one of the most unique systems that enters Moreton Bay or for that matter, the entire east coast. Visitors to the area are staggered by the huge variety of southern and tropical species the river supports. Add to this the fact that one of our largest Australian dwellings sits astride the river and it is easy to be impressed by the Brisbane River fishery.

History suggests that the river was crystal clear in the early days of development of the city of Brisbane. Industry and urban development may have dirtied the face of the river but the location continues to provide impressive fishing. The Brisbane River remains one of the few areas that continue to sustain a healthy population of the prized threadfin salmon. In addition to catching bread and butter species, the river also offers anglers the opportunity to catch a variety of pelagic and reef species such as longtail tuna, cod, snapper and sweetlip. There would be few systems along our coastline that can lay claim to such a fishery. Although the location of the Port of Brisbane prevents some fishing access in the lower reaches, the majority of anglers spend their time targeting fish near to the mouth of the river. In saying this, there are still plenty of boat and shorebased fishing options further up the system. Many of the species that are commonly targeted around the mouth of the system can be caught year-round. This includes the bread and butter brigade and other sought after species such as snapper, sweetlip, cod, threadfin salmon and jewfish. Fishing for many of these species improves following some river flushing rain. The movement and location of prawns and baitfish within the river often dictates where anglers will discover improved fishing for a variety of species. Upriver of Brisbane, the Wivenhoe Dam controls flow to the system. Beneath the dam, the Brisbane River is host to a thriving freshwater fish population that includes species such as the prized Australian bass and other sought after species such as golden perch.

RIGHT: The Brisbane River supports a handy population of threadfin salmon.

Map 26 No. 1 The Compass Adjustment Buoy
(Diver whiting, squid)

The Compass Adjustment Buoy near the mouth of the river fishes well for winter diver whiting. It is also a popular location to hunt up a few squid and sand crabs in the winter.

Map 26 No. 2 Brisbane River Mouth & Channel
(Snapper, mackerel, tuna, estuary cod)

The shipping channel leaving the mouth of the Brisbane River is demarcated by beacons. These beacons provide shelter for baitfish and this means the predators are often not far away. Anglers targeting the beacons with bait and lures will often encounter mackerel, tuna and snapper. A pilchard rigged on gang hooks and drifted down towards the base of the beacons will tempt fish feeding throughout the water column. Baits fished around the base of the beacons will tempt local cod and snapper. Alternatively, soft plastic lures fished alongside the beacons will tempt snapper feeding on resident baitfish. A common approach when targeting mackerel and tuna here is to drop 25 to 55g metal lures (slugs) to the base of the beacons and then retrieve them to surface as fast as possible. Maintain a mobile approach and aim to fish all of the beacons and you are sure to locate fish along the way. The periods around the turn of the tide provide the easiest time to fish the area as the current can push strongly through this region.

Map 26 No. 3 Fisherman Islands Outer Walls
(Snapper, threadfin salmon, jewfish, bream, flathead, luderick, estuary cod)

The Fisherman Islands are an ever-changing area. The reclamation of land results in the topography varying frequently. The outer walls that line the area provide local anglers with some great fishing at times. The front edges of the Fisherman Islands are a popular spot to target bream, snapper and flathead. Casting soft plastics tight against the structure so they can be jigged close to the bottom of the wall is a favoured approach for catching these fish. The rock structure that lines the Brisbane River drops into deeper water and predators spend their time chasing baitfish and prawns along its reaches. The area commonly hosts prized threadfin salmon, jewfish, snapper as well as bream, flathead and luderick. The tide can run hard in this spot so aim to fish around the turn-of-tide periods. Snapper are best targeted on the top of the run-in tide while threadfin salmon and jewfish are best targeted on the latter stages of the run-out tide. Popular baits for the threadfin and jewies includes live-baiting with mullet or herring and night time fishing can often produce some of the best results. These fish commonly follow the mullet schools up and down the wall, so locate the schools of bait and you are in the right place to catch a fish. Soft plastics and lipless crankbait (also known as vibration baits) are favoured lures types when targeting threadfin salmon and jewies here. Locate fish holding around the edge of the drop-off features out from the wall and then jig or slowly retrieve lures in front of them. A sounder is the angler's best friend in this scenario.

Brisbane River Fishing Tips

Threadfin salmon can be found in many parts of the river. They are most commonly caught in waters from the Breakfast Creek area to the mouth of the river. These fish will hold tight against ledges that run along the channel and will also congregate around shallow water flats adjacent to these ledges. Threadfin salmon spend most time feeding on local prawns and baitfish such as herring and mullet. Fish are often caught around deeper ledges and the edge of river shallows where the deeper water and shallows meet. Popular spots include areas adjacent to the creeks and draining flats and these locations fish best around the bottom of the run-out tide. A range of lures and baits fished on outfits sporting 10 to 20kg line will produce fish here.

Flathead are found in many areas around the mouth. They are caught all year round but spring and summer produce the best of the fish.

Bream will hold against any form of hard structure. They are found year-round but summer often produces the best of the fishing. This usually coincides with the peak of the prawn numbers in the river.

Jewfish are often caught around the time when some good rainfall flushes the river. Spring and winter fish well for this species. Aim to target them around new and full moon phases and on the turning of the tide.

Snapper are nearly always found close to hard structure such as reef, ledges or the shipping terminals. These fish are caught all year round but are at their best during late winter and spring. They favour the top of the run-in tide as it provides the cleanest water. Target these fish in 10 to 20m of water and be prepared to find them as far up-river as Hamilton.

Map 26 No. 4 Luggage Point *(Bream, flathead)*

The Luggage Point area is home to a sunken rock wall that is popular with local bream. Anglers that frequent this location are often targeting these fish. Night time sessions fishing with yabbies rigged on near weightless rigs produces some big fish. If fishing the area by day, try using shallow diving hardbody lures fished tight against structure on a high tide. The area also produces some good flathead.

Map 26 No. 5 Boggy Creek
(Flathead, whiting, bream, jewfish, threadfin salmon)

The creek is home to shallow flats and the mouth is associated with the fish attracting oil pipeline. The flats of Boggy Creek fish well for whiting on a building tide and flathead on the run-out. Worm and yabby baits are popular when targeting these fish. The oil pipeline

The mouth of the Brisbane River is a popular place to target jewfish.
(Photograph by Dean Silvester)

MAP 26 BRISBANE RIVER MOUTH

is targeted by anglers trying to catch jewfish, threadfin salmon and bream. The structure attracts bait supply which in turn tempts the predators to the area. Fishing the bottom of the tide when targeting this structure will provide a good opportunity for tangling with some quality fish.

Map 26 No. 6 Pinkenba Wall
(Bream, Snapper, Threadfin Salmon, Mangrove Jack)

A submerged rock wall extends through this area towards the tip of Bulwer Island. The structure attracts bream, snapper and the odd threadfin salmon and jewie. The shallows inside the rock wall produce some good whiting at times. Anglers using baits of yabby and prawns produce solid bream on a night time high tide. Anglers also catch these fish using diving hardbody lures fished against the structure during a high tide. A good tip is to make sure you bump the rock with a lure during your retrieve. This is the catalyst to catching these fish feeding along the wall. Anglers jigging soft plastic lures and lipless crankbaits along the deeper sections of the wall stand a good chance of hooking resident snapper, jewies and threadfin salmon. The feature is also known for producing some solid jacks for anglers fishing live mullet and herring tight against the wall.

Map 26 No. 7 Pelican Banks
(Whiting, Bream, Flathead, Snapper, Luderick)

The shallows around Pelican Banks are a great place to target whiting on a building tide. These fish push up into the flooding mangroves and feed actively on yabbies, prawns and worms. Surface luring or fishing with the aforementioned baits will promote success. The deeper water out from the Pelican Banks and towards the Boat Passage bridge hosts some patchy reef bottom. Although the tide pushes hard through the area, the slack tidal periods can be used to target snapper here. The rock wall near the bridge is a popular spot to target luderick on weed baits during the cooler months.

Area of Interest

A patch of reef that drops into deeper water in this location demarcates the feature known as Clara's Rocks. This is a very popular location to target snapper, jewfish, threadfin salmon and estuary cod. A red channel marker can be used to identify Clara's Rocks and what is recognised as one of the most consistent places to catch jewies. The green channel marker and cardinal marker in close proximity to Clara's Rocks denote a solid ledge structure. This area provides some great snapper fishing at times.

Map 27 No. 8 Clara's Rocks to Bulimba Creek Channel
(Snapper, Jewfish, Threadfin Salmon, Bream, Flathead, Estuary Cod)

The channel in this area contains some structure that is well worth fishing. The river is lined with rock walls and various drains and creeks run into the channel in places. The edges of the channel are lined with ledges that drop down into deeper water and these areas host several shipping terminals and docks. This structure provides the appropriate shelter and feeding grounds for a wide variety of species. A popular fishing strategy is to drift along the channel with lures or baits put into prime fish holding territory. Try to find concentrations of prawns and other bait along these structures and the sought after predators are usually not too far away. The locations that provide draining points into the river on the run-out tide offer the chance to catch flathead and threadfin salmon. The flats adjacent to Bulimba Creek are one such area. These species often lie in wait in such places and ambush food that is pushed into striking range. The ledges, rock walls and shipping terminals will provide good fishing for bream, snapper, jewfish, threadfin salmon and cod.

Map 27 No.9 Eagle Farm Channel and Gateway Bridge
(Snapper, Jewfish, Threadfin Salmon, Bream, Flathead, Estuary Cod)

This stretch of river contains similar structures to those regions of channel towards the mouth. This stretch includes the notable structure of the Gateway Bridge. The bridge is one of the more popular jewfish spots along the river. Anglers fishing with live bait of mullet and herring around the bridge take some good jewfish and threadfin salmon, particularly when fishing through the night. Bait of pilchards and squid will also produce results. The edges of the channel and dock structure along this stretch fish well for bream, flathead, threadfin salmon, snapper and cod.

Map 27 No. 10 Hamilton Channel and Breakfast Creek
(Snapper, Jewfish, Threadfin Salmon, Bream, Flathead, Estuary Cod)

The edges of the channel and boat mooring facilities hold some good fish through this stretch of river. It surprises some anglers that snapper can be caught this far from the mouth but some good catches of squire size snapper are regularly caught in the area. The shores around the mouth of Breakfast Creek provide some of the best shorebased fishing along the river. Anglers fishing in the area regularly tangle with threadfin salmon, jewies, snapper and the

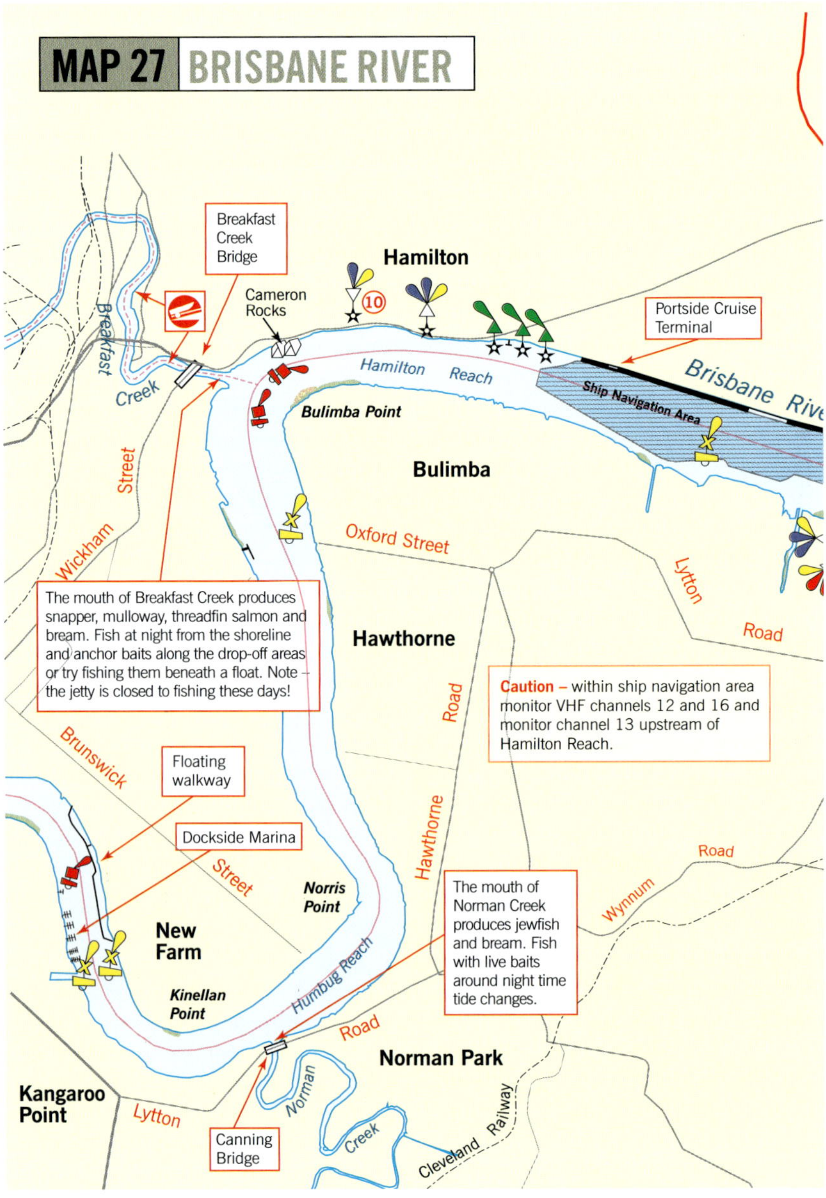

bread and butter species. Targeting the ledges and boats around the mouth with live baits is a popular approach. Big fish are often hooked here when fishing at night, but retrieving these fish through the abundant local structure can result in losses. The southern side of the creek that hosts the jetty is most popular with local anglers. These days you must fish from the shoreline walkways as the jetty is closed to fishing. The added attraction of the spot includes the ability to catch local live bait. Boat anglers fishing the area also take some good fish around the mouth of this creek. The shallow water opposite the mouth is a known location for catching threadfin salmon, particularly when the prawns are concentrated here.

BRISBANE RIVER UPPER REACHES

(BASS, GOLDEN PERCH)

The upper reaches of the Brisbane River provide some good fishing for freshwater native species. The areas close to the Wivenhoe Dam fish very well at times. There are several shorebased access points near the township of Lowood. These areas can be used to cast lures or baits and also to launch a small vessel such as a kayak.

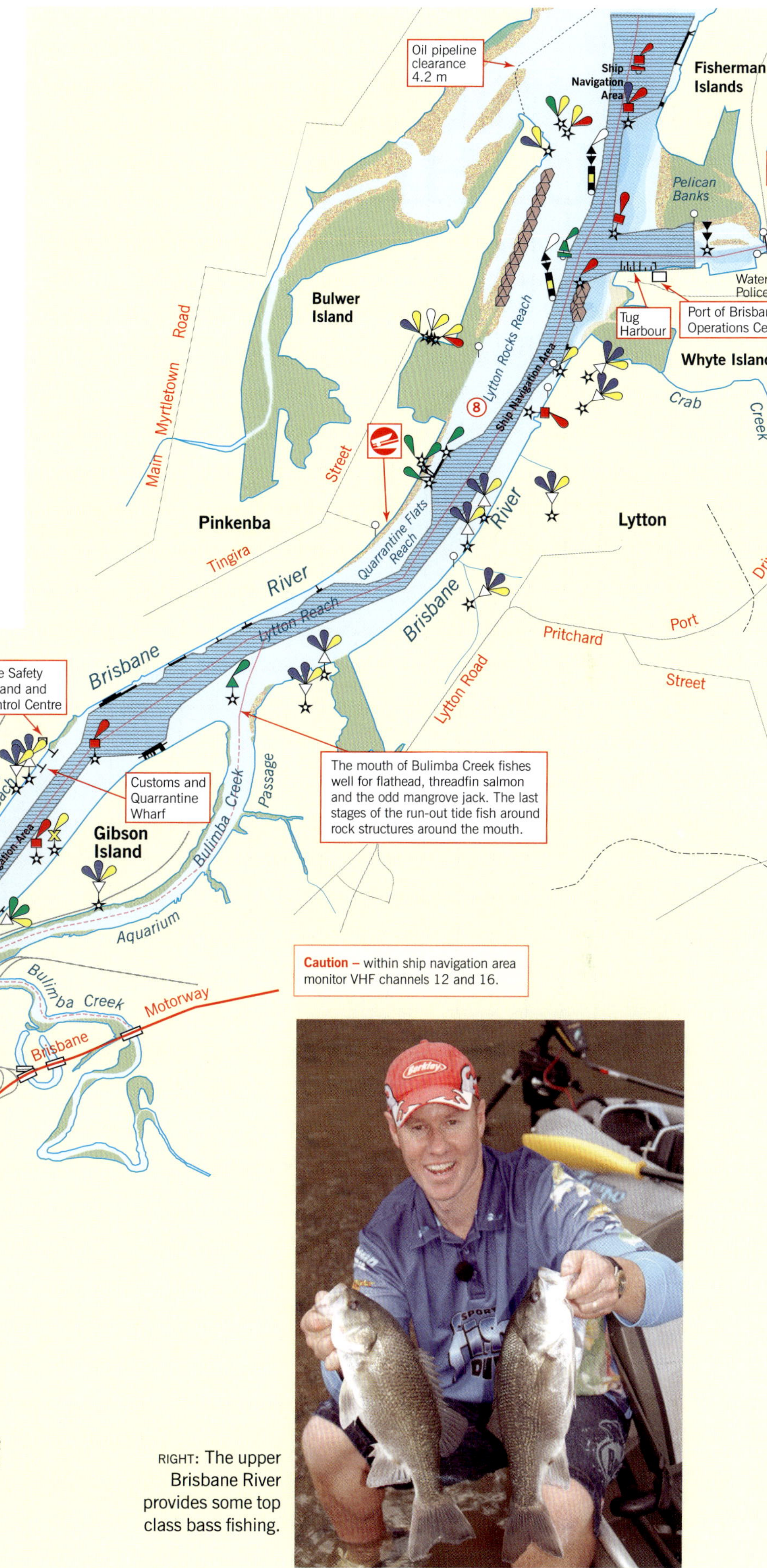

RIGHT: The upper Brisbane River provides some top class bass fishing.

CHAPTER 4

NORTH EAST AND SOUTHERN MORETON BAY

Including Moreton, Mud, Green Islands, northern section of North Stradbroke Island and southern bay islands

ABOVE: The backdrop for the city of Brisbane, the picturesque Moreton Bay and its islands provide some surprisingly good fishing.

INTRODUCTION

Chapter three has covered the fishing options along the north-western shoreline of Moreton Bay. The remaining waters of the Bay can be broadly split into two areas: the expansive waters of the north-eastern bay and the more restricted waters to the south. The northern bay waters provide the most open areas found anywhere within the Bay. This location is host to the main shipping pathway into the Port of Brisbane, a plethora of small channels and sand banks, several mid-bay islands and the large sand mass of Moreton Island. Moreton Bay has a long fishing history with many game fishing records set for species captured in and around the area. Although the region experiences a lot of angling pressure, the bay continues to provide great fishing for a variety of species. The summer months produce top class pelagic fishing for a range of speedsters whilst the open waters, shipping lane markers and islands host schools of baitfish. This in turn brings about marauding predators such as mackerel, longtail and mackerel tuna, kingfish, cobia, trevally and tailor. The reef, sand shallows and ledges provide good fishing for snapper, sweetlip, bream, flathead, whiting, trevally, jewfish and estuary cod. For those with an interest in surf fishing, head to the eastern side of Moreton Island which offers kilometres of beach that produce tailor, bream, whiting, flathead, dart and the occasional larger pelagic. The beauty of fishing Moreton Bay lies in the fact that many of the species just listed can be caught all year round! Anglers that are planning to fish the area for the first time must be aware of restricted fishing areas. The government publication 'Moreton Bay Marine Park Users Guide' describes all Green Zone protected areas and anglers must be aware of these.

The upper regions of south Moreton Bay are widest between Cleveland and the northern tip of North Stradbroke Island. The southern bay waters then gradually thin toward the lower bay reaches around Redland Bay. There are many different types of structures to be found in this area. Extensive sand flats are found adjacent to the open ocean access around the top of North

Stradbroke Island. The shallows and channel waters here are home to a great mix of pelagic, reef and bread and butter species. Deeper water in the mid-southern bay areas are home to significant island structures. Peel, Coochiemudlo, Bird and Goat islands host fringe reef areas that are home to a plethora of reef species and roaming pelagics. The shallow shoreline waters around the southern bay are lined with mangroves and home to plenty of bream, flathead and whiting. The far southern extremities of the bay become increasingly choked with islands. These structures make navigation more challenging but anglers are well compensated by the great fishing these islands provide.

Most of the species caught in the northern bay waters are also found in the southern reaches. The type and movements of local bait provides the main difference between the two areas. This factor affects the behaviour of predatory species; anglers that wish to have consistent results across all areas of the bay need to be tuned into the patterns of bait movement across the two areas. The most common bait sources that local species spend their time hunting includes: hardyheads, bay anchovies, rock crabs and the larger baits of squid, whiting, tailor and pike. Lures that replicate these varied bait types will work well across the bay.

Facilities

The bay waters are serviced by many of the facilities detailed in chapter three.

Moreton Island can be accessed via boat or vehicle aboard the ferries that travel to the island. Boating anglers are able to traverse Moreton Bay and access the western side of the island. Alternatively, there are ferry services such as the Moreton Island MiCat that will transport vehicles across to the island. Anglers planning to access Moreton Island by vehicle need to be aware that permits are required. To find out more; head to the website *www.derm.qld.gov.au*

Stradbroke Island can be accessed via barge or taxi, both of which leave from the Cleveland area. Boating anglers are able to traverse Moreton Bay and access the western side of the island. Anglers planning to access the island by vehicle need to be aware that permits are required and various driving restrictions are in force. To find out more; head to the Redland City Council website. The southern bay waters are serviced by a number of boat ramps. The most popular boat ramps used by anglers to access the area include those found at Manly, Wellington Point, Cleveland Point and Victoria Point.

NORTH MORETON BAY WATERS LOCATION GUIDE

Map 28 No. 1 Open Waters

(longtail tuna, mackerel)

Many anglers push through these waters on their way to other fishing destinations. These areas are home to cruising pelagic species and anglers that use their eyes while travelling can often stumble upon some great fishing in the middle of the bay. Surface feeding activity or signs of large amounts of bait on the fish finder often highlight where pelagic species are to be found. Bird activity close to the surface of the water as well as surface swirls and splashes indicate that fish are actively feeding; this means anglers stand a good chance of catching them. This style of fishing can often be chaotic and anglers sometimes lose the ability to think through how best to approach this type of activity. A good tactic is to sit and watch briefly before approaching a school of surface feeding fish. Establish the direction that the school is feeding and have a guess at the size of bait they are eating. Then move ahead of the fish and cut the noisy engine; tie on a similar sized lure to the baitfish in the area, and cast ahead of the travelling fish. Retrieve the lure as fast as possible through the school and hopefully drags will be screaming soon after. If the fish leave the surface of the water as the boat approaches, don't be afraid to cast a lure ahead of where you believe the fish to be travelling and let it sink to the bottom. Then retrieve the lure back through the water column; you will be surprised how often this results in a hook-up. A good choice of lures for these speedsters includes 3–5 inch minnow style soft plastics, metal slugs in the 25 –55g size, streamer style flies, sinking and floating hardbody stickbait lures as well as vibration style lures such as blades.

The open waters of the bay are home to patchy bottom reef. Locating some of this structure in the middle of the bay can result in the discovery of a good fishing location. Small patches of reef in the midst of expanses of sand are often home to a variety of reef species such as snapper, sweetlip, tuskfish and nannygai.

Above: Pelagic species such as school mackerel can be caught in Moreton Bay open waters through much of the year.

MAP 28 MORETON BAY OPEN WATERS

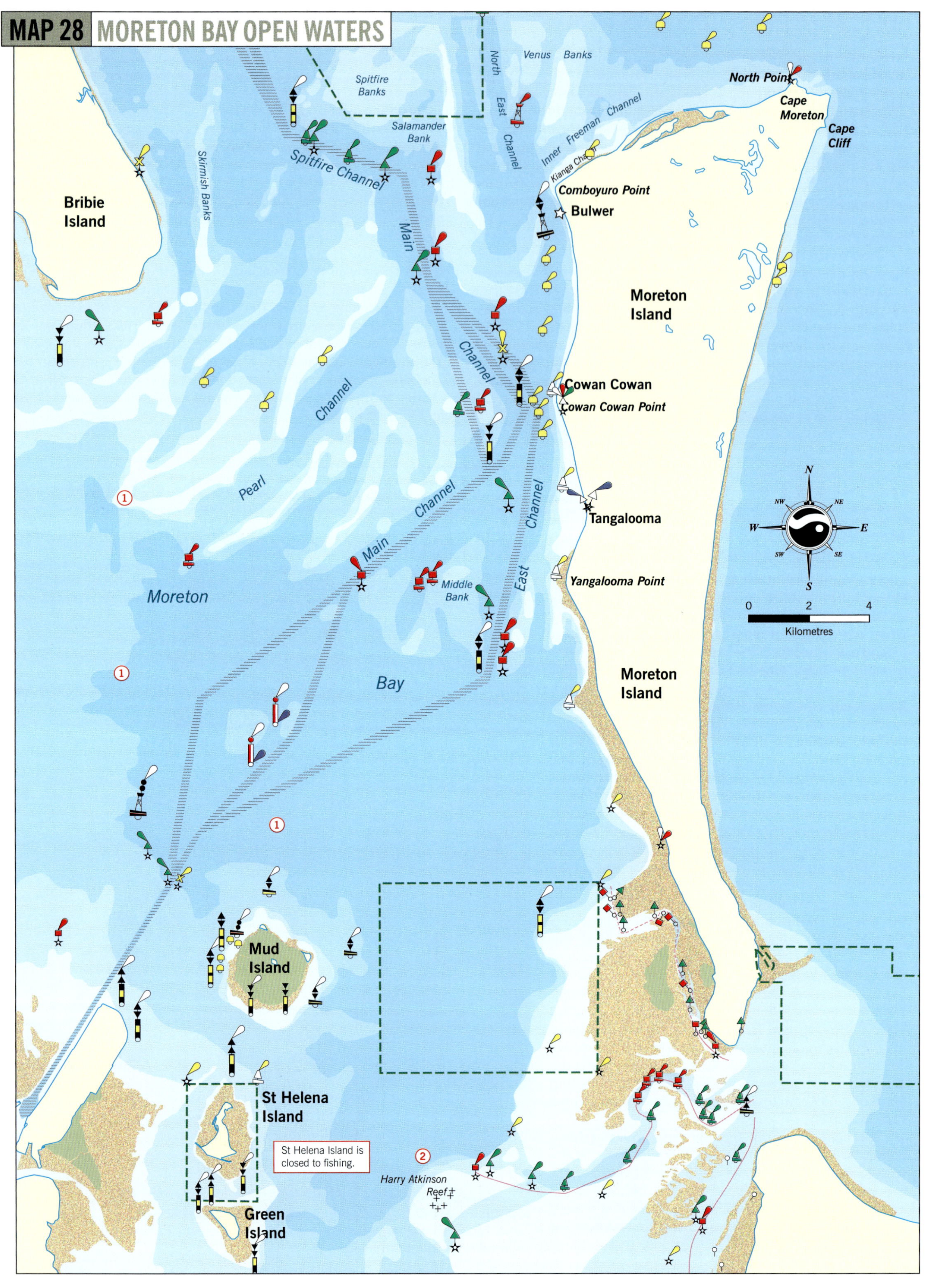

MAP 28 NO. 2 HARRY ATKINSON ARTIFICIAL REEF *(MACKEREL, TUNA, SNAPPER SWEETLIP)*

The Harry Atkinson Artificial Reef is a popular location to target mackerel, tuna and reef species such as snapper and sweetlip. Spotted and school mackerel will chase baitfish holding near to the reef. Dropping metal slugs to the bottom and then retrieving them back to the boat will bring about the undoing of these fish. Anchoring away from the reef and drifting baits of pilchard on single and gang hooks back towards the reef will produce mackerel, snapper and sweetlip. The reef rises to 5m at its shallowest. *Note:* Harry Atkinson has recently been added to quite extensively.

GPS Marks to Get You Started

Latitude	Longitude
2724532	15318304
2724439	15318450
2724604	15318411
2724537	15318527
2724404	15318386
2724350	15318675
2724262	15318704

MAP 29 GREEN ISLAND *(SNAPPER, BREAM, SWEETLIP, LONGTAIL TUNA, ESTUARY COD, WHITING, TAILOR)*

The hard structure of the island sits in the midst of sand and rubble flats. The shallows expand towards a ledge that drops into deeper bay waters. The late stages of the run-in tide are a prime time to target bream and whiting in the shallows as they head into new ground to feed. Some quality fish are taken on bait and lures fished close to the mangroves during these times. Baits of white pilchard, prawn, yabby, worm and small strip baits will tempt local fish here. Anglers fishing shallow diving and surface hardbody lures tight to the mangroves fare well on quality fish here. The outer ledge drops into deeper water that contains mixed sand and patchy reef. These edges are the prime place to catch snapper, sweetlip and cod. A ledge runs south-east from the red marker on the north of the island. This ledge produces snapper, sweetlip and roaming pelagics such as tailor. The waters further out from the ledge often hold cruising longtail tuna. Surface feeding splashes will often highlight the location of these larger pelagics. Popular approaches to catching fish around the island include anchoring and fishing with baits in a berley trail as well as drifting through the area while using lightly weighted baits of pilchard, squid and strip bait. Lure anglers often choose to drift and jig 3 – 5inch soft plastic lures along the ledge and bottom structures. Low light periods of the day fish best for most species.

GPS Marks to Get You Started

Latitude	Longitude
2725185	15313125

ABOVE: Surface feeding activity often indicates the presence of predators such as mackerel and tuna.

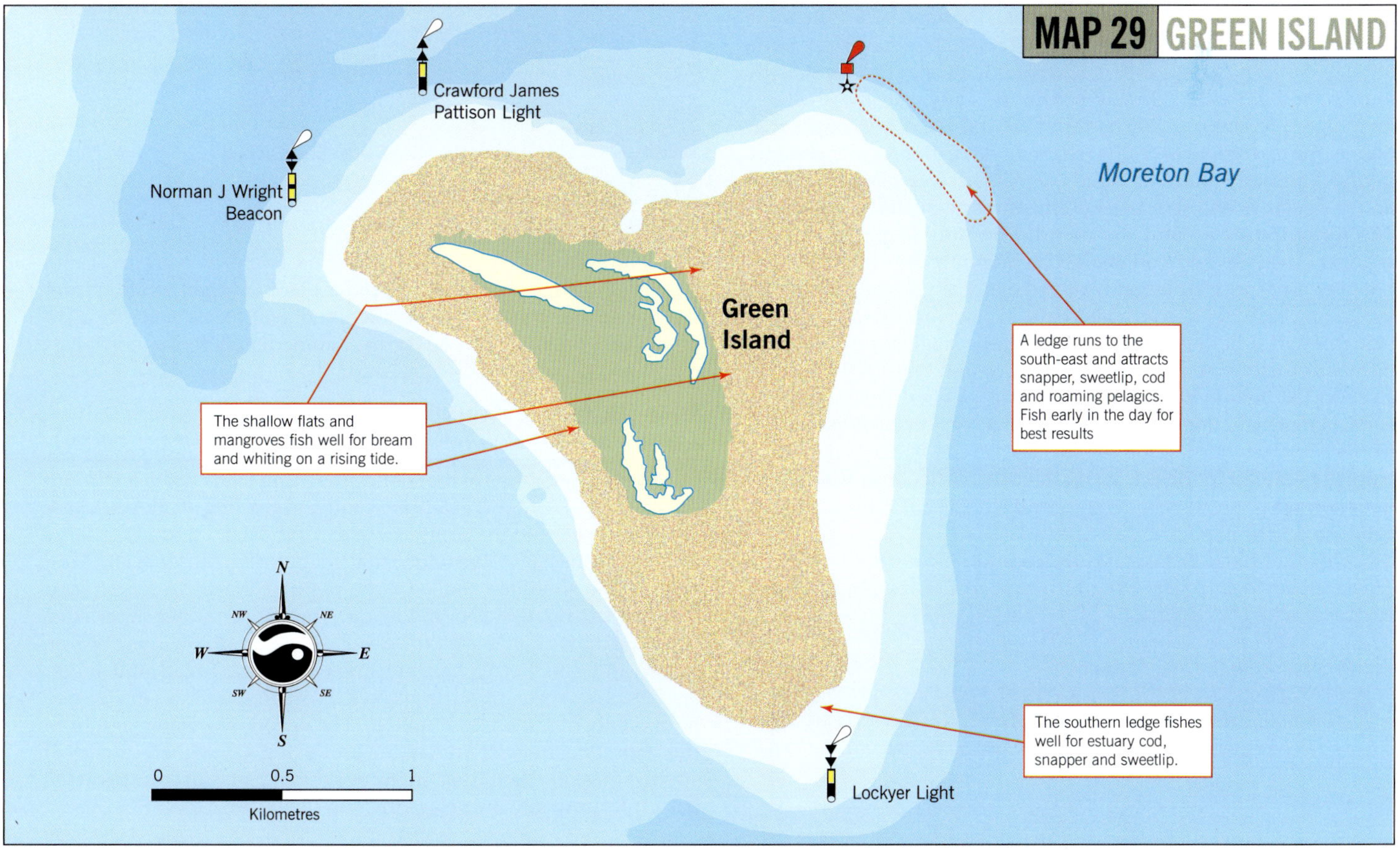

MAP 29 GREEN ISLAND

Crawford James Pattison Light

Norman J Wright Beacon

Moreton Bay

Green Island

The shallow flats and mangroves fish well for bream and whiting on a rising tide.

A ledge runs to the south-east and attracts snapper, sweetlip, cod and roaming pelagics. Fish early in the day for best results

The southern ledge fishes well for estuary cod, snapper and sweetlip.

Lockyer Light

N NE E SE S SW W NW

0 0.5 1

Kilometres

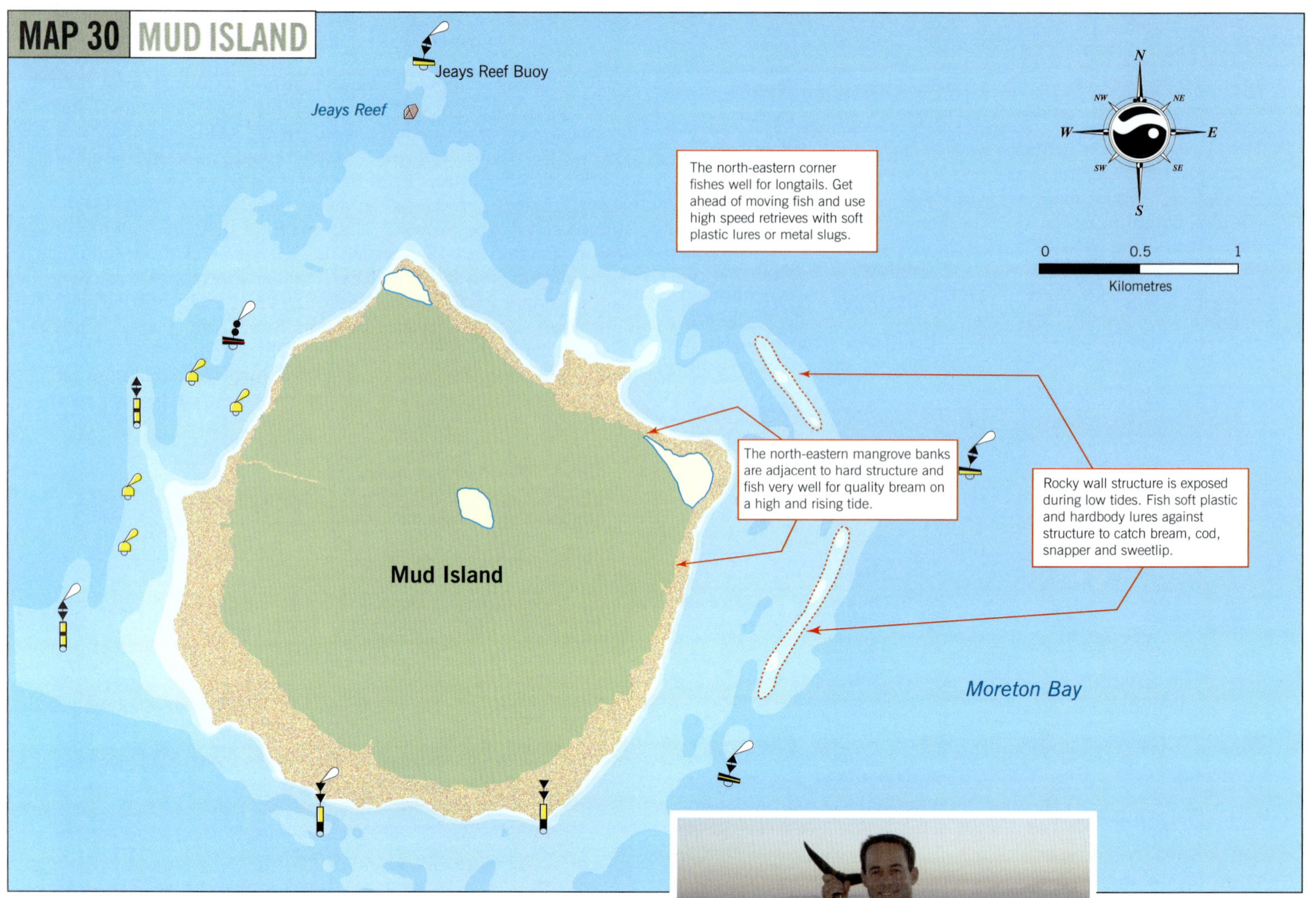

Map 30 Mud Island *(Snapper, Bream, Sweetlip, Longtail Tuna, Estuary Cod, Tailor, Trevally, Mackerel)*

Mud Island is situated further into the bay than neighbouring Green Island but offers similar fishing options. The island is surrounded by shallow sand, mud and reef shallows; these provide attractive feeding grounds to fish as the tide pushes up towards the mangrove lined edge. Quality bream are caught in the shallows on a high tide, but can also be taken around the rocky ledges that define the extremities of the shallow flats. Retrieving shallow diving hardbody lures or lightly weighted soft plastics against island structure will see the undoing of many quality bream here. The rocky ledges around the island drop into deeper water and snapper, sweetlip and cod can all be caught along this structure. Snapper are a popular target here and many anglers anchor off the island and sink lightly weighted baits of pilchard, squid and strip bait through a berley trail. The soft plastic anglers catch a good number of fish around the area. Drifting and jigging these lures close to the bottom produces some good catches. Pelagic species such as mackerel, longtail tuna and tailor feed in close proximity to the island at times. Look for surface activity as these fish drive baitfish to the surface and feast on them. As with Green Island, low light periods of the day that correspond with a turn of the tide often produce best results.

A marker buoy demarcates the location of nearby Jeays Reef. This area is worth prospecting for snapper and roaming pelagics such as mackerel and tuna.

GPS Marks to Get You Started

Latitude	Longitude
2720173	15313791
2720290	15316232

LEFT: Longtail tuna are a popular angling target in Moreton waters.

Map 31 No. 1 Kooringal *(Whiting, Bream, Dart, Flathead, Tailor)*

The southern tip of Moreton Island is home to Kooringal and Reeders Points. This area is a popular place to target whiting from the beach. Baits used to tempt whiting will also attract resident bream and flathead. The surf zones immediately to the north-east offer good fishing for tailor and dart.

Map 31 No. 2 Kounungai *(Sand and Diver Whiting, Bream, Dart, Flathead, Tailor)*

The western shoreline of the island stretching to the north and south of Kounungai contains extensive sand and weeded shallows. These shallows extend to the south towards Crab Island and into a large area of Marine Park Green Zone that lies between Moreton and Mud Island. The shoreline shallows are popular places to target sand whiting, bream, flathead and squid. The deeper water outer edge of the shallows fishes well for diver whiting in the winter. Worm, yabby and small strip bait are great for these bread and butter species. Anglers using surface lures across the shallows in summer have plenty of fun on local species. The deeper bay waters out from this shoreline are well known for producing some good catches of spotted mackerel and tuna. In the event that bait concentrates in the bay off Kounungai, the pelagic fishing can be top class.

White (or Camel) Rock
Moreton Island
Gonzales Beach
Shark Spit
Sandy Peak
South Pacific Ocean
Toompani Beach
'Big' Sand Hills
Gebelum
Kilometres
Kounungai
Sovereign Beach
'Little' Sand Hills
Toulkerrie
Frasers Gutter
The Blue Hole
Hendersons Gutter
Crab Island
Clohertys Peninsula
Lagoon Mirrapool
Coonungai Bank
Airfield
Days Gutter
Note – shoals less than half a metre at low tide.
Kooringal
Campbell Point
Mays Hole
Reeders Point
Moreton Banks
Browns Gutter
Black Gutter
Rous Channel
Boolong Banks
Fishermans Gutter

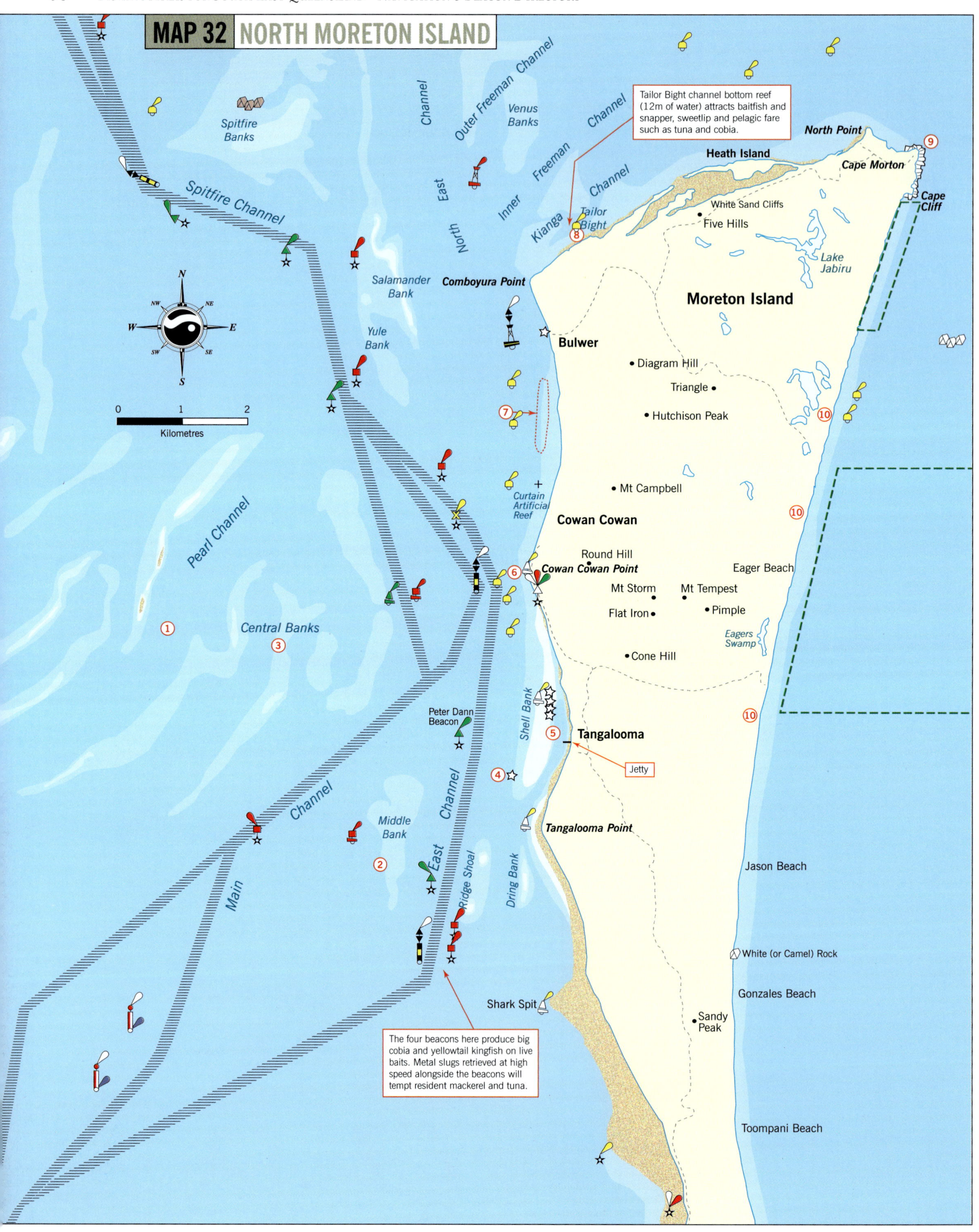
MAP 32 NORTH MORETON ISLAND
Tailor Bight channel bottom reef (12m of water) attracts baitfish and snapper, sweetlip and pelagic fare such as tuna and cobia.
The four beacons here produce big cobia and yellowtail kingfish on live baits. Metal slugs retrieved at high speed alongside the beacons will tempt resident mackerel and tuna.
Spitfire Banks
Spitfire Channel
Outer Freeman Channel
Venus Banks
North East Channel
Inner Freeman Channel
Kianga Channel
Tailor Bight
North Point
Heath Island
Cape Morton
Cape Cliff
White Sand Cliffs
Five Hills
Lake Jabiru
Moreton Island
Salamander Bank
Comboyura Point
Yule Bank
Bulwer
Diagram Hill
Triangle
Hutchison Peak
Kilometres
Curtain Artificial Reef
Mt Campbell
Cowan Cowan
Pearl Channel
Round Hill
Cowan Cowan Point
Eager Beach
Mt Storm
Mt Tempest
Flat Iron
Pimple
Central Banks
Eagers Swamp
Cone Hill
Shell Bank
Peter Dann Beacon
Tangalooma
Jetty
Main Channel
Middle Bank
East Channel
Tangalooma Point
Jason Beach
Ridge Shoal
Dring Bank
White (or Camel) Rock
Gonzales Beach
Shark Spit
Sandy Peak
Toompani Beach

Map 32 No. 1 Pearl Channel (school and spotted mackerel, longtail tuna, snapper, sweetlip, tuskfish)

The Pearl Channel waters are home to deeper water and patchy bottom reef structure. A quick sounding exercise with a fish finder will show where solid structure lies beneath. Bait is attracted to the area and in turn the likes of mackerel, snapper and other reef species are never too far away. The current pushes hard through this area when the tide is in full motion, so aim to fish the slack tide periods if you want to target fish near the bottom. Anglers drifting through the area whilst jigging soft plastics along the bottom experience some good reef fishing at times. Alternatively, fishing at anchor and dropping bait through a berley trail will also secure some of the fish that live here. Mackerel can be targeted by dropping metal slugs to the bottom and then retrieving at high speed whilst surface feeding tuna can be caught here when they are preying on abundant baitfish supplies.

Map 32 No. 2 Shipping Channel Beacons (school and spotted mackerel, longtail tuna, snapper, cobia, yellowtail kingfish)

The Main and East Channels are demarcated by several beacons. The water out from Tangalooma contains a good cluster of these great fish attracting structures; they are popular places for anglers to target a variety of pelagic species as well as the odd snapper. Drifting past the beacons and dropping metal slugs to the base of the structure before retrieving at high speed is a common approach when targeting mackerel and tuna. Dropping live bait around the beacons is a good way to tangle with local cobia and kings. These fish fight hard and at times, dirty, so aim to be equipped with suitably weighted gear. Strong tidal flow through the area can hamper fishing efforts here.

GPS Marks to Get You Started

Latitude	Longitude
2709510	15320162

Map 32 No. 3 Central Banks (school and spotted mackerel, longtail tuna, snapper)

This area contains several smaller channels and these contain small patches of bottom reef in places. These structures hold handy populations of snapper at times. In the event that concentrations of baitfish are holding over the area, schooling pelagics such as tuna and mackerel will be hunting throughout the location. The outer edges of the Central Banks drop into the deeper waters of the Main Channel. A good fish finder will highlight patches of bottom reef in some of these areas. These will always hold a few reef fish such as snapper.

Map 32 No. 4 Captain Nelson Wreck (snapper, tuskfish, school mackerel)

The remains of the Captain Nelson wreck off Tangalooma hold some big fish at times. The wreck lies in approximately 12 – 14m of water and attracts good schools of baitfish. Divers often report sightings of sizeable tuskfish and snapper cruising the ledges around the structure. Anglers that fish the wreck often choose to target periods of slack water to do so. Drifting lightly weighted pilchards down to the structure is a reliable method for hooking resident fish; however, landing them isn't always that easy!

GPS Marks to Get You Started

Latitude	Longitude
2711129	15320019

Map 32 No. 5 Tangalooma (bream, flathead, whiting, trevally, yellowtail kingfish, snapper)

Tangalooma provides plenty of opportunity for anglers wishing to target a range of species. The area is home to great accommodation, plenty of beachfront, a jetty and a line of old wrecks that are home to plenty of hard fighting critters. The shallow sandy flats produce whiting, bream and flathead for lure and bait anglers. The jetty offers access to deeper water and anglers that cast metal slugs and baits have caught everything from flathead to mackerel from this platform. The wrecks are home to big kingfish, bream, trevally and the odd reef species. Casting lures and baits tight against the structure is the best method to catch fish here. The fish get to see a lot of anglers in crystal clear water so don't expect to find them easy to catch. Light line classes, smaller offerings and fishing low light periods of the day around waning tidal phases will go a long way towards producing bites around the wrecks.

Map 32 No. 6 Cowan Cowan Point (bream, flathead, whiting, trevally, mackerel, tuna, snapper)

The point lies adjacent to deeper water of the Main Channel. A ledge lies at the front of the point and this holds patchy reef in places. In the old days, this was a popular place to troll for marlin and Spanish mackerel. Nowadays the location still offers anglers the chance to tangle with pelagic species such as tuna and mackerel. The bottom structure produces snapper and other reef species for bait and lure anglers. Alternatively, you can try your hand at catching a few bream, flathead and whiting. The flathead are often in good numbers through the area from September to April.

Map 32 No. 7 Bulwer Ledge and Shoreline (mackerel, tuna, snapper, cobia, bream, flathead, whiting)

The ledge adjacent to the Bulwer shoreline drops into deeper water and hosts plenty of coffee rock structure. The ground holds good baitfish at times and the current that pushes through the area makes

Longtail tuna often frequent the Pearl Channel.

it an ideal hunting ground for species such as mackerel, tuna and cobia. The location produces Spanish, spotted and school mackerel for anglers that put in time on the water here. Trolling live and dead baits as well as lures produces many of these fish each season. The ledge produces some big snapper and other reef species. These fish start to become active as the tidal flow eases along the drop-off. The shorebased angler will encounter some good fishing for bread and butter species along this beach. Winter sees tailor turn up here whilst summer produces excellent whiting fishing. The Curtin Artificial Reef is positioned along the drop-off below Bulwer and can be found in approximately 20m of water. The reef attracts pelagic and reef species.

GPS Marks to Get You Started

Latitude	Longitude
2706605	15321755

MAP 32 NO. 8 TAILOR BIGHT
(BREAM, FLATHEAD, WHITING, TAILOR)

The location offers surf fishing without excessive swell as the area is largely protected from prevailing southerly wave activity. Casting baits of worm, yabby, pipi and flesh baits of tuna and pilchard will provide good fishing for whiting and flathead in the summer, and bream, dart and tailor in the winter. A patch of bottom reef can be found in the channel out from Tailor Bight. The structure attracts baitfish and snapper, sweetlip and pelagics such as tuna and cobia.

GPS Marks to Get You Started

Latitude	Longitude
2701233	15323157

MAP 32 NO. 9 CAPE MORETON
(BREAM, WHITING, TAILOR, MACKEREL)

The north-eastern corner of Moreton Island provides an option for local rock fishing exponents. Rocky outcrop offers anglers the chance to cast baits and lures into deeper water. The rocks produce bream, tailor and whiting and occasionally larger pelagic fare such as mackerel. Caution must be exercised when fishing this area as it is exposed to dangerous swell at times. The area is largely surrounded by Marine Park Green Zone so be mindful to look for signage of the protected regions and be careful to avoid fishing in such zones.

MAP 32 NO. 10 EAGER BEACH
(BREAM, DART, WHITING, FLATHEAD, TAILOR, JEWFISH)

The eastern side of Moreton Island is home to kilometres of beach. The surf beach contains plenty of gutters that host bream, dart and tailor in winter and whiting, flathead and the occasional mackerel in summer. Consistently successful anglers tend to use a running rig with 50cm of trace to a single or gang hook rig baited with worm, pipi, tuna strip or pilchard. Low tide periods are favoured for whiting and high tides for bream, dart and flathead. Low light periods of the day and night time sessions are most often utilised to catch tailor in the area.

SOUTH MORETON BAY WATERS LOCATION GUIDE

MAP 33 NO. 1 OPEN WATERS
(LONGTAIL TUNA, MACKEREL)

The open waters of the southern bay are frequented by pelagic species as they migrate through the area during the year. A watchful eye while travelling towards a specific destination will often detect signs of surface feeding fish. Target these fish in the same manner as that prescribed for open water pelagics in the northern bay reaches and you are well on the way to experiencing screaming drags and lots of fun!

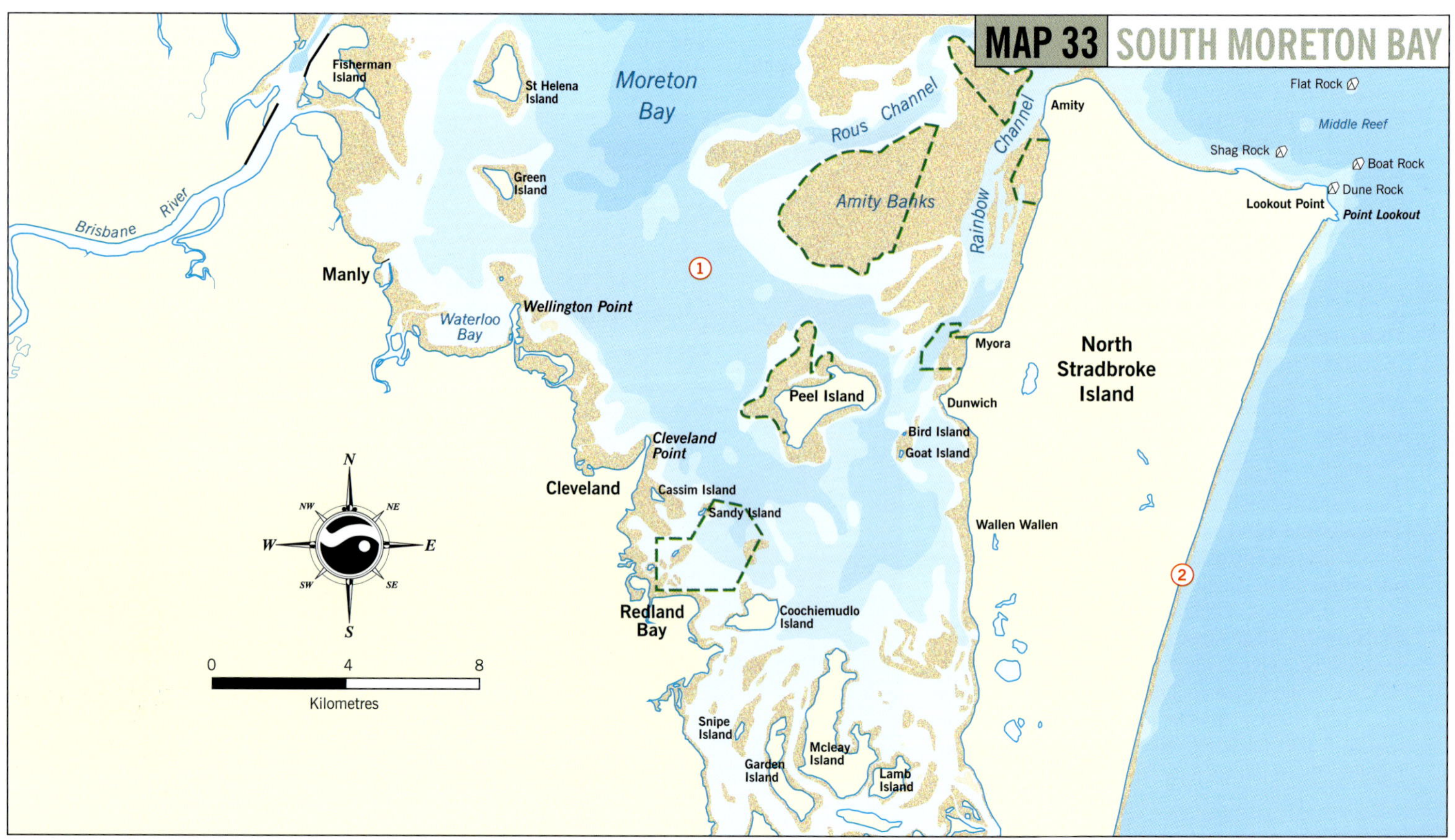

ABOVE: The southern bay islands fish well for jewfish around new and full moon phases and particularly after some good rain.

Map 33 No. 2 North Stradbroke Island East Surf Beaches

(Bream, whiting, flathead, dart, tailor)

The area offers plenty of surf beach fishing real estate. Look for near-shore gutters that will provide good summer time fishing for whiting, swallowtail dart and flathead as well as winter time tailor and bream action. Popular baits include pilchards, garfish, worms and pipis.

Map 34 No. 1 Tingalpa and Lota Creeks

(Whiting, flathead, crabs)

The mouth of Lota and Tingalpa creeks are popular places to target whiting and flathead. A channel cuts through extensive shallows and fish use this as a feeding pathway. High tide sees fish pushing up over the shallows to feed on yabbies and worms, while the run-out tide has fish retreating back into deeper channel waters. Tingalpa Creek is mangrove lined and the edges of the system are worth investigating with baits and lures for flathead, bream and whiting. This is a popular place for anglers hunting up a feed of crabs.

Map 34 No. 2 Waterloo Bay

(Whiting, flathead, bream, mangrove jack)

The shoreline shallows between Cleveland Point and Lota fish well for bream, flathead and whiting, particularly on a building tide. Yabby, worm and prawn baits produce good catches along the length of these western shorelines. Anglers cruising the shallows at high tide will catch some good bream here at times. Retrieve lures close to shoreline mangroves as well as any hard structure sitting in the midst of the shallows. Long casts and lures twitched along the bottom or surface will tempt local fish.

The Aquatic Paradise canals provide good fishing for bream, whiting, mangrove jack and estuary cod. Live bait anglers catch some good fish at night as do the lure brigade trolling bibbed lures or fishing surface offerings around structure. Soft plastics fished around man-made structure produces some quality bream during winter.

Map 34 No. 3 Wellington Point Ledge and Shoreline

(Snapper, sweetlip, whiting, bream, flathead)

A 4 – 5m ledge runs parallel with the shoreline out from the Wellington Point area. The ledge holds patchy bottom reef associated with some slightly deeper water and this attracts reef species such as snapper and sweetlip. The predominant catches of these fish come from the northern and southern ends of the ledge. Drifting along the area and jigging 3 to 5 inch soft plastic lures down the ledge produces a lot of fish. The snapper fishing is best in late winter and the sweetlip become increasingly active into the summer months. The middle areas of the structure fish well for diver whiting in winter and these tasty fish can be caught on small strip baits of squid, peeled prawn and worm.

The shoreline areas inside this ledge produce bread and butter species when the cleaner high tide water pushes up on to the shallows.

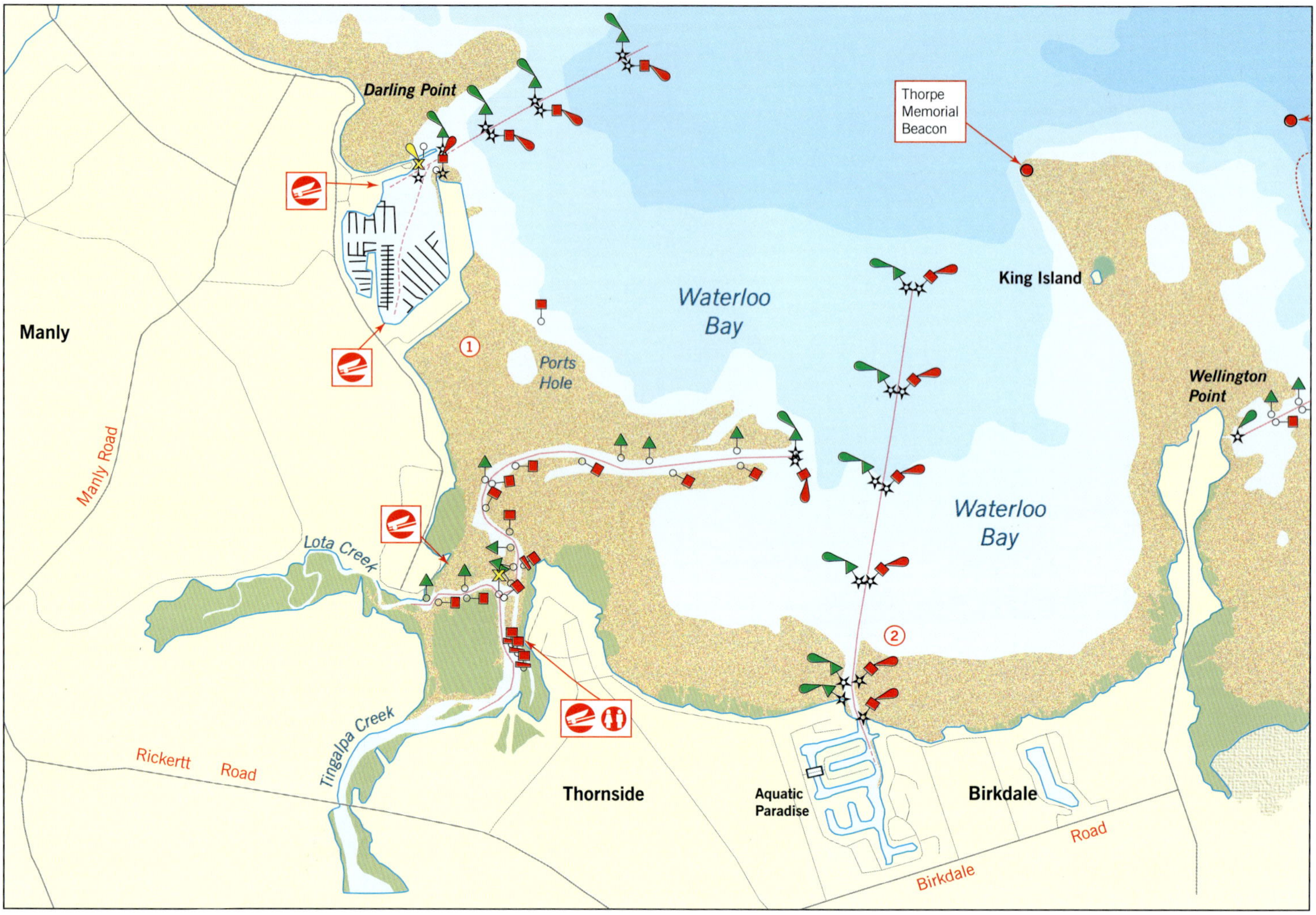

MAP 34 NO. 4 RABY BAY SHORELINE AND CANALS

(BREAM, WHITING, FLATHEAD, MANGROVE JACK, ESTUARY COD, TREVALLY)

The shallows in Raby Bay are lined with mangroves and scoured in places by slightly deeper channels. The channels and occasional hard structure lying in the shallows will attract cruising bream, flathead and whiting. The cleaner waters of the rising tide fish best here.

A good strategy for lure anglers when fishing this entire shoreline is to cover as much water as possible while casting and retrieving an assortment of hardbody lures. Quality bream anglers such as Anthony Wishy and Chris Britton favour a mobile approach while using lure choices that enable them to 'prospect' as much local water as possible: a favoured lure choice of the pair includes the 50–65mm surface stickbait variety. Experience for such anglers dictates that fish in these areas hang out in dispersed groups and a kilometre of fishless shoreline will suddenly be broken by a flurry of fish. The key is to keep moving while fishing!

Raby Bay marks the entrance to a broad canal system that provides ample structure for bream, flathead, estuary cod and lesser flathead, whiting and trevally. Casting lures tight against available hard structure is a popular approach. Be careful not to interfere with residential property as this will ensure anglers are welcome to return in future times.

MAP 34 NO. 5 CLEVELAND POINT LEDGE AND SHORELINE

(SNAPPER, SWEETLIP, WHITING, BREAM, FLATHEAD)

The drop-off from the shallows away from Cleveland Point provides similar fishing to that found off Wellington Point. The structure may not be as expansive as the ledge found off Wellington Point but the area still produces squire sized snapper and diver whiting during the winter months.

LEFT: Trevally are suckers for lures fished around the canal structures.

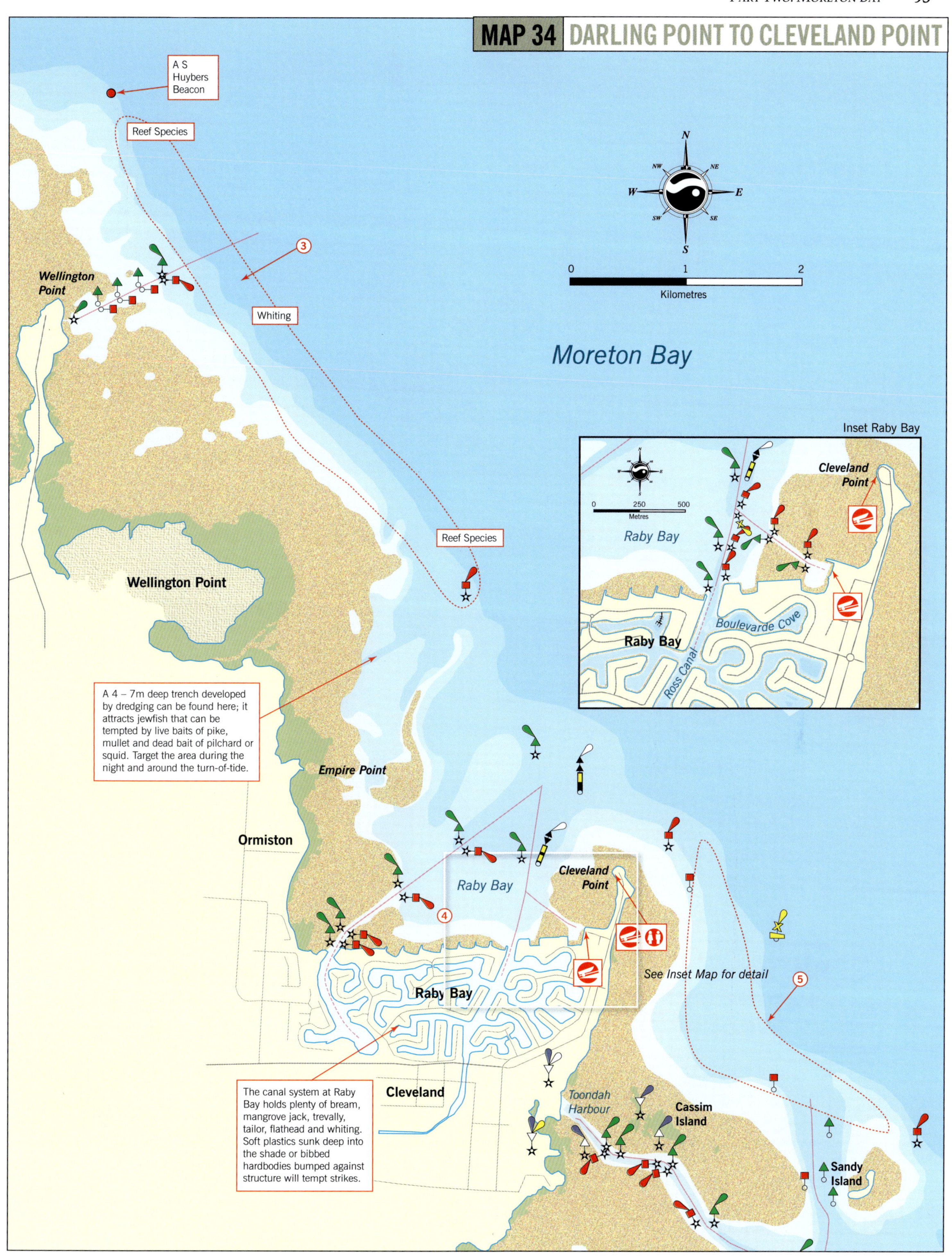
MAP 34 DARLING POINT TO CLEVELAND POINT
A S Huybers Beacon
Reef Species
Wellington Point
Whiting
Moreton Bay
0 1 2
Kilometres
N
S
E
W
NE
NW
SE
SW
Inset Raby Bay
Cleveland Point
Raby Bay
Boulevarde Cove
Ross Canal
0 250 500
Metres
Reef Species
Wellington Point
A 4 – 7m deep trench developed by dredging can be found here; it attracts jewfish that can be tempted by live baits of pike, mullet and dead bait of pilchard or squid. Target the area during the night and around the turn-of-tide.
Empire Point
Ormiston
Raby Bay
Cleveland Point
See Inset Map for detail
Raby Bay
The canal system at Raby Bay holds plenty of bream, mangrove jack, trevally, tailor, flathead and whiting. Soft plastics sunk deep into the shade or bibbed hardbodies bumped against structure will tempt strikes.
Cleveland
Toondah Harbour
Cassim Island
Sandy Island

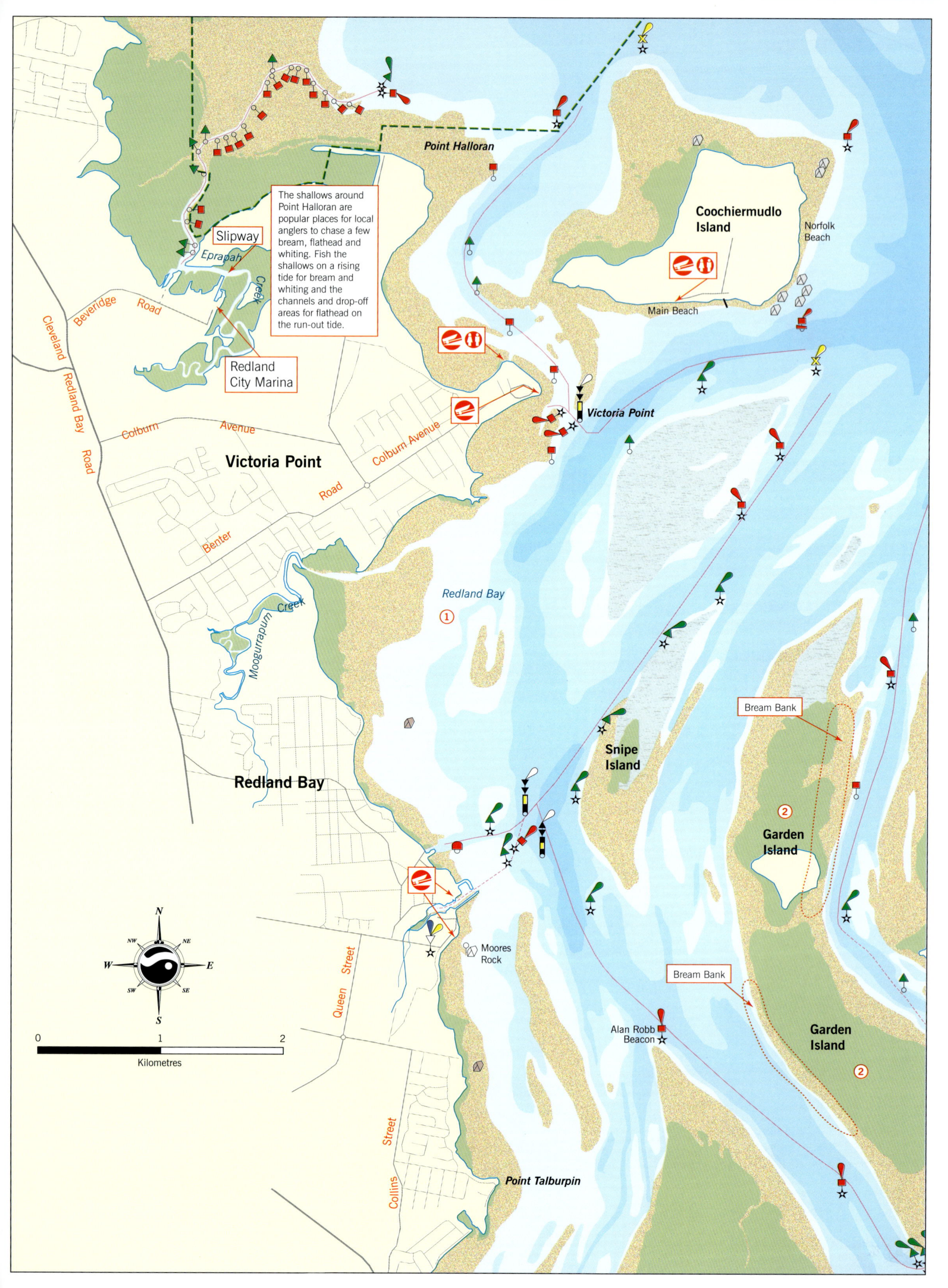
Point Halloran
The shallows around Point Halloran are popular places for local anglers to chase a few bream, flathead and whiting. Fish the shallows on a rising tide for bream and whiting and the channels and drop-off areas for flathead on the run-out tide.
Slipway
Eprapah Creek
Redland City Marina
Beveridge Road
Cleveland Redland Bay Road
Coochiermudlo Island
Norfolk Beach
Main Beach
Victoria Point
Colburn Avenue
Colburn Avenue Road
Benter
Redland Bay
1
Moogurrapum Creek
Snipe Island
Bream Bank
2
Garden Island
Redland Bay
Moores Rock
Queen Street
Collins Street
Alan Robb Beacon
Point Talburpin
N
NE
E
SE
S
SW
W
NW
0
1
2
Kilometres

MAP 35 ISLANDS OF SOUTH MORETON BAY

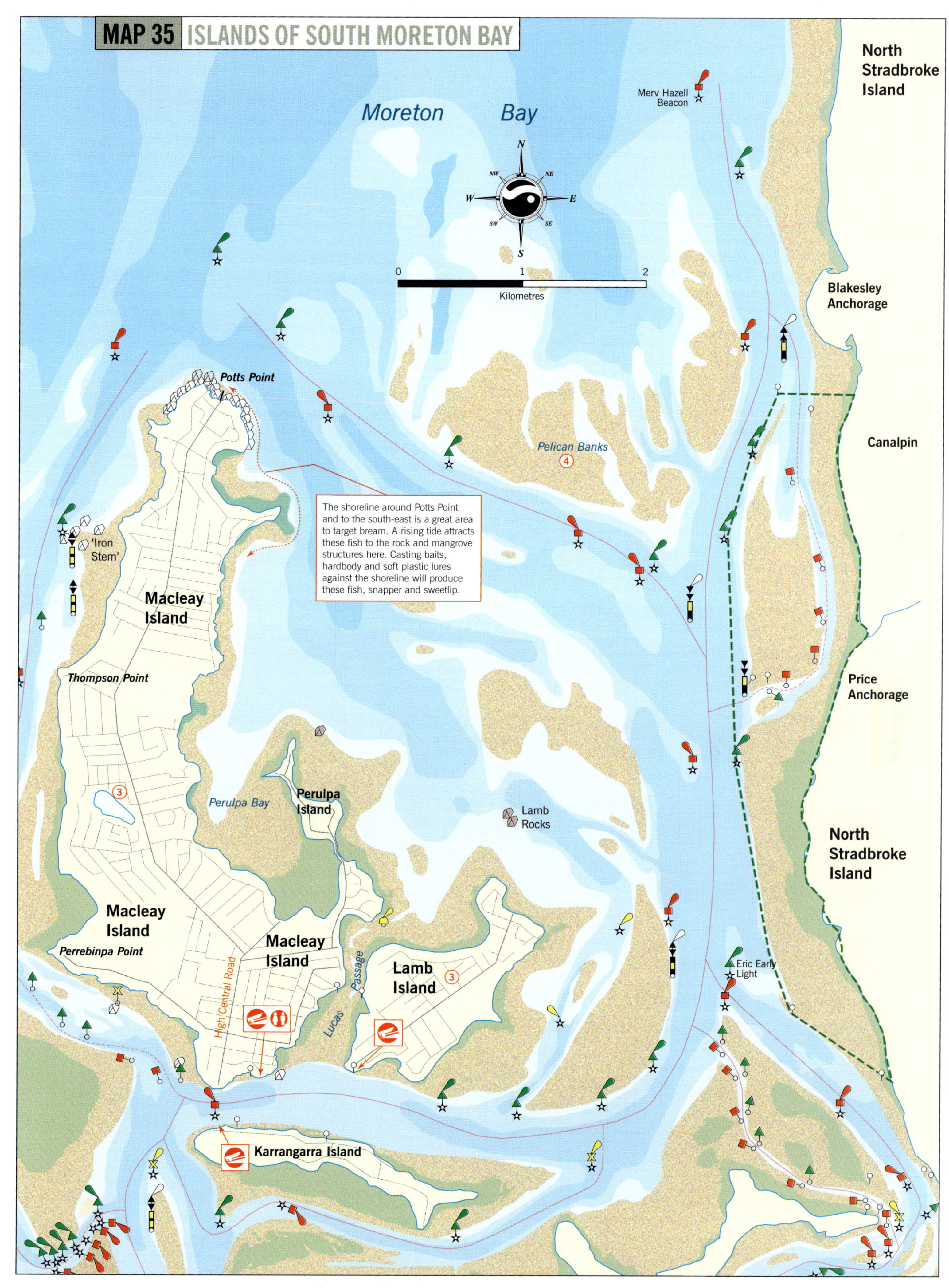

MAP 35 NO. 1 REDLAND BAY
(BREAM, WHITING, FLATHEAD)

The waters of Redland Bay are home to a relatively shallow channel, plenty of sand and mud, as well as weeded flats within a mangrove clad shoreline. The shallows fish well for bream and whiting on a building tide. This is a popular place to retrieve surface and shallow diving hardbody lures. Channels within the shallows produce flathead on run-out and building tides. Large zones of weeded shallows lie opposite Redland Bay; these are similar to the shallows that engulf Snipe Island. Targeting these shallows with surface lures produces plenty of bream when they are schooled up in the area. Alternatively, target the drop-off ledges around the shallows with sinking and diving lures as this strategy accounts for some quality bream and flathead.

MAP 35 NO. 2 GARDEN ISLAND
(BREAM, WHITING, FLATHEAD, TAILOR)

The north-eastern and south-western shorelines of Garden Island are well known for producing some good bream fishing. This typically occurs when the rising tide floods the mangroves. A popular strategy for fishing any of these southern bay islands is to explore the area at low tide. This will enable identification of significant channels and hard structure within the mud and sand shallows. These areas are almost certainly going to hold fish when they fill with high tide water. Bream and whiting will often use deeper channels to move into very shallow mangrove edges around the high tide. If you know where they are going to be, you have half the battle won. The north-eastern bank is the most popular of the island shorelines as it consistently produces some good fish for anglers.

MAP 35 NO. 3 MACLEAY AND LAMB ISLANDS
(BREAM, SNAPPER, WHITING, FLATHEAD, TAILOR)

Local bream and snapper anglers spend more time fishing these islands than most others in the area. This is greatly attributed to them containing a wealth of fish holding structure; anglers are usually able to find a few fish here if some time is invested looking for them. The islands are mostly surrounded in mud, sand and weeded shallows that are lined with shoreline mangroves. Channels and rock structures within the flats hold fish for much of the time. The high tide periods usually see resident fish move into the shallows to obtain an easy feed. Potts Point is the most northern tip of Macleay Island and it contains plenty of shoreline rock that drops into deeper water. The shoreline rocks produce some quality bream whereas the deeper water drop-off's produce snapper and sweetlip. Surface luring for bream and squire sized snapper is a popular pursuit in this area.

The bank to the south east of Potts Point is a great bream fishing location. Patches of weed and flooded mangroves fish well for bream and whiting. The northern waters off Lamb Island are home to a chunk of rock known as Lamb Rocks which fishes well for bream. Extracting these fish can be challenging as they know how to get back to shelter in short time. The southern points of Lamb and Macleay islands are home to rocky shorelines and deeper water. They produce some good bream and prawns at times. A yellow marker in the bay to the south of Perrebinpa Point on Macleay Island demarcates shallow rocks. These rocks fish well for cruising bream during the high tide. The two bays to the south west of Potts Point on Macleay Island contain scattered weed and rock structures within the shallows. These areas fish well for bream, whiting and at times, squid. A solid chunk of rocky structure is marked by yellow beacons here and is known as 'Iron Stem'. This area is a popular place to target snapper and bream on lures. The tide can push hard through this area so aim to fish the turning stages of the tide.

MAP 35 NO. 4 PELICAN BANKS *(WHITING)*

The area known as Pelican Banks consists of a maze of sand banks separated by several deeper channels. The area is a popular spot for whiting fishers and crabbers. Using baits of yabby, worm, prawn or small strip bait will produce sand whiting in summer and diver whiting in the winter. Good catches of crab are also taken here. The area attracts some pelagic activity at times, with the most common visitor being bay tailor.

ABOVE: The shallow shorelines are ideal areas to chase species such as bream and whiting on surface lures. (PHOTOGRAPH BY DEAN SYLVESTER)

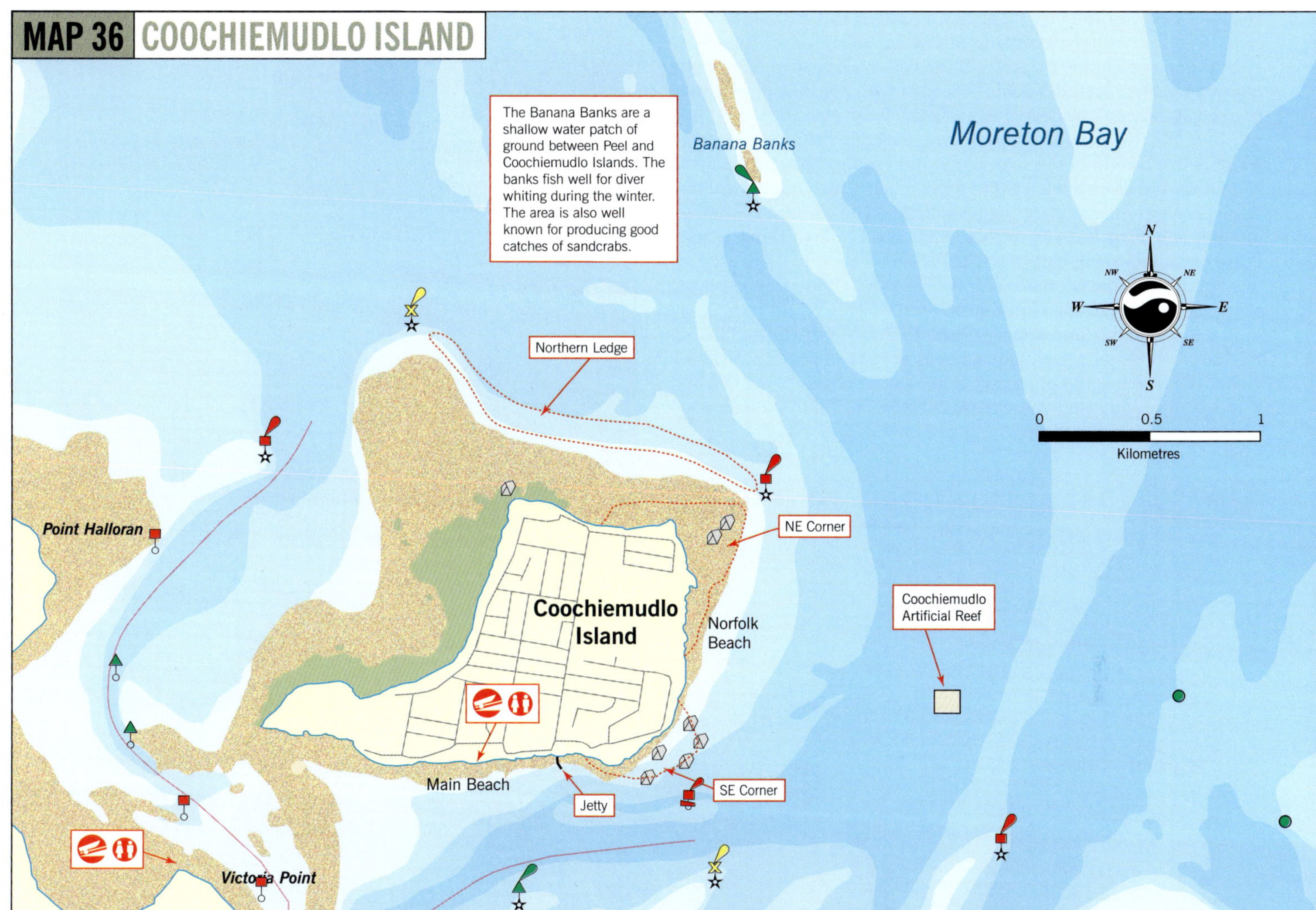

MAP 36 COOCHIEMUDLO ISLAND
(SNAPPER, SWEETLIP, BREAM, TAILOR)

Coochiemudlo is a prominent island in the lower regions of the southern bay. The island contains shallow flats with mixed sand, mud and rubble on the western side of the island. These flats are lined with mangroves and produce a few bream and whiting on a building tide. In saying this, it's the shoreline on the bay side of the island that attracts most angling attention. The north-eastern and south-eastern corners of the island host rocky shoreline outcrop adjacent to a deeper water drop-off. These areas fish very well for bream on a building tide. Casting shallow diving hardbody lures across the reef so that the lure is bumping structure during the retrieve is the way to hook these fish; however, landing them can be a more complex task! The north-eastern corner is marked with a red beacon and a deeper water ledge runs between this beacon and a yellow beacon to the north-west. Anglers targeting this ledge with baits and lures fare well on some quality snapper and sweetlip. The turn of the tide fishes well for these species, and this is accentuated when combined with low light periods of the day. An artificial reef has been installed to the east of Coochiemudlo. The area is worth prospecting for reef species.

Coochiemudlo Artificial Reef GPS

Latitude	Longitude
2734273	15320961
2734283	15321036
2734143	15321040
2734108	15321180
2734058	15321163

MAP 37 NO. 1 GOAT AND BIRD ISLANDS
(BREAM, SNAPPER, SWEETLIP, ESTUARY COD, TAILOR, JEWFISH, SQUID)

Two separate rock and coral outcrops sit abroad a raised patch of ground here; although small, these chunks of rock are given two separate names. The water surrounding the two isles is a mixture of mud, sand and reef that gradually drops into deeper water. A sharper ledge dropping into deeper water is found to the east and southern areas of Goat Island.

The northern patch of outcrop is Bird Island and it is visibly the small sister in this relationship. Some anglers are bemused that this insignificant patch of rock is given the credit of being an island. The shallow rocky substrate around this small island however, is a haven for bream and some quality fish are caught here every year. Retrieving soft plastics, shallow diving and surface hardbody lures across the shallows is a popular and effective approach. Casting near-weightless 3 inch soft plastic lures into windblown areas of rock here produces some cracking bream at times. Do not be surprised to find the bream feeding in water barely deep enough to cover their bodies.

Goat Island is easily the bigger of the two islands and provides quality shoreline reef structure around most of the feature. A rising tide pushing new water over the shallow reef and into the mangrove edges attracts good numbers of bream and squid. The slightly deeper reef structure away from the shoreline regularly produces snapper, sweetlip and tailor. The north-eastern and southern drop-off is well known for producing the odd jewfish for anglers that spend time specifically targeting these fish. A consistent approach to catching a few includes fishing the area with live pike during the hours of darkness. The deeper water to the south of Goat Island also produces the best of the snapper and sweetlip fishing; some big snapper are caught here each winter and spring. This area is also a good spot to catch a few yakkas for live bait which might explain why it is also home to some bigger snapper. The western shoreline of Goat and Bird Island produce some good tailor fishing when these fish are chasing bait in this part of the bay. If you are after a few squid, then the southern and western shorelines are the place to cast a jig. An effective approach when chasing squid here is to follow the high tide and cast jigs right up into the shallows. This is a good way to catch a few tiger squid as they head in close to catch crabs. The arrow squid often hold a bit deeper, so aim to work a jig through the depths and you will quickly establish if there are a few of these species in the area.

Mike Connolly with a couple of lovely Peel Island snapper.

MAP 37 GOAT, BIRD AND PEEL ISLANDS

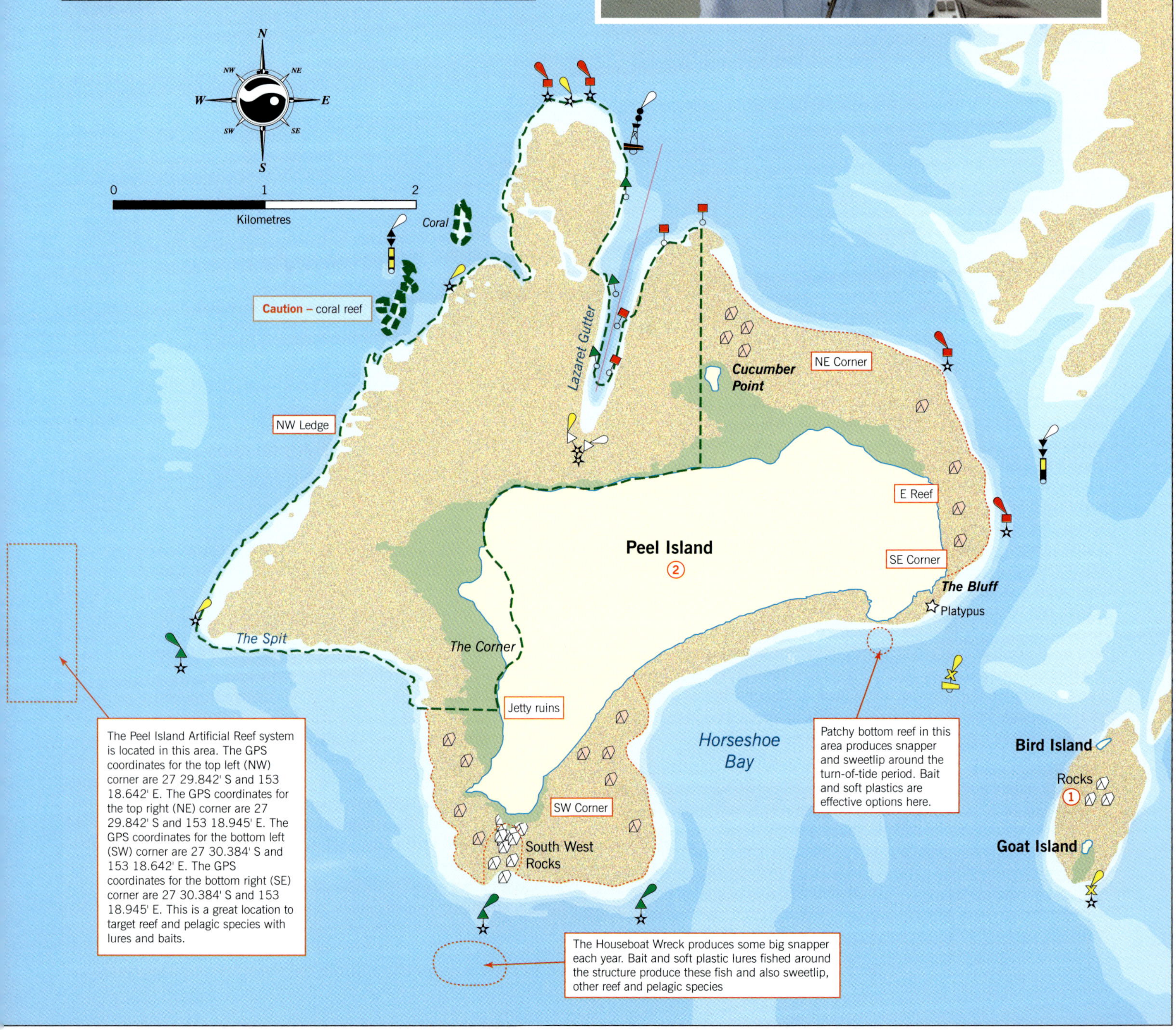

N
NW
NE
W
E
SW
SE
S
0
1
2
Kilometres
Coral
Caution – coral reef
Lazaret Gutter
NW Ledge
Cucumber Point
NE Corner
E Reef
Peel Island
2
SE Corner
The Bluff
Platypus
The Spit
The Corner
Jetty ruins
SW Corner
South West Rocks
Horseshoe Bay
Bird Island
Rocks
1
Goat Island

The Peel Island Artificial Reef system is located in this area. The GPS coordinates for the top left (NW) corner are 27 29.842' S and 153 18.642' E. The GPS coordinates for the top right (NE) corner are 27 29.842' S and 153 18.945' E. The GPS coordinates for the bottom left (SW) corner are 27 30.384' S and 153 18.642' E. The GPS coordinates for the bottom right (SE) corner are 27 30.384' S and 153 18.945' E. This is a great location to target reef and pelagic species with lures and baits.

Patchy bottom reef in this area produces snapper and sweetlip around the turn-of-tide period. Bait and soft plastics are effective options here.

The Houseboat Wreck produces some big snapper each year. Bait and soft plastic lures fished around the structure produce these fish and also sweetlip, other reef and pelagic species

MAP 37 No. 2 PEEL ISLAND (*BREAM, SNAPPER, SWEETLIP, FLATHEAD, ESTUARY COD, TAILOR, JEWFISH, LONGTAIL TUNA, TUSKFISH, NANNYGAI, SQUID*)

Perched in the middle of the southern bay waters, Peel Island is the largest of the open water bay islands. Although a large part of its waters are designated Marine Park Green Zone, the remaining area and good fishing options available at Peel Island make it a popular fishing destination. The island is surrounded by an extensive reef system and much of the northern reef consists of Marine Park Green Zone designation. The shallow reef areas to the south and east of Peel Island offer good fishing on a building tide. Bream, whiting, sweetlip, trevally and flathead will feed in shallow reef waters as the tides rises. Anglers casting diving and surface hardbody lures and lightly weighted soft plastics are in with a good chance of catching these predators. The reef around South West Rocks and between The Bluff and Cucumber Point are the pick of the locations. Lure fishing against shoreline structure is effective at the top of the tide. The mangroves around South West Rocks and Cucumber Point and the rocky shoreline around The Bluff fish well for species such as bream, whiting, sweetlip and squid. Care must be taken when targeting the shallows as a dropping tide and shallow reef can catch anglers in a tough predicament.

The edge of the shallow reef where the Peel Island shoreline drops into deeper water provides some of the best fishing in the bay. Anglers fishing bait at anchor or drifting and casting lures towards the edge encounter a huge variety of species. Snapper and sweetlip are a common catch around the edge of the South West Rocks and Horseshoe Bay reef system. Pelagic species such as tailor, trevally and mackerel are also caught throughout this area; the fishing can be very good when fish herd baitfish against the reef edge in Horseshoe Bay. Fishing with lures that match the size of the bait is a key to catching a variety of species in this event. The reef drops into deeper water in the vicinity of The Bluff. It is common to see boats anchored in the water out from the wreck. Anglers in these boats are often targeting snapper, sweetlip and pelagics hunting around patchy bottom reef in the area. The reef edge that runs around the eastern side of Peel Island offers similar fishing to that around South West Rocks. The waters around Lazaret Gutter fish well around the high tide. Anglers that drift quietly and fish the Yellow Zone waters of this trench often catch snapper, sweetlip, bream, whiting, flathead and tailor. The Naval Reserve Banks are located to the north of Peel. These waters are home to schools of longtail tuna in June to August; if these fish can't be found then this time of year is perfect for hunting up a feed of diver whiting here. The Peel Island Green Zone protects the entire reef along the north-western side of the island, however, anglers are able to fish the waters immediately outside of this reef edge. This provides an extensive area of great fishing options for the Brisbane angler. Anglers can choose to anchor away from the reef edge and drift baits through a berley trail with pilchard, squid and live bait all being popular choices here. The key to catching fish on bait in this location is to fish as light as possible as the fish see plenty of boats and baits. Another effective strategy is to drift along the outer reef edge and cast soft plastic and harbody lures to the deeper sections of the reef edge. Fishing along this area provides great fishing for species like snapper, sweetlip, cod, flathead, trevally and tailor. The location is producing plenty of jewfish catches these days which is a pleasing sign. A late summer session with a storm front on the horizon is known for producing the odd coral trout; a true bonus when fishing such parts of the bay. The north-western area is well known for producing some good longtail tuna captures. These fish are usually in the area around June to August.

The waters off Peel Island are home to deeper sunken structures. The Peel Artificial Reef is located out from the western point of the island. The structure sits in approximately 10–12m of water and produces some good fishing for reef and pelagic species. Snapper, sweetlip, cod and the occasional tuskfish and nannygai are caught here. The Houseboat Wreck is a popular fishing location out from the reef edge at South West Rocks. There are two popular approaches to fishing these deeper structures: anglers will either drift baits down to the target area from an anchored boat, or drift over the area and jig soft plastic or other sinking lure types. These deeper water structures attract some bigger predators at times. Several big snapper are caught here each year. Big Moreton Bay snapper are characterised by fish over the 65–70cm length.

Peel Island Artificial Reef GPS Marks

Latitude	Longitude
2729881	15318726

ABOVE: Longtail tuna hunting bait to the north of Peel Island.

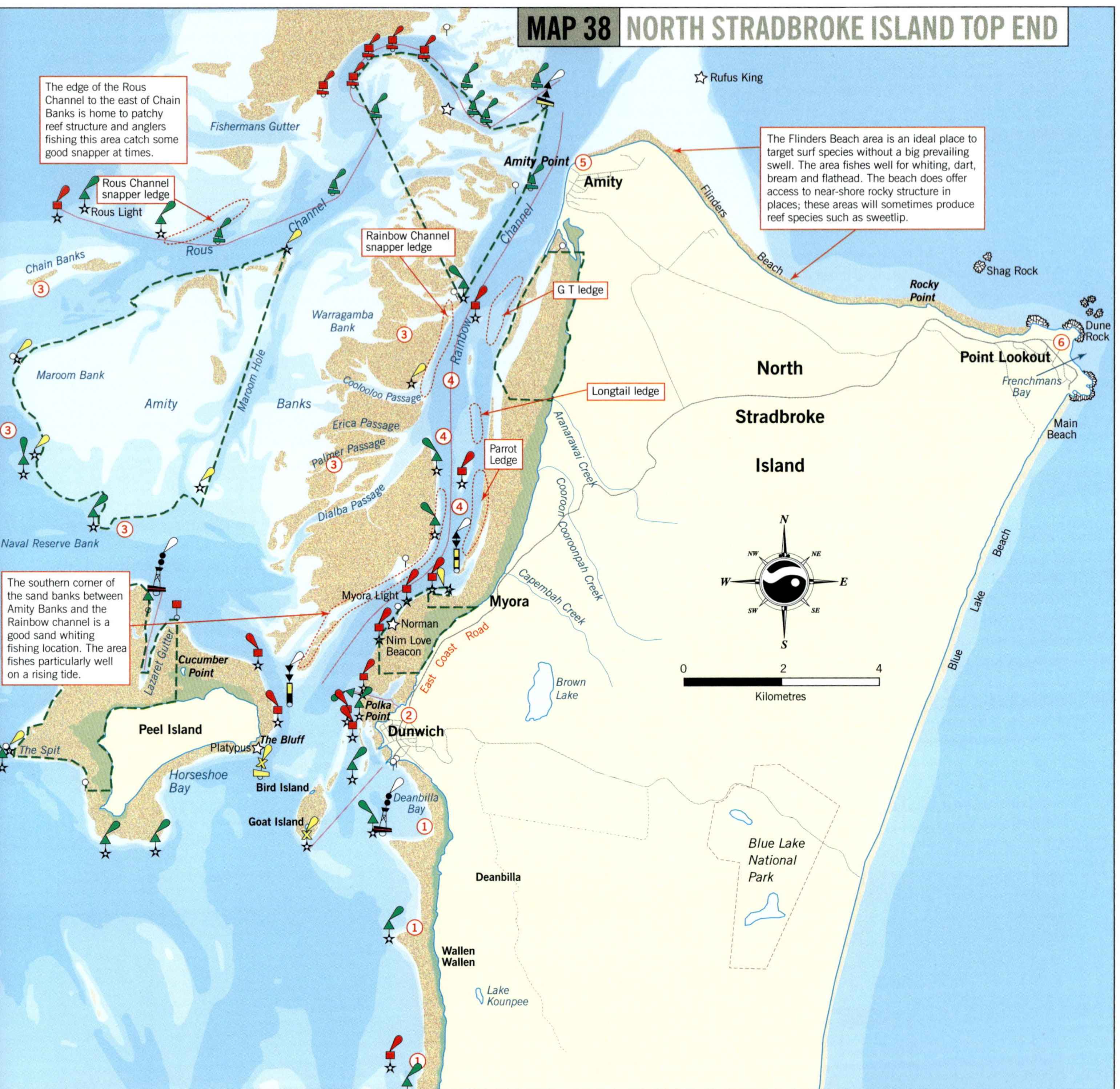

Map 38 No. 1 Wallen Wallen Shoreline to Deanbilla Bay

(Bream, Whiting, Flathead, Golden Trevally, Mackerel, Tailor)

This stretch of shoreline is characterised by extensive sand and weed shallows hugging a mangrove lined bankside. The shallows drop into deeper bay water and attract pelagic and bread and butter species to the area. Lure anglers chasing bream, whiting and flathead catch some good fish in this area by drifting along the lengthy shoreline. Casting lures over the shallows and into the mangrove shoreline while staying on the move is an effective approach. The northern sections of this shore towards Deanbilla Bay are home to old oyster rack structures that fish well for a range of species. The shallows around Deanbilla Bay are a popular sight fishing destination. The odd surprise catch in the way of species such as golden trevally are known to occur in this area. Deeper waters around these shallows are commonly inhabited by pelagic species such as tailor, mackerel and tuna when they are moving through the area.

Map 38 No. 2 Dunwich

(Bream, Trevally, Snapper, Yellowtail Kingfish)

The Dunwich shoreline is home to plenty of jetty, rock and pylon structure. This real estate attracts bream, trevally, yellowtail kingfish and snapper. The fish can be spooky here, so early or late in the day may be the best bet when setting out to catch a few. Alternatively, try using smaller lures or baits and lighter lines; there is a risk of losing the odd fish but you will ultimately get more bites.

MAP 38 NO. 3 CHAIN AND AMITY BANKS *(WHITING)*

The Rous and Rainbow channels guide the flow of water through the gap between Moreton and North Stradbroke islands. Extensive sand banks exist around these channels. The Chain Banks occupy an area to the north-west of the Rous Channel. The sand banks here are popular with whiting anglers. The edge of the Rous Channel to the east of Chain Banks is home to patchy reef structure and anglers fishing this area catch some good snapper at times. Much of the large stretch of sand between the Rous and Rainbow channels is known as Amity Banks. Like Chain Banks, this area produces plenty of whiting as well as the occasional pelagic. The Amity Banks edge adjacent to Naval Reserve Banks is well known for producing cobia when they are hunting in this part of the bay. The southern corner of the sand banks between Amity Banks and the Rainbow Channel are a good sand whiting fishing location. The area fishes particularly well on a rising tide. The north-eastern junction between Amity Banks and the Rainbow Channel forms a drop-off that hosts patchy reef structure. This ledge produces some good snapper when they are resident in the channel. The tide can move strongly through this area; fishing during slack tidal periods is recommended when targeting fish here.

MAP 38 NO. 4 RAINBOW CHANNEL
(LONGTAIL TUNA, TREVALLY, SNAPPER, TUSKFISH, WHITING, BREAM, FLATHEAD, TAILOR)

The Rainbow Channel is a major pathway via which water is exchanged between the southern bay and ocean. As such, the area is prone to strong tidal flow. The channel is also a main conduit for fish moving between the ocean and bay waters. Any available structure in the channel is often occupied by a variety of species. The shoreline between Myora and Amity fishes well for bread and butter species. The ledge that marks the edge of the Rainbow Channel produces a good mix of reef and pelagic fare. A section of the channel edge to the immediate north of Myora is known as Parrot Ledge and produces some big tuskfish for anglers that target them using baits such as crab. The middle sections of the Rainbow Channel are often occupied by longtail tuna. These fish often herd baitfish along the ledge against North Stradbroke Island. The Rainbow Channel ledge to the south of Amity is associated with strong tidal flow. Anglers fishing popper style lures over the ledge here encounter feisty giant trevally. The area is also often home to longtail tuna.

ABOVE: Tuskfish are a popular catch when fishing the Moreton Bay reef systems.

ABOVE: Sweetlip are common captures when fishing the fringe reef in Moreton Bay.

MAP 38 NO. 5 AMITY POINT
(BREAM, WHITING, FLATHEAD, LONGTAIL TUNA, TREVALLY, TAILOR)

Amity Point is a popular angling destination for boat and shorebased anglers. The area offers structure that hosts a variety of species. The near-shore sand and weed flats, rock walls and jetty structures make it a great place for bream anglers. These areas produce plenty of whiting and flathead to complement the bream catch. The Amity Rock Wall is a popular shorebased spot to chase these species. The deeper channel waters that can be located close to shore in this area attract trevally, tailor and longtail tuna. Local anglers catch plenty of squid from the near-shore structure in the area.

MAP 38 NO. 6 POINT LOOKOUT
(BREAM, WHITING, FLATHEAD, DART, TAILOR, SWEETLIP)

This area offers a good shorebased fishing location, providing the ocean swell is not too dangerous. A good mix of beach and rock fishing options can be found here. There is some access to deeper water and areas of near-shore reef. Fishing baits or spinning with metal lures from the shore produces plenty of fish here. The offshore waters immediately out from this location provide some top quality reef and pelagic fishing; it stands to reason that some good catches are to be had from shore here. Anglers will commonly tangle with bread and butter species as well as sweetlip, tailor and the odd larger pelagic such as trevally and mackerel.

PART 3

THE JUMPINPIN AND GOLD COAST

ABOVE: Evening fishing at jumpinpin. (PHOTOGRAPH BY DAVE HODGE)

The open expanses of Moreton Bay give way to more classic estuarine waters to the south. The southern reaches of the bay become a maze, choked with islands and channels that meander down towards the Jumpinpin Bar where the estuarine and bay waters meet the ocean. With its dense cluster of islands and channels, this area is locally referred to as 'The Pin'. This is the transition zone to the more open waters of the Gold Coast Broadwater. The Broadwater is a favourite playing ground for many Queenslanders and tourists and forms the foreground for the large urban dwelling of the Gold Coast and its highrise skyline. Two significant river systems, the Nerang and Coomera rivers empty into the Broadwater. The Gold Coast area also offers fishing destinations in the way of its great beaches and the small but scenic Tallebudgera and Currumbin creeks.

Many species that are available in these waters are caught all year round. That being said, the seasons do affect the quantity and size of various species that can be targeted in these waters. The species which are caught in the southern reaches of Moreton Bay are all able to be caught in the Gold Coast waters during similar stages of the season. Two species stand out when talking about fishing quality around the Gold Coast; summer fishing is particularly good for decent numbers of sizeable mangrove jack and whiting in these parts. These fish form part of the great fishing that anglers can experience in this popular location.

A vast amount of water along this part of the coastline ensures plenty of exploration for local anglers; however, the reality is, they'll never be able to fish it all extensively. Many resident anglers spend their time fishing the abundant estuary channel structures. These areas offer good fishing for bread and butter species as well as some bigger estuarine fare such as jewfish, tailor, trevally and mangrove jack. The deeper parts of the estuary, particularly those near to the mouth offer special surprises such as the odd mackerel, kingfish, tarpon, giant trevally and reef species. Understanding the effect of local seasonal and tidal variations will go a long way towards quickly providing you with success in these waters. The ensuing chapters provide you with a broad guide to fishing the Jumpinpin and Gold Coast waters that will see you catching fish in no time.

Chapter Six of this book thoroughly explores the fishing in The Pin area and provides a comprehensive guide to fishing The Broadwater, Coomera and Nerang Rivers, Tallebudgera and Currumbin Creeks and the wonderful beaches of the Gold Coast area.

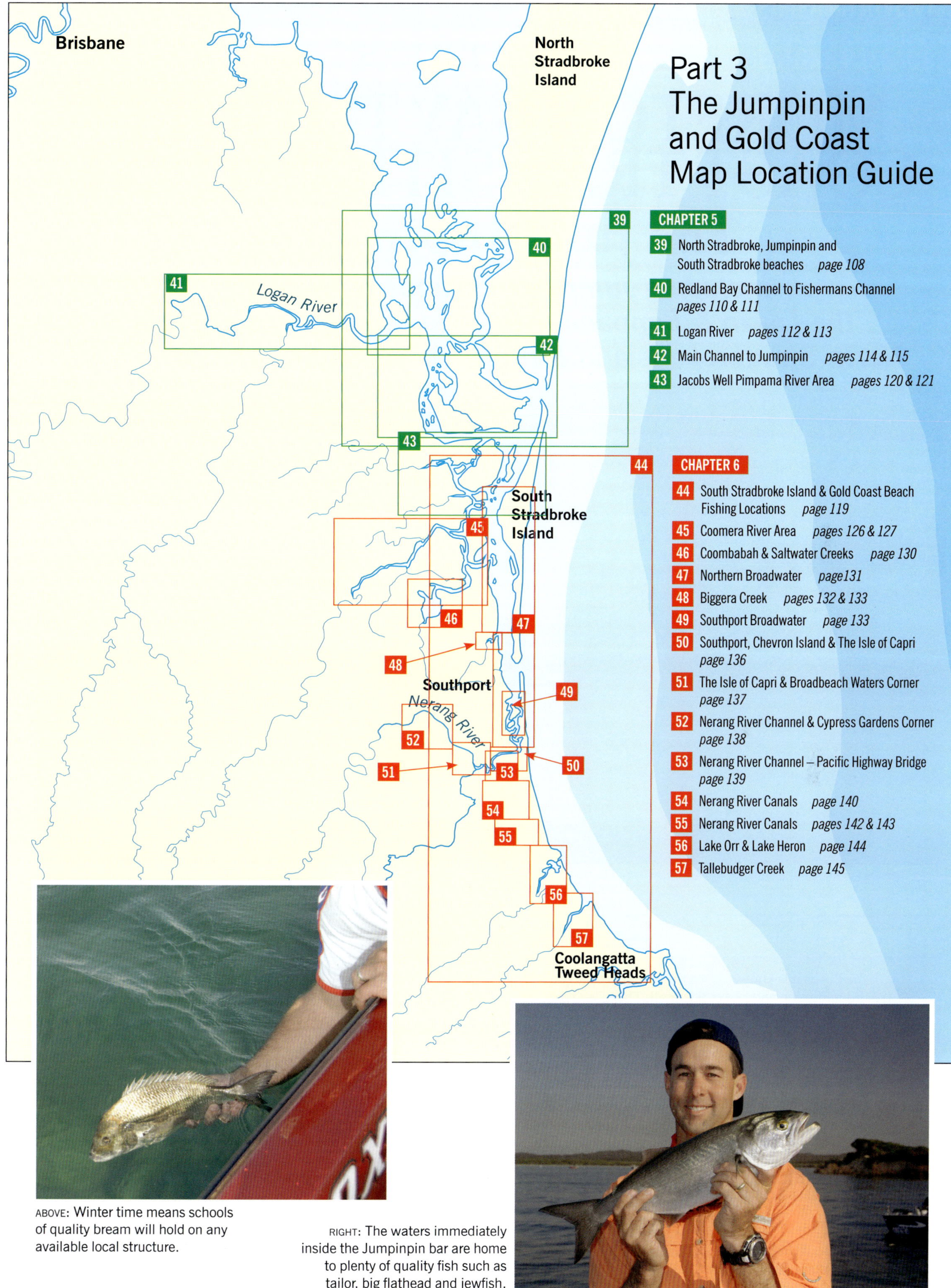

ABOVE: Winter time means schools of quality bream will hold on any available local structure.

RIGHT: The waters immediately inside the Jumpinpin bar are home to plenty of quality fish such as tailor, big flathead and jewfish.

CHAPTER 5

MORETON BAY TO GOLD COAST TRANSITION ZONE

The Jumpinpin Area

Including Jumpinpin islands & channels, the Logan & Pimpana rivers and the beaches of lower North Stradbroke Island & northern South Stradbroke Island

ABOVE: The vast waters in the Jumpinpin area offer myriad fishing opportunities for the shorebased and boating angler.

INTRODUCTION

The Pin as it is known, is such a vast area that you could spend a lifetime and never fish it all. There are rivers and creeks, flats, mangroves, deep water, coffee rock, snags, and rock bars which all hold numerous fish. Some of the more famous spots include: Kalinga Banks, entrance to Swan Bay, Short Island, Cobby Passage, Crusoe Island and Tiger Mullet Channel to name just a few. The Pin offers the chance to catch a variety of bread and butter species as well as various other reef and smaller pelagic fare. Many of these can be caught all year round. Word of warning; you can get lost here so make sure you carry a good map or GPS!

FISHING NOTES FOR JUMPINPIN AND THE GOLD COAST

WINTER: Bream school in the lower reaches to spawn from May to August. Big schools of males hang in the deeper holes waiting for the larger females to arrive. Fish the run-in tide then the first quarter of the run-out for best results. The use of a good sounder to find the schools will improve catches. Favoured baits for these fish include: whitebait, chicken gut, pilchards, yabbies, worm and tailor or tuna fillet. They bite best around the turn of the tide period and in particular, the high tide.

Flathead are an all year species with the winter months producing the majority of the school fish in the 40–50cm range. Concentrating on the shallow flats during the warmer part of the day, especially towards the top of the tide, should see a nice bag of fish. The Pin and Seaway are famous for spring time flathead. Large females congregate around the river mouths and lower parts of the estuaries and this is the place to find that trophy fish. Large females up to one metre are always a chance; these fish love large lures and baits and can turn up anywhere. Favourite local baits include live mullet, herring, prawn or pilchard and strip baits. Look for where the water funnels off the flats into deep water for your best chance of tangling with these beasts. The annual Gold Coast Flathead Classic is held in spring each year as this is the time that anglers are most likely to record some impressive captures.

Luderick are abundant in the cooler months and for the specialists, fishing the deeper snaggy banks towards the estuary mouths with floats and weed baits will score some great fish.

Jewfish (mulloway) are present all year round with the majority of fish being schoolies. It is the cooler months however that see the influx of larger adult fish into the system, feeding on the abundant schools of tailor, bream, mullet and luderick that are present. Working the slack tides will give you your best chance at catching a fish of a lifetime. Favourite local baits include live mullet, prawn, bunched sandworm and tailor, mullet and bonito strip baits. Soft plastics and a variety of hardbody and metal lures also produce many fish here each year.

Tailor school in large numbers, feeding on the abundant schools of hardyheads that also congregate around the lower reaches from May to August. Australian salmon can occasionally show up at a similar time of year and feed in the same manner as the tailor schools. Best time to target tailor is early or late in the day around the top of the tide.

Snapper in the 30 – 45 cm range are caught in various locations around The Pin, Broadwater and Seaway. These fish often hold around areas of deeper water and patchy reef and will respond well to bait and lures.

SUMMER: Mangrove jacks become increasingly active as the water starts to warm up. Jacks love snags and anywhere that holds deep water adjacent to solid structure will provide a chance to hook one. Once hooked they will power for the snags and most times will make it back before you can turn them. Don't be disappointed as this is par for the course. With persistence, a heavy drag and a bit of luck you will land the odd fish. Favourite baits include live mullet or herring. These fish will respond aggressively to a selection of lures that are presented tight against the holding positions of these fiery predators.

Whiting are present all year round but it's the summer months that see larger fish caught throughout the system. They can be caught from the shallows to the deeper holes. For the lure fishermen; shallow water fishing with poppers is the latest craze. If bait is your thing then the best baits are usually blood- or sandworms followed by yabbies (nippers), prawns and small soldier crabs that will often tempt the bigger fish. Yabbies can be pumped from the softer sandy banks throughout much of the area and are one of the top all-round baits for many of the region's bread and butter species. The building tides leading up to the new and full moons are the best times to target whiting. The Nerang River system is one of the most impressive whiting fisheries along the coast and produces several old fashioned 'elbow slappers' each summer.

Mudcrabs are targeted throughout the summer months with catches tapering off into the months of April/May.

The beaches along the Stradbroke Islands and the Gold Coast are home to plenty of bream, whiting, flathead, dart, tailor and jewfish. Clear water gutters that offer deeper water shelter near to the beach provide quality whiting, flathead and dart fishing in the summer and bream, tailor and jewfish in the winter.

FACILITIES

The Jumpinpin region is a sheltered waterway that is ideal for smaller vessels. Channel markers provide anglers with ample clues on where fish should be available as they mark deep channels for navigational purposes. Deep holes are perfect for catching bream whereas the sandbanks are better for flathead and whiting. Watch the depth of water though, especially if fishing on sandbanks during an outgoing tide. Plenty of anglers are caught out and can be stuck on sandbanks for many hours waiting for the tide to come in! The waters between the Jumpinpin and southern Moreton Bay reaches can be accessed via the bay boat ramps of Cleveland Point, Victoria Point and Redland Bay, or the ramps at Cabbage Tree Point, Jacobs Well and Diamond Head.

ABOVE: The surf zone adjacent to the Jumpinpin bar provides first class shorebased fishing for species like tailor, flathead and jewfish.

TRANSITION WATERS LOCATION GUIDE

Map 39 No. 1 North Stradbroke Island East Surf Beaches *(bream, whiting, flathead, dart, tailor)*

The North Stradbroke Island beaches offer plenty of surf fishing options. Look for near-shore gutters that will offer good summer time fishing for whiting, swallowtail dart and flathead as well as winter time tailor and bream action. Popular baits include pilchards, garfish, worms and pipis.

Map 39 No. 2 Jumpinpin Beach *(bream, whiting, flathead, dart, tailor, jewfish)*

The surf zone around the Jumpinpin bar area attracts a lot of beach species. The ready food supply moving in and out of the estuary makes this a good place to target bream, tailor, whiting, flathead and the odd jewfish. Big tailor schools will often hold just inside the wave zone at the bar. Schools of diving birds will sometimes give away their position. The big tailor schools are often shadowed by some big jewies. The start of the run-out tide is a good time to be fishing here.

Map 39 No. 3 South Stradbroke Beach *(bream, whiting, flathead, dart, tailor, jewfish)*

Cleaner water gutters found near to shore offer good fishing for bream, whiting, dart, flathead, tailor and jewfish. Low light periods of the day that coincide with the top of the tide produce good results. The area adjacent to The Bedrooms is a popular spot with local beach fishing anglers. Garfish baits fished in deeper water gutters produce some huge tailor here each year whilst big strip baits of tailor and bonito account for big jewfish when they are stalking the beaches. Beach anglers will find schools of larger pelagics moving near to the beach on rare occasions. Schools of spotted and school mackerel will chase baitfish close to the beach and can occasionally be targeted with metal slugs. A good cast followed by a high speed retrieve is usually required.

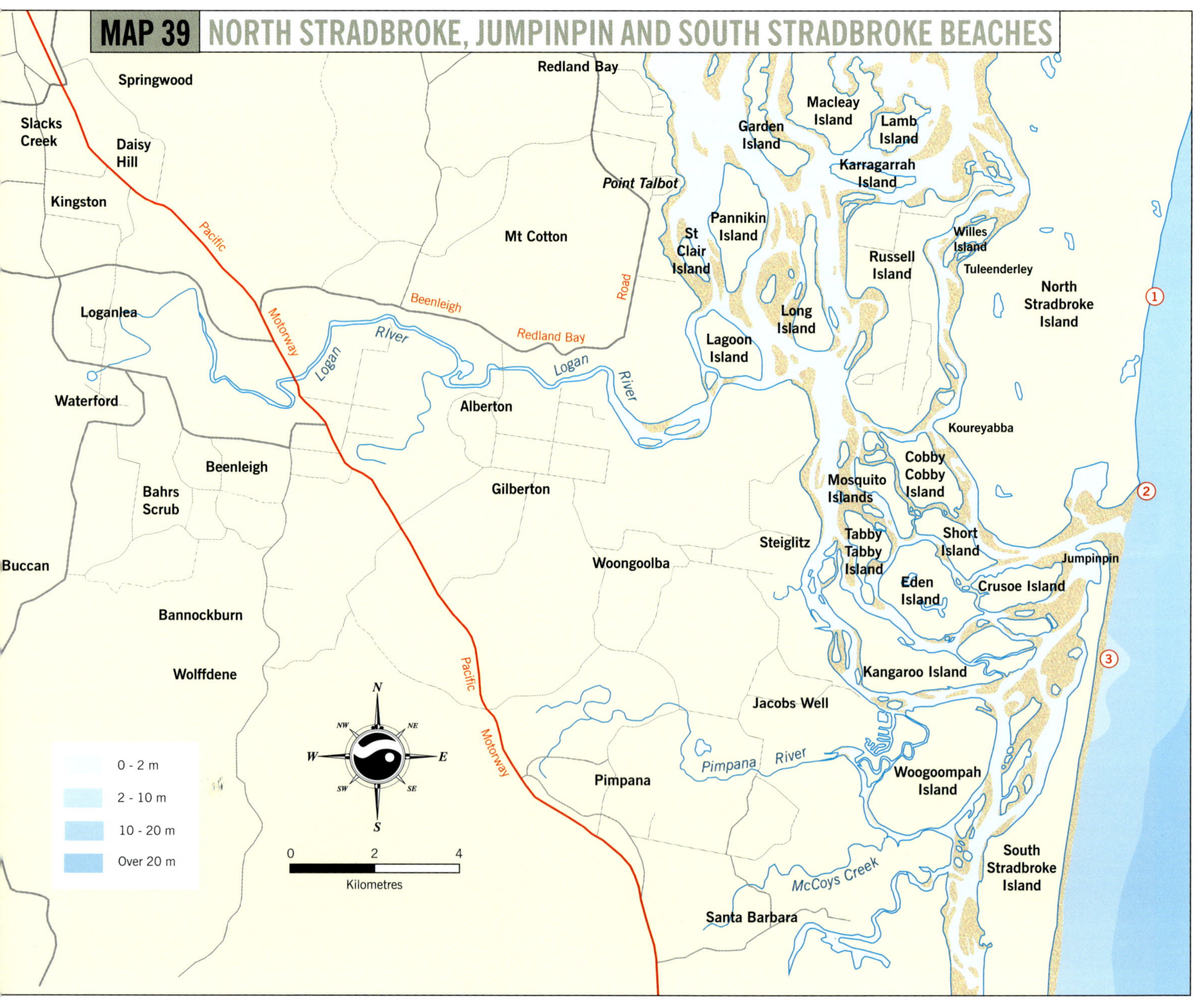

MAP 40 NO. 1 REDLAND BAY CHANNEL
(BREAM, WHITING, FLATHEAD, CRABS)

The Redland Bay Channel runs into the Logan River through the waters between St. Clair and Pannikin islands. The shallow water that lies adjacent to deeper channels fish well for bream and whiting on a building tide. This is a popular place to retrieve surface and shallow diving hardbody lures for these species. These deeper locations will also produce flathead on run-out and building tides.

MAP 40 NO. 2 GARDEN AND LONG ISLANDS JUNCTION
(BREAM, WHITING, FLATHEAD, CRABS)

The channel is highlighted here by a number of markers. The flats fish well for bream and whiting on a building tide as do the base of the channel markers as the tide starts to ebb. Shallow diving hardbody lures fished across the flats and blade and soft plastics cast around the channel markers will produce fish. Baits and sinking lures fished in the channel will provide flathead for anglers. The area is also a popular crab spot.

MAP 40 NO. 3 KARRAGARRA ISLAND
(BREAM, WHITING, FLATHEAD)

Karragarra Island provides similar fishing options as those found at nearby Macleay and Lamb islands. The mud and rocky shorelines that are lined by mangroves fish well for bread and butter species. Scattered rocks and channels etched into the muddy shoreline shallows attract bream, whiting and flathead as the tidal water pushes up towards the mangroves. A tour at low tide will highlight the areas that should be targeted during the building tide. Productive rock shorelines can be found on the south-west corner and middle of the northern shoreline. The northern shoreline hosts plenty of moored boats and the shade beneath these hulls often holds good numbers of bream.

The channel between Karragarra and Russell Islands fishes well for flathead and prawns whilst the shorelines along Russell Island in this area fish well for bream and whiting. The shoreline adjacent to the moored boats near High Street fishes well for flathead, bream and whiting.

MAP 40 NO. 4 CANAIPA POINT AND OONCOONCOO BAY
(BREAM, WHITING, FLATHEAD, JEWFISH)

The north-eastern corner of Russell Island is host to deeper channel waters that rise to shallow mangrove flats. The tidal waters moving past this area divide to move through either the Canaipa or Main Channels. The shallows around Canaipa Point and Ooncooncoo Bay produce bream and whiting for anglers that fish up into the shallows with the rising tide. The high tide masks several channels that cut through the sand and mud bottom; resident fish use these channels during a rising tide to access shallow water feeding grounds. A bigger channel cuts through the shallow mangroves and runs parallel to Canaipa Point. This forms a prominent feeding pathway. Flathead, bream and whiting are all caught in proximity to this location.

Kibbinkibbinwa Point is a rocky peninsular that juts into a deep near-shore channel. The deeper waters produce flathead and jewfish for anglers that fish live bait around the turn of the tide and the new and full moon phases.

MAP 40 NO. 5 CANAIPA PASSAGE – RUSSELL ISLAND STRETCH *(BREAM, WHITING, FLATHEAD, JEWFISH)*

The northern reaches of Canaipa Passage separate Russell Island from North Stradbroke Island. The channel cuts through islands and mangrove lined shorelines and provides a wealth of fishing opportunity. Steeper eastern banks make this a sheltered location to fish when easterly winds are blowing. The shoreline structures include shallow sand, mud and weed flats, timber, rock, jetty and moored boat features. These attract a variety of species. The channel water depths fluctuate and any areas that offer deeper water in proximity to structure will hold fish such as flathead and jewfish. The channel waters around Willis and Double islands are well known for producing some good catches of flathead and the odd jewie. The shallows around Double Island produce flathead, whiting and bream. The Willis Island shallows are protected by Marine Park Green Zone so keep away from these areas. Drifting the channel waters with bait or jigged soft plastic and blade lures is a good strategy for covering water and getting bites from local flathead and jewfish. Target the deeper corners around the channel and sandbank corners. The current is deflected in such areas and makes for an ideal location for larger predators to shelter and ambush prey. The shoreline adjacent to Barcelona Terrace on Russell Island supports a busy boat mooring facility. The area holds plenty of structure to attract bream, trevally and the odd mangrove jack.

MAP 40 NO. 6 MAIN CHANNEL – NORTH RUSSELL ISLAND STRETCH
(BREAM, WHITING, FLATHEAD, JEWFISH, SNAPPER, CRABS)

The top of Main Channel runs between Russell and Long islands. The shallow banks along the edges of Russell Island produce bream and whiting on a rising tide. The water is relatively clean around the high tide in this area; it becomes increasingly turbid through the run-out stages. The channel will produce a few flathead during the run-out however local anglers that regularly fish here spend most of their time targeting the run-in tide. The most notable structure in this area of Main Channel includes Giants Grave. The peninsular at the northern end of Browns Bay transects the deeper channel that runs into the bay. The tip of the peninsular is home to some chunky rock structure and it is this area that most locals refer to as Giants Grave. The combination of some deeper water and shoreline rocks make this a popular spot from which to target bream, squire sized snapper, flathead and the odd jewie. Lures fished tight against the shoreline structure produce some quality bream at times. Live bait fished along the drop-off to the channel produces some good jewfish and flathead during the periods around the turn of the tide. The waters out from the lower reaches of Long Island are a popular spot to throw a cast net for prawns in summer. This also makes them a popular bait to use in the vicinity. A note of warning to anglers choosing to fish this stretch of water in smaller vessels; a strong southerly wind combined with a run-out tide can make this area very dangerous. Large standing waves can meet boaters that get caught in a change of weather.

MAP 40 NO. 7 MAIN CHANNEL – ROCKY POINT
(BREAM, SNAPPER, FLATHEAD, WHITING, JEWFISH, TAILOR, TREVALLY, MANGROVE JACK, MOSES PERCH)

The Main Channel around Rocky Point hosts a range of different structure and as such, a variety of piscatorial species. The area forms the junction between the Main Channel and Logan River waters. It is home to extensive sand, mud and weed flats and some solid channel structure. The area features some solid pylon structures that support the powerline crossing to Russell Island. Locals often refer to this location as The Powerlines. The pylons sit in deeper channel waters and are immediately adjacent to the rocky and shallow channel corner that is known as Rocky Point. With all of their available structure, the deeper channel waters attract plenty of fish. Boats are often anchored here, and anglers fishing with bait encounter flathead, jewfish, snapper, mangrove jack, tailor, trevally and moses perch. Positioning live or dead bait close to rock or pylon structure often tempts the bigger predators. Smaller baits fished in the channel during winter are responsible for catching good numbers of diver whiting.

The shallow rock structures around Rocky Point are a haven for bream, snapper, sand whiting and flathead. This is a popular destination for lure anglers targeting these species. Bumping the rock with hardbody and soft plastic lures is a good strategy for getting bites here. Targeting the deeper outer edges of the drop-off around the rocks with lures produces flathead, jewies and jacks. This is a popular area to troll larger and deep diving hardbody lures for bigger fish. The tide can flow furiously through this area at times, and anglers targeting fish in deeper water will find that fishing the turn-of-tide periods is a lot easier and more productive. The area can become dangerous for smaller vessels when wind and tide are opposed or large vessels throw significant wake as they pass through.

MAP 40 NO. 8 RUSSELL AND COBBY COBBY ISLAND CHANNEL

(BREAM, FLATHEAD, WHITING, JEWFISH, TAILOR, TREVALLY, LUDERICK, MANGROVE JACK)

This channel is referred to locally as Fishermans Channel or Cobby Passage and separates Russell and Cobby Cobby islands. Marine Park Green Zone designation prohibits fishing in much of the shallows around Cobby Cobby Island. The junction of Main Channel and Fishermans Channel is characterised by extensive shallow sand and weeded flats. A tightly marked channel must be followed to prevent boats becoming stuck on these shallows. This area is a haven for sand whiting, bream and flathead. It is a popular location to cast baits of worm, yabby and prawn around the top of the tide. Targeting the channel waters here with soft plastics and diving hardbody lures provides good catches of flathead and bream.

The channel into the western entrance of Fishermans Channel is marked with four red and three green channel markers. The two western red channel markers are located in the area known as Flat Rock. The spot is well known for good catches of bream, squire sized snapper, flathead, jewfish and lesser trevally and tailor. Anglers targeting the deeper water in the area with bait and lures produce some quality fish here. Trolling along the edges of the channel is a popular approach in this location and along much of the southern Russell Island shoreline. The channel cuts along a deep bank on the south-eastern corner of Russell Island. The shoreline is littered with coffee rock and timber here which makes it easy to locate. The ledge is a prime place to target winter luderick, schooled bream as well as the odd school jewfish and big flathead. Drifting a weed bait suspended under a float is the most effective way to catch luderick when they are schooled up here. The tide pushes hard through this location; anglers are best served to fish around the turn of the tide periods as the water starts to build velocity. This is when the resident fish are most likely to bite. The gutter on the opposite side of the channel runs alongside Oak Island. The shallows are occupied by Marine Park Green Zone here but the deeper water often holds a few flathead and bream. If you are fishing in the area, it is well worth a look here.

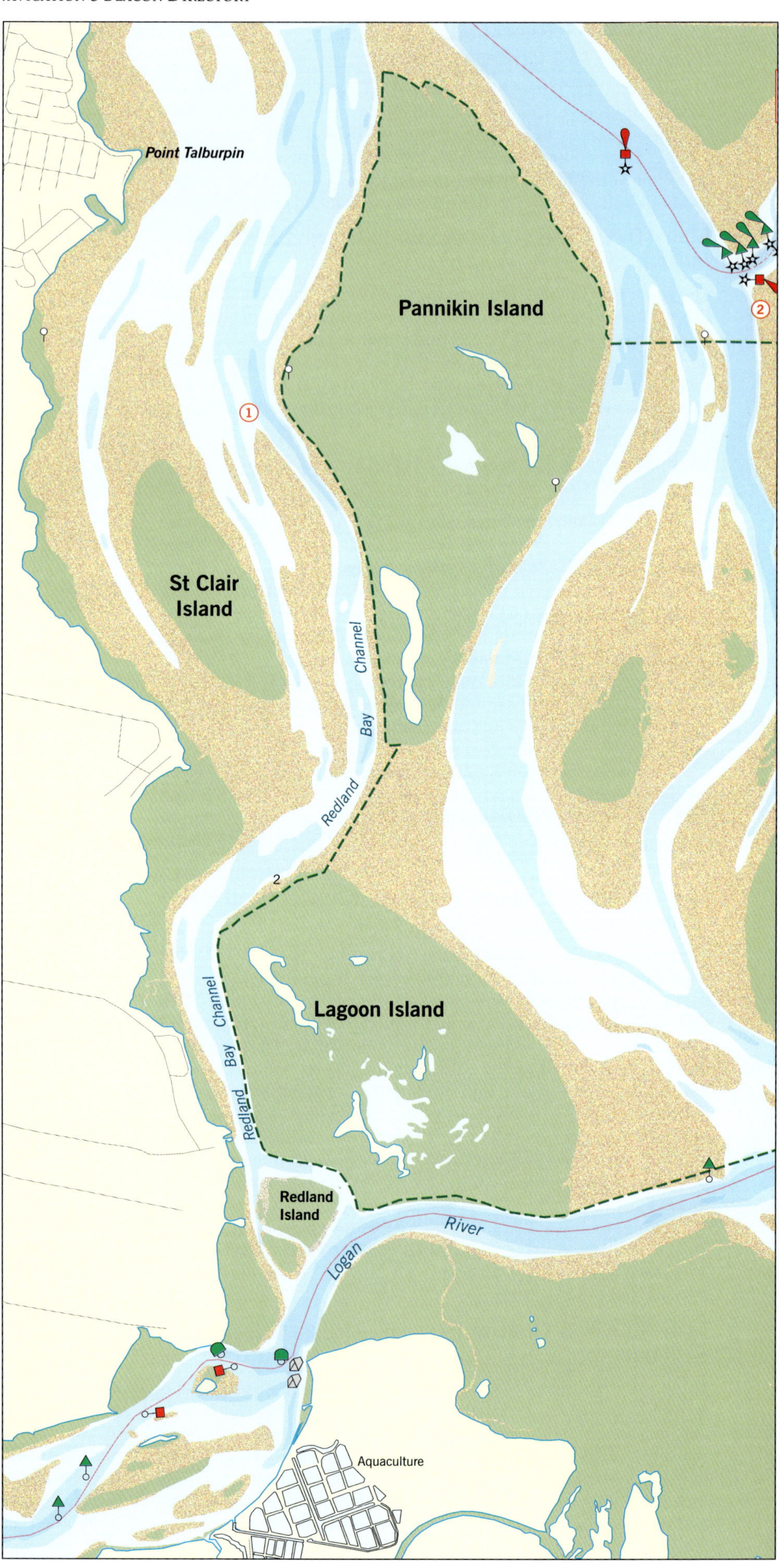

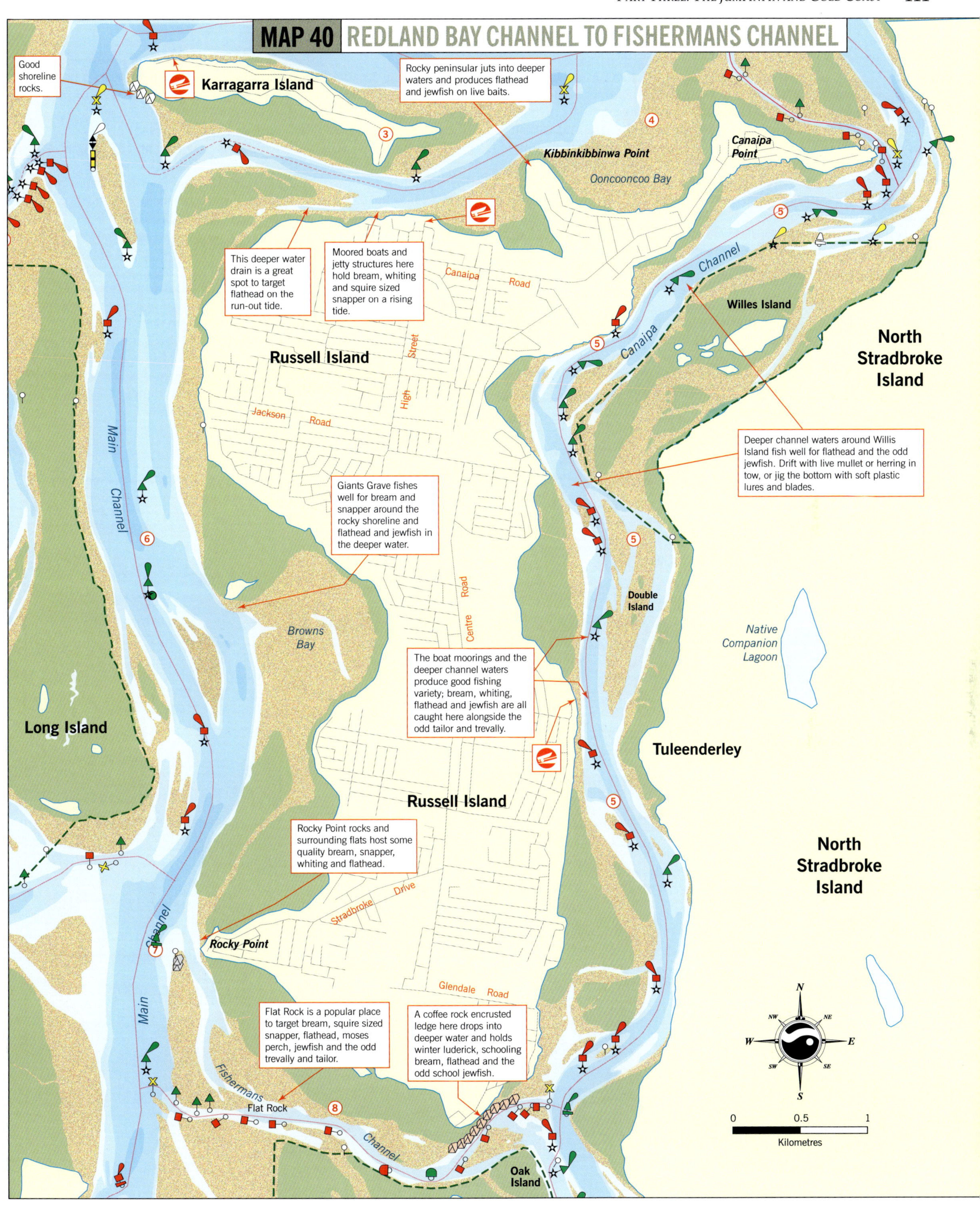
MAP 40 REDLAND BAY CHANNEL TO FISHERMANS CHANNEL
Good shoreline rocks.
Karragarra Island
Rocky peninsular juts into deeper waters and produces flathead and jewfish on live baits.
Kibbinkibbinwa Point
Ooncooncoo Bay
Canaipa Point
This deeper water drain is a great spot to target flathead on the run-out tide.
Moored boats and jetty structures here hold bream, whiting and squire sized snapper on a rising tide.
Canaipa Road
Canaipa Channel
Willes Island
North Stradbroke Island
Russell Island
High Street
Jackson Road
Main Channel
Deeper channel waters around Willis Island fish well for flathead and the odd jewfish. Drift with live mullet or herring in tow, or jig the bottom with soft plastic lures and blades.
Giants Grave fishes well for bream and snapper around the rocky shoreline and flathead and jewfish in the deeper water.
Double Island
Browns Bay
Centre Road
Native Companion Lagoon
The boat moorings and the deeper channel waters produce good fishing variety; bream, whiting, flathead and jewfish are all caught here alongside the odd tailor and trevally.
Long Island
Tuleenderley
Russell Island
North Stradbroke Island
Rocky Point rocks and surrounding flats host some quality bream, snapper, whiting and flathead.
Stradbroke Drive
Rocky Point
Glendale Road
Flat Rock is a popular place to target bream, squire sized snapper, flathead, moses perch, jewfish and the odd trevally and tailor.
A coffee rock encrusted ledge here drops into deeper water and holds winter luderick, schooling bream, flathead and the odd school jewfish.
Fishermans Channel
Flat Rock
Oak Island
N NE E SE S SW W NW
0 0.5 1
Kilometres

LOGAN RIVER LOCATION GUIDE

The Logan River is a popular fishing destination amongst many locals; however, it is sometimes avoided by Brisbane and Gold Coast anglers because it looks dirty at times. It is well known for sustaining good bull shark and catfish populations, but it also offers some good fishing for various other sought after species. The majority of local anglers spend most of their time fishing the area from Pitts Rocks to the mouth of the system. It is often found that good amounts of rain result in fish pushing out of the river for a short period before returning. Don't let the sometimes murky coloured waters fool you though; this system is good at trying to disguise some really good fishing options.

MAP 41 NO. 1 LOGAN RIVER MOUTH FLATS
(WHITING, BREAM, CRABS)

The shallow flats to the south of the Logan River mouth produce some good whiting catches each summer. Baits of bloodworm, sandworm, yabby and prawn produce some good fish on a building tide. The high tide stages three to four days around the new and full moon phases seem to produce the best results.

MAP 41 NO. 2 MARKS ROCKS *(BREAM, JEWFISH, FLATHEAD, MANGROVE JACK, THREADFIN SALMON, SHARKS)*

A rocky ledge drops into deep water along this corner of the river and is a popular location amongst local bait anglers. The tide can run very hard through the area; fishing is made easier and more effective during smaller tides and the turn of the tide periods. Live bait of herring, mullet and prawn, or flesh baits of tailor, mullet and bonito are often used here to tempt jewfish, mangrove jack, flathead, sharks, the odd cod and sometimes threadfin salmon. The deeper water is often home to schools of winter bream. Deeply fished soft plastics, blades and baits of mullet and chicken gut will bring these fish undone. The shallow rocky shorelines fish well for bream and flathead on lures. This is a popular place to cast surface lures when the prawns are active through the area.

MAP 41 NO. 3 SHALLOW BEND ROCKS
(BREAM, WHITING, FLATHEAD, CRABS)

The bank opposite Marks Rocks is home to a shallow rocky corner. Bream use this area to feed when the tide pushes new water up and over the rocks. Drifting in the deeper water and retrieving shallow diving hardbody lures produces some good bream here. The deeper hole immediately up-river of this corner holds schools of winter bream and luderick at times. The shoreline and island banks in this area have produced some quality flathead for anglers fishing away from the sometimes crowded Marks Rocks area.

MAP 41 NO. 4 AGESTON SANDS
(BREAM, WHITING, FLATHEAD, CRABS)

The corner of the river to the north of the channel markers consists of an extensive sand bank. The channel and sand shallows are very

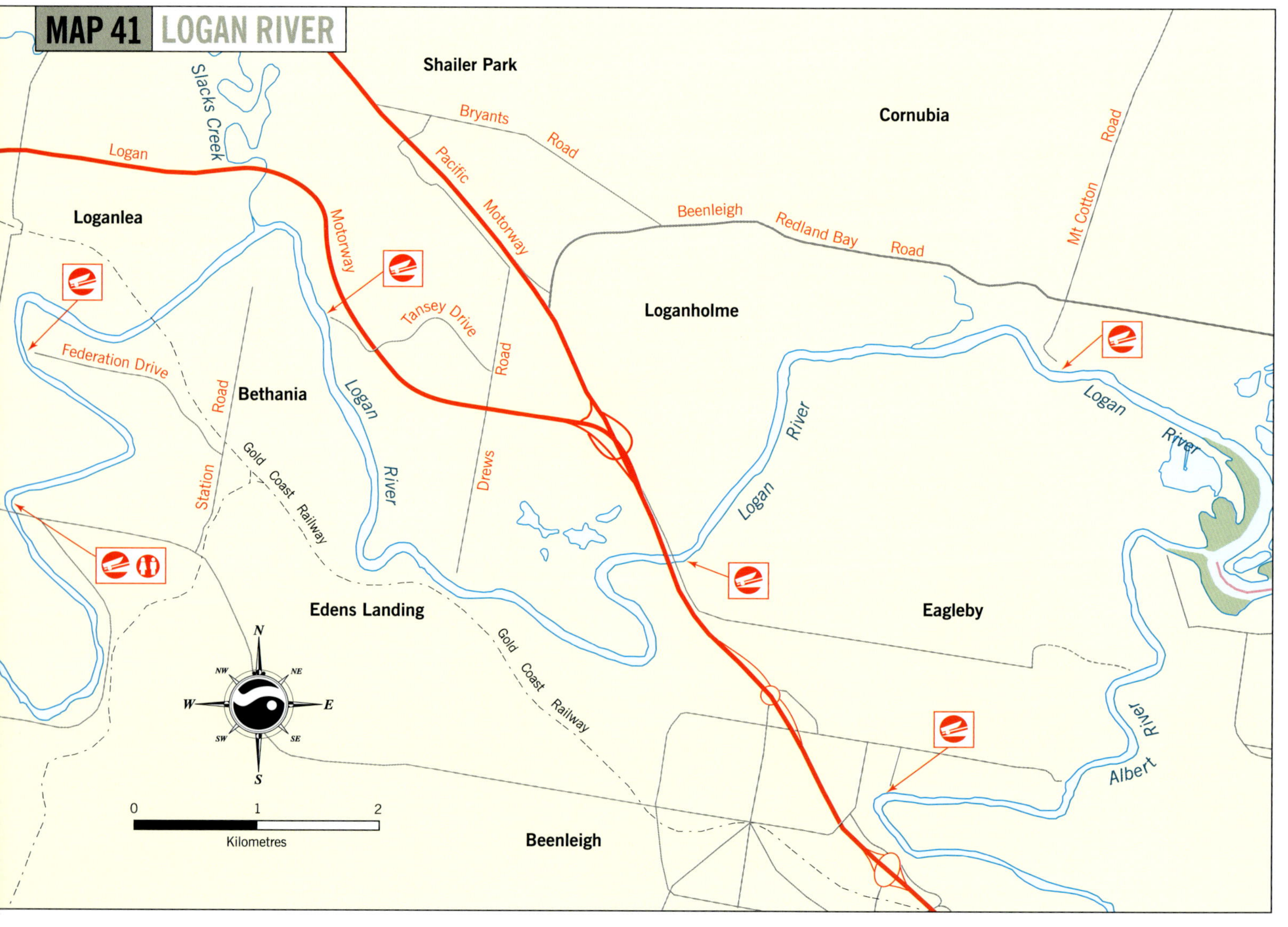

popular spots to target whiting and lesser bream and flathead. Anglers anchoring and fishing with worm, yabby and prawn baits fare well on tasty summer whiting here. The channel and markers produce flathead and bream.

MAP 41 NO. 5 PITTS ROCKS
(BREAM, WHITING, FLATHEAD, CRABS)

The shoreline of the channel in this area is home to rocky structure. The rocks and deeper channel waters hold bream, flathead, mangrove jack and the odd jewfish. This is a popular location to drift and retrieve lures around the deeper structures. Anglers choosing to anchor and fish live bait close to the rocks and deeper water will also tempt local predators.

MAP 41 NO. 6 THE ELBOW TO THE JUNCTION
(BREAM, WHITING, FLATHEAD, CRABS)

The channel becomes more turbid in this area and the banks are lined with mud and sand foreshores. This area and the channel up-river towards the junction of the Logan and Albert rivers produce whiting, the odd jewfish and plenty of sharks. The waters below The Junction are known for producing whiting, and lesser flathead and jewfish.

MAP 42 NO. 1 MAIN CHANNEL – LITTLE ROCKY POINT
(BREAM, SNAPPER, FLATHEAD, WHITING, JEWFISH, TAILOR, TREVALLY, MANGROVE JACK, MOSES PERCH)

The location offers similar fishing prospects to Rocky Point to the north. The local prawn farm outflow does plenty to attract local predators to the area. A small protruding peninsular sits adjacent to a rocky ledge and patches of shoreline rock are scattered throughout the mud and weeded shoreline. The area is marked by a red beacon as the rocks here can quickly damage a boat travelling across the shallows whilst the outer edge of the rock drops into deeper water in the vicinity of the red beacon. The ledge produces bream, snapper, flathead, moses perch and the odd jewie and jack. The location fishes best when bait is holding up against the rocks. Deep jigging lures such as soft plastics and blades in this area produces some good fish. Drifting the shoreline around Little Rocky Point allows the angler to cast lures across the scattered shoreline rocks. Soft plastic lures and hardbody offerings tempt bream, flathead and snapper that feed tight against the rocks. The immediate northern edge of the shoreline rocks drop into a deeper gutter. This gutter holds some good flathead and bream at times. It fishes best on the run-in tide. The shallow flats either side of Little Rocky Point fish well for bream and whiting on a building tide. Small structures such as lone pieces of timber lying across the flats will hold fish once water has filled the shallows.

MAP 42 NO. 2 MOSQUITO ISLAND FLATS
(WHITING, BREAM, FLATHEAD)

Mosquito Island Flats are an extensive area of sand, mud and weeded shallows that are cut by several channels. The entire area fishes well for whiting, bream and flathead when it has a good covering of water. Drifting across it and casting lures is a popular approach. Local flathead anglers troll shallow diving bibbed hardbody lures that produce some very big flathead each spring.

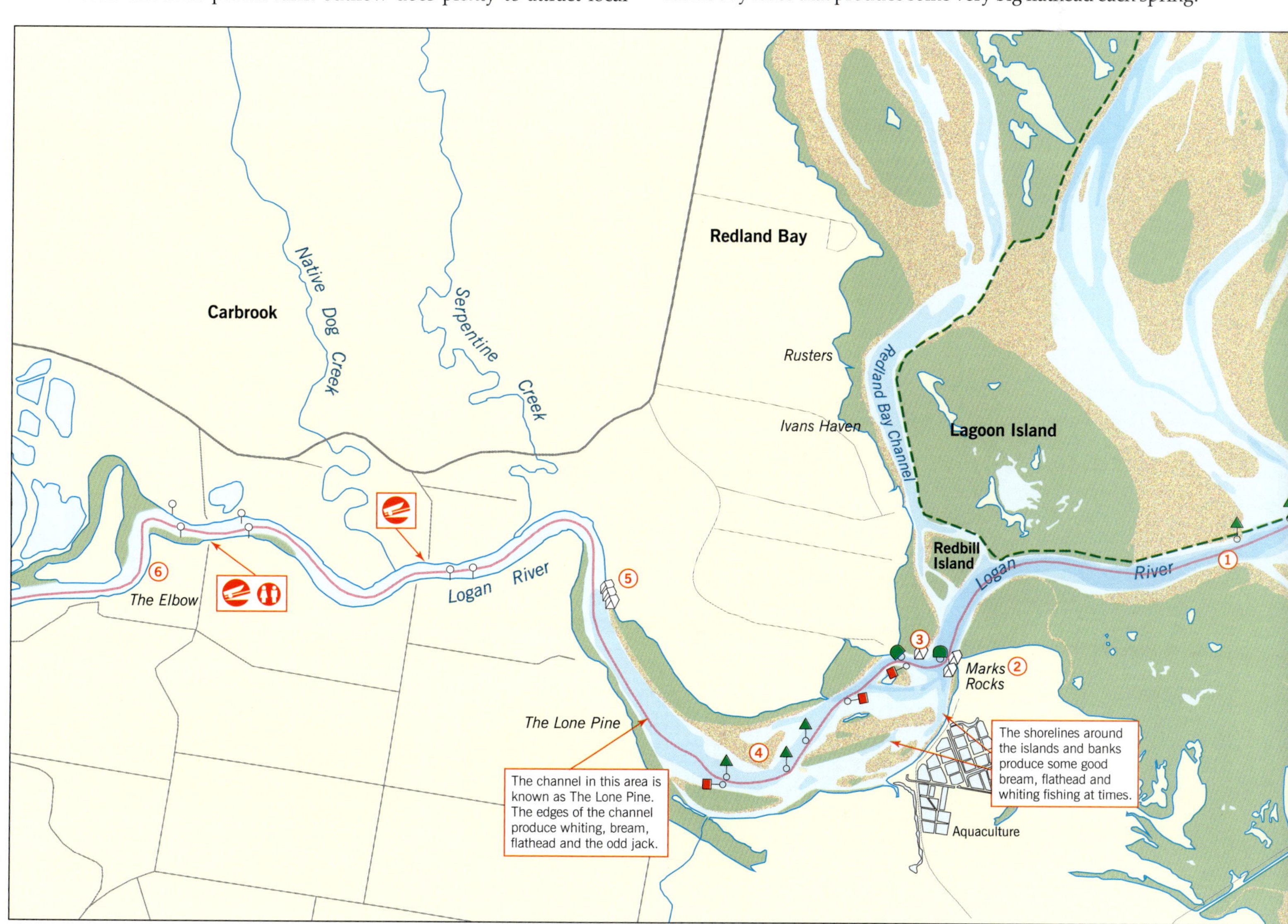

Logan River
CAUTION – these waterways may contain submerged flood debris. Navigate with caution.
Marks Rocks
Main Channel
Russell Island
Fishermans Channel
Flat Rock
Oak Island
Little Rocky Point
1
2
2
Cobby Cobby Island
Cobby Passage
Mosquito Islands
5
Rocky Point Road
Holmstead Road
Aquaculture
The channel forms deeper water here and often holds good flathead on the run-out tide.
Cabbage Tree Point
Point Road
Cabbage Tree
Tabby Tabby Island
Steiglitz
10
Walkers Jetty
8
Road
Point
Cabbage Tree
10
Jacobs Well Road
Meridien Marinas Horizon Shores
Good shoreline fishing.
Eden Island
11
Woongoolba
Behm Creek
Limit of navigation
Behm Creek
Deeper water.
The mouth of Behm Creek is a renowned producer of flathead during the early and late stages of the run-out tide.
Kangaroo Island
11
Good bankside structure on both margins.

MAP 42 MAIN CHANNEL TO JUMPINPIN

An angler casts lures at Little Rocky Point.

BELOW: Flathead love holding along channel edge drop-offs.

A kayak angler chases schooling tailor and mackerel behind the surf zone at Jumpinpin.

Map 42 No. 3 Canaipa Passage – Slipping Sands *(Bream, Flathead, Whiting, Jewfish, Tailor, Trevally, Luderick, Mangrove Jack)*

The Canaipa Channel runs between Cobby Cobby Island and Slipping Sands in this area. The shallow shoreline on the edge of Cobby Cobby Island is protected by Marine Park Green Zone. Deeper waters on either side of the channel hold some good fish throughout the area. In particular, those banks that offer snag and patchy reef structure, hold bream, flathead, jewies and the odd mangrove jack. Live baits fished tight against these structures produce some good fish, as does drifting likely looking sections whilst retrieving lures. Trolling the channel with lures kept close to any available structure is always a good option here. The eastern bank of Cobby Cobby Island is host to deeper water with several submerged snags positioned along the bank. The area holds good bream, jacks, the occasional jewfish and sometimes schools of luderick in winter. A deeper hole wraps the point directly opposite the junction between Fishermans Channel and Canaipa Channel. Live bait fished in this hole around the start of the run-out tide has produced many a big flathead and jewfish. The shallow sandbanks found within the channel usually have some good whiting searching for food around the high tide stage.

Map 4 No. 4 Canaipa Passage – Cobby Passage Junction *(Bream, Flathead, Whiting, Jewfish, Tailor, Trevally, Luderick, Mangrove Jack)*

The junction of the Canaipa and Cobby Passages has a variety of fishing options on offer. Broad sand and weeded flats can be found at the south-eastern point of Cobby Cobby Island. The shallows are a great place to drift with lures to target bream, whiting and flathead. Local guide Brad Smith speaks fondly of this location, experiencing plenty of good sessions here. The odd piece of submerged timber strewn across this flat is renowned for attracting good numbers of bream. The shoreline shallows in this area are Green Zone so stay well away.

Above: Drifting the channel edges in this area of the Pin will mean you cross paths with plenty of flathead.

The bank immediately to the east of the Cobby Cobby Island corner is a great ledge to fish; it drops into deeper water, has plenty of submerged timber lining the bank and contains some nasty bottom rock structure. This is a great bank to drift or anchor along whilst dropping live and dead baits on the available structure. Drifting or trolling the bank and ensuring hard and soft lures are positioned tight against structure will produce some solid hook-ups here. The bank holds bream, flathead, big jewfish and jacks as well as pelagic fare such as tailor, trevally and salmon when they are moving through the area. Thick luderick schools are also common here in winter. Popular approaches include fishing live mullet, herring and prawn baits around the turn of the tide. The low light hours of the day, prior to boat traffic increasing in the area, produce some quality fish here.

Map 42 No. 5 Cobby Cobby Island and Mosquito Island Channel *(Bream, Flathead, Whiting, Jewfish, Tailor, Trevally, Luderick, Mangrove Jack)*

Locally known as Cobby Passage or Little Cobby Passage, this channel intersects plenty of very fishy structure as it weaves between Cobby Cobby and Mosquito Islands. A deeper hole can be found off the south-eastern corner of Cobby Cobby Island. This occurs just prior to Cobby Passage meeting the Canaipa Passage waters. This location produces good numbers of flathead at times as they school up and await passing food. The spot fishes well at the top and bottom of the tide. A small island is located in the middle of Cobby Passage. The western corner of this island marks the location of a rockbar that traverses the channel. Navigation through this area needs to be completed with caution. The adjacent bank of Cobby Cobby Island contains shoreline rock structures which make it easy to identify the approximate position of the rockbar. The water to the immediate east of the rockbar drops into deeper water and the entire area attracts plenty of fish. The shallow rocks are a great place to retrieve a variety of lures for bream, jacks, trevally and tailor. Baits of yabby and prawn are often productive here around the high tide stage. The deeper water often holds bait and in turn, a large variety of predators. Bream, flathead, tailor, jewfish, jacks and trevally are all caught through this area on a regular basis. Deeply worked lures and baits of live mullet, herring, prawn or dead pilchard and strip bait should produce results. Luderick are also caught through some of the deeper waters here.

The area can suffer an influx of drifting weed at various stages of the year. In the event that the channel is found full of the annoying brown weed, it is often best to move elsewhere. The western parts of the channel provide plenty of options for flathead along the drop-off and bream and whiting in the shallows. Targeting the channel waters here with soft plastics and diving hardbody lures provides good catches of flathead and bream. This type of fishing opportunity extends across the shallow flats to the west of Cobby and Mosquito islands. This area is responsible for plenty of huge flathead captures over the years. Many of these are caught on lures while drift fishing or trolling through the sometimes shallow waters.

Map 42 No. 6 Short Island South-Eastern Junction *(Bream, Flathead, Jewfish, Tailor, Trevally, Luderick, Mangrove Jack)*

The south-eastern corner of Short Island is central to two great fishing banks. The lower eastern shoreline is largely lined with mangroves and hosts a near-shore vertical ledge; the ledge drops into deeper water that is home to myriad submerged snags. Anglers drifting along this bank will often see bream and luderick flashing as they roll amongst the snags. At the base of these snags and the ledge, larger species such as mangrove jack, flathead and jewfish will take up prime ambush stations. The deep hole immediately off the south-eastern corner of Short Island is a well-known jewfish location. The tide pushes hard through these areas at times, making it difficult to present lures and baits to resident fish; targeting the area during minimal periods of tidal flow is a good option. This is a popular location for anglers fishing with soft plastics. An effective approach when using these lures is to cast against the shoreline and then let it sink into deeper water as the current drives the boat; progressively jigging the lure down the face of the ledge means fish throughout the area will get a good look at it. This is a proven way of catching fish along many of The Pin ledges. Soft plastics in the 2–5 inch size range are a good choice in this area.

The water to the north of the deeper ledge accommodates anglers that wish to camp. The area is known locally as 'The Huts'. The shoreline waters near The Huts are not as deep as those to the south, but there are several big trees lying along the bottom of the channel. These structures are found in 2–4m of water and usually hold good bream, flathead and mangrove jack.

The southern bank of Short Island faces Crusoe Island and contains a steeper drop-off in the vicinity of the corner. Here, the deeper water offers similar fishing options to the bank on the eastern side of the island. The bank produces some quality bream, flathead and jewfish.

Map 42 No. 7 Short and Eden Islands Channel
(bream, flathead, whiting, jewfish, mangrove jack)

The channel between Short and Eden islands offers some good edge-of-channel fishing. There are plenty of banks to fish in the area and many of them are productive. One of the more productive sections of bank is found against the outer corner of the channel where it turns around the northern tip of Eden Island. The bank hosts a steeper ledge that contains submerged snag structures which usually holds a few good bream and flathead. Anglers fishing here report the occasional school jewfish and jack. The shallow banks throughout the channel fish well for whiting on a summer rising tide.

Map 42 No. 8 Tabby Tabby Island
(bream, flathead, whiting)

Tabby Tabby Island sits amongst a wealth of shallow flats. The flats contain sand, mud and weeded shallows that are occasionally dissected by deeper channels. The flats to the south of the island are well known for producing some larger summer whiting and high tides around the new and full moon phases will produce these fish when using baits of worm, yabby or prawn. The channels provide good fishing for flathead and bream. The best channel spots to target fish include those that traverse the north-east and western sides of the island.

Map 42 No. 9 McKenzies Channel
(bream, flathead, whiting)

The junction of McKenzies Channel and the Crusoe and Short islands channel typically holds bream, flathead and whiting. Sections of shoreline channel can be found in conjunction with fallen timber structures. As the tide starts to push water through this area, the local fish start to become active. Some quality fish can be caught very close to shore here.

Map 42 No. 10 Steiglitz Channel; Cabbage Tree Point – Jacobs Well *(bream, flathead, whiting)*

Serviced by a quality boat ramp, the channel that runs through this area produces many bread and butter species every year. The shallows adjacent to Cabbage Tree Point fish well for whiting and bream. Where the shallows drop into deeper channel waters, good flathead fishing can be encountered. The odd squire sized snapper, tailor, trevally and mangrove jack can also be caught here. The channel to the south of Cabbage Tree Point is a 6 knot zone and is home to plenty of jetty and boat mooring structure. Due to this, the area offers fishing options for the landbased, kayak and boat angler. The local structure is home to plenty of bream, flathead and lesser jacks. The rock wall sections along the western shoreline fish well for all of these species. The eastern shoreline of the channel

ABOVE: The channel ledges and shallow flats provide some hectic bream fishing at times.

has some great structure and targeting fallen timber and deeper shoreline water during the high tide produces some chunky bream, flathead and whiting. The mouth of Behm Creek is a renowned producer of flathead during the early and late stages of the run-out tide. The banks directly opposite Behm Creek produce good bream and whiting on hardbody lures during the last 2 hours of the building tide. The channel markers throughout the area usually hold a few bream schooled at the base of these structures.

Map 42 No. 11 Eden and Kangaroo Islands Channel
(bream, flathead, whiting, mangrove jack, jewfish)

The channel between Eden and Kangaroo islands offers good deeper water channel fishing. It is often surprising how few boats are seen fishing in this area compared to the other areas around The Pin. The shoreline corner bank on Kangaroo Island immediately to the south of Tabby Tabby Island is home to deep near-shore water. The availability of some good shoreline structure means it attracts some good fish. Lure and bait anglers catch good bream, flathead, jewfish and jacks here. The shallows on the Tabby Tabby Island side of the channel are a good location to chase a few whiting. Immediately to the east of the Tabby Tabby Island shallows and adjacent to the mid-point of Eden Island is a good fishing bank. The bank runs tight against the Eden Island shoreline and forms a deeper hole in this location. The spot produces flathead and jewies for anglers fishing baits at anchor. Drifting and casting soft plastics and hardbody lures against the bank will tempt local bream, flathead and jewfish. The section of channel that runs around the southern corner of Eden Island offers a good stretch of bankside fishing. The channel that wraps the southern corner of Eden Island offers good fishing prospects. The bank that lies alongside Kangaroo Island hosts a near-shore ledge with plenty of available structure to attract and hold local predators. Drifting, trolling or anchoring and fishing with live and dead baits produces bream, flathead and the odd jewie and jack. The northern bank of the small island that sits to the south of Eden Island is a great spot for chasing bream and flathead. The deeper snags invariably hold the odd jack or two here as well.

Map 42 No. 12 Tiger Mullet Channel
(Bream, Flathead, Whiting, Mangrove Jack, Jewfish, Luderick, Trevally, Tailor)

Tiger Mullet Channel is central to a number of local hotspots. The channel separates the Green and Gold Banks and provides a good deep water mooring location. The Tiger Mullet Channel includes a stretch of water that is deepest along its southern bank and this makes for a great fishing location. This is a popular spot to target winter schooling bream and spring flathead. Schools of 25–30cm bream will stack in here at times and these concentrations will often include a few bigger fish. The channel also provides good winter fishing for luderick. In the event that good schools of baitfish are staging in the channel, anglers will find concentrations of jewfish, tailor and trevally. The deeper water snags that are found along the bankside ledge are usually home to mangrove jack. The western reaches of Tiger Mullet Channel intersect the Five Ways location to the north and Whalleys Gutter to the south. Deeper water is found immediately adjacent to the Five Ways location and the mouth of Whalleys Creek where it enters Tiger Mullet Channel. The deeper water in all of these locations produces bread and butter species. The turn of the tide fishes well for bream and flathead on lures and bait. The eastern reaches of Tiger Mullet Channel intersect the area known as the Gold Banks. The channel shallows here but remains a great place to target flathead on the last 2 hours of the run-out tide. These fish will hold in any depression along the bottom and lie in ambush mode awaiting food to come to them. Drifting through this area and jigging soft plastic lures along the bottom works very well.

Map 42 No. 13 Whalleys Gutter
(Bream, Flathead, Whiting)

Whalleys Gutter is a popular bream and flathead fishing location. The edges of the channel fish well for bream and whiting around the top of the building tide. Target flathead at the ends of the creek during the last of the run-out tide.

Map 42 No. 14 Crusoe Island
(Bream, Flathead, Whiting, Mangrove Jack, Jewfish, Trevally, Luderick, Tailor)

The quality bankside structure and channel country that is found around Short Island and Tiger Mullet Channel is also found along Crusoe Island. The northern shoreline and north-eastern tip of the island are wrapped by mangrove lined banks that offer plenty of near-shore structure and deeper channel waters. The north-eastern bank is home to plenty of weed and patchy rock structure. This area is a haven for bream, whiting and flathead. Bream often school here in winter and can provide anglers with a fish-a-cast style action. The bank is also a popular spot for the luderick angling brigade. The north-eastern corner of the island is close to deeper channel waters. Bait anglers catch some big flathead, jewfish, trevally and tailor in this location. The eastern edge of the island catches water draining from Green Bank. There is a steeper ledge that runs along this shoreline and this area attracts local bream, flathead and the odd jewie. The southern shoreline is a very productive patch of water to fish. A deep channel is positioned between Crusoe Island and Green Bank. Rock and timber structure can be found scattered along the shoreline and drop-off area. Anglers fishing live and dead bait along the ledge produce bream, big flathead, school jewfish, luderick and jacks. Drifting the bank while retrieving lures along the deeper water ledge will also produce fish here. The McKenzies Channel to the west of the island is a popular spot to target flathead and the odd bream or whiting. The ends of the channel fish well for flathead on a run-out tide, particularly in the Five Ways area.

Map 42 No. 15 Five Ways
(Flathead, Bream, Mangrove Jack, Jewfish)

Deeper channel waters near the southern shore of Crusoe Island and McKenzies Channel is locally known as the Five Ways. Bait anglers fishing live bait around the smaller tides and the turn-of-tide score well on flathead, bream, jacks and the odd jewie. Live mullet, herring, prawn and flesh baits work well here.

Map 42 No. 16 North Heads Bay *(Bream, Whiting)*

The western shore of the northern tip of South Stradbroke Island holds a broad shallow bay. This inlet usually holds plenty of weed. The sand and weed shallows are home to plenty of bream and whiting. Shallow diving hardbody lures and surface options will tempt these fish to strike. Worm and yabby baits around the deeper sandy stretches will also tempt fish. The location fishes well towards the top of a building tide. Bream and whiting feed actively around the weed as new water pushes in to the location. The area always fishes best when there is some wind blowing.

Map 42 No. 17 Kalinga Bank
(Bream, Flathead, Whiting, Mangrove Jack, Jewfish, Trevally, Tailor, Snapper)

This is one of the most popular flathead and bream spots in the area. The south-eastern bank of Stingaree Island drops into deep water. The ledge holds hard mud, patchy rock and timber. The area experiences strong tidal flow and is exposed to swell coming from the ocean at times. The characteristics of the location make it a haven for resident and travelling species. It is not uncommon to see large numbers of boats anchored and drifting through the area on a weekend. The most productive time to fish the location is during low periods of tidal flow, so aim to be fishing around the turn of the tide or during smaller tides. Fishing the area at first and last light or into the night will produce better results as the boat traffic reduces during these times. Presenting live mullet, herring, prawn, yabby, worm or flesh baits along the ledge and deeper water bottom structures will often produce a variety of species. Mullet and chicken gut are popular bream baits here. Bream will school in large numbers during winter whilst flathead are prolific in spring and summer. Pelagic and reef species will often move in from the ocean and hold along this area. Jewfish, mangrove jack and luderick are often encountered along Kalinga Bank and it is this type of variety which keeps bringing anglers back to fish the location.

Map 42 No. 18 Jumpinpin Bar *(Bream, Flathead, Whiting, Mangrove Jack, Jewfish, Trevally, Tailor)*

This is one of the more popular boat and shorebased fishing locations in the area and offers a similar style of fishing to Kalinga Bank. The bar forms the access point for much of the local water entering and leaving the system. The current can be very strong in this area and the channel geometry reflects this. The area contains deep water ledges that are home to some solid timber and reef structure. The location is adjacent to Swan Bay and usually hosts a variety of resident and travelling species. The channel here is often home to some big fish. The Pin bar channel is best known for its catches of bream, flathead and jewfish. This area is one of the go-to jewfish spots in the whole system. September and October are prime times to tangle with jewfish and huge flathead in this area. Large flathead, jewfish and bream will often hold tight against channel structures as the tide pushes hard through the area. As the tidal flow eases towards a change of the tide, these fish leave the structure behind and go in active search of food. This is the optimal time to be fishing this location. The most popular approaches when fishing here are to anchor and bait fish, or drift through the channel and jig sinking lures along the bottom. Anglers fishing the area with soft plastics catch some very good fish here. Schooled bream can provide cricket score catches of fish whilst fishing the bottom with 5–7 inch soft plastics is a popular strategy when targeting big flathead and jewfish. Bait anglers fishing live bait around the smaller tides and the turn of the tide score well on bream, flathead, tailor, trevally, jacks and jewies. Live mullet, herring, prawn and flesh baits work well.

The shoreline ledge is home to plenty of fallen timber. This area attracts plenty of bream, flathead and the odd jack. These areas are popular with boat and shorebased anglers.

The surf zone adjacent to the bar offers some top class fishing at times. Many anglers travel across North Stradbroke Island in 4WD vehicles to fish the sandy stretches around The Pin bar. Shorebased anglers often fish with surf fishing equipment and cast baits into the channel. Fishing around periods of lower tidal flow produce some good fish for shorebased anglers. The waters just inside the bar are renowned for holding big schools of tailor when these fish are in the area and casting baits into the surf zone will often tempt them.

The sandy shallows on the southern side of the bar are home to big schools of whiting at times. These can be targeted from shore or boat; however, boat anglers are urged to always watch the swell moving through the area.

Map 42 No. 19 Gold Bank
(bream, flathead, whiting)

Gold Bank and the South Stradbroke Island waters opposite this location are home to extensive sand flats that sit either side of the channel. The area is popular with whiting and flathead anglers as these fish move on the shallow grounds to chase a feed during high tide. Worm, yabby and soldier crab baits will tempt the whiting whilst trolling the edge of the shallows with small hardbody lures and plastics will catch the flathead.

Map 43 No. 1 Jacobs Well
(bream, flathead, whiting, mangrove jack)

The mangrove islands of the Jacobs Well area are ideal for crabbing and fishing for whiting, bream and flathead. The waters around Jacobs Well are home to plenty of moored boats, jetty and pontoon structure as well as some near-shore bottom reef. A jetty and public access points near the water mean there are several places for the shorebased angler to wet a line here. Anglers that follow Jacobs Well Road to the water will find a short section of beach east of the boat ramp. This is a popular spot for anglers to soak live and dead baits in the channel. Baits fished early and late in the day have produced some quality bream, jacks and flathead from this location. The jetty at Jacobs Well offers similar if not more crowded fishing at times. The eastern shoreline of the channel, the moored boats behind the island above Jacobs Well, the jetty structures and the channel markers are all worth investigating with lure and bait. Bream, flathead and whiting are taken throughout the channel.

Map 43 No. 2 Dinner Island Marina
(bream, flathead, whiting, mangrove jack)

The Dinner Island area hosts channel and marina structures. The channel shorelines produce some good bream and whiting at times. The new marina will attract more bream and mangrove jack as the structure matures. The outer walls are currently producing the odd quality bream and jack.

Map 43 No. 3 Tipplers Passage Shallows and Islands *(bream, flathead, whiting)*

Expansive shallows and mangrove islands choke the waters of the Broadwater around Tipplers Passage. A broad chunk of shallows can be found to the north of Couran Cove and contain the Never Fail, Couran and Tulleen islands. A further patch of shallows is found on the eastern side of Tipplers Passage and these are home to Tipplers and Pandannus islands. The shallow stretch of islands is one of the more productive bread and butter fishing areas in the system. It is rare to put time on the water here and go away empty handed. Bream, whiting and flathead will cruise or lie in ambush across the weeded, sand and gravel shallows during a rising tide. Fish can be caught here all year; however the best of the fishing generally occurs in spring. Anglers drifting the flats and casting and retrieving lures around the features within the shallows generally fare well. The features consist of weed patches and sand edges as well as the occasional patch of rock and gravel structure. Colour changes often denote their locations. The use of shallow diving hardbody and surface lures are popular in this area. Drifting the flats with the wind and making long casts that enable a lure to be bumped across the bottom as it is retrieved, are keys to success. Positioning baits of worm, yabby, prawn or strip bait in front of fish will also entice shallow cruising predators. The edge of the shallows usually holds good fish. The middle stages of the run-out tide and early parts of the run-in will often see fish holding along the drop-off ledge of the flats. Drifting the margins of the area whilst retrieving lures can produce solid bream and flathead. Alternatively, trolling lures and drifting with bait in tow can also be productive. The channel markers that are positioned along the edge of the shallows are great fish attracting structures. Good catches of bream, trevally and the odd school jewfish are taken from these features. A popular edge to locate fish includes the one at the junction between the Jacobs Well channel and the Tulleen Island area.

Map 43 No. 4 Pimpama River *(bream, flathead, whiting)*

The Pimpama River system is shallow throughout much of its reaches; navigating upriver of the big house at Diamond Head can be very tricky at low tide. The deeper water towards the mouth results in most anglers targeting fish between this point and the area known as The Stockyards. The river offers a single lane boat ramp that is quite steep at low tide. The ramp can be found at the end of Coleman Road. The Pimpama River is best fished when the waters are cool, although the areas around Diamond Head and the oyster racks to the left of the river mouth produce some big jacks when the water warms. The river between the Stockyards and the mouth produces good winter whiting on mudworms and yabbies. Target the edge of the flats on the run-out and look for fish high in the shallows during the building tide.

Above: The waters adjacent to the Pin are popular for targeting bigger flathead in spring.

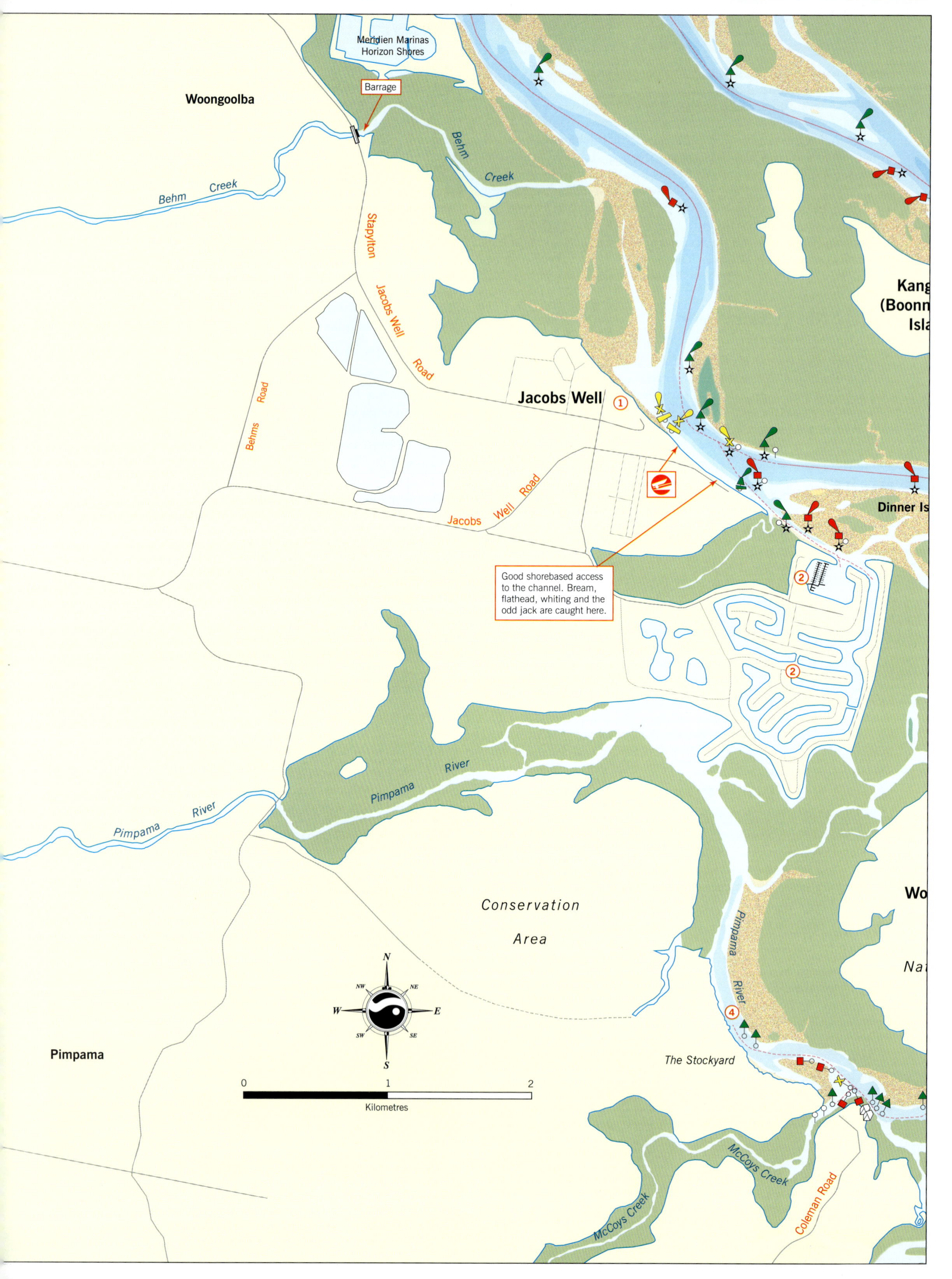

Meridien Marinas
Horizon Shores
Barrage
Woongoolba
Behm Creek
Behm Creek
Stapylton Jacobs Well Road
Behms Road
Jacobs Well
Jacobs Well Road
Kang
(Boonn
Isla
Dinner Is
Good shorebased access to the channel. Bream, flathead, whiting and the odd jack are caught here.
Pimpama River
Pimpama River
Conservation Area
Pimpama River
Wo
Nat
Pimpama
The Stockyard
McCoys Creek
McCoys Creek
Coleman Road
0
1
2
Kilometres
N
S
E
W
NW
NE
SW
SE

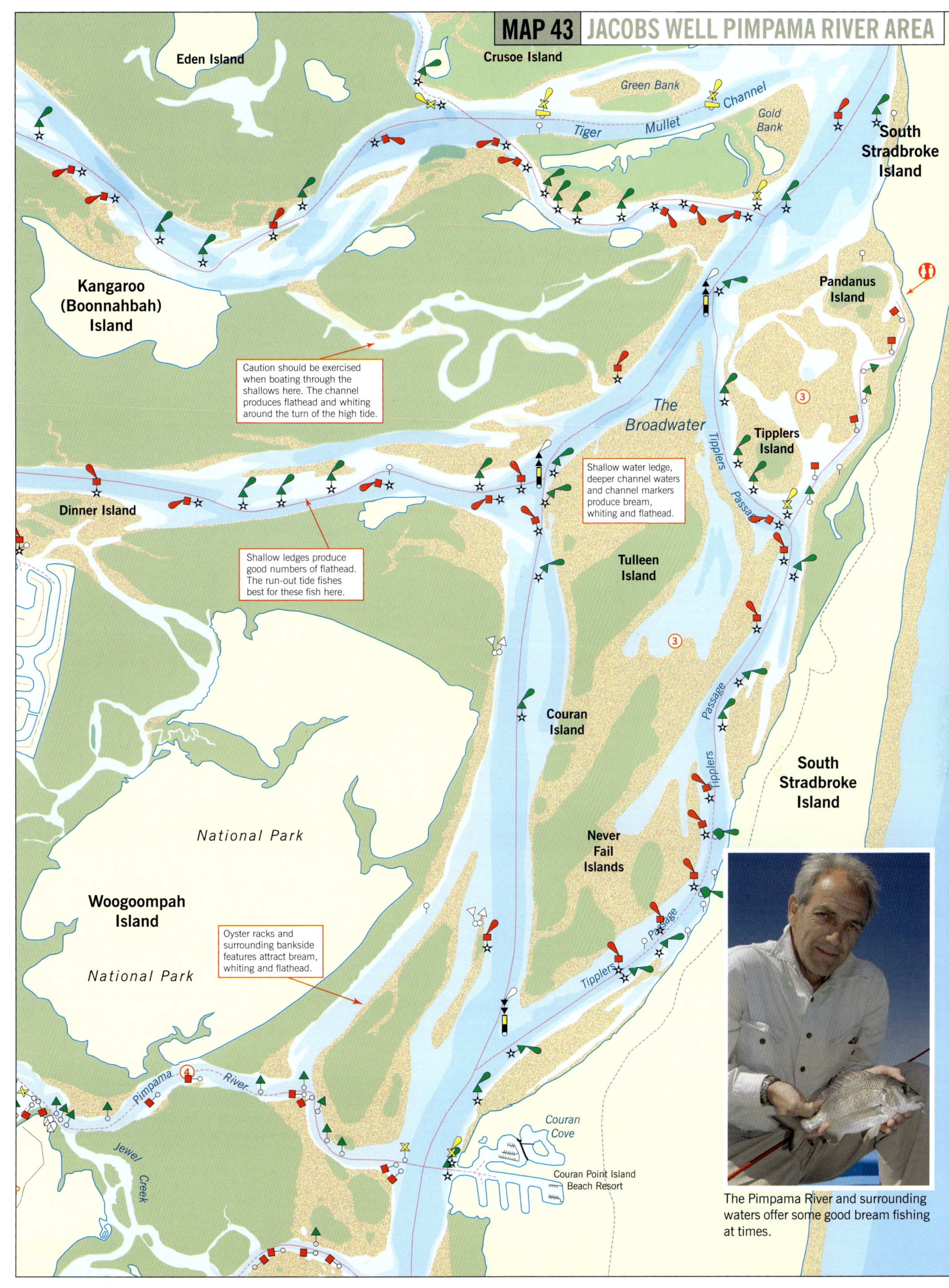

The Pimpama River and surrounding waters offer some good bream fishing at times.

CHAPTER 6

THE GOLD COAST

Including The Broadwater, the Coomera and Nerang Rivers, Tallebudgera and Currumbin Creeks and the beaches of South Stradbroke Island and the Gold Coast

ABOVE: Fishing deep jigged lures is a popular strategy in the Gold Coast Seaway.

INTRODUCTION

The Gold Coast waterways can be broadly classified into six key parts. The vast area encompassed by these valuable fisheries forms the backdrop to many kilometres of beachfront. The *beaches* of South Stradbroke Island and the Gold Coast provide endless beach fishing opportunities. *The Broadwater* as the name suggests is an expansive body of water that snakes between the mainland and South Stradbroke Island and links the waters of the Jumpinpin and Gold Coast city regions. *The Coomera River* system has its junction in the midst of the northern Broadwater reaches. *The Nerang River* feeds a multitude of canal systems and meets the southern parts of The Broadwater where the waters of the Gold Coast Seaway and ocean meet. Immediately to the south of the Nerang System are two small but popular fisheries in the way of *Tallebudgera* and *Currumbin creeks*.

Many of the species that frequent the Jumpinpin waterway are caught in the neighbouring southern waters. A large variety of our favourite recreational species can be caught in good numbers all year round in the Gold Coast area. Surprises that show up throughout the year here include species such as tarpon, cobia, mackerel tuna, kingfish and small queenfish. With the vast number of species available for capture in this area, the Gold Coast waters are some of the busiest in the country. Care must be taken when navigating as large and small vessels often share the same water here. Boat traffic is a key consideration when choosing when and where to wet a line. It is no coincidence that some of the best catches occur early and late in the day and often on a weekday.

The area is largely free of commercial fishing nets; a deterrent to commercial activity seemingly has a lot to do with urban development straddling much of the system. As a result, the Gold Coast waters offer some of the best estuary fishing in the state.

Facilities

Another drawcard to fishing around the waters of the Gold Coast includes the availability of plenty of fishing access for boat, kayak and shorebased anglers. The concentration of development around the area makes it appear as though there is limited area for the shorebased angler to wet a line but this is certainly not the case. There are multitudes of parks, walkways, bridges and through-road points that offer waterfront access. We have marked many of these in the maps of this book, and the rest can be found by looking at the Gold Coast street directory. There are many areas around this beautiful part of the world where the family angler can bring the kids for a play and enjoy a fishing session at the same time. Many of these areas also make great launching sites for kayak anglers.

Good quality ramps can be found at Marine Parade in Labrador.

FACT BOX

BOAT RAMPS

There are several good quality ramps around the Gold Coast area.

Coomera and Broadwater Area:
Paradise Point Boat Harbour
Jabiru Island
Santa Barbara
M1 Highway Bridge at Oxenford/Upper Coomera
Coombabah Creek near Daisy Elms Park at Paradise Point

Broadwater Area:
Centenary Drive at Hollywell
Ray Street at Anglers Paradise

Nerang River and Broadwater Area:
Marine Parade at Labrador (Harley Park)
Marine Parade at Labrador (Leonard Fox Park) at the base of the Gold Coast Highway Bridge
Anzac Park in Southport (at the pool):
This ramp can be busy and sandy at times.
Muriel Henchman Drive at The Spit: *Ramps at either end of a big car park.*
Waterways Drive at Main Beach:
Two single lane ramps and a floating pontoon.
Birt Avenue at Surfers Paradise: *Single lane ramp with limited parking.*
St. Andrews Avenue at Isle of Capri: *Single lane ramp with limited parking.*
Carrara Road at Benowa: *Single lane ramp with limited parking.*
Nerang Connection Road at Nerang (Arthur Earl Park):
Double lane ramp with good parking.
TE Peters Drive at Broadbeach (opposite Convention Centre):
Single lane ramp and limited parking.

Tallebudgera Creek
Awoonga Avenue on Burleigh Heads side of the creek
Murlong Crescent On the Palm Beach side of the creek
Currumbin Creek
Thrower Drive on the Palm Beach side of the creek
Duringan Street on the Currumbin side of the creek

CHARTERS AND GUIDED FISHING

Several guides offer fishing charters in the Gold Coast area. All of them have extensive experience in the area and offer a good selection of bait and lure fishing services.

Thomas Seebach of Coastal Sport Fishing Safaris, ph: 0412 691 929, or visit *www.coastalsportsfishing.com.au*

Ross McCubbin of Lucky Strike Charters, ph: 0428 729393

Brad Smith Guided Fishing Tours, ph: 0419 028704, or visit *www.bradsmithfishingcharters.com*
Brad operates throughout the Broadwater area as well as Tallebudgera, Currumbin Creeks and the Tweed River.

SOUTH STRADBROKE ISLAND AND GOLD COAST BEACH FISHING LOCATION GUIDE

The southern sections of South Stradbroke Island and the Gold Coast are famous for their surf beaches and anglers will love the fact that whiting, dart and bream are all year-round prospects and with good conditions, the gutters will hold plenty of them to keep you busy. Looking for deeper water with a green tinge to it and no waves breaking is the secret to locating fish. Often, taking a high view point from a hill or even your motel room can help locate deeper water.

Tailor can be taken all year round but are more common from May through to September. Best time to be fishing is during the low light periods of either early morning before dawn or late afternoon and into the night. Best baits are W.A. pilchards or whitebait. Smaller pilchards are ideal when 'chopper' (small) tailor are biting. Best areas include the beach around Narrowneck and near Main Beach. Flathead will often show up on the beaches around September also and fall for a range of baits including pilchards, worms and fish strip baits. Winter is best along the beaches for better catches of bream. Mullet and tailor flesh baits fished during the early morning, afternoon light and into the night is a popular approach to catching a few. Beach worms and pipis are also popular local baits for the bream, whiting and dart. Whiting are a good proposition along the beaches during the summer months and fishing shallow gutters with worm and yabby baits is popular. Swallowtail dart are available all year round with worms and yabbies being the best baits. Small metal lures can also be used if there are schools of fish present.

Map 44 No. 1 North Currigee Beach
(Bream, Tailor, Jewfish)

The gutters along the southern beaches of South Stradbroke Island are renowned for producing good catches of bream, tailor and the odd jewfish. This area attracts the first of any piscatorial food running from the Seaway following a storm event. Jewfish moving from the Broadwater will often stop at some of these gutters for a feed before moving on.

Map 44 No. 2 The Spit
(Bream, Tailor, Swallowtail Dart, Whiting, Jewfish)

The Sand Bypass Jetty is accessible from the car park at the Seaway and for a small fee you have access to some good surf fishing for dart, bream, tailor, whiting and mulloway. Bait and tackle is available from the canteen on the jetty. Surf fishing is good over the winter months during low light periods of pre-dawn and dusk. Bream and tailor are often caught here around the top of the tide. The Sand Pumping Jetty is a good spot for tailor and whiting. Yabbies and worms or small metal slugs will provide hours of entertainment on local dart. Phillip Park provides anglers with good access to the beach here.

Map 44 No. 3 Broadbeach
(Bream, Tailor, Swallowtail Dart, Whiting, Flathead)

The beaches here offer good gutter waters near to the shore. The area can be busy so it pays to fish early and late in the day. The usual beach suspects of bream, tailor, whiting, dart and flathead can all be caught along this stretch.

Map 44 No. 4 Palm Beach *(Bream, Tailor, Swallowtail Dart, Whiting, Flathead, Jewfish)*

The northern end of Palm Beach provides good gutters to target bream, tailor and the odd jewfish during low light periods of the day. A rising tide during these times will often produce the best results. These gutters will also fish well for whiting, dart and flathead. The wave break around the mouth of Tallebudgera Creek produces some good catches of tailor in winter.

Map 44 No. 5 Currumbin *(Bream, Tailor, Swallowtail Dart, Whiting, Flathead, Jewfish)*

The gutters close to shore along the beach at Currumbin provide good whiting fishing in summer whereas bream and tailor show up around the rocks and river mouth in winter. Elephant Rock is a popular place to target bigger winter tailor early in the morning. The rocks along the beach attract bream and whiting that will feed close to shore during a rising tide. Baits and lures fished around these areas will often produce some quality fish. Fishing these spots at night is a popular approach when targeting bigger fish.

Above: An angler casts a line into a Gold Coast gutter.

COOMERA RIVER LOCATION GUIDE

The Coomera River marks the northern extent of concentrated Gold Coast urban development. The southern side of the river is heavily populated with bankside housing and canal estates along much of its reach. The northern shoreline however is naturally structured with mud, sand and mangrove lined shores adorning its length. This river offers stark contrast with regards to the structure available for local fish and this may have something to do with the high quality of fishing it has to offer. Landbased fishing can be restrictive in areas due to the canal and marina development along the river. The system offers some very good bream, whiting and flathead fishing although species such as jewfish, estuary cod, luderick, tailor and trevally are also common targets in the system. In saying this, it is the mangrove jack population in the river that really excites local anglers. The variety and amount of structure in the river means jacks are able to feed with good protection, and the relatively clean waters of the estuary make it a hospitable environment for them to prosper.

FACT BOX
COOMERA RIVER JACKS

Many of the Coomera River fishing die-hards are mangrove jack fanatics and with good reason: this river is one of the best mangrove jack fisheries in the south-eastern corner. The trick to catching these fish is learning how to antagonise them and then how best to land them. The river holds plenty of rock, deep water, and hard man-made structure such as bridges and jetty pylons. Most of these areas are occupied by a territorial jack or two waiting in ambush for their next meal. Although live bait of mullet, herring and prawn account for good numbers of fish here, it is the lure fishing brigade that seem to produce the most consistent results. This may have a lot to do with the fact they cover a lot of water in their pursuits to tangle with these fish. The variety and quality of lures and tackle we now have at our disposal allows anglers to effectively present lures in front of fish. Anglers such as Michael Horn are well known around the Gold Coast for catching good numbers of jacks. Mick is a talent when it comes to putting a variety of lures close to structure and then being able to extract fish on very light lines at times. He dispels some of the myths that heavy lines only are required to tame jacks. Small to medium sized bibbed hardbody lures are staple fare for Michael when it comes to targeting jacks. Rolling or twitching these lures deep beneath shade-throwing structures is a key technique for this angler when it comes to catching local jacks.

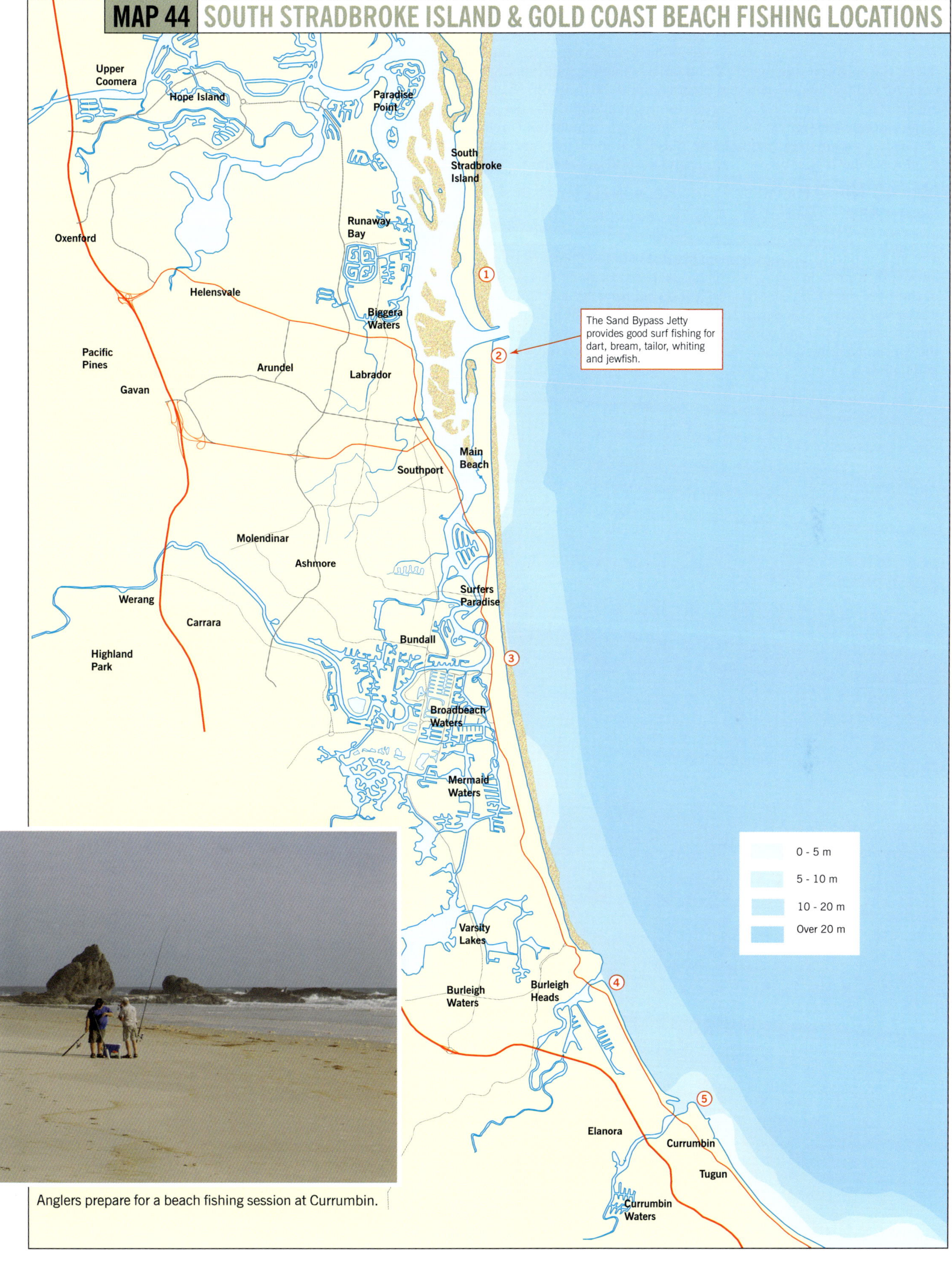

Anglers prepare for a beach fishing session at Currumbin.

Map 45 No. 1 River Mouth Flats and Ledge – South Arm *(whiting, flathead, bream, trevally)*

The mouth of the southern arm of the Coomera has an expansive mud flat on the northern side that drops off quickly into the main channel. Look for flathead on the flats and bream around the drop-off. Sharks are also common here and are regularly caught at night. The deeper waters around the sign on the northern side of the channel hold areas of patchy bottom reef. Jigging soft plastics around this structure produces some bigger bream, trevally and the odd jack at times.

Map 45 No. 2 Paradise Point Rock Wall – South Arm *(mangrove jack, estuary cod, flathead, bream, trevally)*

The rock walls that line the Coomera River at Paradise Point are a well-known mangrove jack haunt; trolling deep divers along this section of the river over the years has also produced trevally, cod and even a surprise catch of threadfin salmon. Landbased fishing along this stretch is best from the park at the end of Paradise Parade. Drifting the wall and fishing with soft plastics and blades also produces bream and flathead.

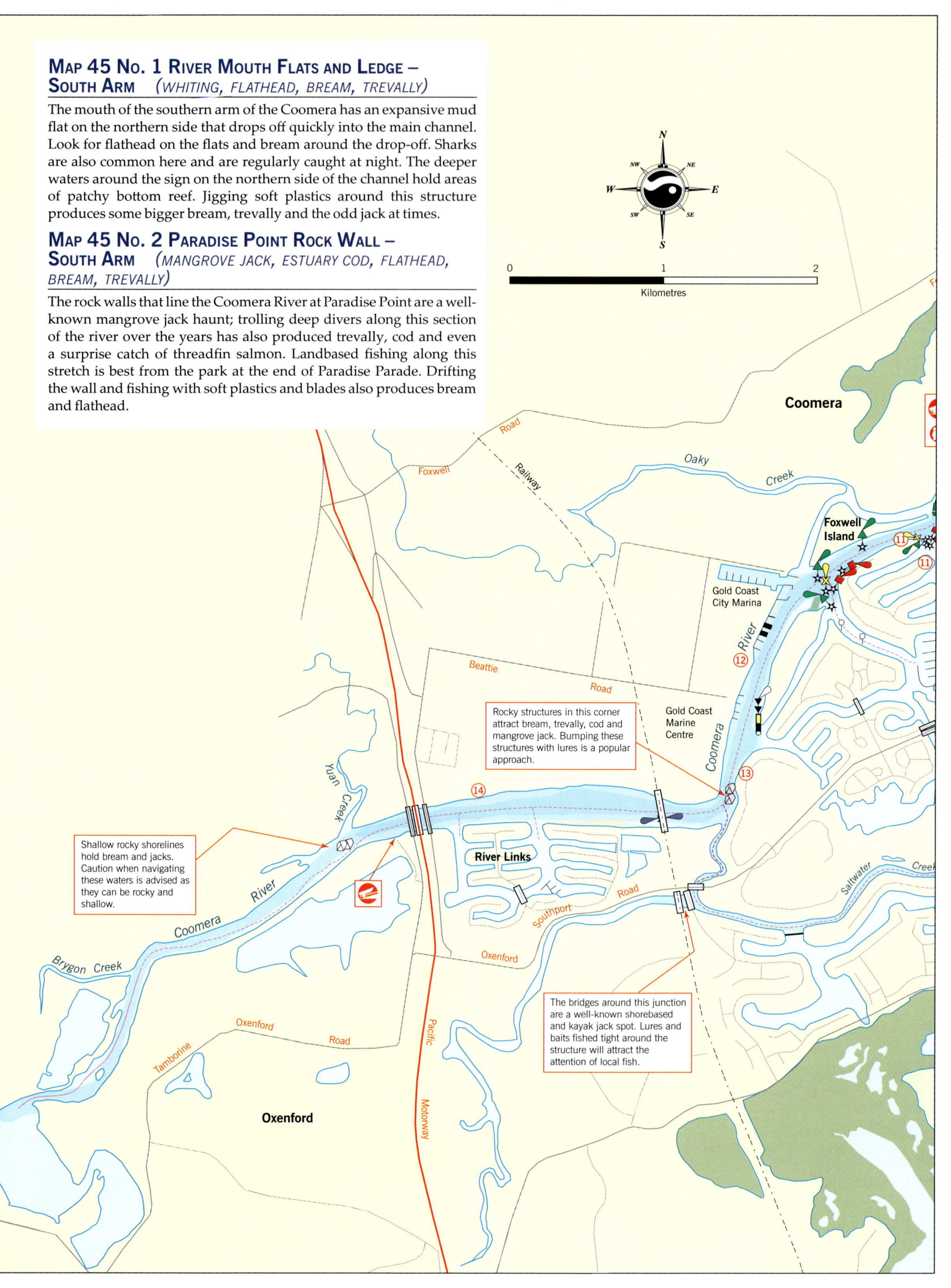

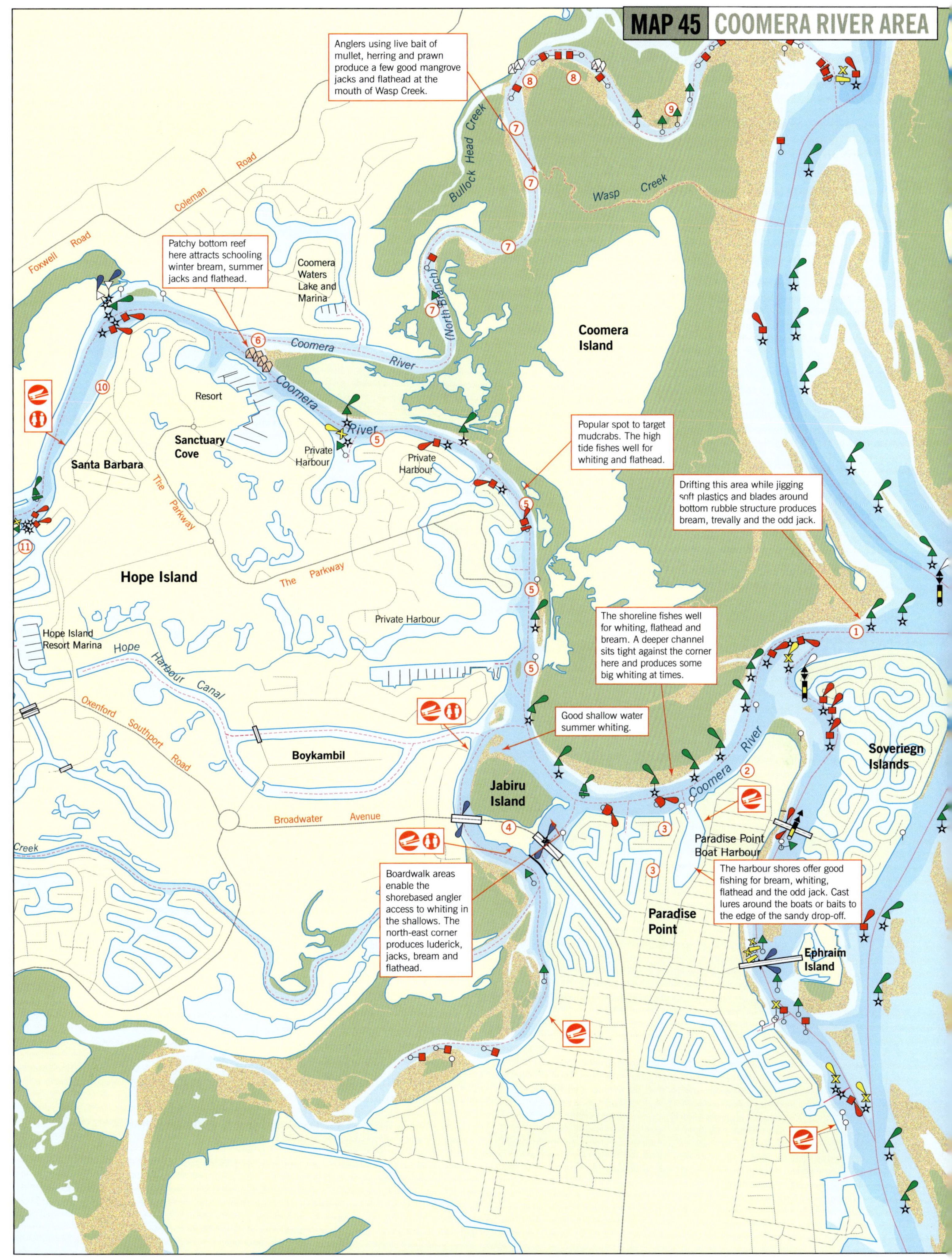

Anglers using live bait of mullet, herring and prawn produce a few good mangrove jacks and flathead at the mouth of Wasp Creek.
Patchy bottom reef here attracts schooling winter bream, summer jacks and flathead.
Popular spot to target mudcrabs. The high tide fishes well for whiting and flathead.
Drifting this area while jigging soft plastics and blades around bottom rubble structure produces bream, trevally and the odd jack.
The shoreline fishes well for whiting, flathead and bream. A deeper channel sits tight against the corner here and produces some big whiting at times.
Good shallow water summer whiting.
Boardwalk areas enable the shorebased angler access to whiting in the shallows. The north-east corner produces luderick, jacks, bream and flathead.
The harbour shores offer good fishing for bream, whiting, flathead and the odd jack. Cast lures around the boats or baits to the edge of the sandy drop-off.
Coleman Road
Foxwell Road
Bullock Head Creek
Wasp Creek
(North Branch)
Coomera Waters Lake and Marina
Coomera River
Coomera Island
Resort
Sanctuary Cove
Santa Barbara
Private Harbour
The Parkway
Hope Island
Hope Island Resort Marina
Hope Harbour Canal
Oxenford Southport Road
Boykambil
Broadwater Avenue
Jabiru Island
Creek
Paradise Point Boat Harbour
Paradise Point
Soveriegn Islands
Ephraim Island

Map 45 No. 3 Paradise Point Boat Harbour and Rock Wall – South Arm

(Bream, mangrove jack, whiting, flathead, trevally)

The canals and rock walls to the west of Paradise Point Boat Harbour host a variety of species. The boats and pontoons within the canals and harbour offer protection to bream, mangrove jack and trevally whereas the shoreline sand and ledges host whiting and flathead. Several 3kg bream bags have come from these canals in local bream tournaments so don't discount them as good fishing spots. The sand flats and boats at Paradise Point Boat Harbour can be easily fished from the shore and a quality two lane boat ramp can also be found here. The rocks that skirt the south wall around these canals produces some good bream, jacks and the odd luderick whilst the mud and sand bank on the northern corner is a proven whiting and flathead producer. The deeper water close to the mangrove bank fishes well at high tide with worm and yabby being the preferred baits.

Map 45 No. 4 Jabiru Island

(Bream, mangrove jack, whiting, flathead, trevally)

Jabiru Island sits at the junction of Coombabah Creek and the Coomera River South Arm. Deeper water and patches of rock wall attract a variety of fish that can be targeted from land, boat or kayak. The island is well equipped with boardwalk areas that enable shorebased anglers some good fishing access. The shallows around the south and north-western corner fish well for whiting on bait whilst surface luring in summer is popular from the shore here. The deeper water around the north-eastern tip of the island fishes well for luderick in the winter and the odd jack in summer. The hole also produces bream and flathead. The boats moored around the island fish well for bream at times. Bridge structures host a variety of predators and the western bridge with its adjacent rock walls fishes well for mangrove jack and trevally.

Map 45 No. 5 Coomera River South Arm Channel – Jabiru Island to Private Harbour

(Whiting, bream, flathead, mudcrabs)

The channel in this area features rock wall and canals on the southern bank and natural vegetation on the northern bank. The shallow northern shoreline is a popular whiting and mudcrab area. The hard structure on the south bank produces the odd jack, trevally and good numbers of bream at times. Drifting the rock wall and retrieving lures that hug the structure is a popular approach.

ABOVE: The Coomera River is a renowned jack fishing location. (PHOTOGRAPH BY MICK HORN)

ABOVE: Solid winter bream provide great sport around Coomera River structure. (PHOTOGRAPH BY MICK HORN)

Map 45 No. 6 Coomera River South and North Arm Junction

(Bream, flathead, mangrove jack, whiting)

The deeper channel water adjacent to the island outside Sanctuary Cove holds patchy bottom reef. This reef and the deeper water drop-off around the junction corner produces bream, flathead and jacks. Anglers anchored and fishing live bait of worm, yabby, mullet and herring produce fish around the turn of the tide. Drifting through the area and jigging soft plastics along the bottom is a popular way to catch winter school bream. Trolling through the channel with deep diving lures produces flathead and jacks whilst the shoreline adjacent to the channel fishes well for bream and flathead. The northern corner is home to rocky shores and plenty of pontoon and jetty structures. Deeper waters around this bank attract bream, flathead, mangrove jack, trevally and the odd jewfish. Positioning live bait in deeper water close to structure, or drifting through the area and retrieving lures produces fish. Diving hardbody lures twitched beneath these structures puts you in with a good chance of annoying resident jacks. The period where the tide starts to gain momentum is a prime time to be targeting these fish.

Map 45 No. 7 Coomera River North Arm – Coomera Waters Stretch

(Bream, flathead, whiting)

The north arm of the Coomera is only accessible by boat. The channel can be shallow but is reasonably well-marked. While best known for its summer flathead fishing, the shallow water warms up quickly during the day which puts the flathead off the bite, so early mornings and the cooler rising tides are best.

The section of channel below the junction of the two arms is lined with mangroves and shallow bankside foreshores on either margin. The area is popular with anglers chasing a few whiting, bream and flathead while they await mudcrabs to enter their pots. The hour either side of the top of the tide fishes well in these parts. The junction of Wasp Creek is a popular place to target mangrove jack on live bait.

Map 45 No. 8 Coomera River North Arm – Bullock Creek Corner

(Bream, flathead, whiting, mangrove jack)

The northern bank of the wide corner contains rocky outcrop at either end. The channel waters and rocky foreshores combine to attract local jacks, flathead and bream. Lures and baits fished around the channel drop-off in the vicinity of the rocks stand a good chance of being eaten by resident predators. The shoreline shallows fish well for school size bream and whiting at times.

Map 45 No. 9 Coomera River North Arm Lower Channel *(bream, flathead, whiting)*

The lower reaches of the Coomera River North Arm contain extensive sand and weeded shallows. This area is popular with local anglers using baits of prawns, yabbies and worms. These baits produce whiting, bream and flathead in the channel and shallower waters. Deeper sections of the channel produce the odd winter luderick.

Map 45 No. 10 Coomera River – Santa Barbara Stretch *(bream, flathead, whiting, trevally, mangrove jack)*

The channel around Santa Barbara contains shallow shores and natural structure on the northern bank whereas the southern shoreline is home to plenty of man-made and rocky features. The jetties, pontoons, rocks and moored boats offer the opportunity to catch bream, trevally and mangrove jack from beneath their shaded margins. Retrieving lures tight against these structures works well here. The shallows and shoreline ledges produce whiting and flathead. The channel markers are good staging points for bream during the run-out stages of the tide.

Map 45 No. 11 Coomera River – Foxwell Island Stretch *(bream, flathead, mangrove jack)*

The channel and canal areas opposite Foxwell Island fish well for bream when they are concentrated in this part of the river. Schools of fish will sit beneath any available structure and lures or baits fished around them will be aggressively attacked. The man-made and natural structure along the banks will produce the odd jack and flathead.

Map 45 No. 12 Coomera River – Gold Coast City Marina Stretch *(bream, flathead, mangrove jack)*

The channel is quite deep in places through this stretch of the river. There is also a variety of structure that holds resident fish. Marina docks and moored boats provide plenty of shelter for fish, as do the natural bankside structures on the eastern side of the channel. Sinking soft plastic lures deep into shaded spots, or retrieving deeper diving hardbody lures through these areas produces some solid bream and jacks. The odd school jew and big flathead can also be caught around the base of these structures at times. The boats in the middle of the channel often hold good numbers of bream beneath them. Anglers anchored in the channel and fishing live baits into the night produce some big jacks and cod.

The shoreline upriver of the Gold Coast City Marina holds patchy rock and mangrove structures. The ledge that runs along this bank produces flathead and jacks. Lures fished in the shallows on a rising tide are a good option for bream.

Map 45 No. 13 Coomera River – Hope Island Stretch *(bream, flathead, mangrove jack, trevally)*

This corner of the river is home to shallow water rocks and bridge structures that sit adjacent to the main channel. These hard structures attract bream, trevally and mangrove jack. Bumping lures along the hard structure is a common way to take fish here. Noisy and flashy lures will often produce the goods when the water is slightly discoloured.

Map 45 No. 14 Coomera River – Motorway Bridge Stretch *(bream, flathead, mangrove jack, trevally, jewfish, estuary cod)*

The river is lined with rock walls, bridges and pontoons along this stretch of channel. The abundant hard structure associated with deeper channel waters means it holds plenty of aggressive jacks. Anglers fishing soft plastics, deep diving hardbody lures and live baits hook good numbers of these fish each summer. Working the bridge pylons is a good strategy in this location. The shorebased angler has plenty of access to fishing the bridge structure and the area is a great place to target a jack, bream, flathead, jewfish or cod. Live baits fished through the night produce some big jacks, cod and the odd school jewfish. Live mullet, herring, prawns, yabbies and worms are all productive baits. Soft plastics fished around pontoons in the adjacent canals produce good numbers of bream. The channel upriver of this area becomes increasingly rocky and shallow. The area holds some good fish but it is hard to navigate.

Right: The rock walls in the lower Coomera provide some awesome jack fishing at times. (Photograph by Mick Horn)

Map 46 No. 1 Coombabah Creek Lower Channel
(Bream, flathead, mangrove jack, estuary cod, jewfish, trevally)

Saltwater Creek enters Coombabah Creek in amongst a section of shallow flats. These flats produce some good whiting on worm baits on a rising tide, but it is the opposite side of the channel that attracts most attention. A deeper section of channel runs along a rock wall from Jabiru Island upriver to the Daisy Elms Park. The fishing in this section produces bream, flathead, mangrove jack, trevally and lesser cod and jewfish. The corner of the wall can be fished from the shore and good bream fishing can be experienced here when the higher tides push towards the top of the wall. Good shorebased fishing access can also be found from the jetty at Daisy Elms Park boat ramp and along The Esplanade.

Map 46 No. 2 Saltwater Creek
(Bream, flathead, mangrove jack, whiting, mudcrabs)

Saltwater Creek offers shoreline shallows, overhanging natural structure, rock wall and jetty features. The shallow shorelines fish well for whiting and flathead. The rock walls, pontoons and fallen shoreline timber attract jacks and bream.

Map 46 No. 3 Monterey Keys
(Bream, flathead, mangrove jack, trevally)

This canal system is locked and boat access is gained only by permit holders. There are various shoreline access points where shorebased and kayak anglers can gain access to the area. The waters here are home to big trevally and jacks, as well as plenty of bream, whiting and flathead. The odd surprise species such as tarpon, giant herring and hairtail can show up in these waters.

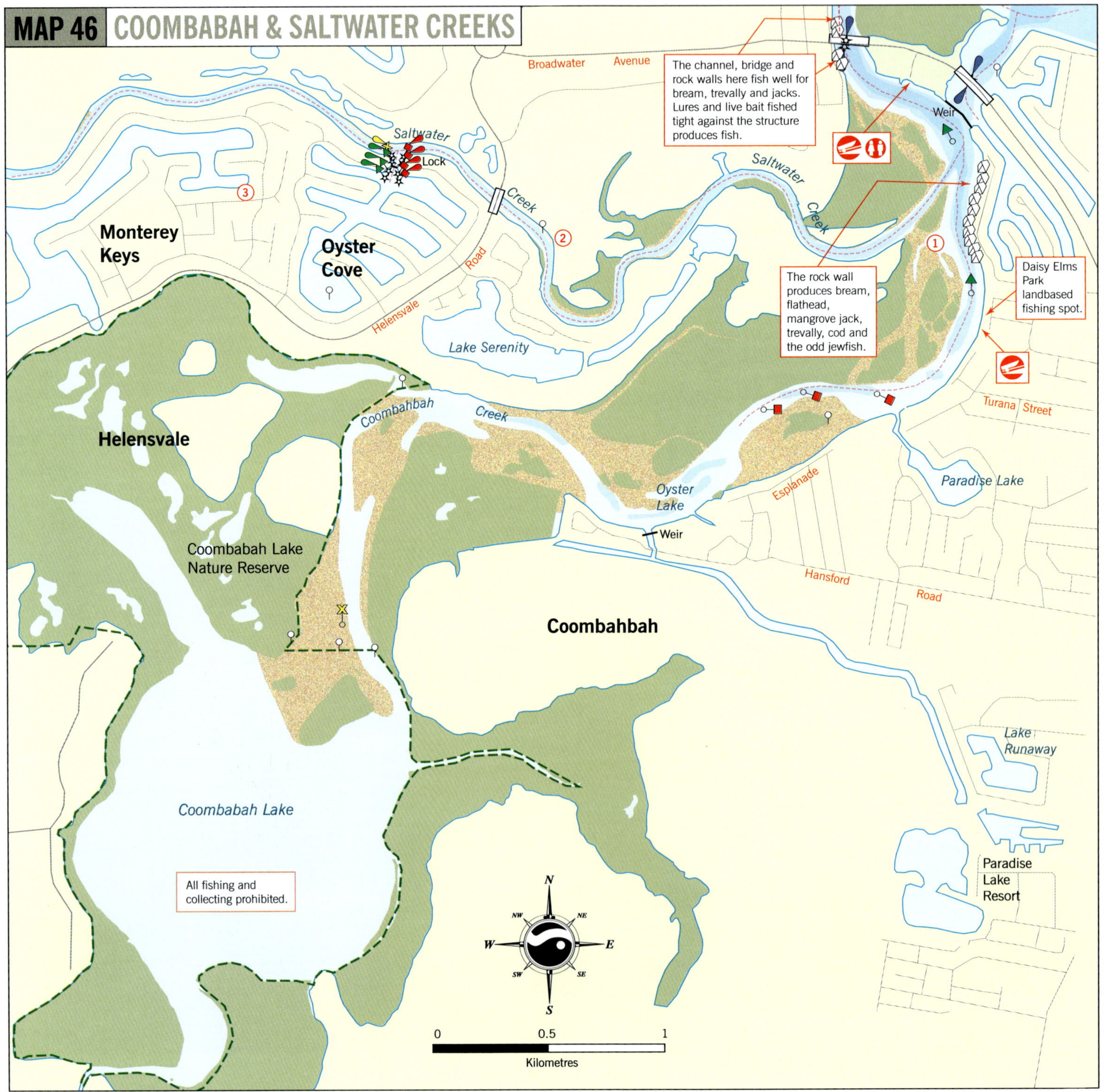

BROADWATER LOCATION GUIDE

As the name suggests, this stretch of channel forms an expansive patch of estuarine water. It is split into two key areas: the Northern Broadwater and Southport Broadwater. The Northern Broadwater links the Jumpinpin and Gold Coast waters and is the bigger of the two areas. The Southport Broadwater refers to the area stretching from approximately Wavebreak Island to the Sundale Bridge vicinity. A true water sports playground, The Broadwater can be extremely busy on weekends so it's a better mid-week option but even with all the hustle and bustle, the location provides some great fishing.

Map 47 No. 1 Coomera River North Arm Entrance Flats

(Bream, whiting, flathead, garfish, crabs)

The waters adjacent to the mouth of the Coomera River North Arm form extensive sand, weed and mangrove lined shallows. A flooding tide often results in good numbers of fish feeding on yabbies, worms and prawns throughout the area. Fishing bait at anchor or drifting while retrieving lures works well here. The edge of the shallow water forms a drop-off into the main channel and fishes well for flathead and bream during the run-out tide. Trolling this edge with lures produces some good flathead.

Map 47 No. 2 North Channel

(Bream, whiting, flathead)

The channel is a good bread and butter fishery. The drop-off on either side of the channel fishes well for bream and flathead, and the shallows produce whiting. A popular tactic here is to target bream and the odd flathead around the base of the channel markers. The run-out tide often coincides with concentrations of fish holding around the base of the markers. Jigging soft plastics and blade lures through the depression situated at the base of these hard structures will produce fish somewhere along this stretch.

Map 47 No. 3 North Channel Flats

(Bream, whiting, flathead)

Referred to as 'The Aldershots', an expansive stretch of shallows is found in the middle of the main channel. A channel cuts through the weeded sandy shallows and the area produces some good fishing on a rising tide. The adjacent channels are used by a variety of fish to move on to these flats to chase the abundant food supply they offer. Derelict oyster rack structures provide added attraction to predators seeking shelter while they feed on local prey. Drifting these flats while casting and retrieving a variety of hardbody lures enables anglers to cover ground while targeting fish here. Fishing baits of worms, yabbies and prawns in depressions across the flats is also a successful approach here. The flats produce the odd tailor and trevally at times when these pelagic species chase baitfish into the shallows on a high tide.

Map 47 No. 4 Brown Island

(Bream, whiting, flathead)

Just out from South Stradbroke Island is the little mangrove island of Browns Island as well as the

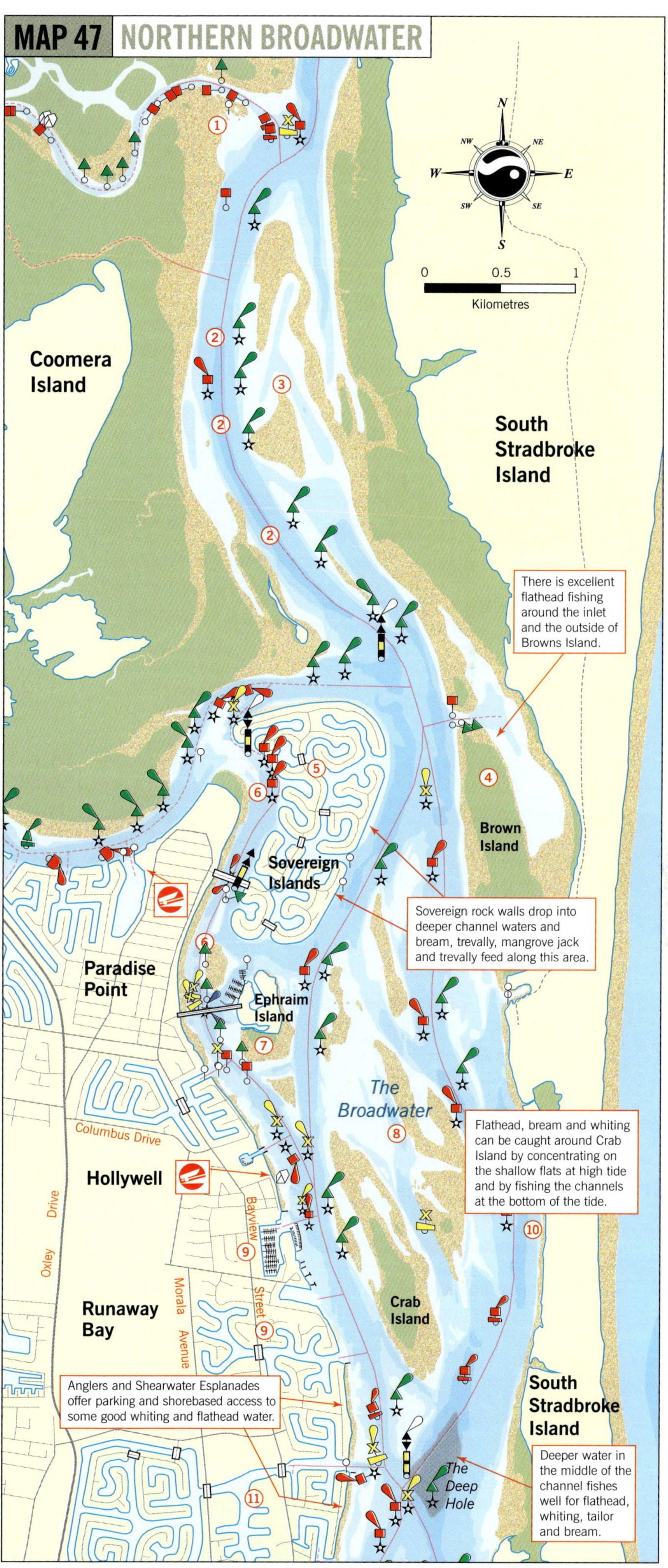

anchorage of Browns Inlet. There is excellent flathead fishing both on the outside of Browns Island as well as the inlet itself. The area makes for a sheltered location to chase a few bream and whiting.

Map 47 No. 5 Sovereign Island *(Bream, Whiting, Flathead, Mangrove Jack, Trevally, Tailor)*

Sovereign Island does not allow for any landbased fishing from the estate but getting out in a boat will put you in touch with some incredibly diverse fishing. The structures around the island and its location act as a strong fish attractant. The island is located at the junction of the South Coomera River and the Northern Broadwater. This area offers deeper water and plenty of bottom reef and man-made canal structure.

The canals are a haven for bream, jacks, flathead, whiting and trevally. The shaded structures such as bridges and pontoons hold jacks, bream and trevally whilst the canal shorelines will often see whiting and flathead cruising in search of a feed. The deeper water around the corners of the island and canals are where baitfish are herded and preyed upon by trevally, jacks and tailor. Twitching and pausing slowly retrieved hardbody lures beneath pontoons and around bridges will tempt the local jack and bream population.

The outer eastern rock wall of Sovereign Island attracts a large variety of species. The rocks, deeper water and current offers shelter and a ready food supply for bream, flathead, trevally, tailor and jacks. Patches of reef along the bottom of the channel here produce the occasional reef fish like snapper, sweet lip and tuskfish and will also hold winter luderick schools. Retrieving or trolling lures along these structures produces good fish around the turn of the tide periods. The northern shoreline along the mouth of the Coomera is renowned for holding solid trevally and jacks and these fish are reputed for destroying anglers tackle in a very short time.

Map 47 No. 6 Paradise Point Foreshores *(Bream, Whiting, Flathead, Mangrove Jack, Trevally, Tailor)*

The foreshore of Paradise Point is a great location for families with a huge park that boasts a number of playgrounds, picnic tables, BBQ and toilets. The public pontoon is a great spot to teach young ones to fish as bream, whiting, flathead and squid are commonly caught from both the pontoon and along the length of the beach. The public pool and the bridge are harder structures that attract a variety of predators and these can be fished from boat, kayak or the shore. Baits and lures fished tight against these structures produce some good bream, flathead, trevally and the odd jack and jewfish.

Map 47 No. 7 Ephraim Island *(Bream, Whiting, Flathead, Garfish)*

The large sand bar on the southern side of Ephraim Island has good numbers of whiting and flathead. Legal sized bream and garfish are also caught through this area at various stages of the year. The weeded sand stretches attract feeding fish on a rising tide. The marina on the island is not open to fishing, but the outer edges can be targeted for the odd bream, trevally and jack.

Map 47 No. 8 Crab Island *(Bream, Whiting, Flathead, Garfish)*

Flathead, bream and whiting can be caught around Crab Island by concentrating on the shallow flats at high tide and by fishing the channels at the bottom of the tide. In late summer and early winter, large schools of garfish can be found on the southern weed beds. The combination of a high tide, strong southerly wind and overcast skies make this area a great place to fish. Drifting across these flats and retrieving small and shallow diving hardbody lures will tempt many of the predators that access these flats to feed during a blow. Summer time surface lure sessions can make for some great fishing here. The mangrove edges of Crab Island attract some big bream and whiting around high tide. Fish will push into shallow water at the base of the mangroves to search for a feed so lures and baits fished subtly will prove the undoing of some of these fish.

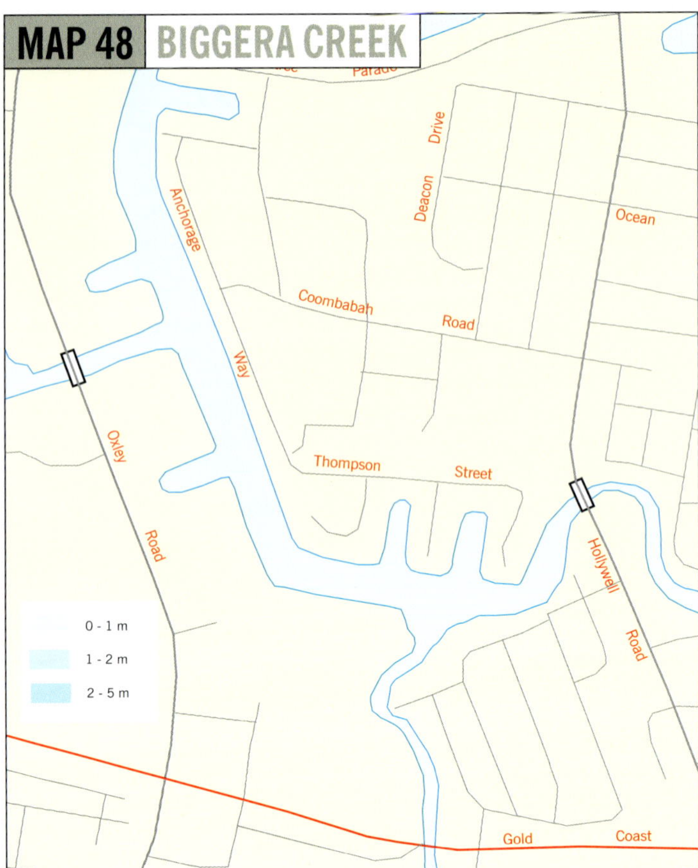

Map 47 No. 9 Hollywell Canals and Runaway Bay Marina *(Bream, Whiting, Flathead, Trevally, Mangrove Jack)*

The abundant man-made structure spread throughout these areas is home to good numbers of bream, trevally, mangrove jack, whiting and lesser flathead. The whiting and flathead can be targeted around the sandy foreshores on bait and lures. The lure anglers produce some good catches of bream and lesser jacks and trevally in these locations; strategically targeting any structure that throws shade on to the water is an effective approach. The rock walls that border Runaway Bay produce some big bream and jacks around a low light turn of the tide.

Map 47 No. 10 Currigee Camp Shoreline *(Bream, Whiting, Flathead, Trevally)*

The western shoreline of South Stradbroke Island is a good spot for catching bread and butter species. A long shoreline sandy drop-off hosts cruising whiting, bream and flathead and trolling lures along the drop-off is a popular method for taking flathead here. Baits of worm, yabby and prawn accounts for many bream, whiting and flathead.

Map 47 No. 11 Runaway Bay Canals *(Bream, Whiting, Flathead, Trevally, Mangrove Jack)*

The rock walls, bridges and pontoons throughout the area produce good bream, trevally and jacks. The sandy stretches and drop-off areas around the shoreline are a good place to prospect for whiting and flathead. There is limited access for shorebased fishing but small boat and kayak anglers are able to fish some good structure in the area. The sandy beaches at either side of the entrance to Runaway Bay Canals offer plenty of shorebased fishing access. Anglers and Shearwater Esplanades offer parking and shorebased access to some good whiting and flathead water. Cast baits of worms, yabbies and prawns to areas of deeper water to tempt these fish. Rising tides fish the best here.

Anglers Paradise
Street
Marine
Parade
Labrador
Channel
Biggera
1
Creek
Burrows
Street
Biggera Waters
N
NW
NE
W
E
SW
SE
S
0
0.5
1
Kilometres
Highway

MAP 49 SOUTHPORT BROADWATER
South Stradbroke Island
1
Carters Bank
North Channel
Good shorebased fishing for whiting, flathead, bream, tailor and trevally. The northern areas of the channel are deepest.
Good near-shore channel and snags. The area attracts some good bream and whiting.
Warning – care should be exercised when navigating the Seaway, particularly under ebb tide conditions when strong tide flows can be experienced. For further information on the condition of the Seaway contact Seaway Tower, Main Beach.
Marine
Parade
WE
WB
WC
WA
E
F
Wave Break Island
3
2
Labrador
Channel
WH
Porpoise Point
A
4
C
Gold Coast Seaway
B
Nerang Head
D
Sand Bypass Jetty
Good shorebased fishing along the rock wall for big flathead, bream, luderick, tailor and trevally.
WF
WG
5
Deepwater Point
The Spit
Jetty
The Broadwater
Marine Stadium
"The Logs" is a good night-time bream spot. Anglers fishing this area with bait produce the best catches on a rising tide.
South Pacific Ocean
Jetty
5
Gold Coast Highway
All lit beacons marking South Channel are synchronised.
South Channel
Caution – sea planes use this area.
6
5
Gold Coast Highway
6
Sea World
Smith Street
Helicopter pontoon - keep clear 30 m.
5
6
Carters Basin
Trawler Berths
7
8
Marina Oceanus
7
7
The Basin
N
NW
NE
W
E
SW
SE
S
0
0.5
1
Kilometres
Southport Yacht Club Marina
9

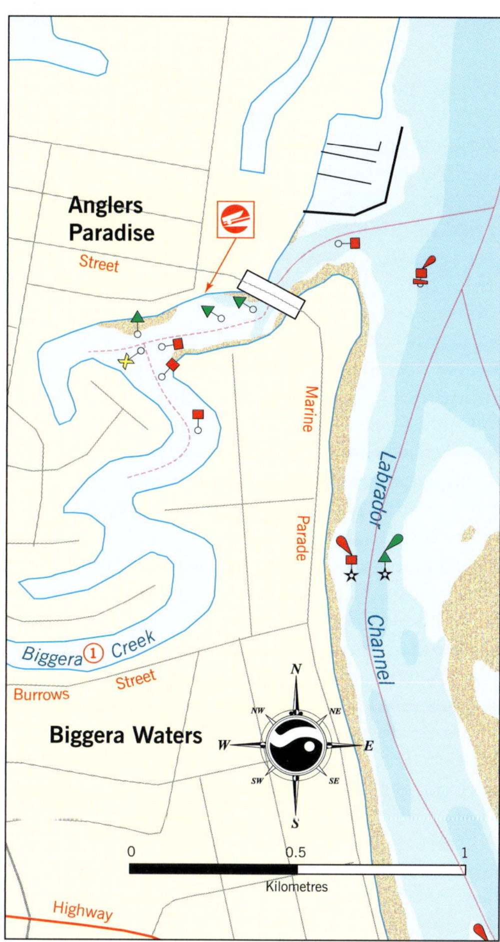

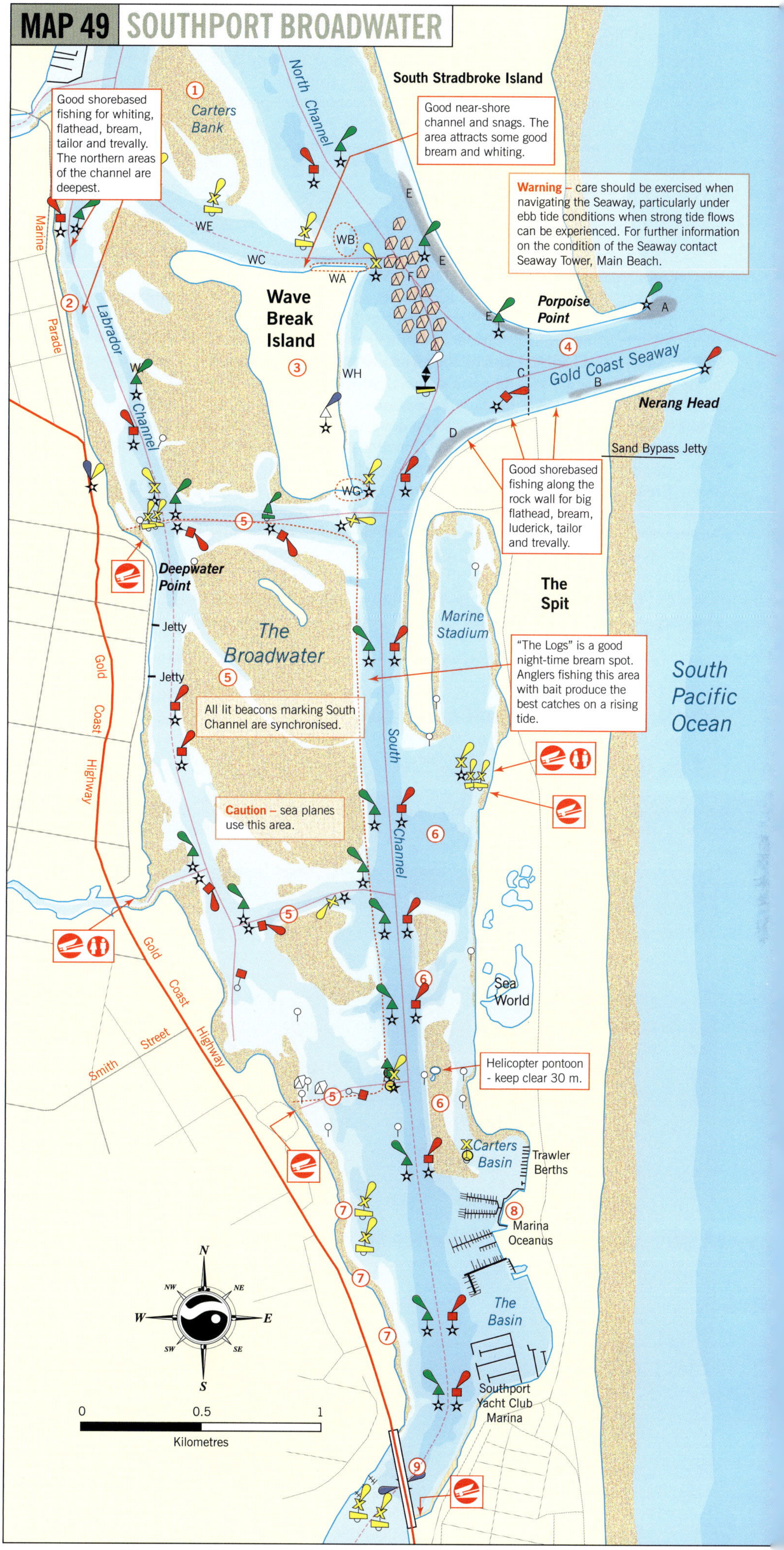

MAP 48 NO. 1 BIGGERA CREEK

(BREAM, WHITING, FLATHEAD)

The creek offers kayak anglers a good opportunity to target bread and butter species and the odd jack and trevally. Lures and baits fished on the sandy drop-offs account for whiting and flathead. Lures fished around bridges, rock walls and pontoons produce bream and the odd jack. The mouth of Biggera Creek, known as Lands End, fishes well for bream and flathead; boat fishing out from here can be productive if you use a sounder to locate the effluent pipe that runs from Lands End to the Seaway. It is also possible to sound out small patches of coffee rock just north of the Bayview Towers Marina.

MAP 49 NO. 1 CARTERS BANK

(WHITING, BREAM, FLATHEAD, GARFISH)

These shallows to the north of Wave Break Island fish well for whiting. The deeper channels and weeded areas within the shallows attract whiting and also bream and the odd flathead. Winter time often has schools of gar moving over these shallows. The deeper drop-off around the southern edges of Carters Bank produces the best of the flathead fishing.

MAP 49 NO. 2 MARINE PARADE FORESHORE

(WHITING, BREAM, FLATHEAD, TREVALLY, TAILOR)

The beach areas along Marine Parade offer plenty of shorebased access. Anglers

fishing baits and lures along this stretch catch good whiting and flathead in spring and summer. Winter fishing provides the odd bigger bream, tailor and trevally. Worms and yabbies are best for the whiting while pilchards and flesh strip baits produce bream, flathead, tailor and trevally. The northern areas of the channel are deepest.

MAP 49 NO. 3 WAVE BREAK ISLAND

(WHITING, BREAM, FLATHEAD, TREVALLY, TAILOR, JEWFISH, LUDERICK, KINGFISH, SNAPPER)

The Wave Break Island has rock walls both to its north (WA) and south banks (WG) where jewfish can be targeted after dark. The deep hole (WB) around the yellow marker at the north wall sees plenty of species including snapper and other reef fish being caught while trevally and luderick can be found around the north wall and an incoming tide often sees kingfish school up in the area. The sandy northern shoreline (WC) hosts a near-shore channel and fallen snags. These snags usually attract some good bream, whiting and the odd flathead. Lure and bait fishing during lower light periods of the day will produce the best results here. The channel between Wave Break Island and Carters Bank (WE) is a good place to drift with baits and jigged soft plastics while targeting flathead. The western shoreline contains extensive shallow sandbanks. The rising tide often has summer whiting pushing towards the shoreline in search of a feed. The deeper drop-off around this area holds flathead during spring and summer. The eastern shoreline is host to deeper channels along the northern and southern parts. These waters are a good place to soak a bait for whiting and flathead. Post spawn bream will often head to this location to feed-up immediately after spawning.

MAP 49 NO. 4 THE GOLD COAST SEAWAY

(BREAM, FLATHEAD, JEWFISH, MANGROVE JACK, TREVALLY, TAILOR, LUDERICK, KINGFISH, SNAPPER)

Fishing The Seaway from a boat can produce almost anything! A list of the common suspects includes: jewfish, tailor, trevally, mangrove jack, flathead, bream and small kingfish. Seasonal visitors to The Seaway include mackerel tuna, tarpon and schools of small queenfish.

ABOVE: Big flathead school in The Seaway in spring.

A deep hole (A) immediately off the northern wall fishes well around the turn of the tide. The start of the run-in tide is a prime time to be fishing here and often produces jewfish and big bream. The tidal flow can be very fast through this area during the middle stages of the tide. Resident jewfish, bream, trevally and luderick will use the slack water tidal periods to venture into open water and search for food. Landbased anglers can toss metal slugs from the walls or use surf rods for bait fishing to help with landing fish over the rocks. Similar fishing options are available along a deep water ledge (B) along the middle of the southern wall. The Pipeline (C) is one of the most prominent features in The Seaway. The pipe runs close to the bottom across the width of the channel. This hard structure attracts jewfish, big giant trevally, mangrove jack and kingfish to name a few of the predators encountered here. Schools of baitfish often hug the pipe and are a beacon for any predators moving through The Seaway. Fish such as trevally, tailor, tarpon and kingfish can be caught around the pipe by retrieving metal slugs from the bottom at high speed. The shoreline fishing around the Pipeline offers anglers a good chance of tangling with luderick, bream and flathead. Luderick will school up around the pipe during winter and are best targeted with weed baits suspended 2–3m under light pencil floats. Spring provides good fishing in the area for big flathead and jewfish. The southern corner channel (D) is a good shorebased location to target flathead, winter school bream, tailor and trevally. This location also produces some good luderick at times. A similar type of structure on the northern corner (E) offers boat anglers the chance to target a variety of species. Fishing bait from an anchored boat or kayak, or drifting and retrieving lures near to the rocks and bottom is a good option during periods of lower tidal flow. Areas along the bottom of The Seaway hold patchy concentrations of reef. The area between the northern corner of Wave Break Island and South Stradbroke Island (F) holds an extended patch of reef. Anglers drifting through this area and jigging blades and soft plastics along the bottom catch some great fish here. Winter months offer good bream and snapper fishing while spring produces good jewfish and flathead. Bait anglers fishing live baits at anchor also produce some good catches here.

This area is one of the busiest boating areas in the country. Boat and kayak anglers are warned to take care when fishing and navigating these waters. The area is shared by boats of all sizes, kayaks, divers, surfers paddling across the channel and jetskis.

MAP 49 NO. 5 WESTERN CHANNEL FORESHORE AND SAND BANKS

(WHITING, BREAM, FLATHEAD, TREVALLY, TAILOR)

The maze of sand bars in the middle of the Southport Broadwater are loaded with whiting. The warmer months are better and baiting up with worms or yabbies is best.

Bream, whiting and flathead can be caught along the foreshores between Labrador and Southport. Good spots include around the mouth of Loder Creek as well as the rock wall that follows Marine Parade at Labrador.

MAP 49 NO. 6 MAIN CHANNEL – SEAWAY TO SEA WORLD

(WHITING, BREAM, FLATHEAD, TREVALLY, TAILOR)

The channel linking The Seaway with the Nerang River is deep. A straight section is located along the stretch between The Seaway and Sea World. The channel markers attract bream, tailor and trevally. The edges of the channel along the eastern side make for good shorebased whiting and flathead fishing. This area can be accessed via The Spit. The western side of the channel opposite the dredge is host to piles of logs sitting on the bottom and as such is locally referred to as 'The Logs'. This is a good night-time bream spot and anglers fishing this area with bait produce the best catches on a rising tide.

Map 49 No. 7 Main Channel – Marina Mirage to Southport Yacht Club *(Whiting, Bream, Flathead, Mangrove Jack, Trevally, Tailor)*

The stretch of water between Marina Mirage and the Gold Coast Bridge is one of the busiest waterways in Queensland but bream in the thousands live around the boats in Marina Mirage. While fishing inside the marina is prohibited, finding a quiet corner outside of the marina will provide plenty of action. Here the dense man-made structure is home to some solid mangrove jack and trevally. The boats in the middle of the channel offer protection for bream, trevally and tailor.

Across from Australia Fair at Southport is a huge park with a massive array of amenities for kids and some good quality whiting can be caught from the shore. Bream, flathead and the odd trevally and tailor can be found around the outside of the swimming pool enclosure and respond well to soft plastic lures. Good shorebased fishing access can be gained along this shoreline.

Map 49 No.8 Sundale Bridge *(Whiting, Bream, Flathead, Mangrove Jack, Trevally, Tailor, Jewfish)*

The Sundale Bridge is a popular spot amongst shorebased, boat and kayak anglers. A number of pylons anchor the bridge in deeper water and offer protective feeding grounds for a variety of predators. The periods around the change of tide are optimal here as the tidal flow can be strong during mid-tide stages. Anchoring baits and retrieving soft plastic, blade and diving harbody lures around the bridge produces trevally, bream, jewfish, flathead and the odd mangrove jack. Live baits fished around the bridge pylons at night produce some of the best catches.

Top right: The Sundale bridge attracts a variety of fish species and makes for a great landbased fishing location.

Right: Quality bream can be caught from the Sundale Bridge pylons.

NERANG RIVER LOCATION GUIDE

The Nerang River is an angler's paradise; forget Surfers Paradise as this is a fisher's paradise. The fishing here can be fantastic with all the pontoons, jetties and bridges; the structure is endless and has created a haven for all species. There are some popular spots that produce great fishing at times, including: The Southport School (TSS), Bundall Bridge, Lake Intrepid and the Council Chambers to name a few. To fish this place you will need a street directory. This may sound strange but without it you could get lost here, there are that many canals!

The Nerang River is a waterway that is surprisingly productive given its situation in the heart of one of Queensland's busiest cities. Large numbers of boats use the river and although the fishing is best Monday to Friday and during the evening, plenty of fish can still be caught during the busy times. When anchoring, ensure that you are not in a channel which can hinder other boats trying to traverse the sometimes narrow stretches of river.

The labyrinth of man-made canal systems hasn't been detrimental to fishing as rock retaining walls, pontoons and jetty pylons are home to bream, mangrove jack, estuary cod and trevally. A well placed lure in amongst this structure is bound to receive attention from the local fish residing in the area.

The lower reaches of the river fish best when the water is muddied from heavy downpours of rain. In this instance it's best to fish towards the mouth of the river, particularly during the run-in tide.

Bridge pylons are home to mangrove jack, estuary cod and bream so it's worth fishing these areas. The same fish you catch in the Broadwater you can catch here: bream, flathead, luderick, jewfish, tailor, trevally, whiting and mangrove jack to name a few.

FACT BOX
NERANG WHITING

The Nerang River is most renowned for extra large whiting that can be caught over the undulating sandy bottom of this system. Live worms are the best bait to use however small black soldier crabs and yabbies can produce fish as well. Best places to catch fish are the shallow sandy areas at night however increased boat traffic can see whiting move into the deeper sections of the river. Popular whiting haunts include the mouth of the Nerang River, Budds Beach, Council Chambers and Isle of Capri area.

FACT BOX
LANDBASED FISHING

Fishing Nerang River landbased can be done at most of the park areas situated along the banks. A Refidex street directory will direct shorebased anglers to many parks, bridges and open access points where anglers can wet a line from the shore.

LEFT: The retaining walls and reef around The Southport School and Chevron Island fish well for jacks, bream, trevally and the odd sizeable cod. (PHOTOGRAPH BY MICK HORN)

RIGHT: The Nerang and Gold Coast waters produce some cracking whiting each summer. (PHOTOGRAPH BY MICK HORN)

MAP 50 NO. 1 THE SOUTHPORT SCHOOL (TSS)
(BREAM, TREVALLY, MANGROVE JACK, FLATHEAD, JEWFISH)

Commonly referred to as TSS, this location receives a lot of attention. The stretch of channel contains significant reef along the bottom. This forms a ledge that drops into deeper water along the eastern bank which is home to retaining wall and pontoon structures. The tide can run hard through the area and it is a busy section of the river with regards to boat traffic. This being said, the location produces some quality fish every year. The waning and building periods of the tide stimulate fish feeding activity and bream, trevally, tailor, mangrove jack, flathead and school jewfish are all caught here. Summer time produces good jacks along the ledge and pontoons while winter is a good time to encounter big schools of spawning bream. Drifting the area while jigging blades and soft plastics, or trolling with deep diving lures are popular approaches here. Commodore Drive on the eastern shore offers a good shorebased fishing location that provides access to deeper rocky waters. The canal system to the east of the main channel provides good fishing for bream, trevally, flathead, whiting and mangrove jack. The back reaches of these canals are great places to cast and retrieve surface lures for bream, trevally, whiting and jacks. Deeper diving hardbody lures and soft plastics will catch resident species sheltering beneath the abundant jetty and boat mooring structure.

MAP 50 NO. 2 CHEVRON ISLAND
(BREAM, TREVALLY, MANGROVE JACK, FLATHEAD, WHITING)

The southern shores of Chevron Island provide a rock wall that drops into deeper channel waters. The wall hosts several jetties and pontoons and the area attracts bream, trevally and mangrove jacks. Drifting along the bank and retrieving lures tight against the ledge and jetty structures will tempt resident fish; however, many good fish are lost around the sharp structure here. The channel markers and sandy shallows on the opposite bank produce good whiting and bream. This shoreline is adjacent to the Council Chambers and offers some good landbased fishing access. Worms and yabbies fished along this stretch produce some big whiting each summer. The eastern corner of this shoreline is a rocky point that drops into deeper water. This is a popular shorebased luderick spot in winter.

The bridges at either end of Chevron Island are well known for producing some quality bream and jacks. Live baiting at night or retrieving and banging hardbody lures against the pylons are favoured approaches.

MAP 50 NO. 3 COUNCIL CHAMBERS TO ISLE OF CAPRI
(WHITING, BREAM, TREVALLY, MANGROVE JACK, FLATHEAD)

An undulating sandy bottom with patches of deeper water characterise this stretch of river. The area is a popular whiting spot. It is common to see many boats and shorebased anglers scattered through the area. These anglers are invariably targeting whiting on worm, yabby and crab baits. The summer fishing is best with a rising tide around the full and new moons the pick of the conditions. The rock walls and bridge pylons around the Capri Bridge fish well for bream, jacks and trevally. The shallows around Girung Island are great backwaters to chase whiting on a building tide. Surface luring these speedy battlers is popular in summer here. Shallow diving hardbody lures retrieved around local weed and rock around the islands will produce bites from bream and flathead.

MAP 51 NO. 1 NERANG RIVER – ISLE OF CAPRI AND SORRENTO CHANNEL
(BREAM, TREVALLY, MANGROVE JACK, WHITING)

This stretch of river fishes well for much of the year. A host of canals drain into the channel in this area. These drain points are home to bridges (A), rock walls and pontoons. The bottom of the channel is largely sandy throughout, however some solid reef is located in the vicinity of the Bundall Road Bridge (B). The sandy stretches here are home to some good whiting for much of the year. The hard structure produces good jacks, bream and trevally. Rolling diving hardbody lures along the rock walls, beneath the pontoons

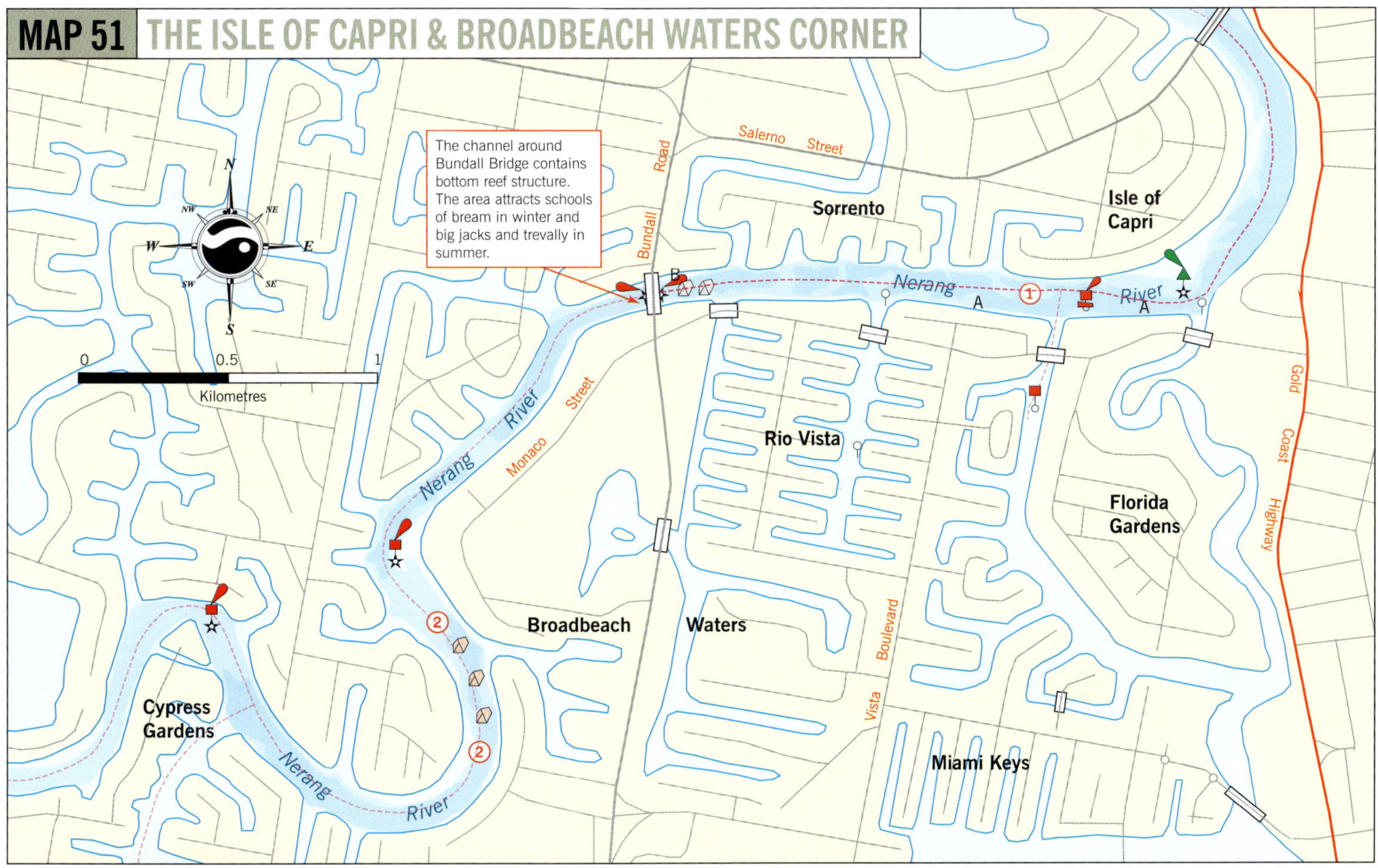

and around the bridges throughout this area results in some good strikes from jacks and bream. Trolling diving hardbody lures along the rock walls and around bridges is a popular way to catch jacks here. Jigging blades and soft plastics along the channel bottom reef areas is a great way to catch some good winter schooling bream. Retrieving lures at speed through the areas where the canal drain points meet the Nerang River channel is a sure fire way to hook some big trevally and herring. There is shorebased access to the bridges in this area via Monaco Street. Fishing live bait and lures around the bridges accounts for some quality jacks here; this is particularly the case for anglers that fish into the night.

MAP 51 NO. 2 BROADBEACH WATERS CORNER *(WHITING, BREAM, TREVALLY, MANGROVE JACK)*

The southern corner of this bend in the Nerang River channel produces good fishing at times. The bottom of the channel contains patchy reef throughout this area. The rock walls along the bank and the bottom reef attracts schooling winter bream and the odd trevally and mangrove jack in summer. Drifting the channel and jigging soft plastics and blades around the reef produce some good catches. Bumping the rocks along the southern wall with diving hardbodies is a popular approach to catching bream and jacks here. The sandy and shallower stretches on either side of the corner are well-known whiting grounds. In particular, bait anglers fishing the sandy corner adjacent to Monaco Street produce good catches of whiting. The shallows and deeper channel fish well for big whiting on the larger building summer tides.

MAP 52 NO. 1 CYPRESS GARDENS CORNER *(BREAM, TREVALLY, MANGROVE JACK, WHITING)*

A deeper rocky bottom is found along the northern corner of the channel here. The deeper water sits adjacent to a rock wall adorned with jetty and pontoon structures. The tide runs hard through this area at times. Targeting the deeper water structure with blades and soft plastics produces fish here. Anglers fishing live bait at anchor also take some good fish in this spot. Fishing around low light periods of the day and a turn of the tide often provide the best results.

MAP 52 NO. 2 NERANG RIVER CHANNEL – BENOWA *(BREAM, TREVALLY, MANGROVE JACK, WHITING)*

This stretch of the river is home to plenty of jetty, pontoon and rock wall structure. Where salinity levels are favourable and concentrations of prawns are found in these upper areas, the fishing can be very good. Retrieving or trolling lures along the face of channel structures provides good fishing at times.

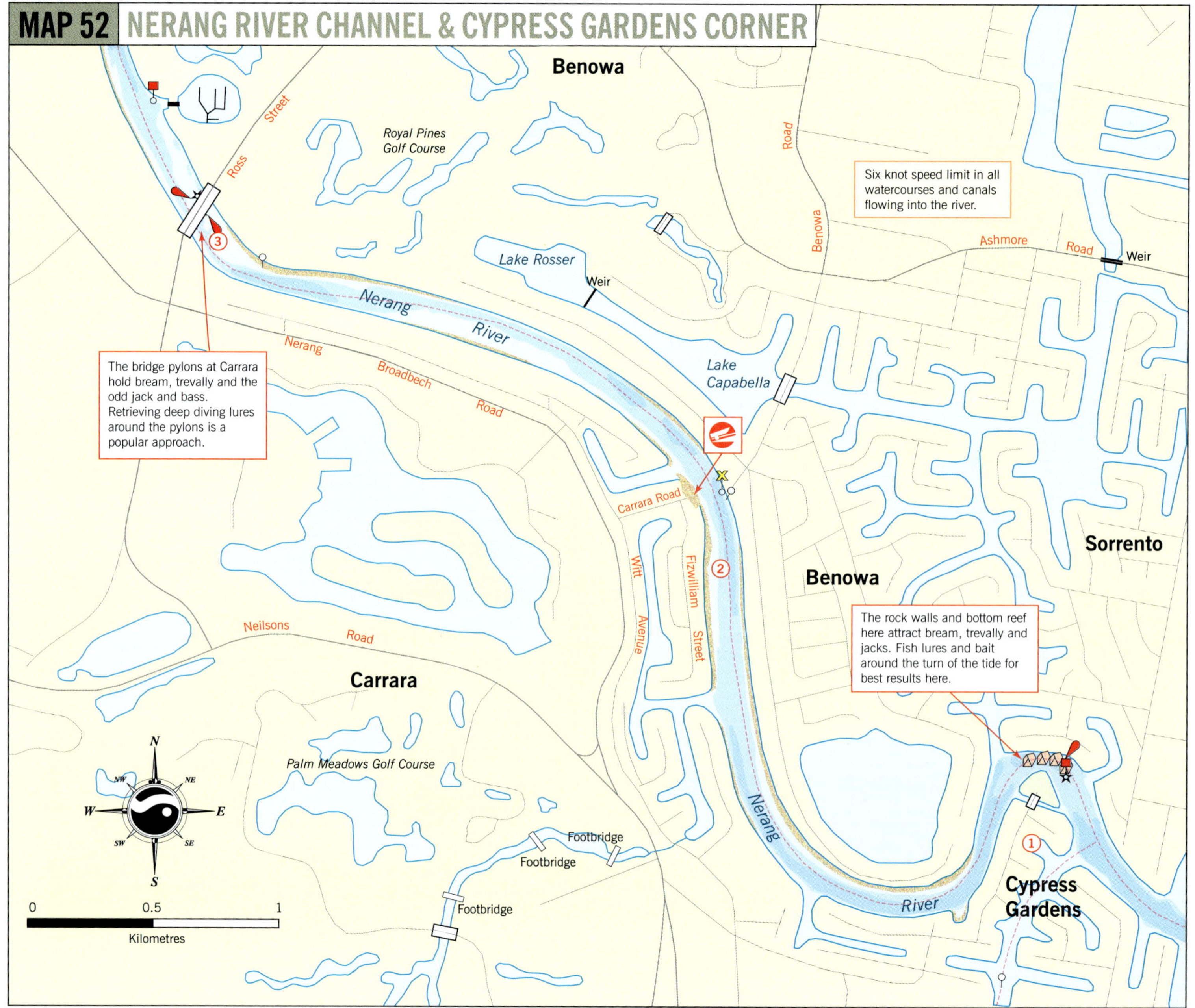

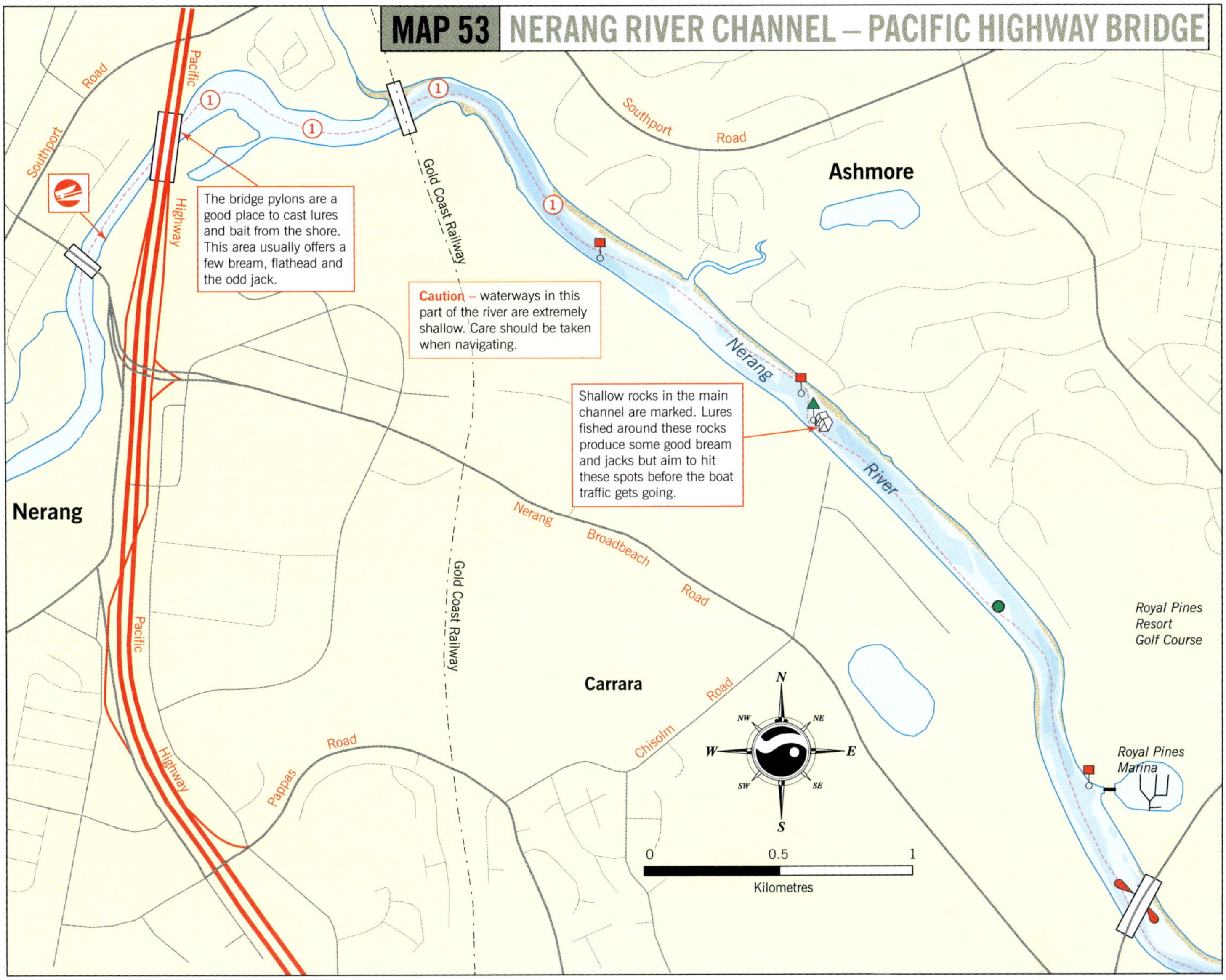

MAP 53 NERANG RIVER CHANNEL – PACIFIC HIGHWAY BRIDGE

Southport Road
Pacific Highway
Gold Coast Railway
Ashmore
Nerang River
Nerang
Nerang Broadbeach Road
Carrara
Chisolm Road
Pappas Road
Royal Pines Resort Golf Course
Royal Pines Marina
0 0.5 1
Kilometres

The bridge pylons are a good place to cast lures and bait from the shore. This area usually offers a few bream, flathead and the odd jack.

Caution – waterways in this part of the river are extremely shallow. Care should be taken when navigating.

Shallow rocks in the main channel are marked. Lures fished around these rocks produce some good bream and jacks but aim to hit these spots before the boat traffic gets going.

Map 52 No. 3 Nerang River Channel – Carrara *(Bream, Trevally, Mangrove Jack, Whiting)*

The rock walls and bridge here hold good numbers of bream, trevally and the odd jack. This stretch of river often produces bass for anglers casting lures around the available structure. The latter stages of the run-out tide have also produced the occasional barramundi for anglers targeting the rock walls with lures in this area.

Map 53 No. 1 Nerang River Channel – Pacific Highway Bridge *(Bream, Trevally, Mangrove Jack, Whiting)*

The stretch of river around the Pacific Highway Bridge fishes well for bream, flathead and whiting at times. The odd bass and barramundi are also caught by anglers using lures in the area. Up-river from the fishing platform located in the Nerang River Parklands, anglers can expect to catch the odd bream, flathead and trevally.

RIGHT: The structure around the Nerang River main channel is a haven for jacks.

LEFT: Retrieving deep diving lures in the canals is an effective way to catch good bream around Jupiters Casino. (PHOTOGRAPH BY ROD WALMSLEY)

Maps 54 & 55 The Canals *(Bream, Whiting, Flathead, Mangrove Jack, Trevally, Tailor)*

The Nerang River canals provide some of the most concentrated man-made fishing structure along the Queensland coast. Many of the local species thrive around the abundant structure which combines to provide shelter and a great feeding spot in a single location. The canals provide a wealth of fishing opportunity for species such as bream, trevally, mangrove jack, flathead, whiting and tailor as well as several others. Boat and kayak anglers have access to many of the Nerang River canals; however, care must be taken when fishing around many of the structures in these areas as they ultimately belong to local residents. Treat property with care and anglers will be welcome to fish here in future years.

There are various approaches that are met with consistent success in the canals. A popular one includes targeting the canals closest to the main Nerang River channel while there is good

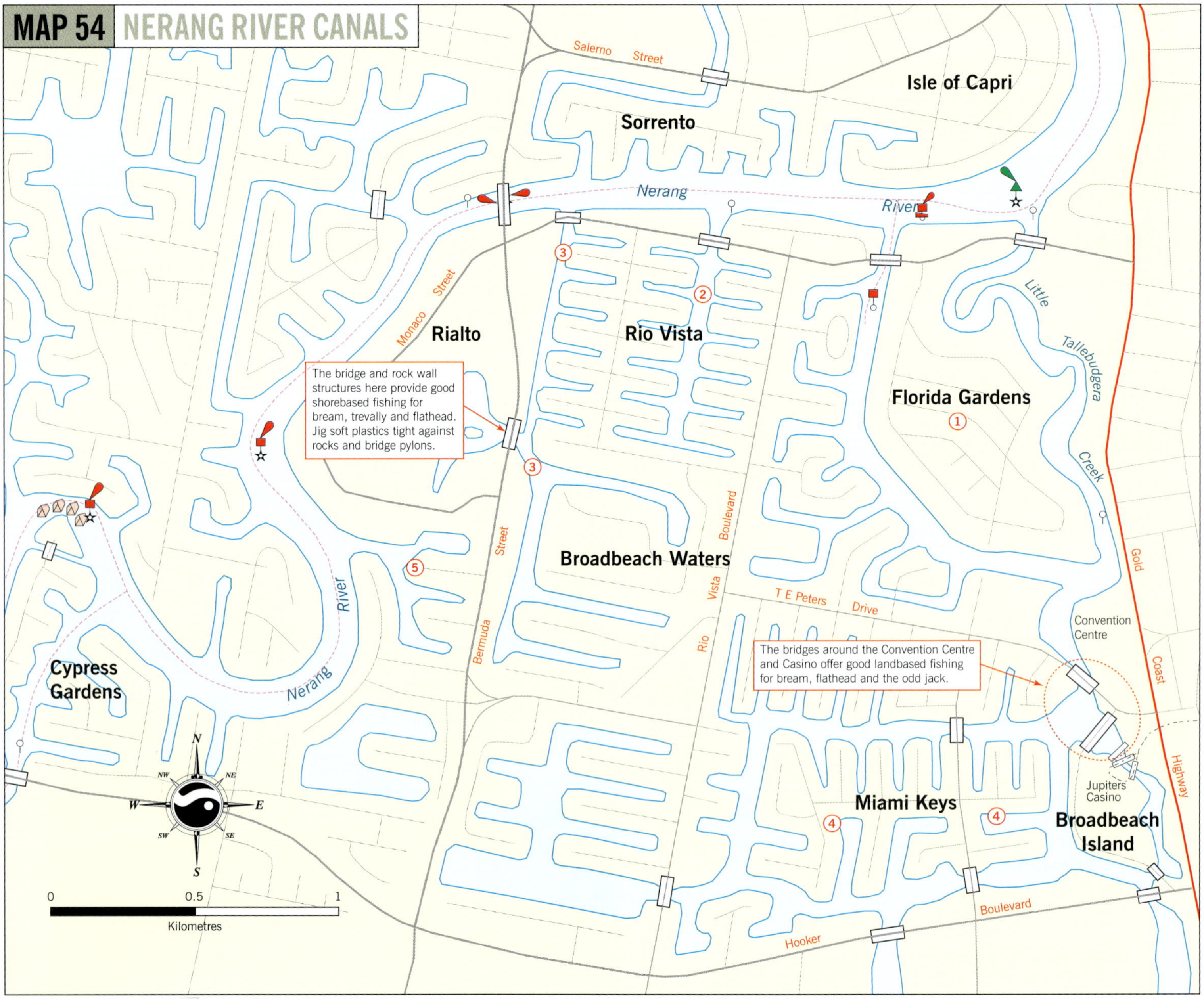

MAP 54 NERANG RIVER CANALS

The bridge and rock wall structures here provide good shorebased fishing for bream, trevally and flathead. Jig soft plastics tight against rocks and bridge pylons.

The bridges around the Convention Centre and Casino offer good landbased fishing for bream, flathead and the odd jack.

Salerno Street
Isle of Capri
Sorrento
Nerang River
Monaco Street
Rialto
Rio Vista
Florida Gardens
Little Tallebudgera Creek
Broadbeach Waters
Bermuda Street
Rio Vista Boulevard
T E Peters Drive
Gold Coast Highway
Convention Centre
Cypress Gardens
Miami Keys
Jupiters Casino
Broadbeach Island
Hooker Boulevard
0 0.5 1 Kilometres

ABOVE: Surface lures fished across canal waters at night are often the way to tempt resident jacks. (PHOTOGRAPH BY MICK HORN)

tidal flow through the river. Exploring the far reaches of canals and distant canal systems during periods of low tidal flow often uncovers more active fish populations. The rising tide is often used by resident fish to leave shaded areas and cruise the shallows in search of food. Surface lures, lightly weighted soft plastics and shallow diving lures will produce fish along the sandy shorelines during such times. A receding tide will drive fish to seek shelter beneath available hard structure and in deeper water holes in the system. Lures and baits have to be presented to fish in deep shaded waters to tempt a bite at these times. Quality fish are nearly always found close to structure. Lures and baits have to be presented tight to these areas to catch such fish. Lures should be bumped against structure wherever possible as this is often the catalyst to getting a response from fish that see a lot of lures and baits. Larger live baits and surface lures fished in the canals during the night are a good strategy for catching mangrove jack and larger trevally. Focus your efforts around deeper water structures and points where tidal flow is focussed to have the best chance of catching these predators. The point at which canal systems enter the main channels are often home to deeper water. Jigging blades and soft plastic lures across these deeper water points is a popular approach to catching bream, flathead and at times, whiting.

Map 54 No. 1 Florida Gardens

The Florida Gardens Canals meet up with Little Tallebudgera Creek which meanders past the Convention Centre. The canals are home to bream, some good whiting and lesser flathead. Little Tallebudgera Creek hosts good rock walls and mixed sand and reef bottom. The rippled sandy bottom usually hosts schools of cruising bream and whiting. The rock walls hold bream and winter luderick. The area offers some good landbased access from the parks that hug the creek shores. The odd jack is caught in the deeper water on live bait fished at night.

Map 54 No. 2 Rio Vista East

There are good canal fishing waters located near to the Nerang River channel. Good bream fishing is found here in winter and spring. The far reaches of the canals fish well at the top of the tide and are good places to retrieve surface lures.

Map 54 No. 3 Rio Vista West

A long line of canals near to the Nerang River channel can be found here. The back end of the southern canal arms fish well for bream and the odd jack. You can experience good summer surface action whereas deep diving hardbody lures are a reliable option in winter and spring.

Map 54 No. 4 Miami Keys

The channel waters to the north of Jupiters Casino fish well at times. Soft plastics around the pontoons or blades jigged around the entrance to canal arms is a sound approach. The bridges in the area are well renowned for producing big bream and jacks in spring and summer. There is plenty of shorebased fishing access from the shorelines around Jupiters Casino. The bridges can be easily fished from the shore here and offer bream, trevally, flathead and mangrove jack fishing options.

Map 54 No. 5 Broadbeach Waters and Sorrento Canals

These canal systems are close to the main channel of the Nerang River. They produce some good bream and jacks at times. Surface fishing the back reaches during summer and slow rolling deep diving lures during winter are proven approaches here. These canal systems often produce fish when most others in the lower reaches are providing tough fishing.

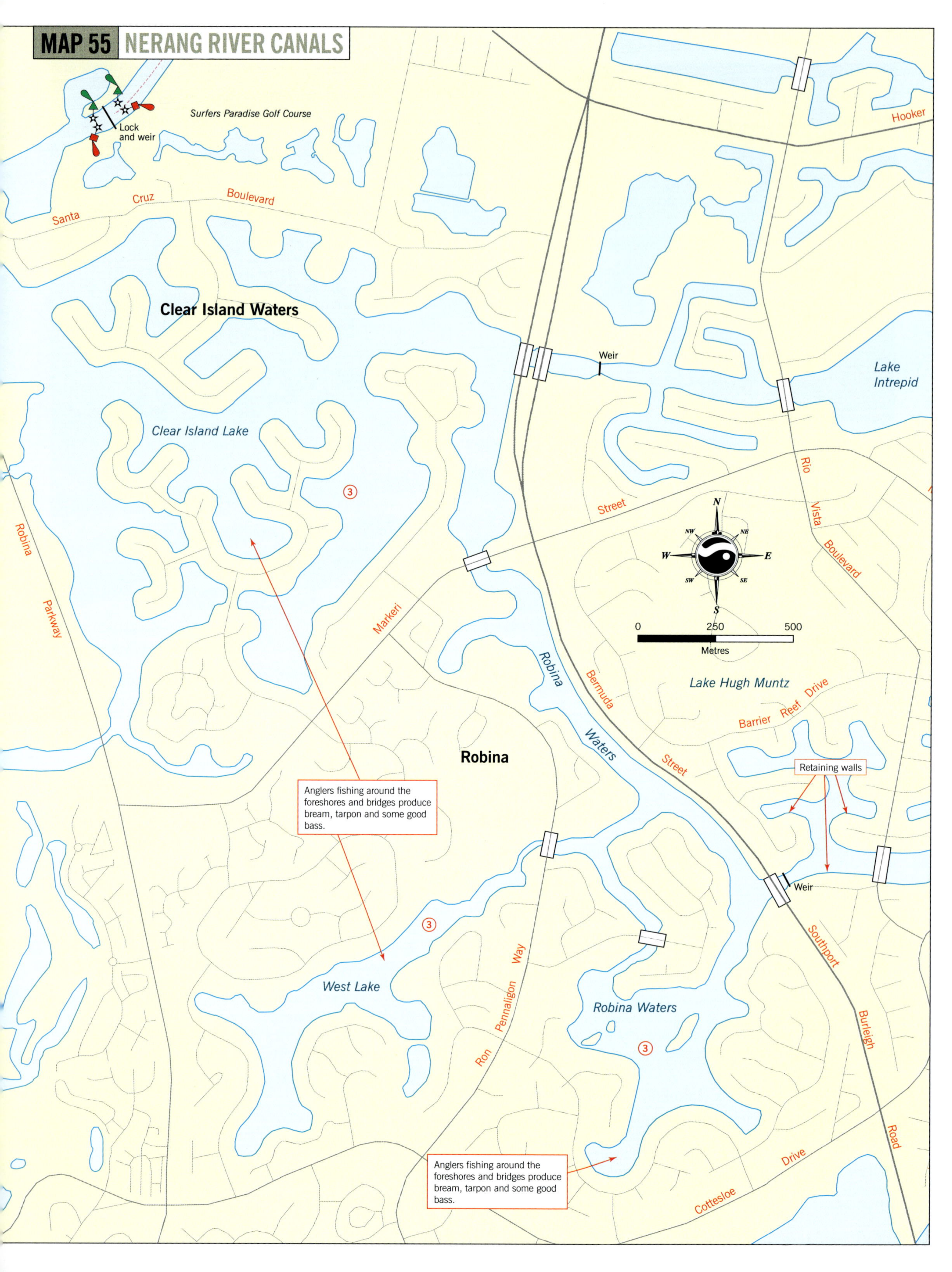
MAP 55 NERANG RIVER CANALS
Surfers Paradise Golf Course
Lock
and weir
Santa
Cruz
Boulevard
Hooker
Clear Island Waters
Weir
Lake
Intrepid
Clear Island Lake
Rio
Vista
Boulevard
Street
Robina
Parkway
Markeri
N
NW
NE
W
E
SW
SE
S
0
250
500
Metres
Robina
Waters
Bermuda
Street
Lake Hugh Muntz
Barrier
Reef
Drive
Robina
Retaining walls
Anglers fishing around the foreshores and bridges produce bream, tarpon and some good bass.
Weir
Southport
Burleigh
Road
Way
Pennaligon
Ron
West Lake
Robina Waters
Anglers fishing around the foreshores and bridges produce bream, tarpon and some good bass.
Drive
Cottesloe
3
3
3

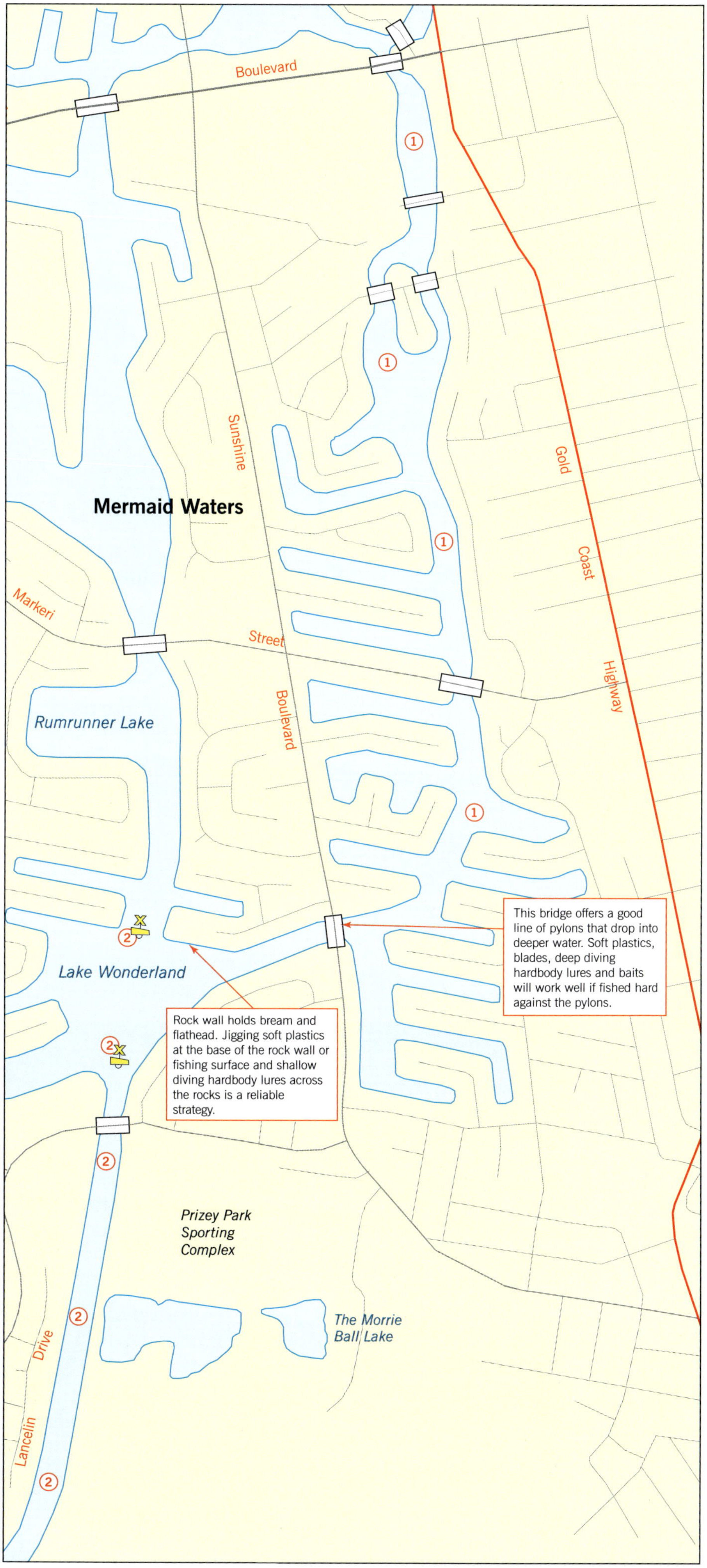

Boulevard

Sunshine Boulevard

Gold Coast Highway

Mermaid Waters

Markeri Street

Rumrunner Lake

Lake Wonderland

This bridge offers a good line of pylons that drop into deeper water. Soft plastics, blades, deep diving hardbody lures and baits will work well if fished hard against the pylons.

Rock wall holds bream and flathead. Jigging soft plastics at the base of the rock wall or fishing surface and shallow diving hardbody lures across the rocks is a reliable strategy.

Prizey Park Sporting Complex

The Morrie Ball Lake

Lancelin Drive

ABOVE: The Gold Coast canals produce quality bream in winter and spring.

MAP 55 NO. 1 MERMAID WATERS EAST

This is often a productive stretch of canals to fish. The bridges and rock walls usually hold a few good bream and the odd jack. The sandy shorelines around these canals fish well for bream and whiting on a building tide. Surface lures and lightly weighted soft plastics fished in the shallows works well here. The bridges all offer shorebased access and provide good fishing. Jigging soft plastics and blades around the base of bridge pylons produces some big bream and the odd jack and trevally. The rocky and sandy shallows around the bridges are often a haven for whiting and lesser flathead.

MAP 55 NO. 2 LAKE WONDERLAND AND LANCELIN DRIVE

The lake waters fish well for trevally at times. Surface luring will quickly bring these fish out to play if they are around in numbers. The shoreline shallows fish well for bream and whiting on a building tide. The bridges and pontoons in the area fish well for bream and jacks on the run-out tide. Big bream are known for cruising the base of the retaining concrete walls in this area and lightly weighted soft plastics cast tight against these walls will usually attract the attention of fish. The Lancelin Drive Channel holds deeper water and patchy bottom reef. The area often holds schooling bream. Jigging blades and soft plastics along the bottom will quickly receive attention from fish if they are concentrated here. Big fish are often produced from the bridges at either end of the channel.

MAP 55 NO. 3 ROBINA WATERS, WEST LAKE AND CLEAR ISLAND LAKE

These lakes are controlled by weirs; the water can often be fresh. Anglers fishing around the foreshores and bridges produce bream, tarpon and some good bass at times.

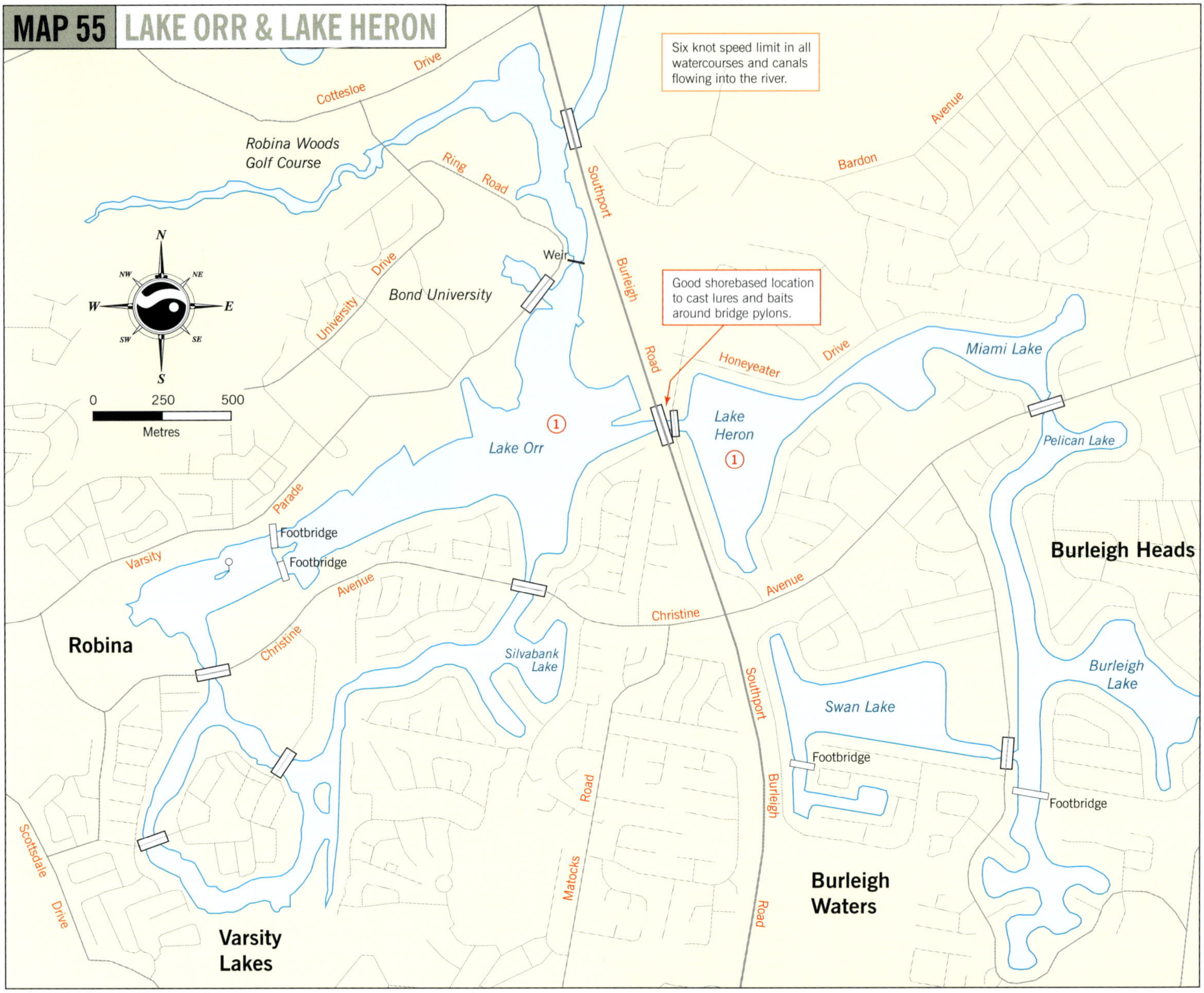

MAP 55 LAKE ORR & LAKE HERON

Six knot speed limit in all watercourses and canals flowing into the river.

Good shorebased location to cast lures and baits around bridge pylons.

Robina Woods Golf Course
Bond University
Lake Orr
Lake Heron
Miami Lake
Pelican Lake
Burleigh Heads
Burleigh Lake
Swan Lake
Silvabank Lake
Robina
Varsity Lakes
Burleigh Waters
Weir
Footbridge
Footbridge
Footbridge
Footbridge
Cottesloe Drive
Ring Road
Southport Burleigh Road
University Drive
Honeyeater Drive
Bardon Avenue
Varsity Parade
Christine Avenue
Scottsdale Drive
Matocks Road
0 250 500
Metres

Map 55 No. 1 Lake Orr and Heron

Lake Orr and Lake Heron produce some good trevally fishing at times. The lakes maintain a population of resident fish that grow bigger each year. The bridges and shoreline rocks produce a few bream, flathead and the odd jack and bass.

TALLEBUDGERA CREEK LOCATION GUIDE

Tallebudgera Creek is a very shallow system with crystal clear water at high tide and huge expanses of golden sand at low water, making it very popular for families. Most of the creek's shallow sand banks are fringed with weed beds and hold good numbers of whiting, bream and flathead. The sand is loaded with yabbies and soldier crabs, making them ideal for catching a feed. The canals are home to some quality bream and there are plenty of mangrove jack in the summer months that hide under the numerous floating pontoons.

Navigating upstream past the canals is difficult at low tide but is ideal for kayak fishing. Providing the tide isn't too full, most of

Night fishing in Tallebudgera produces some trophy jacks for bait and lure anglers. (PHOTOGRAPH BY MICK HORN)

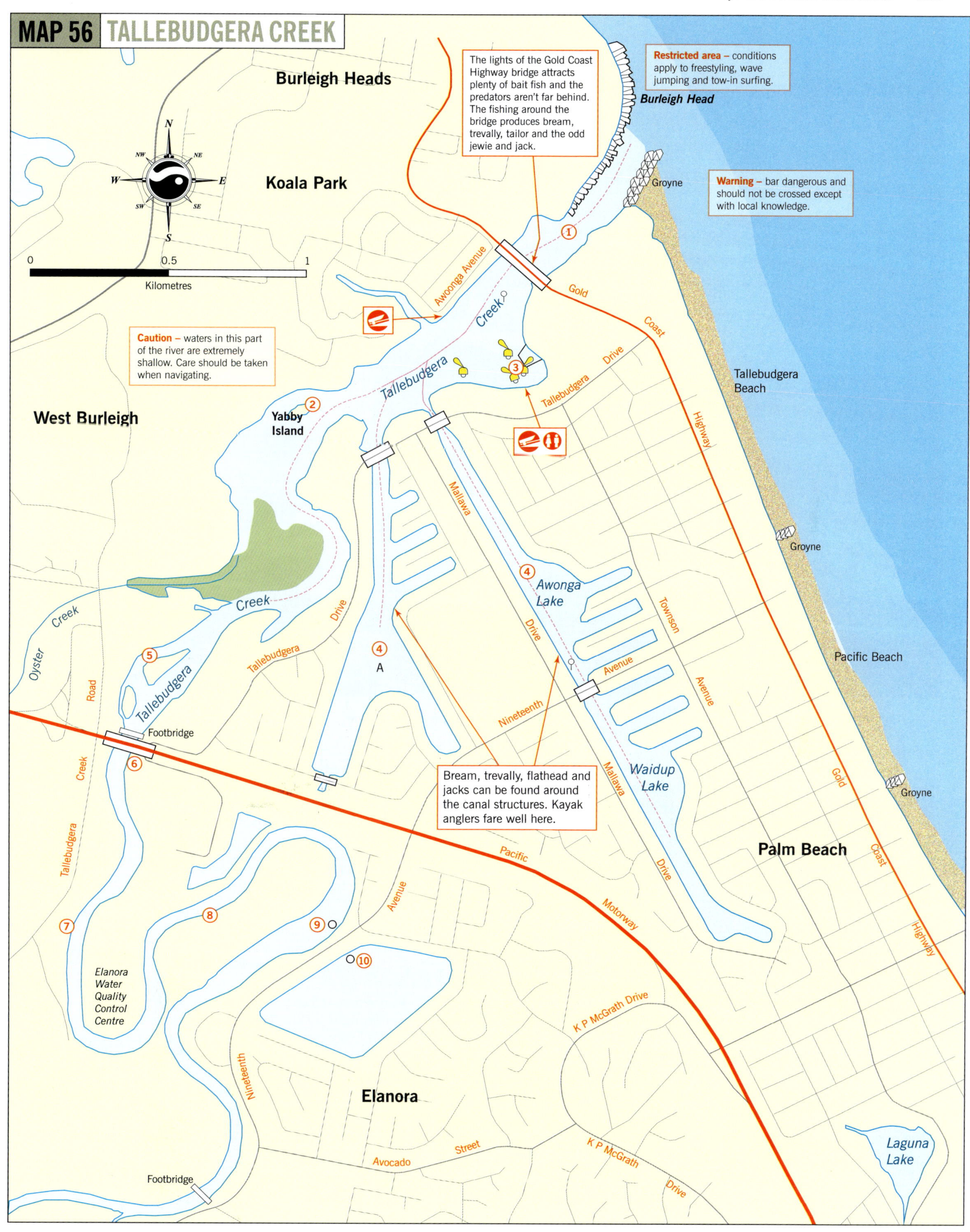

MAP 56 TALLEBUDGERA CREEK
Burleigh Heads
Koala Park
West Burleigh
Burleigh Head
The lights of the Gold Coast Highway bridge attracts plenty of bait fish and the predators aren't far behind. The fishing around the bridge produces bream, trevally, tailor and the odd jewie and jack.
Restricted area – conditions apply to freestyling, wave jumping and tow-in surfing.
Warning – bar dangerous and should not be crossed except with local knowledge.
Caution – waters in this part of the river are extremely shallow. Care should be taken when navigating.
Bream, trevally, flathead and jacks can be found around the canal structures. Kayak anglers fare well here.
0
0.5
1
Kilometres
Groyne
Tallebudgera Beach
Pacific Beach
Palm Beach
Yabby Island
Tallebudgera Creek
Oyster Creek
Awonga Lake
Waidup Lake
Laguna Lake
Footbridge
Elanora Water Quality Control Centre
Elanora
Gold Coast Highway
Pacific Motorway
Awoonga Avenue
Tallebudgera Drive
Mallawa Drive
Townson Avenue
Nineteenth Avenue
Tallebudgera Creek Road
K P McGrath Drive
Avocado Street

ABOVE: Tallebudgera Creek carries a good reputation for providing good summer mangrove jack fishing. (PHOTOGRAPH BY MICK HORN)

the shore is accessible by foot, making fly fishing or flicking lures a great option. The channel waters, bridges and pontoons attract a variety of larger predators so don't be fooled into thinking that this smaller creek is only home to smaller sized fish.

Map 56 No. 1 Tallebudgera Creek Entrance
(Bream, whiting, flathead, tailor, jewfish)

A rising winter tide just after dark will often see big schools of tailor enter the creek. They can be targeted from the deeper channel at the creek's mouth. This channel follows the southern shore at the mouth before swinging around to the northern shore just before the bridge. A jewfish angler will also be switched on to the fact that the big jewies will often follow tailor and mullet schools into the creek.

The lights of the Gold Coast Highway bridge attracts plenty of bait fish and the predators often aren't far behind. A lot of the surface action that you see under the bridge at night is tarpon and they can be almost impossible to catch on bait. Small soft plastic lures will entice the odd one and when the tailor are in the area, the lure fishing for these fish can be red hot.

Map 56 No. 2 Yabby Island
(Whiting, bream, flathead)

The area is home to shallow water yabby beds. Baits of yabby and worm fished in the area results in some good catches of summer whiting.

Map 56 No. 3 The Swimming Pool
(Bream, trevally, tailor, jewfish)

The swimming pool netting provides a large structure close to the entrance of the creek. Anglers casting lures or baits around the area catch bream, trevally, tailor and the odd school jewfish. Fishing is best early in the day or at night when the area is not being used by swimmers.

Map 56 No. 4 Tallebudgera Creek Canals
(Bream, trevally, flathead, tailor, jewfish)

The two canals that run off Tallebudgera Creek have a bridge just inside the mouth and both are a light tackle angler's delight. Awonga and Waidup Lakes provide the waters for the eastern canal system. This canal provides the pick of the bridges; the southern side of the bridge fishes well at first or last light. Here, there are tailor, tarpon, jewfish, bream and trevally and all will take a well presented lure on light tackle. The odd mangrove jack will make short work of you in the pylons so beef the gear up if it's jacks you're after. The western system (A) has broad open backwaters that are a popular spot to chase trevally on surface lures. The pontoons and jetties are a good spot for boat and kayak anglers to cast lures for bream, jacks and flathead.

Map 56 No. 5 Tallebudgera Creek Road Yabby Flats
(Whiting, bream, flathead)

The shallows along this shoreline are home to good numbers of yabbies. The area fishes well for whiting and bream using baits of yabby and worms.

Map 56 No. 6 Pacific Highway Bridge
(Mangrove Jack, Bream, Flathead, Trevally, Jewfish)

The bottom of the channel around the Pacific Highway Bridge hosts plenty of hard rock structure. This structure makes the bridge area a great place to target tough predators such as jacks, trevally and the odd jewfish. Bream and flathead will also hold position in the waters around and about the area. This location is a very popular place for the local live bait anglers; fishing with live fish and prawns around the bridge at night is an excellent way to hook those resident predators.

Map 56 No. 7 Creek Road Rock Wall
(Bream, Flathead)

The western shoreline holds a good rock wall that sits adjacent to deeper channel water. Drifting the area with baits or casting and retrieving soft plastics close to the structure provides good fishing for bream and flathead.

Map 56 No. 8 Water Treatment Channel
(Mangrove Jack, Bream, Flathead)

The southern bank sits above the deepest part of the channel in this location. The shoreline provides areas of fallen timber that are used by local jacks as prime ambush locations. Casting lures around the timber produces jacks in summer and flathead in spring.

Map 56 No. 9 Lake Outlet
(Mangrove Jack, Bream, Flathead)

The outlet that releases lake water into the creek is located here. A run-out tide pushes water through this area and often attracts local predators. Anglers fishing with live bait and soft plastic lures in summer fare well on night-time jacks in this spot.

Map 56 No. 10 Lake Inlet
(Mangrove Jack, Bream, Trevally, Flathead)

The opposite side to the Outlet; this area fishes best on a run-in tide. Resident bream, jacks, trevally and flathead hold around the Inlet on a run-in tide. These two areas are good shorebased locations.

CURRUMBIN CREEK LOCATION GUIDE

Much of Currumbin Creek is accessible by foot; exploring the area with a light spin rod, handful of lures and backpack can reveal some beautiful and productive fishing locations. The lower sections of the creek are home to deeper channel waters, bridges and extensive shallow flats. These areas are a haven for whiting, bream, flathead and the odd mangrove jack.

Moving upstream, Currumbin Waters Canals can see some excellent surface lure fishing at first and last light for trevally and mangrove jack. Past the Galleon Way Bridge, a more natural looking creek begins to emerge and hiding in the snags are some monster bream and mangrove jacks. Lures cast close to the snags works well during the day, but at night, the fish leave the snags and can be caught on live or fresh fish baits. The creek is a busy little waterway but continues to produce plenty of fish every year.

Map 57 No. 1 Currumbin Creek Entrance
(Whiting, Bream, Flathead)

Just before the Gold Coast Highway Bridge, the creek opens up into what resembles a small lagoon, which is home to some big whiting and bream. This area is a popular swimming hole on weekends but fishes well considering how busy it can get. The shallows to the

Above: The bridges near the mouth of Currumbin Creek host some quality jacks, bream, trevally and the odd jewie. (Photograph by Ben Godfrey)

MAP 57 CURRUMBIN CREEK

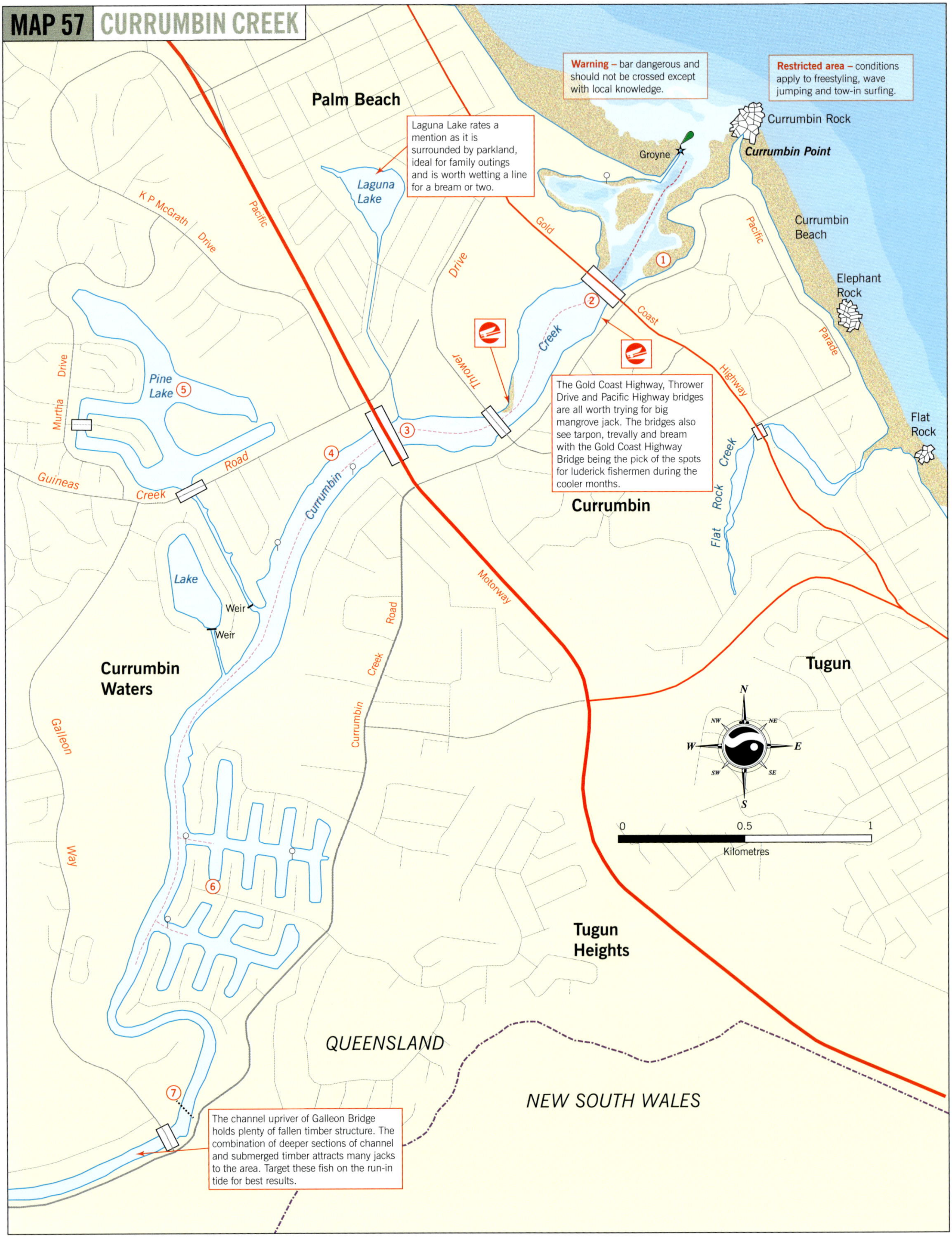

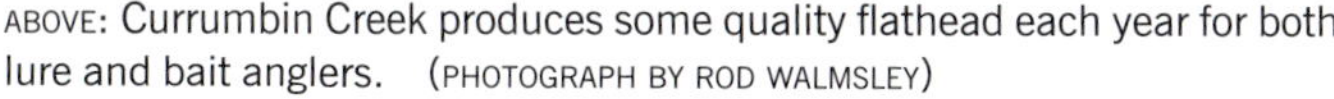

ABOVE: Currumbin Creek produces some quality flathead each year for both lure and bait anglers. (PHOTOGRAPH BY ROD WALMSLEY)

RIGHT TOP: Currumbin Creek produces some sizeable trevally for a small system. (PHOTOGRAPH BY MICK HORN)

RIGHT: The upper reaches of Currumbin Creek provide some good bass fishing during summer. (PHOTOGRAPH BY ROD WALMSLEY)

west of the swimming area are full of yabby beds. A bait fished in this spot before the swimmers and water craft start getting active is a good way to catch resident fish.

Map 57 No. 2 Gold Coast Highway Bridge
(MANGROVE JACK, TREVALLY, LUDERICK, BREAM, FLATHEAD)

The bridge provides good structure around some slightly deeper channel waters. Baits and lures fished around the structure produce summer jacks and trevally and winter bream and luderick. Fishing at night is a good option in this area as the on-water traffic has largely disappeared by this time of day.

Map 57 No. 3 Pacific Motorway Bridge
(BREAM, FLATHEAD, TREVALLY, MANGROVE JACK)

The bridge offers plenty of pylons at which to cast lures and baits; a popular approach here is to drift baits through the area. The bridge always holds a few bream, flathead, trevally and mangrove jack. The spot is a popular night-time summer jack location. The run-in tide produces best results here.

Map 57 No. 4 Guineas Creek Road Flats
(WHITING, BREAM, FLATHEAD)

The channel is lined by shallow flats and baits of yabby and worm produce bream and whiting on a building tide. Lightly weighted soft plastics and surface hardbody lures attract attention from local fish in summer.

Map 57 No. 5 Pine Lake
(BREAM, FLATHEAD, TREVALLY, MANGROVE JACK, TARPON, GIANT HERRING)

Landbased anglers have excellent access to Pine Lake, which is fed by a narrow canal from Currumbin Creek. Most of the shore is accessible from The Pines shopping centre with parks and footpaths around a lot of the lake. Bream, flathead, trevally and mangrove jack are commonly caught here. Fly fishing for tarpon and giant herring provides some exciting action on light fly rods in this location.

Map 57 No. 6 Currumbin Waters Canals
(BREAM, FLATHEAD, TREVALLY, MANGROVE JACK, TARPON, GIANT HERRING)

The canals provide some exciting fishing for boat and kayak anglers. The most popular approach is to cast a variety of lures around the man-made structure here. The water clarity improves in the area during the latter stages of the run-in tide. The fishing is often at its best during these times.

Map 57 No. 7 Powerlines Channel *(FLATHEAD)*

This sandy and weeded section of channel is host to some timber shoreline structure making it a popular location for catching flathead. Drifting and jigging with soft plastics or dragging fresh baits along the bottom should produce fish in this area.

PART 4

OFFSHORE FISHING

ABOVE: The offshore waters of the south-east corner of this state hold plenty of treasures for anglers.

The offshore fishing scene of the south-east corner of Queensland has much to offer the recreational angler. The climate makes fishing in these waters a pleasure and weather permitting, the ocean in the Brisbane and districts areas can be accessed from a number of ports. The offshore angler is faced with a huge number of local fishing options. Deeper water currents are easily accessible and provide some fantastic big game fishing. The Moreton Bay, Gold Coast and Sunshine Coast waters have accounted for a number of gamefishing records. Deep and shallow reef systems provide endless opportunities for anglers chasing reef and pelagic species. Shallow water bommies and exposed ocean rock attract the likes of big giant trevally and other pelagics. There are several locations where fishers float lining for snapper can be sitting alongside boats occupied by anglers popping surface lures for XOS giant trevally: Like I said, the area has a lot to offer!

A great mix of offshore species can be targeted along the south-eastern corner of the coastline; the Brisbane, Gold Coast and Sunshine Coast waters are situated in a geographical zone where northern and southern species mix. The local species hit-list includes but is not limited to the likes of northern bluefin and yellowfin tuna, mackerel, cobia, sweetlip, pearl perch, teraglin, coral trout, snapper, jewfish (mulloway), red emperor, nannygai, gold band snapper, tusk fish, amberjack, marlin, sailfish, dolphin fish, kingfish and sharks.

Offshore water temperatures govern the type of piscatorial activity you are likely to find when venturing offshore in these parts. This variable aside, you are most likely to find that the warmer months provide great pelagic fishing activity for species such as Spanish, spotted and grey mackerel, tuna, wahoo, dolphin fish, sailfish, marlin and cobia although there will be some overlap with some of these species on any given year. Winter pelagic captures are dominated by the likes of the odd cobia, longtail tuna, kingfish and amberjack. The cooler months are very often the domain of the reef angler targeting bottom species. This has a lot to do with improved weather conditions combined with increased numbers of reef species in certain reef areas during the winter months. The cool periods are prime time to target fish like snapper, pearl perch, teraglin, tuskfish and red emperor. Although they can be caught all

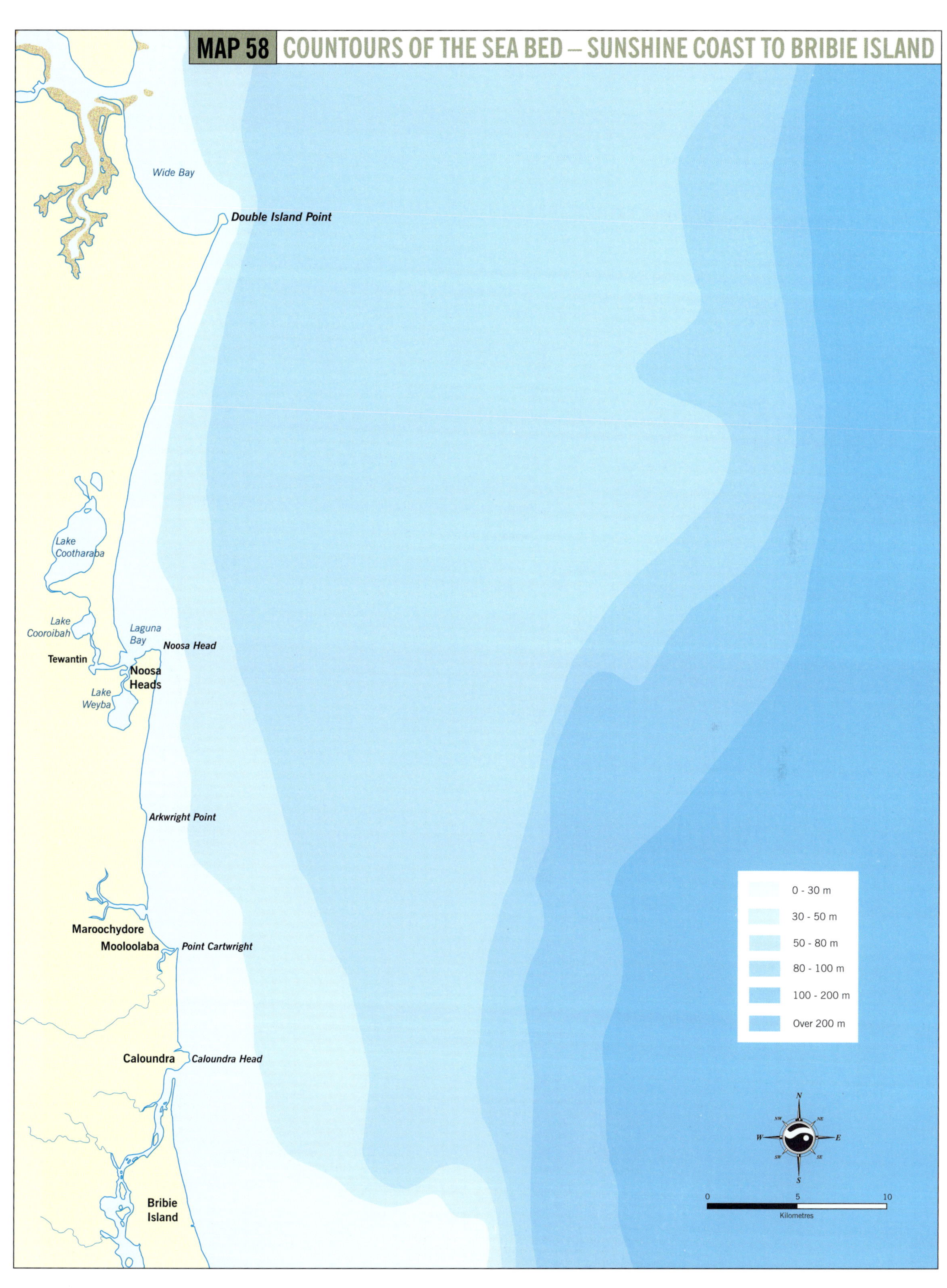
MAP 58 COUNTOURS OF THE SEA BED – SUNSHINE COAST TO BRIBIE ISLAND
Wide Bay
Double Island Point
Lake Cootharaba
Lake Cooroibah
Laguna Bay
Noosa Head
Tewantin
Noosa Heads
Lake Weyba
Arkwright Point
Maroochydore
Mooloolaba
Point Cartwright
Caloundra
Caloundra Head
Bribie Island
0 - 30 m
30 - 50 m
50 - 80 m
80 - 100 m
100 - 200 m
Over 200 m
N
NE
E
SE
S
SW
W
NW
0
5
10
Kilometres

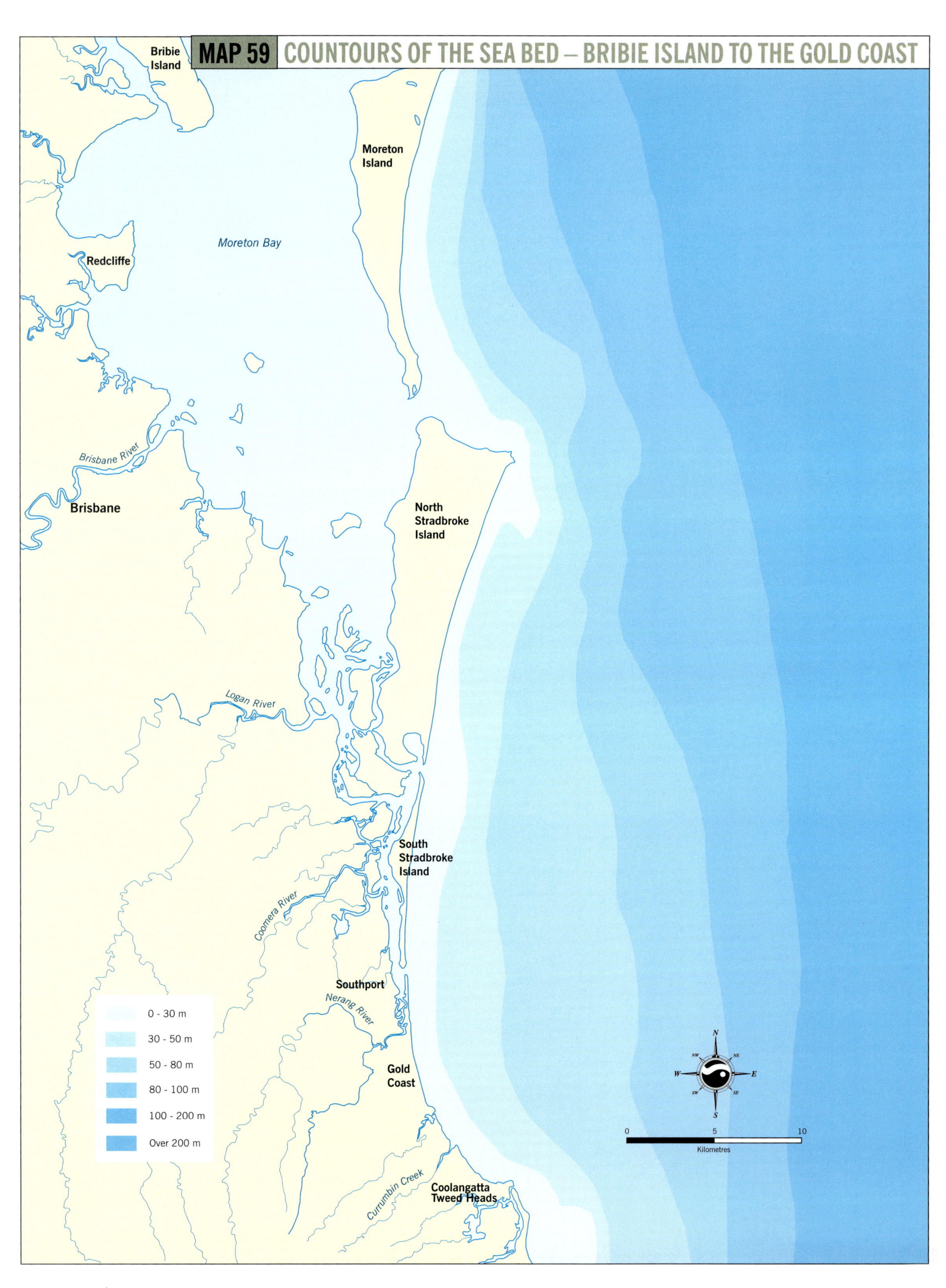

MAP 59 COUNTOURS OF THE SEA BED – BRIBIE ISLAND TO THE GOLD COAST
Bribie Island
Moreton Island
Moreton Bay
Redcliffe
Brisbane River
Brisbane
North Stradbroke Island
Logan River
South Stradbroke Island
Coomera River
Southport
Nerang River
Gold Coast
Currumbin Creek
Coolangatta
Tweed Heads
0 - 30 m
30 - 50 m
50 - 80 m
80 - 100 m
100 - 200 m
Over 200 m
N
NE
E
SE
S
SW
W
NW
0
5
10
Kilometres

year, the summer months often provide a good run of coral trout, sweetlip and snapper.

A unique aspect to fishing along this stretch of the coast is the manner in which fishing conditions change between the northern and southern waters. For example, there is often the scenario where the inshore anglers fishing the Gold Coast and Moreton Island waters are reporting good catches of mackerel, wahoo, trevally and dolphin fish. At the same time, the Sunshine Coast anglers are faring poorly unless prepared to travel a good 60km or so off the coast. Pardon the pun, but the Cape Moreton peninsular provides a major turning point in this stretch of coastline. The fishing conditions change a lot at this precise point, and with good reason. The contour maps we have provided (maps 58 and 59) show the geometry of the ocean floor from the Sunshine Coast to the Gold Coast. The gradient of the ocean floor varies dramatically between Noosa and the Gold Coast. Sunshine Coast anglers wishing to target fish in 70–80m of water have to travel 40–60km before they are able to do so. Moreton Island anglers on the other hand, need travel only 1–2km from the tip of Cape Moreton before they hit the deeper water ledge. This ledge affects the movement of current along the coast considerably. Being that the currents are the fishing lifeline of these waters, it becomes easily apparent why fishing varies from north to south. It explains why the big giant trevally and near -shore dolphin fish and wahoo are readily available a stones throw from Moreton Island and the Gold Coast. Sunshine Coast anglers don't get to see big giant trevally and have to travel 10–20km's before they stand a chance of seeing wahoo, dolphin fish and other blue water current dwellers.

Chapter seven will highlight all the key offshore fishing areas from Noosa to the Queensland and New South Wales border. GPS marks identifying most of these areas have been provided to assist you to find the general location of these fishing spots. The maps of these locations have been split into two key areas to reflect the variability of fishing conditions in the two zones. The Sunshine Coast fishery incorporates the area from Noosa to Bribie Island while the southern waters incorporate those from the tip of Moreton Island to the Gold Coast.

LEFT: Quality reef fishing can be found a stones throw from Moreton Bay.

BELOW: Our south-east waters offer plenty of offshore fishing options.

CHAPTER 7

OFFSHORE FISHING

The Sunshine Coast, Brisbane and the Gold Coast

ABOVE: Sailfish are popular visitors to our local waters.

INTRODUCTION

The offshore fishing from Noosa to the Gold Coast is a sport fisher's paradise. In close proximity to one of our biggest cities and two of Australia's most popular tourist playgrounds, locals and visitors are treated to a world class fishery. A number of shallow and deep water ocean access points and plenty of service facilities make fishing the local Brisbane offshore waters both easy and pleasurable. This is one of the reasons that Queensland maintains some of the highest boat registration numbers per capita in the country. The seasons broadly dictate the types of fishing on offer in this part of the world. In a very broad sense, summer is the season for chasing pelagic and various reef species, while winter is the domain of the reef fishing angler.

GPS Marks

There are extensive shallow and deep water fishing grounds along this stretch of coast. In this chapter we have summarised all of the key locations available to offshore anglers. Global Positioning System (GPS) marks identifying the locations of fishing spots have been listed. These marks are sourced from the many experts that have helped to produce this book and not all can be verified. The variability between different GPS units can provide small discrepancies in the exact location of waypoints. The GPS coordinates we have published can be used to locate the general area of the fishing spots described; several of these marks identify prominent fish holding zones within a particular reef system. Being that much of the local reef consists of broken reef and rubble, it will pay huge dividends to explore the areas around the published marks. Use your sounder to locate features that suit your target species and styles of fishing. Published GPS marks should not be used as a navigation tool.

Green Zones

Every effort has been made to highlight the boundaries of current Marine Park Green Zones. Fishing is prohibited in these areas as they serve to protect fish within their boundaries. These areas are open to change at any time, and as such, anglers must always maintain an awareness of the exact current locations of local Green Zones.

FISHING NOTES FOR OFFSHORE

Fishing Variables

There are certain variables that influence the feeding habits of fish. Experienced commercial and recreational fishers pay close attention to some of these variables which means they should be paid due credit. It is worth understanding some of these factors to ensure you maximise your fishing time on the water.

The ***moon phase*** has an affect on all animals which means we need to consider its influence on fish. Experience suggests that many fish will be increasingly active around the new and full moon periods. The days immediately around and including the full moon are used by many commercial anglers to catch fish during the middle of the night. Seasoned veterans will tell you that reef fishing during the day of the full moon can be a testing experience. The position of the moon in the sky also has an effect on fish feeding behaviour. The periods including the moon being directly overhead and directly underfoot seem to coincide with increased feeding activity levels.

It should come as no surprise that the ***tidal fluctuations*** have an effect on fish feeding activity. Sayings like 'no run, no fun' have been around for a long time. The slack water stages of the tide very often correlate with tough fishing conditions. The best time to be fishing often coincides with the start and end of a tidal cycle. This means that fish will feed most actively as the tide begins to move, and then again just before it starts to lose momentum towards the end of the tide phase.

The movement of the ***barometer*** will have an effect on fish behaviour. More often than not, a dropping barometer will have a negative influence on local fish. The dropping barometer is associated with north-westerly wind in south-east Queensland. Many anglers have learnt that fishing this area during the north-westerly wind makes for tougher fishing.

ABOVE: There are several variables such as moon phase that influence the behaviour of fish.

Many anglers experience improved results during ***low light*** periods of the day. Making the effort to be fishing as the sun is rising or setting can often pay dividends. So too, overcast and cloudy days often coincide with a better catch.

The amount of prevailing ***ocean current*** can dramatically affect the fishing success of a day on the water. It is difficult to predict the amount of current velocity that you will encounter on any given day. Responding to the amount of current is what often sets the consistently successful anglers aside from the rest. Adapting technique to try and effectively present lures and baits to fish is a good strategy. Another good tactic is to move and try to locate areas that are experiencing lower current flow. Often the margin of strong and slowly moving zones of current hold good numbers of bait and predators.

SPECIES AND TECHNIQUE

Local anglers use a number of techniques to target some of our favourite species. A list of some of the popular local targets and the techniques used to catch them is summarised in the following section.

Reef Species

Snapper are one of the most sought after recreational fish in these waters and they are readily caught on baits and artificials. Quality fresh baits fished with a minimum of lead is a proven recipe for success. Fresh fillet baits, live fish, squid and pilchards are some of the most popular baits used by local anglers although live yakka or slimey mackerel will work exceptionally well for the larger snapper. Paternoster rigs fished at anchor is a traditional way of fishing for snapper on the reef; however, it is the anglers that learn to drift or anchor and fish lightly weighted baits that consistently bring home the better catches. This technique is locally referred to as 'float lining'. John Palermo has been bait fishing for snapper in these waters for decades. His outfit of choice includes an 8–10kg monofilament outfit rigged with a no. 5–9 size ball sinker (depending on current) and a ganged two hook rig. John fishes with W.A. pilchards the majority of the time.

Soft plastics are a common choice for snapper these days and almost any 3–5 inch plastic will entice the average snapper up to 3kg. Larger plastics to 7 inch are ideal for targeting those trophy fish that can reach 10kg in weight. These lures can be fished while drifting or at anchor for equally good results. Blade lures, lipless crankbaits and minnow lures are also becoming increasingly popular with snapper anglers as we learn effective methods of catching fish on these offerings.

Large high pressure systems move over southern Queensland in winter. This makes for stable fishing conditions when the snapper are schooled up in spawning mode. This is a prime time of the year to catch some good fish. Spring and early summer are the seasons to catch some really big snapper. Post spawn fish often head into shallower water to feed aggressively and regain condition. Bait and soft plastics fished around the shallower reefs regularly produce

ABOVE: Snapper are a popular offshore target.

fish around that magic 10kg mark. February and March will also produce some good snapper catches but the main action often occurs after dark.

Pearl perch are another very popular reef fish amongst Queensland anglers; they can be targeted with both baits and artificials. Quality fresh baits fished close to the bottom will nearly always entice these fish if they are schooling in the local area. Their big mouth makes them easy to hook but also proves their downfall as a fighting fish. As the mouth of a pearl perch remains open when being brought up, they often feel like nothing more than a heavy weight. Fortunately the eating quality of these fish well and truly compensates for their fighting ability. These fish are suckers for a well presented soft plastic or metal jig. Smaller knife and skirted jigs account for many of them each season.

There are a variety of sweetlip species encountered on local reef systems. Grass, red throat and yellow sweetlip (commonly known as spangled emperor) are the most common varieties encountered by local anglers; they are often caught by fishers targeting snapper, as they are found in similar areas and will eat the same offerings. Grass sweetlip are the most common and many larger specimens are lost due to their tenacious and powerful fighting ability once hooked. Their prime white flesh makes them a welcome catch. Sweetlip are caught all year round but they are most active during the spring and summer months. They are caught on many of our reef systems but seem most common on our shallower reefs. Anglers targeting these fish on baits and lures are well served to decrease the size of baits and plastics. Sweetlip are equipped with a smaller mouth that makes eating larger offerings a challenge at times.

Anglers actively fishing for sweetlip will encounter the prized coral trout as these fish like similar types of structure. Three varieties of trout are found in these waters: the common, coronation and island (bar-cheeked) trout. These fish are most active in the summer months on reef systems that offer generous relief. They are rarely found on the gravel grounds. Sunshine Reef at the northern end of the Sunshine Coast is one of the most consistent producers of trout. These fish are nasty brawlers and expert at finding their way back to a reefy cave when hooked. Anglers that consistently defeat these predators use 20–40kg mainlines. Although trout are taken on soft plastics and jigs at times, in local waters they are most commonly caught on baits. Live fish, pilchard and squid baits fished near to the bottom are a sound approach to tempting one of these tasty fish.

RIGHT: Our offshore waters sustain many species of cod.

BELOW: The distinctive slashing spray of a mackerel chasing baitfish near the surface. High speed retrieves with metal slug lures will tempt these fish.

Above: Nannygai are a welcome catch in our southern waters.

Jewfish (mulloway) are a popular catch on our offshore reefs. Although not a common fish, they are becoming more prolific in our bay and inshore waters. The key to catching these fish offshore is to find the structures that they most favour. This usually comprises of any hard feature with a bit of height. If a structure deflects current, it will house jewies. Common places to find these fish include wrecks, ledges and reef systems with bommies and pinnacles. Large dead and live fish, squid baits and soft plastic lures will tempt these predators. An average offshore jewie is usually in the 10–15kg range so suitable tackle should be used when tackling these hard fighting fish. Winter and spring are the pick of the seasons to catch fish, but they are likely to show up whenever there has been some good rain and the ocean is discoloured. Fishing at night, around the new and full moon and across the turn of the tide are good strategies when chasing jewies.

Teraglin, also known as trag jewfish, are caught when targeting snapper and pearl perch. These fish form large schools over predominantly deeper water reef systems. Trag are not known for their sporting ability but are a great table fish. Average sized fish caught are around the 1–2kg size; however, they do grow upwards of 10kg but it is rare to see fish over 5kg in local waters. These fish will aggressively attack baits and soft plastic lures when they are in numbers and best seasons for them are winter and spring.

A variety of rockcod species call our local reefs home. The most common species caught are the maori and estuary rockcods. These fish have cavernous mouths and happily attack any live, dead bait or lure put in front of them. These fish are caught all year round and fish in the 2–5kg range make excellent eating. Estuary cod grow to huge proportions and fish over a metre are protected. These fish are often seen as protectors of the reef and should be handled gently and returned wherever possible.

Red emperor are a common catch in local waters, however, they are rarely of legal size. The waters around Double Island to the north of Noosa are renowned for producing good numbers of emperor; sadly these big fish are not often seen to the immediate south. The deeper northern gravel reefs of the Sunshine Coast produce the odd legal red, but there are few local anglers that have been lucky enough to catch one here. Targeting these fish is a game of patience in local waters. Fishing the deeper reef in winter with big baits and heavy gear is the way to go if attempting to catch a red.

Tuskfish are often locally referred to as 'parrot' and are a welcome catch for anglers. These fish battle hard and come with a pair of succulent white fillets. Like the sweetlip, they possess smaller mouths which mean suitably sized squid and fish flesh baits will produce the goods. These fish are caught all year but winter is the prime time to catch them. They are caught in similar areas to snapper, sweetlip and pearl perch.

Moses perch, hussar, nannygai and jobfish are some of the other reef species that are caught by anglers chasing snapper and pearl perch. Moses perch and hussar are common throughout most of our reef systems. Species such as large-mouth nannygai and jobfish are less common and are often caught in deeper reef systems. Nannygai show up randomly on the odd shallow water system in local waters.

Pelagic Species

Mackerel are a popular angling target throughout much of the summer months. Spanish, grey, school and spotted mackerel are heavily targeted due to their fighting ability and tasty white fillets. Schools of mackerel often invade these waters around Christmas time each year and are usually gone by May. The seasons are known to change and sometimes there are school sized fish being caught in June. Big Spanish mackerel can be caught all year round, but these larger fish are often loners and consistent catches are hard

Local AJ's will always test out tackle every step of the way.
(Photograph by Roderick Walmsley)

to replicate. Summer run mackerel will follow bait schools and the key to finding them is to search for the bait. Surface feeding expressions make it easy to find them, however they will spend most of their time feeding deeper in the water. Targeting fish around deeper bait schools and reef is the way to go when they can't be seen near the top. Surface feeding schools of mackerel can be targeted with metal slugs (chrome slices) and a high-speed retrieve. Slow trolling with either live and dead baits or deeper diving hardbody lures can produce results when the mackerel are a little deeper. Jigging metal slugs and drifting pilchards on ganged-hook rigs around reef systems and bait schools is a popular approach. Wire and heavier line classes are often required when targeting mackerel as they are adept at chewing through fishing line.

Yellowtail kingfish hunt throughout our offshore waters.

Wahoo are synonymous with warm blue current and any areas that this water permeates will offer the chance to catch these speedsters. The wider grounds on the Sunshine Coast such as Chardons Reef, The Hards and Barwon Banks, the wide reefs off Caloundra and Mooloolaba and then the water off Cape Moreton and the Gold Coast offer plenty of opportunity to tangle with wahoo. Renowned Brisbane wahoo locations include the Hutchinson Shoals, Flinders Reef and off Point Lookout. High-speed skirted lures and bibbed and bibless minnows work a treat on these speedsters. Wahoo between 6–10kg are average sized fish but they can reach over 25kg. Slowly trolled, rigged swimming-baits and bridle-rigged live baits will also work a treat around current lines, bommies, rocky outcrops and exposed reef areas.

Surface feeding schools of longtail (northern bluefin), yellowfin, and mack tuna can be found in our offshore waters throughout the year; they can be caught on lures and baits. The peak of tuna activity occurs in summer, but they can be caught sporadically throughout the year. Longtails are often caught in deeper water on the Sunshine Coast and around Moreton Island in winter. These fish make great sport and anglers spend a lot of time chasing them on lures. Getting close to an aggressive surface feeding bunch of tuna is an exciting affair. High speed spinning with metal slugs and soft plastics is a popular strategy for hooking these fish. Many anglers also choose to troll bibbed and skirted lures in local waters when chasing tuna. Recent times have resulted in more anglers targeting them on surface hardbody lures such as stickbaits and poppers. Tuna will

ABOVE: The wider grounds of the Gold Coast produce some large yellowfin tuna. (PHOTOGRAPH BY RODERICK WALMSLEY)

ABOVE: The waters a stone's throw from the Gold Coast can turn up some fun sized marlin at times. (PHOTOGRAPH BY RODERICK WALMSLEY)

also readily take a well presented pilchard bait or fly. The key is finding where the fish are and presenting a hook to them without spooking the school.

Cobia, also known as black kingfish, are a year-round proposition. Spring and early summer seems to produce a more consistent run of fish but keep your eyes out for them at all times. These fish have a propensity for hanging around big objects such as floating ocean debris, turtles, manta rays and whales. Once spotted, they will often readily take a bait, soft plastic or other type of lure. Cobia are hooked anywhere from top to bottom on live and dead baits including yakkas, slimey mackerel, whiptails, sand crabs and many other larger baits. They spend much of their time hunting fish and crabs and are a species that offer great sport and a very good feed. With the average quality fish around the 8–10kg mark and specimens to over 40kg showing up at times, minimum 15kg main line, 45kg monofilament leaders and 8/0 live bait or circle hooks are required for a positive outcome.

Amberjack (AJ's), yellowtail kingfish and samson fish are without a doubt the thugs of our waters. Most often hooked while targeting other species such as snapper, these fish make a habit of destroying equipment. They love areas where current, structure and baitfish are found together. They can be caught all year round and will respond well to lure and bait techniques. Live and dead baits of fish and squid will tempt AJ's and kings. Lure fishing techniques including deep water knife jigging, soft plastics jigging and surface luring with stickbaits and poppers are favoured approaches for catching these beasts. Tackle needs to be sturdy to win battles with kingfish and amberjack.

Several species of trevally can be caught in offshore southern Queensland waters. The most common species encountered in the waters offshore of the Brisbane area include the giant, brassy (tea-leaf) and golden trevallies. Golden and tea-leaf trevally will school on prominent structures such as wrecks and bommies. The golden trevally becomes more common towards the northern waters around Noosa and Teewah. The most targeted trevally species in the south-east corner is the giant trevally (GT). These fish are rarely caught offshore along the Sunshine Coast as the water here does not hold the type of structure and current that suits these fish. The waters south of Cape Moreton hold some very big giant trevally as the deeper water here rises to shallow bommies and the whole area is often exposed to stronger current. Anglers casting big poppers and stickbaits hook big fish each season; landing them is a very different matter! Sturdy tackle and a dose of luck are required to boat these fish. Large GT's to over 30kg are sometimes caught around the bommies out from Point Lookout, Flinders Reef and Cape Moreton.

The summer months are prime time to catch dolphin fish and the same waters that hold wahoo, sailfish and marlin will usually hold them. These fish haunt any piece of flotsam so areas such as FADs and Wave Buoys are always worth a look through the spring and summer months. These fish will take live and dead baits floated around berley trails on 4/0 to 6/0 hooks however the majority of fish are taken whilst trolling. Fast trolling speeds and skirted lures are a popular way to tempt strikes from dolphin fish. Fish in the 10– 15kg bracket are not uncommon and they put up an amazing fight that involves a great aerial display.

Marlin and sailfish are most often caught along this part of the coast between December and April. The wider grounds of the Sunshine Coast produce the best catches however these fish can be caught considerably closer to land around Cape Moreton and waters to the south. Small black marlin and sailfish are the most commonly caught billfish to be taken inside the continental shelf. Stand-up tackle of 8kg is most often employed to catch these fish. Live baiting in the deeper water or trolling skirted lures and dead baits are the most common approaches taken. Beyond the edge of the shelf is the domain of the heavy game fishing angler. Large blue marlin are prized targets in these waters and are targeted on 24–37kg stand-up gear or the heavier 37–60kg tackle used in conjunction with a chair. Trolling big baits and skirted lures or fishing with live baits is the undoing of many big fish in the area.

FACILITIES AND SERVICES

There are a number of locations from which to access the offshore fishing from Noosa to the Gold Coast.

NOOSA RIVER AND BAR

The northern reefs of the Sunshine Coast can be accessed from the Noosa River. This includes the waters from Coolum to Double Island. The Noosa Bar can be a shallow and dangerous bar to cross at times. The erosion of sand from Noosa Main Beach ultimately deposits material at the nearby river mouth thereby reducing the average water depth. The advantages of using the Noosa Bar include the large protection the Noosa Headland provides from southerly swell. Easterly and north-easterly swell on a run-out tide can make this bar quite hostile. Prior to crossing the bar: research the location of the current channel and plan to cross the bar on a middle to high tide. The channel is often positioned to the north in winter and in the middle and southern parts of the bar in summer. Anglers wishing to learn how to best cross this bar are able to purchase valuable bar-crossing lessons from local trainer Jim Sharpe of the Australian Boating College. Jim can be contacted on 07 5474 1404 or via the website www.abcboating.com/Qld/noosa.

MAROOCHY RIVER

The Maroochy Bar is a dangerous proposition in many cases. Few boaters use the entrance to access the ocean as the deep water Mooloolaba entrance is only a short distance away.

MOOLOOLAH RIVER

The deep water ocean access provided by the Mooloolah River at Mooloolaba is a very popular place. The location offers easy access to north and southern waters for large and small sized vessels. The entrance is generally safe but this does change at times. Deposition of sand around the entrance can produce a wave break here occasionally. A larger easterly swell has turned boats over here in the past.

CALOUNDRA BAR

The northern entrance to Pumicestone Passage hosts the Caloundra Bar. The bar offers access to the southern reef systems of the Sunshine Coast. The bar has a reputation of becoming nasty in short time but in fine weather and with suitable bar crossing experience is relatively easy to cross. Traversing the channel at suitable tidal stages is a key part of successfully navigating this bar. The beaches to the north of the bar such as Moffats Beach are sheltered locations that offer offshore kayak anglers good access to inshore waters.

MORETON ISLAND – NORTH AND SOUTH PASSAGE

The extensive sand build up at either end of Moreton Island require caution when crossing these waters. Many boats use the South Passage Bar and although it may seem docile at times, it has claimed plenty of boats over the years. Inexperienced boaters are advised to seek some form of tuition prior to considering a crossing of the South Passage Bar. Bill Corten has been educating boaters in how to best cross this bar for many years. A phone call to Bill at Reel Affair (07 3286 3647 or 0447 233 247) is well worth the effort.

JUMPINPIN BAR

The Jumpinpin Bar enables access to the northern Gold Coast reef systems around North Stradbroke Island; the bar has claimed many boats over the years. It is a wide area and waves break sporadically across its girth. Only boaters with plenty of bar crossing experience should consider tackling this area when there is some swell about.

THE GOLD COAST SEAWAY

Deeper water ocean access enables fishers to travel to all of the Gold Coast reef systems. The entrance will break in certain conditions so do your homework and safety checks before passing through this area.

TALLEBUDGERA AND CURRUMBIN CREEKS

These systems have shallow water entrances and although boats do pass through them, it is not advised for newcomers.

ABOVE: The bay waters around Mooloolaba attract schools of tuna in summer.

FACT BOX

GUIDING SERVICES

There are plenty of guide and charter services available for the offshore fishing areas of the Sunshine Coast, Brisbane and the Gold Coast. For contact details visit the following websites;

Noosa

Noosa Bluewater Charters – *www.noosabluefishing.com.au*
Fishing Offshore Noosa – *www.noosafishing.com*
Noosa Catch – *www.noosacatch.com.au*

Mooloolaba and Caloundra

Offshore Reef and Game Fishing Mooloolaba – *www.offshorefishingmooloolaba.com.au*
Fish n Crab Charters – *www.fishncrabcharters.com*
Odyssey Fishing Charters – *www.odysseycharters.com.au*
Flat Dog Charters – *www.flatdogcharters.com*
Top Catch Charters– *www.topcatchcharters.com.au*
South Queensland Charter Services – *www.sqcs.com.au*
Outside Edge Fishing Charters – *www.outsideedge.com.au*
Incredible Charters – *www.incrediblecharters.com.au*

Brisbane

Nitro Fishing Charters with John Palermo can be contacted on landline number 07 3821 7900, mobile number 0407 127 405 or web address – *www.nitrocharters.com*
Moreton Island Fishing Charters – *www.moretonislandfishingcharters.com.au*
Reel Easy Charters – *www.reeleasycharters.com.au*
Frenzy Charters – *www.frenzycharters.com.au*

Gold Coast

RU4REEL Fishing Charters – www.ru4reel.com.au; 0449 903 366
Gone Fishing Charters – *www.gonefishing.net.au/*
Down Under Charters – *www.goldcoastfishing.com/*
My Charter Boat Charters – *www.mycharterboat.com.au/*
Lucky Strike Charters – 0428 729 393
True Blue Fishing Charters – *www.truebluefishing.com.au*
Fish The Deep Charters – *www.fishthedeep.com.au*
BK's Gold Coast Fishing Charters – *www.bksfishing.com.au*
Fish n Fun Charters – *www.fishnfun.com.au*
Gold Coast Fishing Charters – *www.goldcoastfishingcharters.com*

SUNSHINE COAST OFFSHORE LOCATION GUIDE

Map 60 No. 1 Coffees Reef: 48 to 55m depth

(Snapper, pearl perch, trag jewfish, cod, tuskfish, mackerel, tuna, sailfish)

The reef here consists largely of broken bottom; a structure that locals refer to as 'grazing country'. Local reference to the reef as coffee rock has earned this patch of ground its name. The area sits to the north of North Reef and is a popular place to look for snapper when they are in spawn mode. This area often sees the first mackerel and other pelagics as they move into the region at the start of summer. Floatlining with pilchards and live bait, as well as jigging the bottom with soft plastics works well on this reef. The fish here are often mobile so find the bait and the predators will often be close at hand. The problem with anchoring here is that the bait and predators are likely to move. Drifting is a good approach to fishing this area to overcome the transient fish here.

GPS Marks to get you started

Latitude	Longitude
2612300	15310700
2612870	15309275
2612085	15312245

Map 60 No. 2 North Reef: 45 to 58m depth

(Snapper, pearl perch, trag jewfish, jewfish, cod, tuskfish, cobia, mackerel, dolphin fish, marlin)

This is an extensive zone of reef that runs from north to south. The southern reaches are the shallowest and can be reached quite easily from Noosa. The deepest sections of reef are found on the north-eastern side of the system. The reef consists of broken rubble and gravel with the odd bommie and wreck. This is a very popular fishing spot for Noosa locals as it provides some of the most consistent local reef fishing; the first mackerel of the season are often caught here. Summer produces the odd dolphin fish and marlin, but the reef fishing is the big attraction. The hard structure produces top class fishing for snapper, pearl perch, trag jewfish and at times cobia and jewies. The biggest winter snapper caught by Noosa anglers are usually taken at North Reef. Fishing baits on the bottom and mid-water around a berley trail is one of the most popular methods used here. Floating live or dead bait often accounts for the fish of the day when anchored in these parts. Drifting with soft plastics and jigs is also known for producing some good fish as is trolling when the pelagics are about.

GPS Marks to get you started

Latitude	Longitude
2617360	15310640
2617090	15314300
2618139	15342450
2618550	15310120
2615500	15310480

Map 60 No. 3 Teewah: 15 to 20m depth

(Mackerel, tailor, jewfish)

The shallow grounds around Teewah are home to patchy bottom reef and the odd wreck. These shallow north shore waters often produce mackerel when most other spots are quiet. A troll through the area will quickly establish if fish are around. It often fishes well for tuna and mackerel from Australia Day to March. Cruising birds will often highlight when fish are hunting in the area.

GPS Marks to get you started

Latitude	Longitude
2618209	15307195

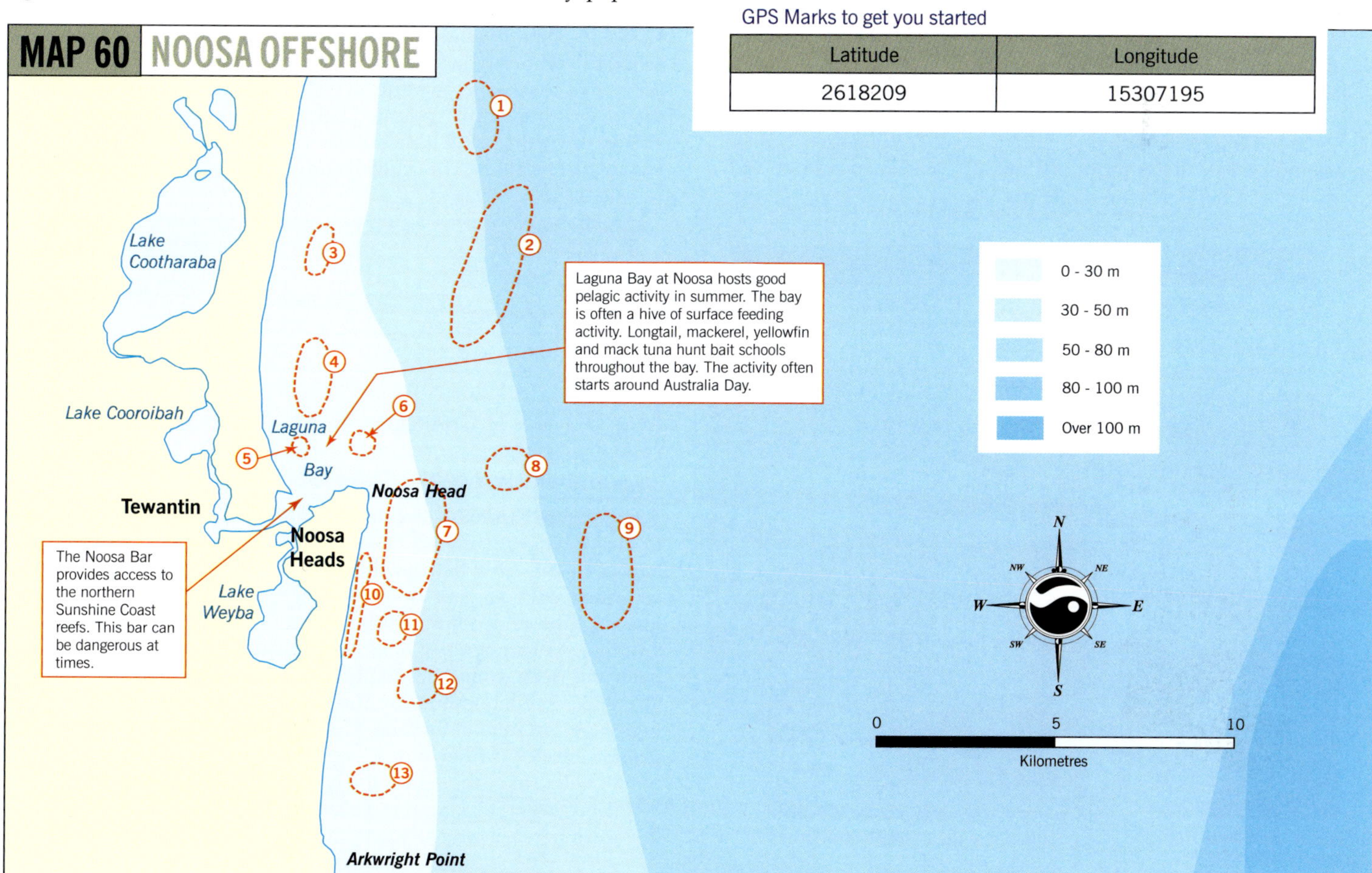

MAP 60 NO. 4 BIG HALLS REEF: 20 TO 30M DEPTH

(SWEETLIP, SQUIRE, COD, TUSKFISH, MACKEREL)

Extensive areas of patchy and broken reef exist throughout this area and these often attract schools of baitfish. This is a popular summer fishing location and can be thick with mackerel at times. It rarely produces quality snapper, but is a haven for sweetlip, cod and tuskfish. Fishing lightly weighted baits and soft plastics through a berley trail will usually produce fish here.

GPS Marks to get you started

Latitude	Longitude
2620275	15305131
2620630	15305180
2620290	15305070

MAP 60 NO. 5 LITTLE HALLS REEF: 13M DEPTH

(BAIT, SWEETLIP, SQUIRE, COD, TUSKFISH, MACKEREL, TUNA)

A ledge runs from north to south along the area. The drop-off attracts a lot of baitfish and is often the first stop for many anglers as they collect live bait. These anglers often encounter various other predators such as mackerel, tuna, sweetlip and cod. Good catches of mackerel can be taken here in January to March.

GPS Marks to get you started

Latitude	Longitude
2612200	15305005

MAP 60 NO. 6 JEW SHOAL: 9 TO 18M DEPTH

(SNAPPER, SWEETLIP, MACKEREL, COBIA, TUNA)

A few kilometres from Noosa is a popular patch of reef. The Jew Shoal contains several bommies amongst broken bottom reef. Some of these bommies rise to within 10 metres of the surface. Despite the name, it is rare to catch a jewfish here. The spot is pressured by anglers and divers but occasionally produces the odd good snapper, sweetlip, mackerel or roaming tuna and cobia. Drifting the area with bait and soft plastic is often the most successful approach. This is a popular destination for kayak anglers as it offers relatively sheltered waters in close proximity to land. Trolling lures and baits behind a 'yak' have produced quality Spanish mackerel and a variety of other pelagic and reef species.

GPS Marks to get you started

Latitude	Longitude
2621860	15306982

ABOVE: Sunshine Reef is a very popular location to target coral trout.

MAP 60 NO. 7 SUNSHINE REEF: 25 TO 35M DEPTH

(SNAPPER, SWEETLIP, CORAL TROUT, PEARL PERCH, TUSKFISH, MOSES PERCH, MACKEREL, COBIA, TUNA)

Also known as Misery Reef, this patch of ground is one of the more impressive reef systems in the area. The bottom contains mixed sand, rubble and plenty of bommies. The area is a stone's throw from the Noosa Headland but is one of the more consistent coral trout producers in this stretch of coastline. The area fishes most productively through spring and summer. Fishing bait and lures from anchor is a proven approach here. Targeting specific bommies from an anchored position is the way to target the local trout. A ball sinker above a pilchard, squid or live bait will get the attention of these aggressive predators if they are active. A lightly weighted pilchard floated out the back of the boat on gang hooks will be found by cruising mackerel, cobia or tuna if they are in the vicinity. The area directly out from the Surf Club is a popular place to troll for Spanish mackerel and downrigging or slow trolling with weighted pilchards seems to work best here. The outer edge of the reef sits in approximately 35m of water. This can be a good place to target when more shallow parts of the reef are not firing.

GPS Marks to get you started

Latitude	Longitude
2623760	15309430
2625120	15309010
2625151	15309204
2624015	15308859
2624448	15309432

MAP 60 NO. 8 MASSOUDS REEF: 45 TO 50M DEPTH

(SNAPPER, PEARL PERCH, TUSKFISH, MOSES PERCH, NANNYGAI, COD, MACKEREL, COBIA)

This reef consists of broken rubble and is found straight out from Noosa in 50m of water. The location is often forgotten by anglers as they head north, east and south from Noosa. Remarkably, this is one reef that seems to perform well when many others are shut-down. Drifting lightly weighted baits to the bottom beneath a ball sinker, or fishing with a paternoster rig usually produces a good feed of reef fish here. The odd pelagic will show up here in summer.

GPS Marks to get you started

Latitude	Longitude
2622550	15310001
2621325	15312360
2621550	15312215

MAP 60 NO. 9 CHARDONS REEF: 48 TO 55M DEPTH

(MACKEREL, WAHOO, DOLPHIN FISH, MARLIN, SAILFISH, SNAPPER, PEARL PERCH, COBIA)

Ten kilometres from Noosa, this reef offers local anglers the chance to target bigger gamefish. The summer current is often running harder in this area than in the reefs closer to Noosa. This often coincides with anglers catching bigger pelagic species. Wahoo, marlin, tuna and dolphin fish are found here when the area is holding good amounts of bait. Trolling skirted lures, live and dead baits and deep diving hardbody lures will soon establish if there are bigger predators hunting the area. This is a good spot to fish following big rainfall on land as dirty water will often push local pelagic species further out to sea. These fish and concentrations of bait will often congregate at Chardons. This can be a very good Spanish mackerel location in February and March. The bottom of the ocean here is home to patchy rubble and the odd bommie. This

ABOVE: Chardons Reef attracts a good run of Spanish mackerel each year.

reef produces some bigger snapper in winter. Chardons Reef is often a hit and miss location. If the fish are there you will have a ball, if not, don't waste too much fuel waiting for them to show up! The last GPS mark listed below identifies the middle of a productive north to south trolling line.

GPS Marks to get you started

Latitude	Longitude
2624240	15315810
2623910	15315477
2624240	15315762
2626310	15314226
2624848	15313791

Map 60 No. 10 Sunshine to Peregian Coffee Rock: 8 to 14m depth

(Mackerel, tuna, snapper, sweetlip)

Plenty of bottom coffee rock can be found a few hundred metres from the beach between Sunshine and Peregian beaches. This structure is often used to anchor the local shark nets. The structure attracts baitfish and as such there are often predators in the area. Trolling lures in this stretch will often produce mackerel when they are around. Soft plastics fished through this stretch of reef during late winter and spring will produce some surprisingly good snapper.

Map 60 No. 11 Victor Baileys Reef: 25 to 30m depth

(Snapper, pearl perch, sweetlip, coral trout, Moses perch, mackerel, cobia)

This reef is found immediately to the south of Sunshine Reef and holds similar structure. The fishing in this area is much the same as that found at Sunshine Reef. Drifting pilchards down a berley trail is a popular approach here. Leaving a crowd of boats at Sunshine Reef to fish the often less popular Victor Baileys can pay dividends at times. This reef is known for producing some big spring snapper. These fish hunt the edge where reef and sand mix and are often in pursuit of whiting. Soft plastic lures and baits fished tight to the bottom will often be the undoing of these fish.

GPS Marks to get you started

Latitude	Longitude
2626041	15308012

Map 60 No. 12 Castaways Reef: 28 to 35m depth

(Snapper, pearl perch, sweetlip, tuskfish, Moses perch, mackerel, cobia)

Broken rubble and several bommies are scattered throughout this area. The reef is a popular place to target snapper in the winter. Floating lightly weighted pilchards down to the reef works well when the snapper are schooling in the vicinity. The area is often alive with spotted mackerel in March. These fish will concentrate around the bommies as these are often used for shelter by local baitfish.

GPS Marks to get you started

Latitude	Longitude
2627050	15308701
2627041	15308810
2627054	15308770
2626970	15308848

Map 60 No. 13 Hancock Shoal: 25 to 30m depth

(Snapper, sweetlip, tuskfish, mackerel, cobia)

Patchy rubble and bommies are found in this area that sits just to the north of Coolum. The location fishes well for snapper in winter and sweetlip and mackerel in summer. The position of this reef means it doesn't get pressured by anglers very much as it sits mid-way between the ports of Noosa and Mooloolaba. This greatly reduces the number of anglers that visit this patch of reef.

GPS Marks to get you started

Latitude	Longitude
2630483	15307143
2630165	15307793
2630360	15307761

ABOVE: Shallow reef systems offer good fishing for sweetlip in summer.

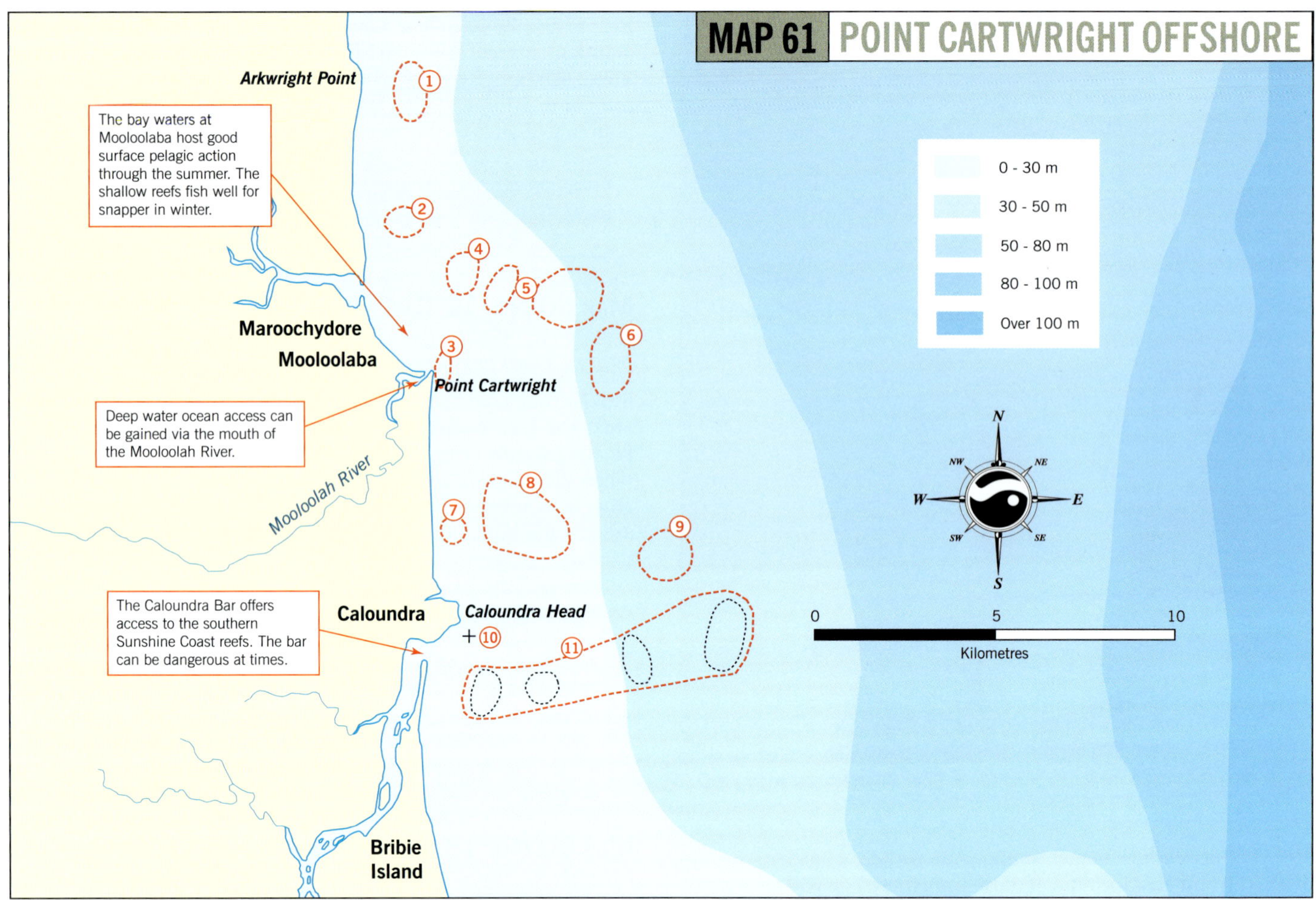

Map 61 No. 1 Arkwright Shoal: 8 to 26m depth *(snapper, sweetlip, tuskfish, mackerel, coral trout, jewfish, tuna)*

Extensive shallow reef lies throughout this area. The reef consists of ledges, bommies and broken bottom gravel. The reef extends to a deeper water ledge on the eastern boundary; the water drops to approximately 25m of depth at this point. The waters out from Coolum are home to plenty of this reef structure. The area fishes very well for sweetlip, tuskfish, cod and the odd trout in summer. Snapper and the occasional jewfish are caught here in winter and spring. The outer edge of the reef attracts summer mackerel and tuna. Drifting is an effective strategy in this area as the reef is shallow for much of its length. Anglers fishing baits at anchor do best during low light periods of the day.

GPS Marks to get you started

Latitude	Longitude
2632430	15307380
2632671	15307842
2632890	15307745
2633205	15310005

Map 61 No. 2 Mudjimba Island: 8 to 14m depth *(snapper, sweetlip, mackerel, jewfish)*

Mudjimba Island can be found to the north of the Maroochy River mouth. Shallow reef lies on the bottom immediately surrounding the island. Low light periods of the day are a good time to cast a bait or plastic in this area. Squire sized snapper, sweetlip and the odd jewie are caught by anglers fishing at these times. Casting soft plastics around the island wash zones can be an effective tactic at times. Trolling lures around the island produces mackerel and tuna in summer.

Map 61 No. 3 Point Cartwright Reef: 8 to 14m depth *(snapper, sweetlip, mackerel, tuna, jewfish)*

Shallow reef hugs the bottom areas around Point Cartwright. These areas hold baitfish at various times of the year. This in turn attracts predators that are hunting in the area. Squire sized snapper and the odd jewie are caught here in winter. Summer provides some good fishing for sweetlip, mackerel and tuna.

Map 60 No. 4 The Inner Gneerings: 12 to 18m depth *(snapper, sweetlip, mackerel, tuna)*

Patchy bottom rubble is found along the bottom here and this often attracts baitfish that are moving through the area. The area receives a lot of pressure but can turn up the odd good catch of snapper, sweetlip and when they are around, mackerel and tuna.

GPS Marks to get you started

Latitude	Longitude
2638745	15309505

Map 60 No. 5 The Outer and Middle Gneerings: 15 to 25m depth *(snapper, sweetlip, pearl perch, moses perch, kingfish, mackerel, tuna)*

Broken bottom reef and the odd bommie are found in this area. The spot is easy to see as it lies in the area surrounding the flashing beacon known as The Blinker. The area receives a lot of pressure so it pays to fish at times when there are no crowds. Evening winter sessions produce some good catches of snapper at times. Drifting baits and soft plastics slowly to the bottom produces good results. Trolling the area offers the opportunity to catch mackerel and tuna in the summer months. The odd kingfish is taken around the Blinker.

GPS Marks to get you started

Latitude	Longitude
2639110	15312038
2638915	15311267
2639245	15312952

MAP 61 NO. 6 MURPHYS REEF: 18 TO 25M DEPTH

(SNAPPER, SWEETLIP, PEARL PERCH, MOSES PERCH, MACKEREL, TUNA)

This is a well-known reef a few kilometres out from Point Cartwright. The area is home to gravel and the occasional bommie. The reef is pressured by anglers but continues to produce good fish for those that fish well-presented lures and baits at peak tidal periods. Fishing this area during the night or at first light is a good option. Drifting the reef while jigging soft plastics near the bottom produces snapper, pearl perch, moses perch and cod. Drifting or trolling with baits and hardbody lures produces mackerel and tuna in the summer months.

GPS Marks to get you started

Latitude	Longitude
2639540	15314082
2640770	15313280
2641209	15313650
2642170	15313899

MAP 61 NO. 7 RAPER SHOAL: 8 TO 15M DEPTH

(SNAPPER, SWEETLIP, MACKEREL)

This is a shallow patch of reef close to the beach making it a popular spot with kayak anglers as it is close to a good launch site. The area breaks when there is swell running here so some caution must be applied when fishing the shoal. Although plenty of fishing pressure is applied to the location by local anglers, the spot produces enough fish to keep them coming back. The waters around the outer edges of the structure produce squire sized snapper on baits and soft plastics. The reef attracts mackerel and tuna in summer. Trolling through the area or casting and retrieving lures at surface feeding activity should put you in touch with a fish or two.

GPS Marks to get you started

Latitude	Longitude
2645410	15309650

MAP 61 NO. 8 CURRIMUNDI REEF: 20 TO 35M DEPTH

(SNAPPER, SWEETLIP, TUSKFISH, MACKEREL, COBIA)

The bottom structure here consists of broken reef and the odd bommie. The spot fishes well in winter for snapper, tusk fish, pearl perch and cod. The odd big snapper is caught here by anglers float lining pilchards or drifting with plastics. The summer congregation of baitfish in this location attract mackerel, tuna and cobia.

GPS Marks to get you started

Latitude	Longitude
2644995	15310558
2645240	15310540
2645604	15310869
2645840	15312908

MAP 61 NO. 9 CURRIMUNDI WIDE: 40 TO 55M DEPTH

(SNAPPER, SWEETLIP, PEARL PERCH, TUSKFISH, MACKEREL, KINGFISH, COBIA)

Broken reef in deeper water attracts some quality snapper and pearl perch in winter. The odd bommie in the area ensures kingfish and cobia are caught here at times. The area fishes well for spotted and Spanish mackerel in summer.

GPS Marks to get you started

Latitude	Longitude
2646668	15314870
2646980	15317100
2647790	15315750

MAP 61 NO. 10 BRAYS ROCK

(SNAPPER, SWEETLIP, MACKEREL)

A chunk of rock can be found out from the headland at Caloundra. The rock is a popular place for kayak anglers to hunt up a few quality fish. The waters around the area fish well for squire and sweetlip, as well as mackerel and other roaming pelagics at times.

MAP 61 NO. 11 CALOUNDRA INSHORE REEFS (3, 5, 9 AND 12 MILE)

(SNAPPER, PEARL PERCH, SWEETLIP, MACKEREL, COBIA)

A line of separate reefs can be found heading east from the Caloundra Bar. These include the 3 Mile (20–30m deep), 5 Mile (25m deep), 9 Mile (30–40m deep) and 12 Mile (40–50m deep) Reefs. The systems do receive fishing pressure from local anglers and the fish can be tough to catch at times. Fishing these areas on weekdays or early and late in the day can overcome this issue. Presenting lightly weighted soft plastics and baits to resident fish will provide anglers with some quality reefies and pelagics when they are in the area.

3 Mile GPS Marks to get you started

Latitude	Longitude
2649840	15310590

5 Mile GPS Marks to get you started

Latitude	Longitude
2649730	15312410

9 Mile GPS Marks to get you started

Latitude	Longitude
2648505	15315060

12 Mile GPS Marks to get you started

Latitude	Longitude
2648220	15316780

MAP 62 NO. 1 THE HARDS: 60 TO 100M DEPTH

(SNAPPER, PEARL PERCH, TRAG JEWFISH, NANNYGAI, RED EMPEROR, TUSKFISH, SWEETLIP, JOBFISH, MACKEREL, WAHOO, DOLPHIN FISH, MARLIN, SAILFISH, TUNA, AMBERJACK, KINGFISH, COBIA)

The Hards is not easily accessed as it is a good 60km run from Noosa. The reef is located to the north of the Barwon Banks and sits adjacent to an eastern ledge that drops into much deeper water. The bottom here is home to gravel reef and scattered bommies and pinnacles. The current can charge through this area at times. The reef is home to a huge variety of species and the beauty about making the long trip out here is that you never know what the day will hold. Winter fishing for snapper, pearl perch, trag and a host of other fish is often superb. The current velocity usually slows in winter and makes fishing here a lot easier. The summer fishery offers a hit list of big predators. Drifting bait through a berley trail or trolling through the area can provide marlin, dolphin fish, tuna and mackerel. This is a popular spot for anglers that live to jig the depths. The pinnacles in the area are home to some big kingfish and amberjack that love taking home lures.

GPS Marks to get you started

Latitude	Longitude
2620600	15335930
2617277	15338540
2620280	15335740
2615800	15339758
2618720	15336880
2615381	15339468

Map 62 No. 2 The Barwon Banks: 55 to 80m depth *(Snapper, pearl perch, trag jewfish, nannygai, red emperor, tuskfish, sweetlip, jobfish, mackerel, wahoo, dolphin fish, marlin, sailfish, tuna, amberjack, kingfish, cobia)*

The Barwon Banks is an extensive section of reef and is a popular spot for anglers leaving the ports of Noosa and Mooloolaba. The northern parts of the reef are a good 40–50km from Noosa. A mix of broken reef and gravel host plenty of bommies and pinnacles. The area earns its name due to the huge rise seen in parts of the system. The shallowest sections of reef rise to 30m while the deepest sit in 80m of water. The reef sits adjacent to a deeper water drop-off and the combination of current flow and raised reef make this a Mecca for a number of species. The winter fishing can be amazing here. Anglers encounter big schools of snapper and a variety of other reef species. The summer months provide plenty of good gamefishing action and it is common to see several game boats working the area when the weather is good. The reef pinnacles and lumps usually hold a few amberjack and kings. Jigging metal and plastic lures can tempt a solid strike; landing them is another issue.

The wide grounds off the Sunshine Coast are one of the few places where it is possible to tangle with larger local red emperor.

GPS Marks to get you started

Latitude	Longitude
2628200	15332160
2630079	15332510
2628275	15332450
2631200	15331747
2628570	15335150
2627820	15332540
2635428	15330369
2636025	15330541
2626780	15333400
2631650	15332050
2629225	15330285

GPS Marks – Shallow Barwon Banks

Latitude	Longitude
2620095	15336293
2623250	15333570
2629120	15332140
2624010	15335540
2628050	15332404

Map 62 No. 3 The Wide Barwon Banks: 60 to 90m depth *(Snapper, pearl perch, trag jewfish, nannygai, red emperor, tuskfish, sweetlip, jobfish, mackerel, wahoo, dolphin fish, marlin, sailfish, tuna, amberjack, kingfish, cobia)*

The Barwon Banks contains a separated section of reef that hugs the drop-off into deeper water. The area is prone to strong current flow, but can hold some good fish at times.

GPS Marks – Wide Barwon Banks

Latitude	Longitude
2627570	15336101
2629075	15334928
2630230	15335075

Map 62 No. 4 The Marlin Grounds: 50 to 70m depth *(Mackerel, wahoo, dolphin fish, marlin, sailfish, tuna)*

This large area is well known for holding good concentrations of bait. This in turn attracts a variety of larger predators. Exploring the area while looking for bird activity, current lines and soundings of deeply holding bait, is a good method for stumbling upon some good game fishing. The area is a popular location among local gamefishers.

GPS Marks to get you started

Latitude	Longitude
2633820	15323800
2630170	15323420
2635201	15317240
2636200	15319925

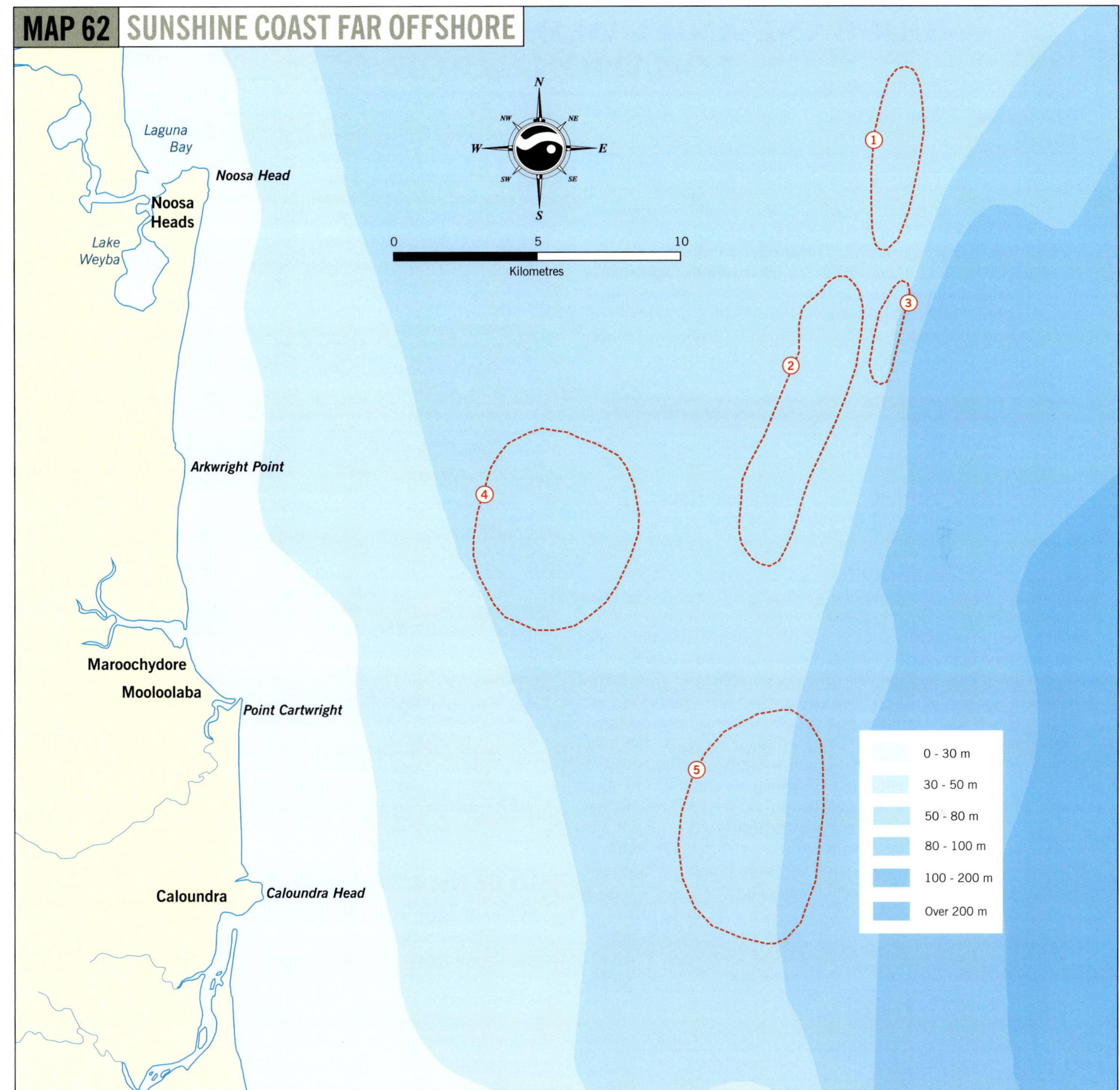

MAP 62 NO. 5 CALOUNDRA WIDE AND CALOUNDRA DEEP: 65 TO 100M DEPTH

(SNAPPER, PEARL PERCH, TUSKFISH, MACKEREL, KINGFISH, COBIA, WAHOO, DOLPHIN FISH, MARLIN, SAILFISH)

These reef systems are located directly east of the Caloundra Bar. Bommies, the odd pinnacle and gravel are found in 65 to 100m of water. The area is a popular winter snapper and pearl perch haunt and local anglers catch some quality fish here each season. Float lining with baits while drifting or at anchor are proven methods here. The odd kingfish and cobia is caught here as the current conditions are often favourable for these predators. Spanish mackerel, wahoo, dolphin fish, marlin and the odd sailfish show up in the summer months.

GPS Marks to get you started

Latitude	Longitude
2643050	15328001
2646830	15327820
2647805	15325204
2650391	15327165
2651470	15325995
2642130	15329671
2646608	15329235
2650447	15329275

BRISBANE AND GOLD COAST OFFSHORE LOCATION GUIDE

Map 63 No. 1 The Trench
(MARLIN, SAILFISH, DOLPHIN FISH, WAHOO, MACKEREL)

This is a popular location with local gamefishers. A significant ledge drops into deeper water adjacent to the shallow waters around Hutchinsons Shoal. The ledge takes a significant change of direction in this location as it wraps around Hutchinsons and the northern tip of Moreton Island. This deeper corner does a great job of deflecting current and makes it a good spot for baitfish and other predators to stage. Many quality gamefish have been caught in these waters. Trolling lures, baits and live baiting here is a good way to tangle with marlin, sailfish, dolphin fish, wahoo and a host of other pelagic hunters.

GPS Marks to get you started

Latitude	Longitude
2656345	15323355

Map 63 No. 2 Hutchinson's Shoal and Reef: 15 to 100m deep *(SNAPPER, PEARL PERCH, TUSKFISH, TRAG JEWFISH, SWEETLIP, MARLIN, SAILFISH, DOLPHIN FISH, WAHOO, MACKEREL, TREVALLY)*

This fishing location is a popular spot for good reason. The area contains shallow water bommies in amongst plenty of deeper water broken reef; a propensity for the current to push hard against the area attracts a huge variety of fish. Locally known as 'Hutchies', it is home to shallow water shoals, pinnacles and bottom gravel. The shallow water sections are known to break in rare circumstances. The harder structures attract reef species and roaming pelagics. Reefies can be targeted at anchor or while on the drift; they will occupy shallow and deeper water reef structures throughout the area. Fresh baits, soft plastics and jigs fished around the hard stuff produces reef species, the odd kingfish and amberjack. Trolling live and dead baits and an assortment of lures around reef and schools of baitfish will attract the attention of summer pelagics. Surface luring around the shallows is a good way to be brutalised by one of the big giant trevally that hunt in this area.

GPS Marks to get you started

Latitude	Longitude
2656473	15329187
2656062	15329413
2657182	15328954
2656824	15329991
2656451	15329578

Map 63 No. 3 Cape Moreton Shallows: 15 to 80m deep *(SNAPPER, PEARL PERCH, TUSKFISH, TRAG JEWFISH, SWEETLIP, CORAL TROUT, MARLIN, SAILFISH, DOLPHIN FISH, WAHOO, MACKEREL, TREVALLY)*

A chain of shallower water shoals sit adjacent to deeper water that falls to depths of 80m to the east. Shallow reef high spots from south to north respectively include Roberts Shoal (12m depth), Brennan Shoal (breaks occasionally), Smith Rock (breaks occasionally) and Flinders Reef that always breaks and is exposed at a half tide. The shallow water reef attracts a variety of species. Large trevally thrive around the reef high spots and can be tempted by big surface poppers. Anglers trolling around the area encounter a variety of summer pelagic species. Slow trolling baits is a popular way to target school, spotted and Spanish mackerel in this area. The depth of water quickly drops away from the shallow reef points. The deeper water ledge to the east of these shallows can fish very well for snapper during winter. Patchy reef and the odd wreck are also scattered through this area. The *Aarhus* and *Marietta Dal* wrecks are located around Smith Rock. The bottom structure in this area and in particular, that between Flinders Reef and Hutchies, fishes well for reef species. Jigging soft plastics or drifting baits down to the reef provides action from reef and pelagics feeding throughout the area.

Flinders Reef GPS Marks to get you started

Latitude	Longitude
2658245	15330178

Smith Rock GPS Marks to get you started

Latitude	Longitude
2700141	15328899

Brennan Shoal GPS Marks to get you started

Latitude	Longitude
2701301	15328892

Roberts Shoal GPS Marks to get you started

Latitude	Longitude
2703597	15329103

Aarhus Wreck GPS Marks to get you started

Latitude	Longitude
2659870	15328700

Marietta Dal Wreck GPS Marks to get you started

Latitude	Longitude
2659965	15328809

Map 63 No. 4 Shallow Tempest: 25 to 50m deep
(SNAPPER, TUSKFISH, SWEETLIP, MACKEREL, TREVALLY)

The reef here consists of undulating rubble with the odd peak and pinnacle. This area is a popular place to target snapper in winter and spring. Drifting the area with plastics and lightly weighted IQF pilchards during low light periods of the day is often a productive approach to catching snapper, other reef species and pelagics here. Shallow points such as Henderson Rock attract the odd bigger pelagic including some chunky giant trevally.

GPS Marks to get you started

Latitude	Longitude
2705690	15328970
2706390	15328850

Map 63 No. 5 Deep Tempest: 80 to 90m deep
(SNAPPER, PEARL PERCH, TRAG JEWFISH, JEWFISH, AMBERJACK, KINGFISH, TUSKFISH, SWEETLIP, JEWFISH, MACKEREL, SAMSONFISH)

Deep Tempest is located to the east of Shallow Tempest. Deeper water reef consisting of low lying rubble and the odd pinnacle are found throughout the area. The reef is well known for producing some big snapper, amberjack, trag jewfish and pearl perch. The location fishes well when there is some current pushing through

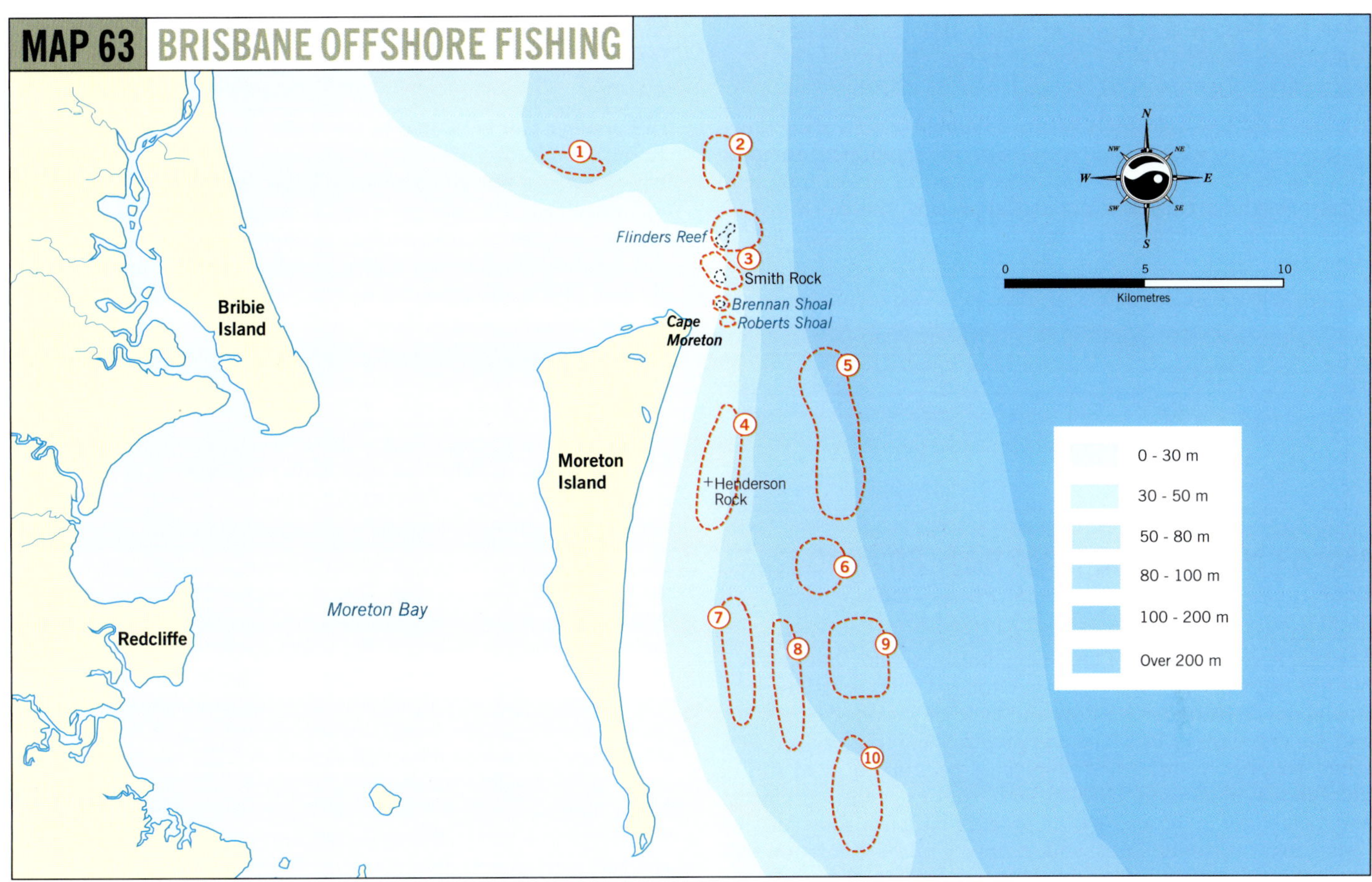

here. Local charter boats take some of their best catches while drifting pilchards rigged with a ball sinker and 1 to 2 hook gang rigs. Changing ball sinker weights so that the bait gets near to bottom slowly while drifting is the key to catching fish on some of the local reefs. Controlling the speed of your drift is often aided by the use of a sea anchor (drogue). Soft plastics and live baits will also produce some good fish along this reef. Knife jigs and live bait are a good option when chasing kings, amberjack and samson fish. Paternoster rigs are favoured when targeting these fish or reef species such as pearl perch. The pinnacles that attract kings and amberjack will also hold the odd solid jewie in winter and spring. Summer months will produce the usual pelagic culprits for anglers trolling, jigging or live baiting here.

GPS Marks to get you started

Latitude	Longitude
2707415	15334677
2707496	15334597
2707720	15334050
2709435	15333871
2707723	15334808

Map 63 No. 6 Round Patch: 68 to 80m deep

(Snapper, Pearl Perch, Trag Jewfish, Amberjack, Kingfish, Tuskfish, Sweetlip, Mackerel, Samsonfish)

Situated to the south of Deep Tempest, this reef produces chunky snapper, pearlies, trag jewfish, kings and AJ's. The reef structure is largely low-lying rubble, but does hold the odd 3–5m ledge and higher pinnacle. Exploring the area with the sounder zoomed in tight to the bottom will assist in identifying small but significant features that can hold good numbers of fish. Floatlining baits or fishing them on a paternoster rig will produce fish here. The current will often dictate the effectiveness of presenting baits and lures to bottom fish in this location.

GPS Marks to get you started

Latitude	Longitude
2710581	15333067
2710729	15334045

Map 63 No. 7 29 Fathom Reef: 60 to 80m deep

(Snapper, Pearl Perch, Trag Jewfish, Amberjack, Kingfish, Tuskfish, Sweetlip, Jewfish, Mackerel, Samsonfish)

The reef here consists of rubble bottom with the odd small rise. Charter operators like John Palermo recommend zooming the sounder tight to the bottom structure to identify any small rise or ledge. Seemingly insignificant undulations within the reef will often hold good concentrations of fish. The northern end of the reef typically fishes well in June. This is a good time to catch big snapper, pearlies and jewies here. The southern areas of the reef produce better catches of trag jewfish, tusk fish and kings. The eastern ledge provides some very good fishing at times so don't ignore this area if fishing is a little quiet elsewhere on the reef. Setting up long drifts along the reef is a popular and very often, effective approach.

GPS Marks to get you started

Latitude	Longitude
2719492	15333021
2716203	15330197
2717725	15330459
2715500	15331980

Map 63 No. 8 33 Fathom Reef: 50 to 70m deep *(Snapper, Pearl Perch, Trag Jewfish, Tuskfish, Mackerel, Dolphin Fish, Cobia)*

The reef here consists largely of broken rubble bottom along much of its extent. The western side is one of the more productive areas to fish. The reef is a well-known snapper producer and drifting with lightly weighted baits is a popular approach. The reef provides good fishing for mackerel, cobia and the odd dolphin fish in summer.

GPS Marks to get you started

Latitude	Longitude
2716738	15330967
2716750	15329675
2717457	15332755
2719200	15333084

Map 63 No. 9 Square Patch Reef: 80 to 90m deep *(Trag Jewfish, Snapper, Pearl Perch, Amberjack, Kingfish, Cobia, Dolphin Fish)*

The reef here comprises of low lying broken bottom that makes it hard to anchor at times. An effective strategy when searching here is to zoom the sounder window and look for shows of bigger fish and not just signs of bait. The reef produces big trag jewfish, AJ's, kings, snapper, pearlies and sometimes provides a good run of dolphin fish in autumn. Drifting with bait or jigging soft plastics and metal lures in the area will all produce local fish. John Palermo nearly always drifts this area while dropping pilchard baits towards the bottom. A common strategy is to free-spool a bait towards the 50m depth mark and then slowly release line for the remainder of the drop. The last 30m of the slowly sinking pilchard's descent will often tempt those bigger and fussier fish to bite. The visible signs of current lines in the area should not be ignored. Drifting in proximity to such zones can provide some very good fishing at times.

GPS Marks to get you started

Latitude	Longitude
2714115	15334625
2714603	15336143
2715087	15336001
2715635	15334258

Map 63 No. 10 35 Fathom Reef : 60 to 75m deep *(Snapper, Tuskfish, Pearl Perch, Amberjack, Kingfish, Cobia)*

The bottom structure is largely low-lying reef with the odd rise and pinnacle. The area fishes well for snapper, pearlies and tusk fish. The southern end of the reef produces good numbers of pearl perch and squire sized snapper in May and June. Patches of wire weed usually hold some good pearlies in winter and spring. The western edge of the reef fishes well for larger snapper during winter. The northern end of the reef produces the best of the amberjack and kingfish fishing.

GPS Marks to get you started

Latitude	Longitude
2619464	15333094
2720731	15335441
2720779	15334919

Map 64 No. 1 Sevens Reef: 65 to 85m deep *(Snapper, Tuskfish, Pearl Perch, Amberjack, Cobia, Wahoo)*

This smaller reef is located to the north of Flat Rock. Broken reef throughout the area provides a good winter snapper spot. Anglers fishing the reef also produce some good catches of tuskfish, cobia and amberjack. The odd nannygai is caught in this area from time to time. Summer pelagics such as mackerel, wahoo, yellowfin tuna and dolphin fish are caught here by anglers fishing live and dead 'floaters' and trolling around the reef.

GPS Marks to get you started

Latitude	Longitude
2722648	15333858

Map 64 No. 2 Middle and Big Halfway Reefs: 20 to 40m deep *(Mackerel, Wahoo, Tuna, Giant Trevally, Snapper, Sweetlip, Kingfish, Cobia)*

The north-eastern corner of North Stradbroke Island offers some unique fishing. A group of shallow and exposed bommies sits in the midst of deeper and current rich waters. The deeper waters around the shallow reef is littered with bottom rubble and gravelly rock. The whole area screams fish. The combination of shallow rock, white wash zones, strong current and schools of resident fusiliers ensures there are some solid giant trevally in the area. Surface lures fished here will tempt these fish as well as tuna, mackerel and the odd wahoo. Anglers trolling around the shallow reef and deeper water margins of Point Lookout report some good catches of mackerel and wahoo. Fishing the bottom reef in this area with baits and soft plastics will offer some good fishing for squire, sweetlip and various other reef fish. Fishing the waters around Middle Reef offer anglers a more sheltered spot to wet a line when the wind is blowing from the south.

Middle Reef GPS Marks to get you started

Latitude	Longitude
2723940	15332450

Big Halfway Reef GPS Marks to get you started

Latitude	Longitude
2725105	15333260

Map 64 No. 3 One Mile Reef: 60m deep *(Kingfish, Pearl Perch, Snapper, Tuskfish, Mackerel, Wahoo, Tuna, Cobia)*

Directly off Point Lookout lies the smaller One Mile Reef. Rubble structure with occasional small pinnacle can be found along the bottom of this reef. The proximity of this reef to zones of good current flow ensures that there is often some good fishing here. The reef produces sizeable kings, pearlies and snapper in winter and spring. The eastern parts of the reef offer good fishing for tuskfish. Summer sees pelagics arrive when bait is stacked up along the reef.

GPS Marks to get you started

Latitude	Longitude
2723170	15334270
2724852	15335050
2725233	15335101
2725160	15334962

Pinnacle Out From Point Lookout

Latitude	Longitude
2729641	15335216

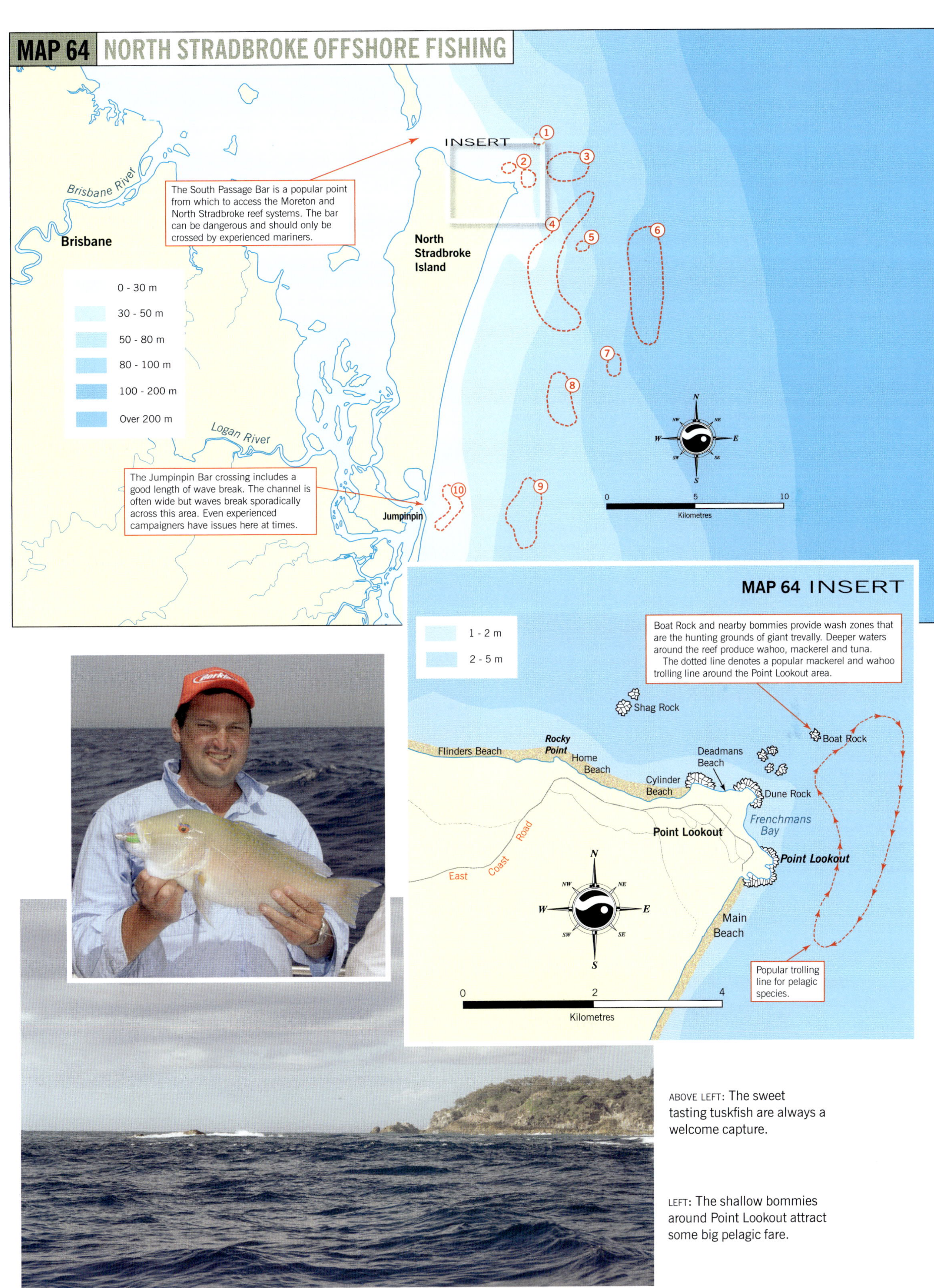

ABOVE LEFT: The sweet tasting tuskfish are always a welcome capture.

LEFT: The shallow bommies around Point Lookout attract some big pelagic fare.

Map 64 No. 4 Inner Cathedrals Reef: 40 to 65m deep *(Kingfish, Pearl Perch, Snapper, Tuskfish, Mackerel, Wahoo, Tuna, Cobia)*

This area offers broken bottom structure interspersed with some large pinnacles. The reef often fishes well for snapper and pearl perch. Summer provides good fishing for mackerel, tuna, cobia and kingfish. This reef is a lure fishers Nirvana. Regardless of whether you enjoy jigging soft plastics or knige jigs, casting surface stickbaits or trolling skirts and diving hardbody lures, there will always be something in this area that wants to eat what you've got!

GPS Marks to get you started

Latitude	Longitude
2730144	15336815
2730398	15336487
1729832	15336725
2740589	15336806
2740256	15336639
2739385	15336749
2739215	15336558

Map 64 No. 5 Waverider Buoy *(Dolphin Fish)*

The Waverider Buoy is located south-east of Point Lookout and will occasionally attract dolphin fish. The spot is a hit-and-miss affair so don't place all your bets on the buoy bringing home the goods for you.

Waverider Buoy GPS Coordinates

Latitude	Longitude
2729751	15337705

Map 64 No. 6 50 Fathom Reef: 90 to 120m deep *(Snapper, Pearl Perch, Trag Jewfish, Kingfish, Amberjack, Samson Fish, Cobia)*

The area is home to bottom reef and pinnacles. The spot fishes well for snapper, pearlies and trag jewfish in winter. The pinnacles attract kings and amberjack. This is a tough spot to fish when the current is working hard through the area. The wire weed structure that can be found in places will often hold schools of pearl perch and snapper.

GPS Marks to get you started

Latitude	Longitude
2727495	15339995
2727571	15341211

Map 64 No. 7 Guys Reef: 60 to 70m deep *(Snapper, Pearl Perch, Trag Jewfish, Kingfish, Amberjack, Cobia)*

This area contains a smaller section of bottom reef with the odd smaller rise and ledge. Drifting the area during winter and using soft plastics and fresh baits will hold you in good position to catch a few snapper, pearl perch and trag jewfish. The odd dolphin fish, marlin and wahoo are caught here when bait is holding on the reef during the summer months.

GPS Marks to get you started

Latitude	Longitude
2740589	15336806

ABOVE: Snapper are often in good numbers here in winter.

Wahoo love the stronger currents that are found in this area.
(Photograph by Roderick Walmsley)

ABOVE: Pearl perch are often caught in similar locations to snapper. (PHOTOGRAPH BY RODERICK WALMSLEY)

MAP 64 NO. 8 SULLIES REEF: 50 TO 60M DEEP
(SNAPPER, PEARL PERCH, TRAG JEW, COBIA, DOLPHIN FISH, MARLIN, MACKEREL, WAHOO)

Extensive areas of bottom gravel are found in this location. The reef holds good concentrations of bait at times. Fishing plastics and baits near the bottom of the water column produces snapper and other reef species. Summer baitball activity will often hold the attention of nearby dolphin fish, marlin, mackerel, wahoo and cobia.

GPS Marks to get you started

Latitude	Longitude
2741911	15333494
2741562	15333593
2741257	15333610

MAP 64 NO. 9 COTTON REEF: 90 TO 100M DEEP
(SNAPPER, TRAG JEW, PEARL PERCH, COBIA, KINGFISH, AMBERJACK, JEWFISH)

Small bottom rises and the odd larger pinnacle characterise this stretch of reef. The area fishes well for trag jewfish, snapper, jewfish and tailor in winter. The shallower lumps hold the odd kingfish and amberjack.

GPS Marks to get you started

Latitude	Longitude
2744224	15333275
2744137	15333374
2744021	15333297
2743876	15333335
2743653	15333412

MAP 64 NO. 10 JUMPINPIN BAR OUTFLOW: 8 TO 12M DEEP *(MACKEREL, TAILOR, TUNA)*

The run-out tide often dirties the water immediately to the ocean side of the Jumpinpin Bar. The edge of the dirty water is a good place to troll hardbody lures and live and dead baits. Slow trolling weighted gars and pilchards or live tailor is a great way to hook school, spotted and Spanish mackerel in the warmer months. There are usually plenty of tailor here in the cooler months.

MAP 65 NO. 1 SEAWAY BAIT GROUNDS: 20M DEEP
(BAIT)

This area is a good place to fill the live tank with bait prior to heading further offshore. The summer months will provide the occasional action on mackerel and tuna that are in the area looking for a quick feed.

GPS Marks to get you started

Latitude	Longitude
2757021	15327084

MAP 65 NO. 2 SEAWAY GRAVEL GROUNDS: 80M DEEP
(SNAPPER, TRAG JEWFISH, JEWFISH)

Small gravel patches and rises are interspersed with the odd pinnacle in this area. The reef fishes well for snapper, trag jewfish, pearlies and the odd jewie in winter and spring. A warm blue current pushing through the area in summer will bring the odd bigger pelagic, including marlin to these grounds.

GPS Marks to get you started

Latitude	Longitude
2755423	15328901
2756536	15329727
2756149	15329671
2758134	15330608

MAP 65 NO. 3 PALM BEACH REEF: 50M DEEP
(SNAPPER, MACKEREL)

Patchy bottom gravel attracts good numbers of baitfish to the area. This attracts predators such as snapper, various other reef species and mackerel in the summer. The reef is a very popular place when the mackerel are biting here. A crowd of boats and kayaks will quickly communicate that this is the case! This is a good location for kayak anglers as it holds some good fish and is easily accessed from the Gold Coast. Float lining pilchards through a berley trail and slow trolling baits are popular approaches to catching fish

ABOVE: Palm Beach attracts quality Spanish mackerel in summer. (PHOTOGRAPH BY BEN GODFREY)

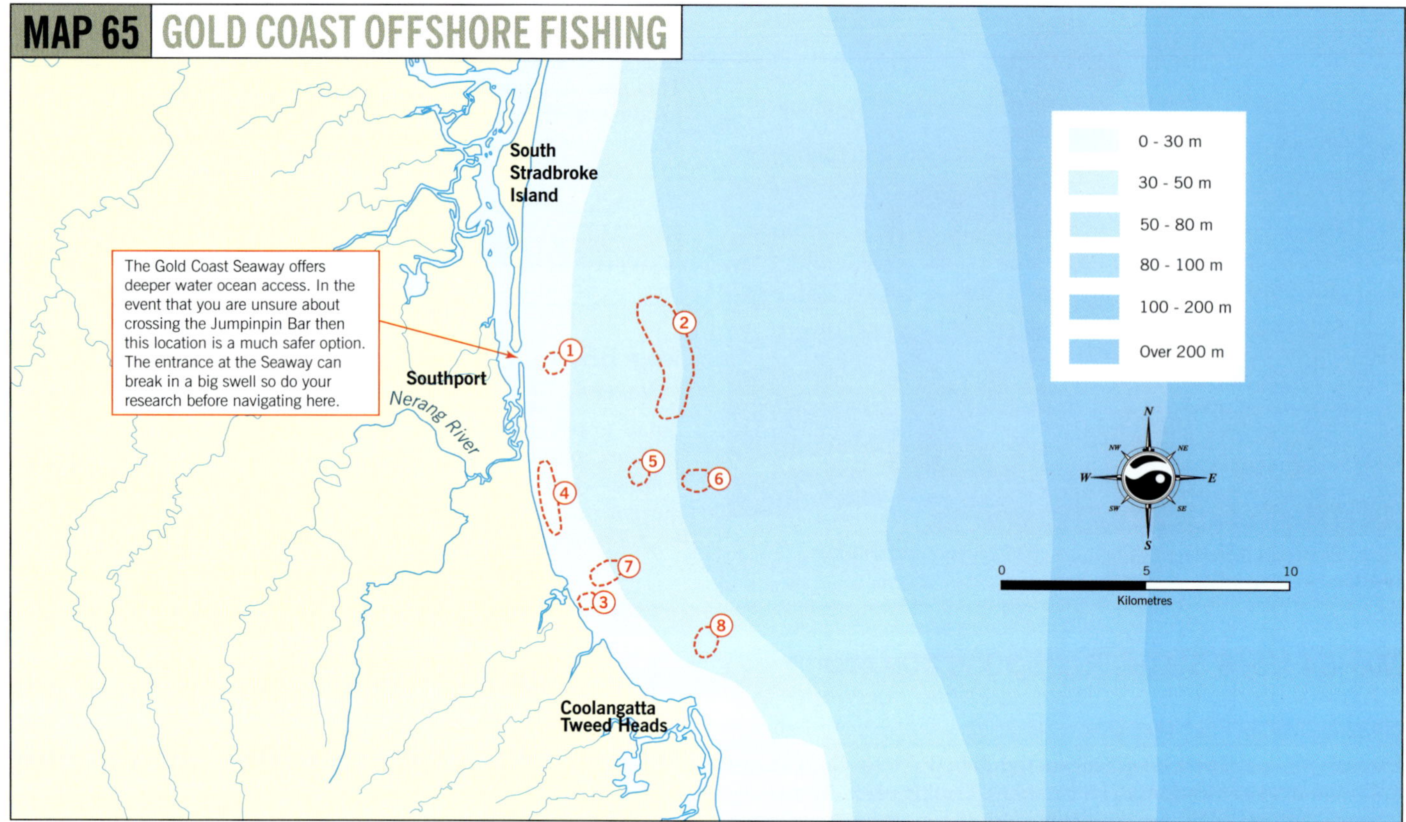

here. Deep trolling live bait on a downrigger is a good strategy to catching mackerel when they are pushed deep by boat traffic.

GPS Marks to get you started

Latitude	Longitude
2806296	15328754

Map 65 No. 4 Mermaid and Broadbeach Reefs: 35 to 50m deep

(Snapper, jewfish, mackerel, cobia, tailor)

These shallower Gold Coast reef systems produce fish for anglers prepared to stay closer to shore. Kayak anglers fare well in this area when weather permits access to these waters. Winter produces squire and the odd larger snapper and jewies are occasionally caught here by anglers fishing live and dead baits and plastics. Cobia are taken on live and dead baits in spring and early summer.

GPS Marks to get you started

Latitude	Longitude
2802520	15327136
2802510	15327198
2801598	15327081

Map 65 No. 5 Focus Reef: 80m deep

(Snapper, trag jewfish, mackerel, cobia, tailor)

The reef consists of bottom gravel and the odd pinnacle. The location is a popular place to chase a winter snapper and trag jewfish. Pelagic species including mackerel, cobia and tailor are caught here at times.

GPS Marks to get you started

Latitude	Longitude
2759606	15328846

Map 65 No. 6 Surfer's Pinnacle: 100m deep

(Snapper, trag jewfish, pearl perch, kingfish)

A shallow section of ground in this area holds some good numbers of snapper, pearl perch and trag jewfish in winter. September is also a good time to tangle with a kingfish here.

GPS Marks to get you started

Latitude	Longitude
2800703	15331268

Map 65 No. 7 Burleigh Heads Gravel: 50 to 60m deep

(Snapper, trag jewfish, mackerel)

Gravel reef in the area attracts good shows of bait at times and fishes well for squire sized snapper in winter. Trolling and floatlining pilchards and live bait works well for mackerel here in summer.

GPS Marks to get you started

Latitude	Longitude
2804215	15329461

Map 65 No. 8 Currumbin Jewfish Reef: 80 to 90m deep

(Snapper, jewfish)

Gravel and shallow bommies are found along this stretch of reef. The area fishes well for snapper and jewies in winter and spring. Lightly weighted live and dead baits and soft plastics produce the best of the fishing here. The start of the tidal flow around a new moon is a good time to be fishing this location.

GPS Marks to get you started

Latitude	Longitude
2807331	15334914

SUMMARY

This book was two years in the making. A large amount of time was dedicated to researching the many fishing locations and opportunities available. My aim when developing maps and published information was to provide you with the best start to successful fishing in the areas listed. Any angler evolves as they learn the nature of a fishing location and the options it presents. I hope to have started you off on the right foot so that you are experiencing the best of our local fishing in a shorter space of time.

A growing threat to any of our natural resources is the pressure we humans place on them. We spend a lot of our time producing products to make you a better angler. This carries a level of responsibility for all of us; continuing to enjoy our local fishing means looking after it in a way that promotes longevity of local stocks and structure. I encourage all anglers to look after all parts of the eco-system every day we are on the water.

The challenge when developing a map based fishing guide is always detailing as much technical information as possible. Unfortunately, the cost of publishing a book always restricts the amount of information that can be printed. To gather more detailed fishing information on techniques, knots, baits and more, feel free to head to your local tackle store or to our website to find information on our many other great media products. The address of the AFN website is *www.afn.com.au*

This sounds extremely clichéd but the rest is now definitely up to you. Having read this book you will have grounding in the type of fishing structure, species and seasons that any location offers. This book will hopefully encourage you to expand your fishing boundaries and have the confidence to try new locations. This publication will hopefully become a great reference guide for many years to come. As always, use up-to-date fishing reports and advice from local tackle stores to plan any trip to improve your success. To assist this process, we have collated the contact details of all local fishing tackle outlets at the time of publication. Good luck with your fishing endeavours in this lovely part of the world, we look forward to seeing you on the water.

TACKLE STORE LOCATION GUIDE

Sunshine Coast Area

STORE	PHONE	STREET ADDRESS	SUBURB
TIN CAN FISHING PTY LTD	(07) 5488 0778	69 GYMPIE ROAD	TIN CAN BAY
TOP TACKLE	(07) 5486 4220	SHOP 6, COOLOOLA SHOPPING COMPLEX	COOLOOLA COVE
DAVO'S TACKLE WORLD	(07) 5449 8099	SHOP 6, NOOSA HOMEMAKER CTR - CNR MARY & THOMAS STS	NOOSAVILLE
HOOKED-ON ANGLING & OUTDOORS	(07) 5449 7541	27 HILTON TERRACE	TEWANTIN
BARRA JACKS FISHING & OUTDOORS	(07) 5444 8618	40B LONGWOOD STREET	MINYAMA
TACKLE WORLD KAWANA WATERS	(07) 5444 0714	8 NICKLIN WAY	MINYAMA
FISHING WORLD MAROOCHYDORE	(07) 5443 2714	22 FIRST AVENUE	MAROOCHYDORE
TIE 'N' FLY OUTFITTERS	(07) 5444 0611	8A PT CARTWRIGHT DRIVE	BUDDINA
WELLSY'S TACKLE P/L	(07) 5493 8264	UNIT 8, LINKWAY COMM.CTR - METIER LINKWAY	BUDDINA
KAWANA BAIT & TACKLE	(07) 5444 5551	SHOP 5, 18 PARKANA CRES, BUDDINA SHOPS	BUDDINA

Brisbane Area and Western District

STORE	PHONE	STREET ADDRESS	SUBURB
ALLROUND ANGLER	(07) 5495 7400	CNR.BEERBURRUM RD & HAZEL STREET	CABOOLTURE
GATTON HOME BREW	(07) 5462 4244	SHOP 7/8 KARL COMPLEX - 279 GATTON HELIDON ROAD	GATTON
HIGHFIELDS BAIT & TACKLE	(07) 4615 4335	14 GLADSWOOD DRIVE	HIGHFIELDS
THE TACKLE SHOP CARSELDINE	(07) 3862 9015	1754 GYMPIE ROAD	CARSELDINE
JONES'S TACKLE PTY LTD	(07) 3350 2054	692 GYMPIE ROAD	CHERMSIDE
TACKLE LAND SANDGATE	(07) 3269 5060	78 RAINBOW STREET	SANDGATE
TACKLE WORLD LAWNTON	(07) 3205 7475	640 GYMPIE ROAD	LAWNTON
THE TACKLE WAREHOUSE	(07) 3398 6500	436 OLD CLEVELAND ROAD	CAMP HILL
MOSSOPS TACKLE SHOPS	(07) 3391 0413	47 BALACLAVA STREET	WOOLLOONGABBA
WATER TOWER BAIT & TACKLE	(07) 3396 1833	10 ERNEST STREET	MANLY
WELLINGTON POINT MARINE	(07) 3207 2235	SHOP 3, 368 MAIN ROAD	WELLINGTON POINT
VICTORIA POINT BAIT & TACKLE	(07) 3820 9581	12A COLBURN AVE	VICTORIA POINT
DAVE'S BAYSIDE BAIT & TACKLE	(07) 3820 9757	SHOP 4/127 COLBURN AVENUE	VICTORIA POINT
BP REDLAND BAY	(07) 3206 8514	721 CLEVELAND REDLAND BAY ROAD	REDLAND BAY
CHARLTON TACKLE & BAIT	(07) 3818 1677	18 KERWICK STREET	REDBANK
WARWICK TACKLE & TUSK	(07) 4667 1756	SHOP 2, 180 WOOD STREET	WARWICK
WARWICK OUTDOORS & SPORTS	(07) 4661 3533	115 PALMERIN STREET	WARWICK
FISH N BITS	(07) 4636 6850	340 ALDERLEY STREET	TOOWOOMBA
TACKLE WORLD TOOWOOMBA	(07) 4632 9770	224A RUTHVEN STREET	TOOWOOMBA

Gold Coast Area

STORE	PHONE	STREET ADDRESS	SUBURB
OXENFORD BAIT & TACKLE	(07) 5580 6851	147 OLD PACIFIC HIGHWAY	OXENFORD
COAST MAPS & CHARTS	(07) 5537 2287	SHOP 56A HARBOUR TOWN S/C - GOLD COAST HIGHWAY	BIGGERA WATERS
GOLD COAST FISHING TACKLE	(07) 5679 0840	SHOP 2 / 57-59 BRISBANE ROAD	BIGGERA WATERS
DOUG BURT'S TACKLE WORLD	(07) 5532 0678	SHOP 4, 142 BRISBANE ROAD	LABRADOR
FAR OUTDOORS	(07) 5463 4114	12 HIGH STREET	BOONAH
THE BOATSHED BAIT & TACKLE	(07) 5525 0338	2 THROWER DRIVE	CURRUMBIN
ANGLERS WAREHOUSE	(07) 5599 4376	141 WHARF ST	TWEED HEADS
SOUTHPORT FISHING & DIVE CENTRE	(07) 5531 2333	HOWARD'S LANDING, 95 GOLD COAST HIGHWAY	SOUTHPORT

Also available at BCF and Anaconda.

FISH COOLER DELUXE RANGE

Keep your catch
ICE COOL for LONGER

Small	915 mm x 460 mm x 300 mm	AC1136
Medium	1220 mm x 510 mm x 300 mm	AC1143
Large	1520 mm x 510 mm x 300 mm	AC1150
Extra Large	1830 mm x 510 mm x 300 mm	AC1167

Small

Medium

Large

Extra Large

KAYAK COOLER DELUXE RANGE

Medium	610 mm length - Top width 180mm - Bottom width x 400 mm	AC1112-11000
Large	910 mm length - Top width 250mm - Bottom width x 510 mm	AC1129-13700

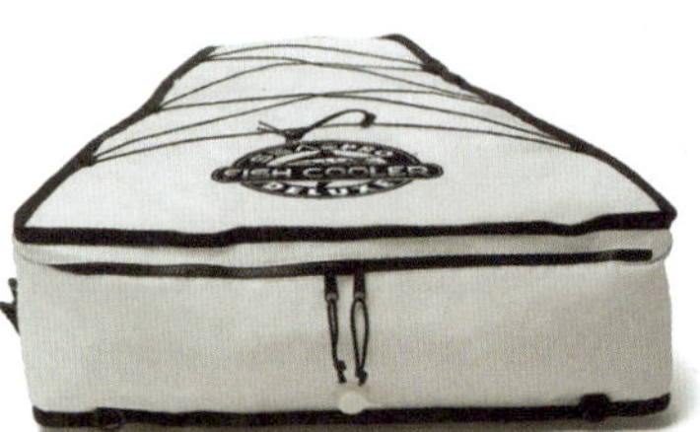

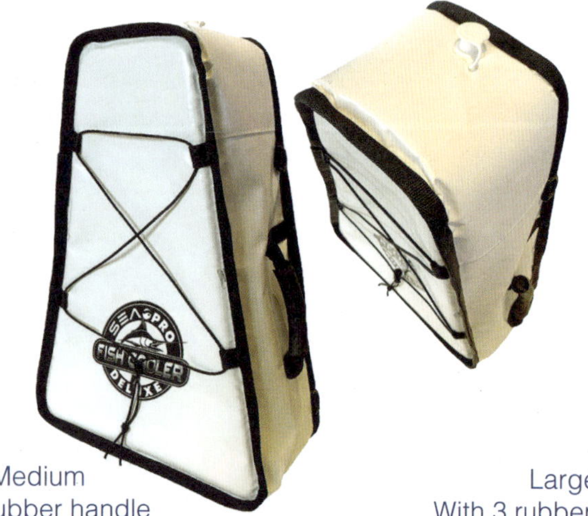

Medium
With rubber handle

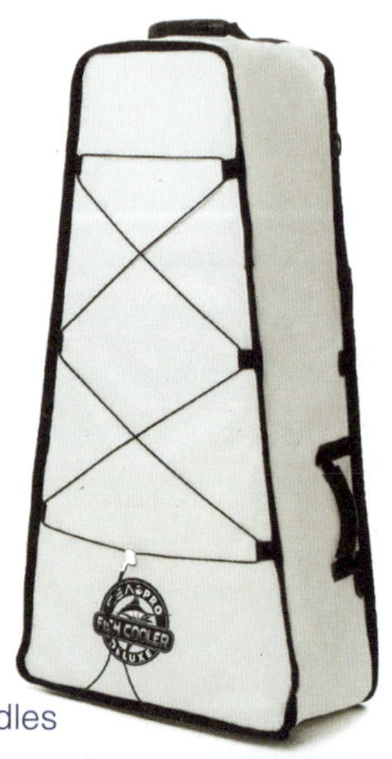

Large
With 3 rubber handles